THOUGH SILENT THEY SPEAK

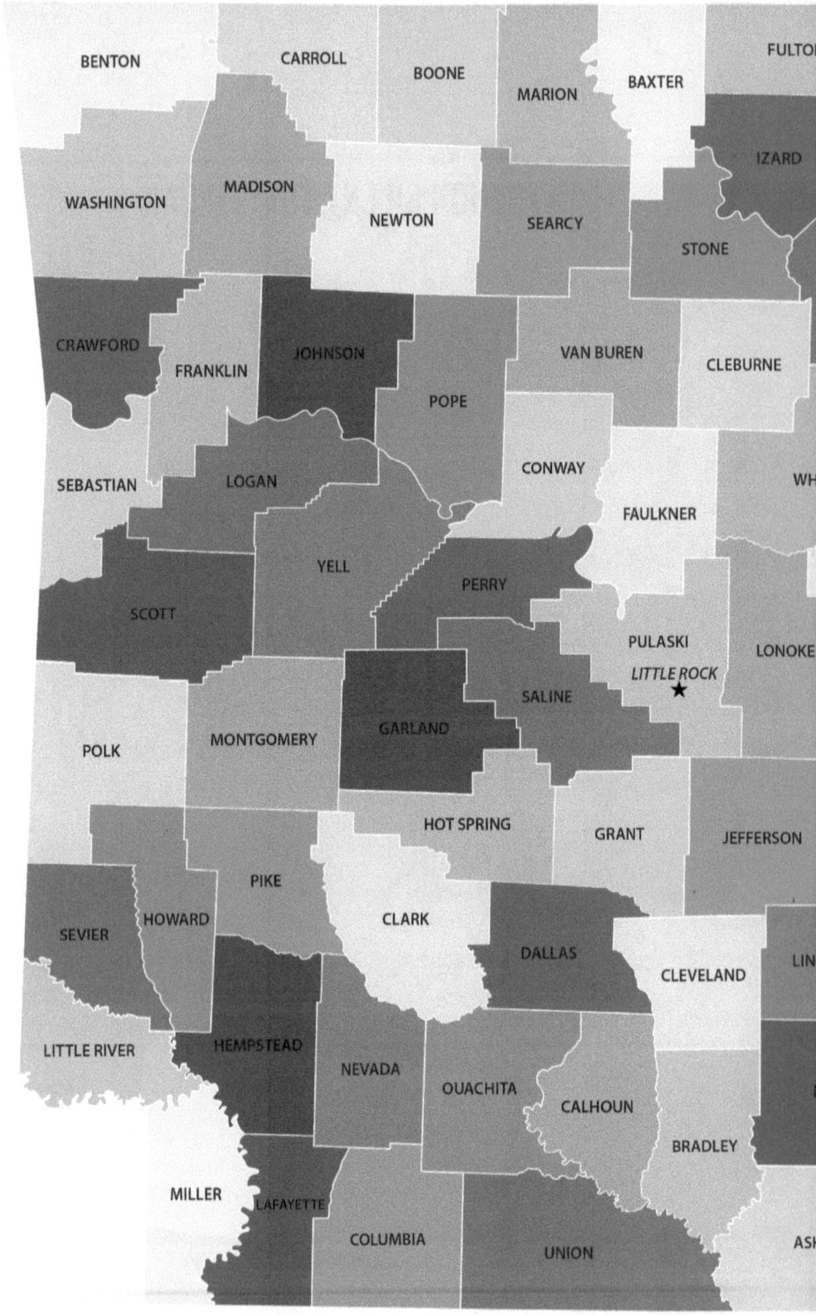
BENTON
CARROLL
BOONE
MARION
BAXTER
IZARD
WASHINGTON
MADISON
NEWTON
SEARCY
STONE
CRAWFORD
FRANKLIN
JOHNSON
POPE
VAN BUREN
CLEBURNE
SEBASTIAN
LOGAN
CONWAY
FAULKNER
YELL
PERRY
SCOTT
PULASKI
LITTLE ROCK
LONOKE
POLK
MONTGOMERY
GARLAND
SALINE
HOT SPRING
GRANT
JEFFERSON
PIKE
SEVIER
HOWARD
CLARK
DALLAS
CLEVELAND
LITTLE RIVER
HEMPSTEAD
NEVADA
OUACHITA
CALHOUN
BRADLEY
MILLER
LAFAYETTE
COLUMBIA
UNION

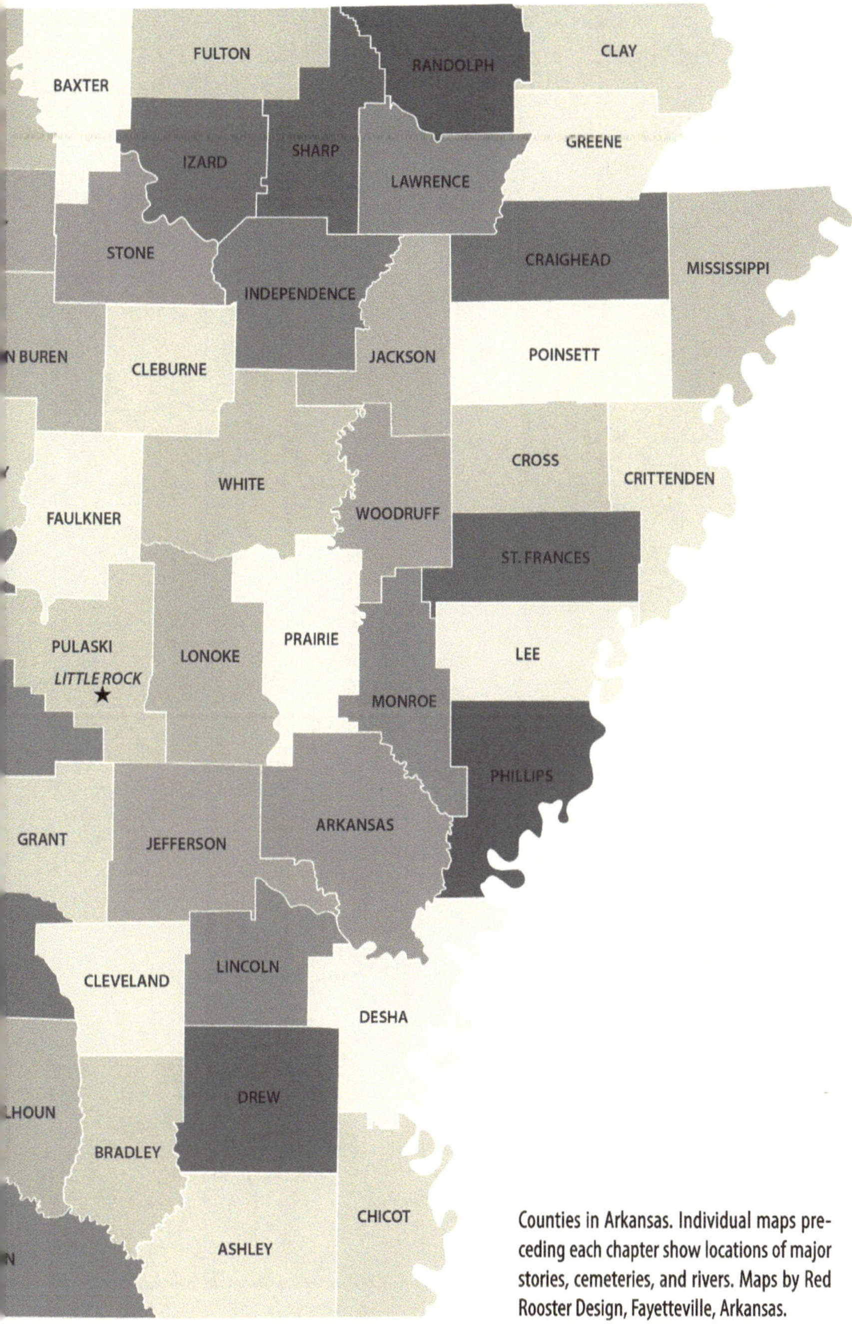

Counties in Arkansas. Individual maps preceding each chapter show locations of major stories, cemeteries, and rivers. Maps by Red Rooster Design, Fayetteville, Arkansas.

THOUGH SILENT THEY SPEAK

ARKANSAS GRAVESTONES AND GRAVEYARDS

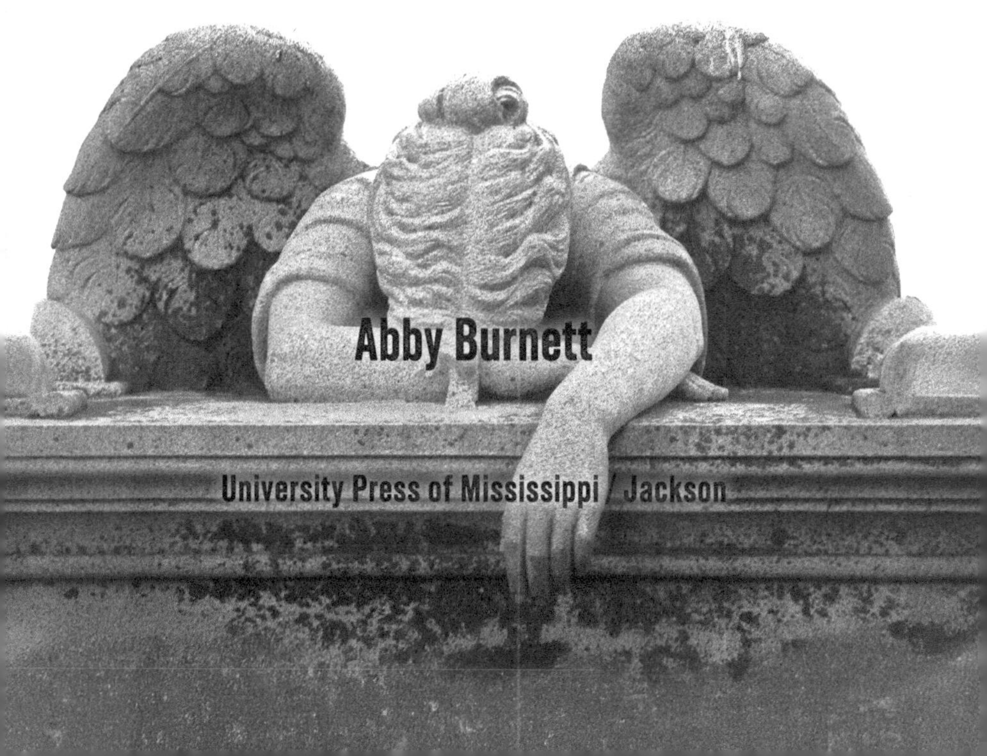

Abby Burnett

University Press of Mississippi / Jackson

The University Press of Mississippi is the scholarly publishing agency of the Mississippi Institutions of Higher Learning: Alcorn State University, Delta State University, Jackson State University, Mississippi State University, Mississippi University for Women, Mississippi Valley State University, University of Mississippi, and University of Southern Mississippi.

www.upress.state.ms.us

The University Press of Mississippi is a member of the Association of University Presses.

All photos taken by the author unless otherwise noted.
Cover photo: Cave Mountain Cemetery (Newton Co.) photographed by Hal Mitzenmacher.
Weeping angel statue courtesy of Carmen K. Sisson/Cloudybright on Alamy Stock Photo.

Manufactured in the United States of America
∞

Publisher: University Press of Mississippi, Jackson, USA
Authorised GPSR Safety Representative: Easy Access System Europe - Mustamäe tee 50, 10621 Tallinn, Estonia, gpsr.requests@easproject.com

Library of Congress Cataloging-in-Publication Data

Names: Burnett, Abby author
Title: Though silent they speak : Arkansas gravestones and graveyards / Abby Burnett.
Description: Jackson : University Press of Mississippi, 2025. | Includes bibliographical references and index.
Identifiers: LCCN 2025037367 (print) | LCCN 2025037368 (ebook) | ISBN 9781496860446 hardback | ISBN 9781496860453 trade paperback | ISBN 9781496860460 epub | ISBN 9781496860477 epub | ISBN 9781496860484 pdf | ISBN 9781496860491 pdf
Subjects: LCSH: Sepulchral monuments—Arkansas | Cemeteries—Arkansas | Epitaphs—Arkansas | Inscriptions—Arkansas
Classification: LCC NB1803.A8 B87 2025 (print) | LCC NB1803.A8 (ebook) | DDC 726/.809767—dc23/eng/20250924
LC record available at https://lccn.loc.gov/2025037367
LC ebook record available at https://lccn.loc.gov/2025037368

British Library Cataloging-in-Publication Data available

MOTTO OF THE WOODMEN OF THE WORLD:
DUM TACET CLAMET
("THOUGH SILENT, HE SPEAKS"),
FOUND ON ALL MEMBERS' TOMBSTONES

This book is dedicated to the memory of my paternal grandfather, Fred Boewe, who instilled in me a love of graveyards and an appreciation for the stories they contain.

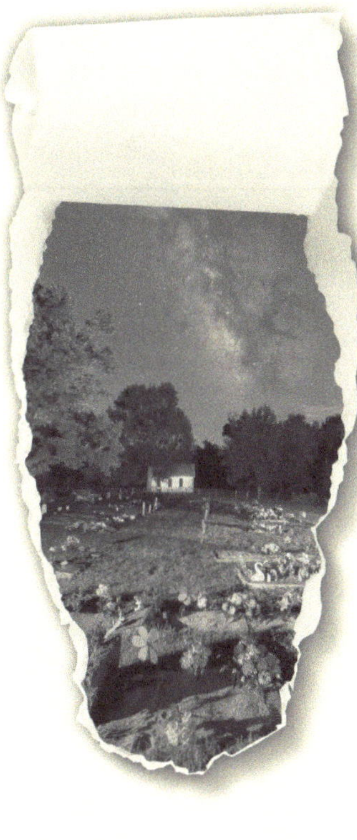

CONTENTS

ACKNOWLEDGMENTS

Graveyard exploration, research, and writing are all solitary occupations, but writers need people, specifically ones who generously share their knowledge. I am indebted to so many who have done just that. I am grateful to fellow gravestone enthusiasts, but also to historians, genealogists, archaeologists, park rangers, cemetery groundskeepers, librarians, and friends and to the readers who meticulously vetted certain sections of this book. All of them generously gave their time, attention, expertise, and encouragement to my project.

I am also grateful to the people I met entirely by chance while exploring graveyards. Time and again, these seemingly random encounters provided me with precisely the information I was seeking, such as the true story of the murder weapon grave marker or the location of an amputated limb's burial. I am so grateful to the people who graciously answered my questions and who then recommended additional graveyards to visit.

Special appreciation goes to the people who read specific sections, or the entirety, of the book's manuscript and offered valuable comments and corrections. My immense gratitude goes out to Vincent Anderson, Morris S. Arnold, Paige Ford, Jim Greene, Melinda Large, Jerry Harris Moore, Joshua L. Segal, and Bob Young, and to Elizabeth Farry, my copyeditor. A special thanks to Ian Brown, who not only carefully scrutinized the entire manuscript but also suggested the book's title.

I am also grateful to members of the Arkansas History Listserv, the Association for Gravestone Studies, and to everyone listed below—alphabetically, for fairness—but also to people whose names I should have recorded, ones who came to my talks and made suggestions, as well as contacts on various Facebook sites dedicated to graveyard exploration, taphophiles who pointed me toward so many interesting graveyards and tombstones I would not have found on my own. This is no small thing because as of this writing the online source Find a Grave (www.findagrave.com) lists 9,004 cemeteries in Arkansas—the number is rising—and, to date, I have visited 1,450 of them, a number that is also rising.

In addition to everyone named above, I wish to thank the following people for their input: Beth Ardapple, Gail Ashbrook, Renee Banks, Whitney Barringer, Cindy Beckman, Cody Berry, Bob Besom, Rosey Bird, Leroy Blair, Bill Bowden, Enoch Bowerman, Jan Kennedy Brown and Cadie Brown, Gary Brown, Kevin N. Brown, Sara Eagle Briggs, Evelyn Burnett, Drew A. Calhoun, Lisa C. Childs, Courtney Moore Clements, Carla Hines Coleman, Ellen Corley, Julienne Crawford, Charlton Cupp, Kip Davis, Erik Ditzler, Richard C. Finch, Sean Fitzgibbon, Mike Forney, Ron Fuller, Gary Masami Funamura, Susan Gallion, Angela Gibbs, Donna Goldstein, Glendle Griggs, Carolyn Hanna, Teresa Harris, Donna Hawkins, J. French Hill, Holly Hope, Bill Horrell, Don House, Louis Intres, Marvin Jeter, Brandon Johnson, Jackie King, Jeff Koone, Carol Lawler, Mollye McCalman, Stephanie McElhaney, Mark McElroy, Jerry McElvey, Sherryl Miller, Hal Mitzenmacher, Natalee Moon, Reine Melson Moore, Andrew Morrison, Melissa Nesbitt, Kate Nessler, Robert Okamoto, Anne Prichard, Wendell Pyles, Randy Ridgway, Elizabeth L. Roark, Elizabeth Robbins, Acadia Roher, Ron Romano, Lexie Rue-Harris, Dolores J. Rush, Joy Russell, Cheryl Shaver, Heather Shelman, Lance Spanke, B. Craig Stinson, George Takei, Teresa Taylor, Leonard Norman Thompson, Bobbie Thurman, Evelyn Jackson Trammel, Elisabeth A. Walker, Jon Walter, Luann Sewell Waters, Phillip Watkins, Bertie Wells, Jeannie Whayne, James Whitlow, Ralph S. Wilcox, Josh Williams, and Blake Wintory.

Finally, I want to thank Jim Binns, my partner of more than a quarter century. Creating this book was a long process, and through it all he patiently listened to me enthuse about my discoveries, made valuable suggestions, accompanied me on several long cemetery trips, and kept the home fires burning—and our dogs fed—when I traveled alone. My gratitude to him, and my love for him, knows no bounds.

THOUGH SILENT THEY SPEAK

INTRODUCTION

Never underestimate the importance of cemeteries. Arkansans haven't always marked every grave, maintained or even remembered the locations of every graveyard, but destroy one at your peril. Governor Orval Faubus used this to his advantage in 1964, when his campaign for reelection was challenged by New York–born Winthrop Rockefeller, the wealthy grandson of Standard Oil founder John D. Rockefeller. After Winthrop Rockefeller had employees clear some of his Arkansas land for farming, Faubus broadcast television spots, supposedly depicting Rockefeller's land, "showing bulldozers hard at work destroying a cemetery."[1]

The actual incident had occurred many years earlier and under very different circumstances than portrayed by Faubus. A bulldozer operator had accidentally knocked over one or more tombstones in an overgrown graveyard on Rockefeller's property,[2] but he restored the stones, then erected protective fencing around them. Despite knowing the truth, Faubus repeatedly campaigned using this story and went on to win a sixth term in office.[3] The dirty trick may have cost Rockefeller that election, but he was elected governor two years later.

Such strong feelings are tied to the Southern tradition of Decoration Day, an event once separate from Memorial Day. Originally this was a time set aside for a "graveyard working," when a cemetery was cleaned and every grave restored and decorated, followed by a potluck meal, sermons, speeches, and hymn-singing. Within rural communities, no two cemeteries held their events on the same day in order to allow families to attend multiple decoration festivities wherever they had friends or family buried. The tradition is fading away today, although there is still an emphasis on placing colorful flower arrangements on the headstones on or before the observance, which is now almost universally held on Memorial Day.

Despite the disappearance of this tradition of respect, cemeteries are still places where the living enjoy spending time strolling or birdwatching. The stones also offer some interesting reading material. Though sometimes challenging to decipher, the poetry inscribed on tombstones—known as epitaphs—may be sentimental, morbid, informative, or unintentionally funny. Such treasures are hiding in plain sight, waiting to be discovered.

That's not to say that such jaunts are perfectly safe—tombstone tourism can be risky. The pamphlet *Tombstone Trail: Final Destinations*, published by Arkansas Delta Byways, a guide to graves and graveyards along the eastern edge of Arkansas, has this to say when giving directions to Crittenden County's Guerrant Cemetery: "Caution is advised, as the turn-off from US-64 is a treacherous pavement drop-off and the cemetery site often houses numerous commercial beehives." Some warnings are issued by the cemeteries themselves, such as the signs posted at Delamar Cemetery (Dallas Co.): "Please close gates. Wild hogs are in the area!"

Still, by exercising a little caution, graveyards can be wonderful places to study such diverse subjects as sculpture, architecture, geology, poetry, biography, portraiture, symbolism, and early photography. The breadth of this field is evident during bus tours at the Association for Gravestone Studies' annual conferences, when attendees exit the motor coaches and fan out, often to the dismay of local guides intent on giving a lecture about their cemeteries. There is no corralling a gaggle of taphophiles (tombstone lovers) after each has spotted something of personal interest: mausoleums with stained glass windows, marble angels in postures of grief, cast zinc obelisks, infants' markers, homemade headstones, or fraternal lodge insignias—to name just a few enticements.

Two more disciplines should be added to the list of subjects to be studied in cemeteries: anthropology and sociology. Though literally silent, a tombstone can speak volumes about the deceased's life, beliefs, virtues, and other attributes, as well as providing commentary on contemporary customs. There's the disparity between the elaborate marble confections, usually carved in Italy, found on the graves of the wealthy, and the roughly shaped and crudely lettered fieldstones or concrete markers of the very poor, when their graves are marked at all. There are the high and dry landscaped parks reserved for whites' burials and, on the other side of a dividing fence, vastly less desirable ground commonly relegated to Blacks. Then there are modern grave goods: figurines, bird feeders, solar lights, unopened beer cans, the deceased's boots or other possessions left on recent burials, and the occasional mailbox situated in a family plot, in which relatives leave letters to the deceased.

Another area of study is the difference between men's and women's memorialization. In the late 1800s, and into the early 1900s, a wealthy man's grave marker was likely to be adorned with his likeness in the form of a statue, bust, cameo, or photoceramic picture, while statuary on a woman's grave would be a generic, petal-dropping angel or an allegorical figure such as Faith, Hope, or Charity. Even inscriptions discriminate. An influential man's showy marble marker is likely to detail his achievements or modestly insist that the deceased's virtues constitute his true monument. In contrast, women are tepidly endorsed: "She hath done what she could," or worse, "Think what a wife should be; she was that."

Men tend to be memorialized by what they accomplished in life, by their military exploits, elected offices, the titles they earned, or the churches they pastored, while women are defined by their relationships to others. According to their tombstone inscriptions, they are the wives, mothers, sisters, and daughters of someone else. Sometimes they are wholly subsumed by their husbands, for example, "Mrs. Marion Pistol, wife of Marion Pistol."[4] Even on modern granite markers, where technology has made all manner of artwork possible, the husband's side of a shared headstone is likely to display emblems showing the crops he raised, the truck he drove, or the team he rooted for. (In Arkansas this will assuredly be the Razorbacks and may include the epitaph, "Calling those hogs in Heaven.") Given the prevalence of Bibles, angels, praying hands, rosaries, or Christian crosses, wives' interests appear to be religion, although generic birds and dogwood blossoms also predominate.

The purpose of this book is to celebrate Arkansas's cemeteries and the most unusual grave markers found in them, ones with interesting stories. In order to locate these stories I talked with residents of towns and cities across the state, describing my project and asking for guidance. This often resulted in being told that the state's third or eleventh or eighteenth governor, or lieutenant governor, or a state supreme court justice, was buried in the town cemetery—always a man, and seemingly always under an immense obelisk. These and the Woodmen of the World's ubiquitous stone tree trunks are the things I was usually urged to see.

With no disrespect to these men and the townspeople who take pride in them, such biographies are not included here. Unfortunately, neither are ones about some of this state's most famous women, such as Hattie Caraway, the United States' first female senator (died 1950, Oaklawn Cemetery, Jonesboro, Craighead Co.) and Martha Mitchell of Watergate fame (died 1976, Bellwood Cemetery, Pine Bluff, Jefferson Co.), whose outsized lives are memorialized with understated markers identical to those of the rest of their family, stones so underwhelming that it takes guidance from cemetery personnel to locate their graves at all.[5] To be fair, this sometimes happens to men as well, as in the case of Senator J. William Fulbright, whose simple marker is obscured by a stand of ornamental grass in Fayetteville's Evergreen Cemetery (died 1995, Washington Co.).

An exception might have been made had any of the state's seventy-five counties been named for a woman but, perhaps predictably, not one was. This feels like a squandered opportunity in a state that named White County after either the White River or Tennessee native Hugh L. White, a failed 1836 presidential candidate. Prairie County was named for a natural feature, while at least five counties were named for water: Little River, Hot Spring, Saline, and the Mississippi and Ouachita Rivers, with Arkansas County perhaps taking its name from the Arkansas River. Other namesakes are even more specific: a tree used as a landmark (Lonoke), the French word for a stump (Chicot), or a county outline that resembles a state (Nevada).[6] At best, and only with a vigorous stretch of the imagination, can women claim the counties of Columbia (an allegorical female figure) or Pulaski, named for Polish Count Kazimierz Pulaski, buried in Savannah, Georgia, and who is now believed to have been born intersex.[7]

After ruling out Arkansas's namesakes and public figures, we turn to some Arkansans who lived extraordinary lives. Unfortunately, the wildest lives are often commemorated with the tamest tombstones. A perfect example of this is the staid marker of William Waddle (1837–1919). By age fifteen he had survived a fall from a third-story window onto a pile of rocks, been stabbed, shot thrice, run over by a wagon, and struck by lightning—all separate incidents.[8] He was wounded a dozen times in the Civil War before he returned home to Pocahontas (Randolph Co.) to farm and (oh, the irony) sell insurance.[9] He finally died of "general disability" two days shy of his eighty-second birthday.[10] If only his columnar monument in Pocahontas's Masonic Cemetery did justice to these events, but his misspelled epitaph notes only that he was "All ways a friend to the poor, widowes and orphans."

An unusual death does not always result in an arresting tombstone or inscription. The Doss family's plot, in Berryville's city cemetery, hints at one story: Winnie Doss and six children share a 1945 death date, all of them killed when a tornado demolished their home. But this plot also contains a strange second death that isn't obvious: widowed Samuel Doss went on to marry Nannie, a woman he met through a "lonely hearts" correspondence club and became the fourth husband (and possibly the ninth or tenth person) she killed using poison. It was this crime that finally got Nannie Hazle Braggs Harrelson Lanning Morton Doss caught. She pleaded guilty and, narrowly avoiding death in the electric chair, was sentenced to life in prison, where she died of leukemia eleven years later.[11]

At least Will Waddle and Sam Doss *have* markers. Lee Trickey (discussed in chapter 8) lies in an unmarked grave. In his case the lack of a tombstone serves as additional commentary on his sad life and abandonment in death.

Given Arkansas's wealth of unusual tombs and their eccentric occupants, it is not feasible to cover all aspects of burial and commemoration. For the most part, modern granite markers, on which it is possible to find laser artwork showing everything from sugar cookie recipes to suicide notes to the deceased's tattoos,[12] are too numerous and too varied to list here, and this includes most modern markers placed on older graves. Other omissions include military cemeteries and war memorials, large-scale burials in times of epidemics and natural disasters, institutional cemeteries (asylums, poor farms, potters' fields), and the burials found within religious communities where monks, priests, and nuns relinquished their individuality in life, then death. Still, exceptions have been made in some of these categories.

When writing about certain subjects (grave houses, tombstones of amputated limbs, shell-covered graves, etc.) I'm merely describing what I've found or have been able to document, not giving an exact count of such markers. Conversely, it is possible that someday a reader will search a cemetery mentioned here and discover that a marker no longer exists. Vandalism is a terrible problem in isolated cemeteries; so, too, is improper cleaning that ultimately renders delicate inscriptions illegible or causes the surfaces of stones to crumble away.

While some authors and websites make a distinction between graveyards (affiliated with a church, and part of a churchyard) and cemeteries (larger burial sites not connected to any church), these terms are used interchangeably here. It is simply not possible to separate these concepts when writing about Arkansas cemeteries, as in some rural communities they are found adjacent to a multipurpose church/school/lodge hall or may have been established by a church that is no longer standing. According to one source, "In our great grandfather's time there was no cemetery as we know it today. In fact, it wasn't even called a cemetery—it was a 'graveyard,' or 'church yard,' or 'God's acre.'"[13] Even the much older-sounding "burying ground" has been used by Arkansans.

In telling the stories of the state's oddest markers—a stone Irish setter, a life-sized carving of a girl being pulled from her grave by an angel, a murder weapon used to mark its victim's grave—I can tell you about the deceased's life and death, but I cannot explain why this particular statue or object was used to mark the burial. While there are accounts of people ordering tombstones from traveling salesmen or local monument yards, none explains why a certain marker, verse, or symbol was chosen. Sometimes a stone must speak for itself.

Sometimes the deceased speaks for himself too. Nathan Ellington (1808–1890), a man who had his coffin built, pre-need, and who carefully preserved his wedding clothing for eventual reuse as his burial garments, maintains ownership of the Ellington Cemetery (Logan Co.) from beyond the grave.[14] Carved on one side of his monument are these words: "All this graveyard square that lies in Section 19 and 30 shall remain the property of Nathan Ellington forever."[15]

Never underestimate the importance of cemeteries!

1. White House Cemetery, Arnett
Tontitown Cemetery
(Washington)

2. Fort Smith National Cemetery
(Sebastian)

3. State Line Cemetery, Texarkana
(Miller)

4. Bellwood Cemetery, Pine Bluff
St. Joseph Cemetery, Pine Bluff
(Jefferson)

5. Pioneer Cemetery, Batesville
(Independence)

6. Sloan site, Crowley's Ridge
(Greene)

7. Tyronza
Augusta Memorial Park
(Poinsett)

8. Arkansas Post(s) & site of Napoleon, near Arkansas River

9. Czech National Cemetery, Hazen
Slovak Catholic Cemetery, Slovak
Russian Orthodox Cemetery, Slovak
(Prairie)

10. Old Mound Cemetery, Arkansas City
Rohwer Relocation Camp Cemetery
(Desha)

11. Scull Cemetery
(Arkansas)

12. Arkansas River | **13.** Mississippi River

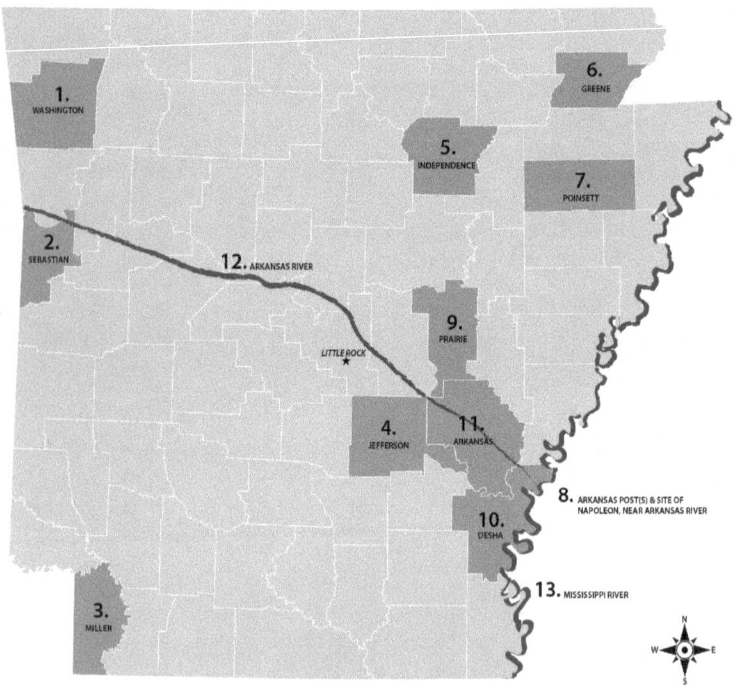

Major locations discussed in chapter 1.
Map by Red Rooster Design, Fayetteville, Arkansas.

Chapter 1

AN OVERVIEW OF ARKANSAS CEMETERIES

Lonely now we'll always roam
Like the cloud, the wind, the wave
Where you've dwelled shall be our home,
Where you died shall be our grave.

Ours the God whom you adored
Your Redeemer shall be ours
We will leave earth's charms deplored
And meet our friend in Heaven's bowers.

—MARGARET INGRUM, 1831–1856, GAINSVILLE CEMETERY (GREENE CO.)[1]

An exploration of Arkansas cemeteries should start with the state's oldest, which would be the one used by the Dalton culture at the end of the Ice Age, known as the Archaic Period (8500 BCE). Located between the Cache River and the western side of Crowley's Ridge (Greene Co.) in the northeast corner of Arkansas, it's not only the state's oldest, it's also "the oldest known formal open-air cemetery in the New World."[2]

Setting aside Native American cemeteries for the moment, the first Europeans to settle in what would become the state of Arkansas lived, died, and buried their dead at each location of the Arkansas Post, the earliest non-Native settlement that, founded in 1686, predated statehood by a century and a half. But although there were several incarnations of the post at various locations along the Arkansas River, "not even the slightest physical trace of a colonial occupation has survived above the ground," though archaeological finds (but not graveyards) have been made at these locations.[3]

One Arkansas cemetery proclaims itself to be the state's oldest, an assertion made by erecting a new tombstone with an antique death date, then using that misdated stone as proof of the cemetery's antiquity. This took place in 2015 when members of the Grand Prairie Historical Society commissioned a headstone for "Pierre Laclede Liguest," a cofounder of the city of St. Louis, and placed it in Scull Cemetery (Arkansas Co.). The tombstone's inscription contains several errors, including a death date of June 20, 1778, and "Ark. Post" as the location where the death occurred.[4] Once this headstone was in place, the Society created new signage for the cemetery: "Scull Cemetery, 1778, Oldest Cemetery in Arkansas."

"Carved in stone" suggests certainty but is never proof of accuracy. Despite this, tombstone inscriptions are exempt from the rule of law that forbids hearsay (statements made outside of court) because, it is argued, the information on a tombstone was supplied by (presumably well-informed) family members intending to leave a factual record.

The errors on Pierre Laclède's modern marker are traceable to more than one early Missouri historian. However, even if Laclède *had* died and been buried at Arkansas Post—he didn't, and he wasn't—in 1778, the post was situated about twenty-five miles downriver from its present and final location, and it is near this final location where Scull Cemetery is located.

According to Morris S. Arnold, the leading authority on the Arkansas Post and author of numerous histories of the post and colonial Arkansas, the Scull family did not come to Arkansas until around 1800. There was no "Scull Cemetery" downriver at the post's previous locations.[5]

The first Arkansas Post was established beside the Arkansas River in 1686 by Frenchman Henri de Tonti. Over the next two and a half centuries, the post moved between several locations and was under the authority of France, then Spain, then the United States. The first location was roughly thirty miles above where the Arkansas River joins the Mississippi River;[6] the Chickasaw destroyed this post in 1749, following the French-Chickasaw war, and the post moved upstream another five miles to a site known as *Ecores Rouges* (Red Bluffs). Seven years later it moved back down the Arkansas River to about seven miles from its confluence with the Mississippi River. There the post remained for the next twenty-three years.

In 1764, Pierre Laclède—his last name, "Liguest," was added for legal reasons, but historians have used the two interchangeably—together with his common-law wife's son, Auguste Chouteau, are credited with founding the Missouri settlement that Laclède named St. Louis. (It should be noted that historian Carl J. Ekberg casts serious doubts on this city's cherished origin story.[7]) Laclède founded the town as a trading post from which to buy furs from the Osage Indians, and his monopoly over this trade made him wealthy. However, he later went deeply into debt, and in 1778, hoping to recoup his fortune, he traveled to New Orleans to obtain merchandise to sell back in St. Louis. Ill and dispirited before he left New Orleans,[8] Laclède died aboard his trading boat while traveling back up the Mississippi River, somewhere near the mouth of the Arkansas River a day or two before May 27.[9] He was forty-eight years old.

At this time the post, located seven miles up the Arkansas River, was under the command of Captain Balthazar de Villiers, whose job as commandant included acting as a coroner. On May 27, 1778, de Villiers traveled downstream from the post to view Laclède's body, pronouncing that "death had occurred naturally."[10] He then inventoried the contents of Laclède's trading boat (itemizing such things as linens, trade goods, and rum), a record he began drawing up *the morning of* May 27,[11] meaning that Laclède died prior to this date.

May is the beginning of warm weather in south Arkansas, and in an era before the availability of embalming or sealed metal coffins, Laclède's body would have required immediate burial. According to St. Louis historian Wilson Primm, who was acquainted with Laclède's natural son Pierre Chouteau, the burial occurred on a bench of land at the juncture of the two rivers, a practical site for the burial of river travelers who died on their journeys.[12] Laclède's body was placed in a coffin built from the oar benches of his trading boat and buried in the forested spot, in what may already have been an established graveyard, as it was one of the few places on the west bank that was usually above water.

Nineteen years after his father's death, Pierre Chouteau was told the burial story and had the graveyard pointed out to him by the same men who had worked aboard Laclède's boat and who would thus have buried his body.[13] Another early St. Louis historian, John F. Darby—who also claimed to have visited this graveyard—wrote that, lacking a tombstone, Laclède's grave was not identifiable.[14]

One year after Laclède's death, in 1779, the post moved back upstream to the previous—and its present-day—*Ecores Rouge* location. In 1803, its ownership was transferred to the United States following the Louisiana Purchase. Today, this site, the post's last location, is the Arkansas Post National Memorial, a state park.

Some accounts give June 20 as Laclède's death date, which was the date his death was recorded in St. Louis. His burial location is not in question, and was something historians Primm and Darby agreed on. According to Darby, "The spot where Pierre Liguest Laclède was buried is . . . just above the town of Napoleon—in a deep, heavy grove of timber, in a light sandy soil, and on that account the place became a famous grave-yard for the last sixty or seventy years, particularly when the cholera and yellow fever raged, and there might be, perhaps, from ten to fifteen dead bodies to bury from a single steamboat."[15]

The rough river town of Napoleon was established four or five decades after Laclède's death,[16] around the time steamboat travel became the norm. (The year 1811 saw the first steamboat on the Mississippi River, though one did not ascend the river as far as St. Louis until 1817.) Even before steamboats increased travel on the Mississippi River, it had long been a conduit for boat trade, and the Arkansas River's confluence with the Mississippi served as a transfer point for goods and passengers. Ultimately this sandy graveyard would hold deceased steamboat passengers; residents of Napoleon who died from natural causes, murders, and epidemics; and the boatmen who died at the US Marine Hospital at Napoleon, in use from 1855 until the building collapsed into the river in early 1868.[17] John Darby—a stickler for accuracy—stated that the graveyard contained several thousand bodies.[18]

The 1860 Census shows that there was a marble dealer in Napoleon, but today only one monument-style marker still stands in the remnants of its graveyard.[19] This damaged obelisk marks the graves of spouses Henry and Cecilia Smith, who died in 1859 and 1871, respectively. Archaeologist T.L. Hodges, who visited the site in 1943, saw this obelisk and two marble tablets, nearby,[20] and wrote that by probing the soil with a rod he found evidence of other markers that had been buried under river silt, although—somewhat surprisingly for an archaeologist—he did not excavate them.[21] Darby wrote that the graveyard soil contained neither clay nor stone,[22] so any resistance to a soil probe was likely to have been a buried tombstone.

The Arkansas and Mississippi Rivers flooded repeatedly, changed course, or, in the case of the Mississippi, had its course deliberately altered during the Civil War, to Napoleon's detriment.[23] A flood in 1874 was severe enough to cause the remaining residents to require rescue,[24] although it took the flood of 1882 to finish washing away all traces of the town. How far the Arkansas River encroached on the graveyard is unclear, but Darby, in 1872, was misinformed about its complete eradication, although likely correct in his assertion that Laclède and many other long-buried bodies had probably washed away.[25] The Arkansas River certainly changed course and very likely cut across at least a portion of this cemetery, as by one account washed-out grave markers were found downstream.[26]

The post had a graveyard at each of its locations, as its Catholic residents required burial in sanctified ground, but none of these earlier sites can be located. Even the final, present location of the post had essentially disappeared by the early 1940s,[27] but a map drawn by an eyewitness in 1832 shows *two* graveyards there. In the half century since the settlement had moved back, the older of the two graveyards may have simply washed away, as the 1832 map identifies it as "the old cemetery, undermined by a gulley,"[28] likely caused by erosion from the Arkansas River, as it was situated near its bank. Although not identified by name, the map's second and more secure burial ground may be the site of today's Scull Cemetery. It is not known how the Scull name came to be associated with this graveyard (Sculls are not known to have been buried in it), but Hewes Scull owned the land next to the older original graveyard, so perhaps the surname was later given to the second burial ground.[29]

Scull Cemetery's oldest known grave is that of Henry Conway, killed in a duel in 1827. At least, members of the Grand Prairie Historical Society believed that the pile of rubble they saw there in 1963 was all that remained of Conway's original obelisk, although at that time the oldest marked grave they found had an 1868 death date.[30] Today, Conway's grave has a modern military marker because his original marker, containing a lengthy inscription, was shattered by a tree.

The town of Napoleon has not survived either, but its graveyard has. What remains is the small portion that was not washed away by the changing course of the Arkansas River, which stranded the graves on an island. Still, the continued existence of the Smiths' remaining grave marker, the fact that two other inscribed tablets were visible there as late as 1968 or 1969,[31] as well as details from Hodge's 1943 visit, provide evidence that this cemetery still exists, though today it is unreachable except by boat, and then only with help from an expert guide.[32]

Laclède's error-riddled modern tombstone is in the wrong location, but its creators had the right idea. The graveyard that once held—or possibly still holds—his remains is, indeed, the oldest (non-Native American) cemetery in Arkansas.

WHERE HAVE ALL THE GRAVEYARDS GONE?

Napoleon's burial ground is lucky to have survived at all, given the speed and power of flooding rivers as they carve away banks and sweep away substantial buildings—not to mention tombstones. This is true of all graveyards near major rivers, even burials initially situated far back from the banks. This was made clear in 1883 when first one sealed metal coffin, then a second one, washed up in Vicksburg, Mississippi. A local newspaper speculated that the first coffin had come from a graveyard at Goodrich's Landing or Lake Providence (both in Louisiana), which "have been caving for some time,"[33] but two weeks later another article added Napoleon's graveyard to the list of possible sources.[34] A year earlier, an "overflow" of the rivers had caused graveyards to disappear, including Wells Ferry, farther up the

Arkansas River near Little Rock. There, families were in a race against the river to exhume and remove bodies, but even so, "many bodies were carried away by the waves."[35]

Napoleon's graveyard was just one option when boat captains needed to bury deceased passengers; they also buried them in the wood yards along the Mississippi River. Steamboats needed huge amounts of cordwood to power their boilers, and this created an industry in places where there were natural landings for the boats. Burying bodies while also taking on fuel was an efficient use of time.[36] It was also a necessity, such as during the 1833 cholera outbreak, when "the disease was rampant all along the Mississippi, with the woodyards becoming burial grounds."[37] Graveyards created under these circumstances have by now almost certainly been lost after rivers changed course. One that survives, however, is the now-abandoned Red Hill Cemetery near the Arkansas River (Faulkner Co.), believed to be the graveyard of river travelers in the early 1800s.[38]

Nature is quick to reclaim any graveyard no longer used or maintained. Historical societies across the state have published lists of lost or endangered cemeteries, many of them too far gone to restore. For example, in 2002, White County compiled a list of its top twenty-five "forgotten" cemeteries,[39] one of which had been used just the previous year. In addition to being abandoned, reasons given for the condition of these graveyards include "headstones are in a forest of trees," "overgrown and vandalized," "trees have fallen on the graves," and "stones have been accidentally bushhogged and broken and are stacked in a heap overgrown with brush." Three of these cemeteries are Black (one is labeled "Old Slave Cemetery"), while two others contain both the enslaved and their enslavers.[40]

Despite laws protecting them, sometimes cemeteries were deliberately destroyed. For example, fifty tombstones are missing from the "Scab Graveyard" (Franklin Co.), which originated during a coal miners' strike in 1898. According to an enumeration of this cemetery, "Some were killed in the strike and the local people would not let them be buried in their cemeteries. Western Coal & Mining Co. owned and donated the land for the cemetery. . . . Someone carried the tombstones away to use in the foundation of a house. No one could say where this house was located. Horses and cows have trampled the cemetery."[41] The fact that the miners were "foreigners" and Roman Catholics meant, according to local people, that they could not be buried in Protestant cemeteries—not that this was offered as an option.

NATIVE AMERICAN BURIAL CUSTOMS

The first Paleoindians, known as the Clovis culture, are believed to have entered what would become Arkansas via the Mississippi River sometime between 11,500 and 8500 BCE.[42] They were followed by the Dalton culture (8500 to 1000 BCE), and it is their cemetery, known as the Sloan site, that was excavated in 1974 on sand dunes near the Cache River (Greene Co.). There, "spatial patterning of the artifacts and bone fragments suggests there may have been about 28 to 30 people buried there," according to the Arkansas Archeological Survey.[43] The artifacts (stone tools) are either offerings indicating the individual's status or objects "intended for use in the afterlife."[44] Furthermore, because there was no evidence of human habitation at the site, according to Dan F. Morse, the archaeologist who oversaw the excavation, "We can assume that the only anthropogenic use of the site was for burial of individuals," thus making it a true cemetery.[45]

Next came the Woodland period (1000 BCE to 1000 AD) and, with it, the beginning of mound building. Some conical mounds were used to contain burials, such as an Early Woodland graveyard (1000 BCE to 200 BCE) in northeast Arkansas, which contained bodies laid out in an east-west orientation, some accompanied by grave goods.[46] During the Middle Woodland period (200 BCE to AD 300) fewer burial mounds were built in Arkansas, but one of the most elaborate was the Helena Crossing site, now destroyed, near the city of Helena (Phillips Co.). Inside five mounds were found both male and female remains, along with pottery, marine and mussel shell cups and spoons, and jewelry. The most lavish burial was that of an adolescent who wore pearls, shell beads, and wolf canine teeth, held earspools in both hands, and had a silver and copper panpipe on the chest.[47]

During the Late Woodland period (AD 300–1000) even more mounds were built, both dome-shaped and platform mounds, some of these the work of the Plum Bayou people. The Mississippian period, the last of these designations, started in AD 1000. This era saw some use of charnel houses ("a type of temporary mausoleum"), thatched structures in which bodies were stored, with grave goods, before being later buried in mounds elsewhere on the site.[48]

The Mississippian period ended with the arrival of Hernando de Soto, in 1541, and is the beginning of written descriptions of Native people, as several survivors of the de Soto expedition wrote memoirs. Another early account, coming a century and a half later in 1721, was written by Father Pierre Charlevoix, who described a Quapaw graveyard in Eastern Arkansas during a smallpox epidemic. It was, he said, "like a wood [forest] of stakes and posts newly erected, on which was suspended almost every thing in use among these barbarians." Mourners poured food onto the graves and built fires near them, which, Charlevoix speculated, was done to aid the deceased.[49]

NEW GRAVEYARDS ON OLD GRAVE MOUNDS

In 1881, archaeologist Edward Palmer arrived in Arkansas to collect data on the prehistoric earthen mounds found along the eastern side of the state. He did so under the auspices of the Smithsonian Institution's Bureau of Ethnology (i.e., cultural anthropology), which had received congressional funding to form a Mound Exploration Division. His (and others') findings "demolished the theory of a lost race of non-Indian Mound-Builders" as having been the creators of the mounds, which were, in fact, "built by the ancestors of the historic eastern North American Indians."[50]

Palmer is often cited for his work on the Plum Bayou Mounds (formerly known as the Toltec Mounds, Lonoke Co.), believed to be the creation of the Plum Bayou people.[51] They built and used the site starting around AD 650, and mound building activity ceased in AD 1050; they used one of the mounds for burials. Native Americans of the Mississippian period used these mounds at a later date, also for burial purposes.[52]

By the time Palmer began his work, an estimated 1,100 Arkansas mounds had been destroyed both by farming and from using the mounds for material with which to create embankments under railroad tracks.[53] Some of the mounds that survived did so because whites buried their dead atop them to keep these graves dry during floods. These elevations weren't always sufficient, however. Akron Cemetery (Independence Co.), atop a seven-foot mound, contains several duplicate tombstones, presumably because "the river would wash markers away, and the family would replace them. The original stones would then surface . . . when the water would recede. There are legends that the Akron gravestones would surface in Newark two miles away following a White River flood."[54]

Situating cemeteries on mounds preserved some of the earthen structures but hindered Palmer. He wrote that one of the Jackson Mounds (Mississippi Co.) was so covered with graves "that no examination could be made of it,"[55] while the Web Mounds (Craighead Co.) "were covered with graves . . . [so] I concluded not to visit them,"[56] although an impassible road also played a part.

Even some of these elevated cemeteries have disappeared over time. Headstones have been destroyed by modern farming methods, and some mounds were intentionally removed. It is difficult to give an exact number of extant white cemeteries atop Native American mounds in Arkansas, but one source puts the existing number at sixty-four.[57] Some sites nominated for the National Register of Historic Places have had their addresses withheld to protect them, but it is easy to spot a mound rising above a plowed field, crowned with a scattering of marble tombstones. What follows is an account of three mound cemeteries that are still in use.

AUGUSTA MEMORIAL PARK, AUGUSTA (WOODRUFF CO.)

A plaque outside the cemetery, erected during Augusta's 1998 sesquicentennial, states authoritatively that the site "was the burial ground for the Chickasaws before the first settlers." Five years later, however, when the cemetery was nominated to the National Register of Historic Places, the claim was modified: "According to local legend, the cemetery may be built upon an ancient Indian burial mound."[58]

In any event, the cemetery's original name, Crescent Hill, came from the shape of the terrain, and its oldest graves sit at the crest of a gentle slope, whose earliest tombstone is that of hotelkeeper Penelopy Simmons (died 1852). There are also several headstones with emblems of Black fraternal lodges inside Augusta Memorial Park, within sight of nearby Mason Cemetery, the African American burying ground, separated by a road.

TYRONZA (POINSETT CO.)

In 1883, Edward Palmer visited what was then called Tyronza Station, where seventeen of the original forty or fifty mounds still remained (today there are just three).[59] The largest mound Palmer saw may have survived because a house had been built on it, while the next largest was covered "by a modern grave yard."[60]

Palmer wrote that he was denied permission to dig into three mounds whose owner used them to pen up livestock during times of high water. Cindy Grisham, in her history of Tyronza, believes that this landowner was Martha Ann Stalker, who ran the boardinghouse where Palmer likely stayed. It is Grisham's belief that a fourth one of Stalker's mounds, situated near her house, was off-limits because it was the burial site of Stalker's son James Baker (her son by her first husband) and Duncan Stalker (her third husband). This mound had been left untouched during the construction of the Kansas City, Fort Scott, and Gulf Railroad earlier that same year[61] but was destroyed in 1919 during highway construction.[62]

Two other mound cemeteries still exist, however. One is the East family's graveyard at the edge of a cotton field, whose oldest marked graves are those of J. H. East (died 1925) and wife Lottie (died 1920). The other, Webber cemetery, is on a large mound at the back of land that became Tyronza's town cemetery in 1926.

MOUND CEMETERY, A.K.A. OLD MOUND CEMETERY, ARKANSAS CITY (DESHA CO.)

Edward Palmer visited this mound in 1882, but as it had been used as a cemetery since at least 1866 (the earliest date found on a tombstone) it contained too many graves for him to excavate. He reported that bones, pottery, and bricks had been turned up by gravediggers—evidence, he said, of the mound "having been inhabited previous to the advent of the Whites."[63] It has been determined to be a Mississippian mound, built between AD 1200 and 1600.[64]

Mound Cemetery is just three miles from the Mississippi River and was affected by the catastrophic flood of 1927, after which levees were raised and fortified. This brought an end to routine spring flooding, known as "the overflow." Palmer described the "novel procession" that attended burials in times of high water: "Should any one depart this life at Arkansaw City during an overflow the remains is [sic] taken to this mound in a boat followed by the inhabitants in various kinds of water crafts."[65]

Today, most of the monuments on the top of the mound are broken, scattered, and in many instances illegible. In contrast, Memorial Garden Cemetery, at the base of the mound, is tidy and well-maintained. According to a metal plaque erected by the Arkansas Black History Advisory Commission in 2008, "Enslaved persons are at the foot of the mound, with whites at the summit." Following the Civil War, "the mound continued to be used as a community burial place" by both races, as evidenced by the large number of tombstones bearing the emblems of Black fraternal lodges.[66] The earliest date found on these markers is 1885.

Though this is clearly an example of whites taking the highest and driest burial spots for themselves, Blacks may have had an issue with using mounds for their burials. Ruth Polk Patterson, in her memoir about growing up near Muddy Fork (Polk Co.), described a taboo from her childhood. "The old Indian mounds were the dwelling place of the dead, of course, and the children were taught to observe the mound with great respect," she wrote of her childhood among extended family in the 1930s. "If a person came upon the mounds in the woods, he was instructed never to walk atop them but to walk

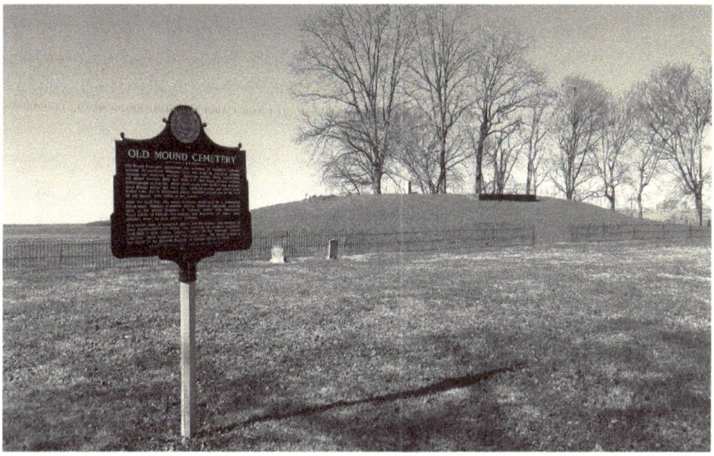

Fig 1.1. Whites once buried their dead on top of this Native American mound, while Blacks were relegated to the flood-prone lower land. Old Mound Cemetery, Arkansas City (Desha Co.).

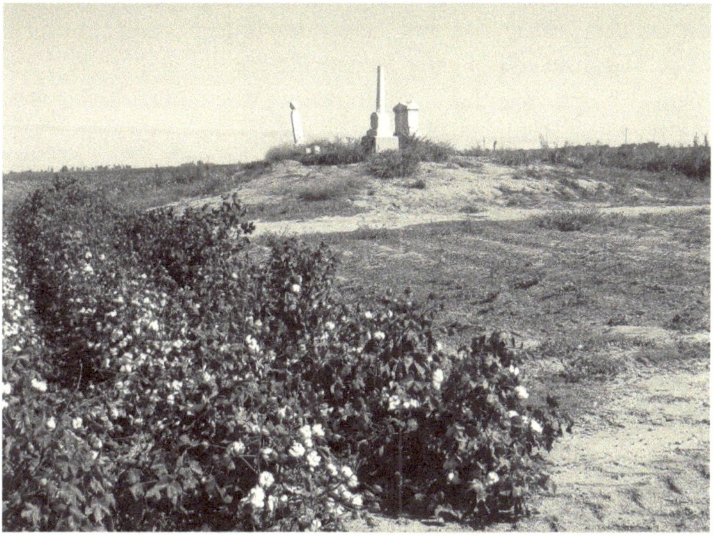

Fig 1.2. Cemeteries on Native American mounds are easy to spot from a distance, such as McFadden Cemetery, surrounded by cotton fields near Wilson (Mississippi Co.).

several yards around them, lest the spirits of the dead Indians come to life and avenge themselves on the intruder."[67] Palmer also recorded this taboo. He was denied permission to excavate a mound belonging to one Captain Cook at Forrest City (St. Francis Co.) on the grounds that Cook's Black tenants "would not rent his land for fear of hants,"[68] a colloquial version of "haunt," a term for ghosts or restless spirits.

OTHER EARLY GRAVES AND GRAVEYARDS

Marking a burial years or even decades after the death is known as backdating, and doing so after the passage of time can result in errors. Whitehouse Cemetery at Arnett (Elkins area, Washington Co.) has backdated itself. The gatepost signage states that the cemetery was "established 1800 with land donated by the Hanna family, 1854." However, the earliest marked grave is Samuel Hanna's, who died in 1837. (His marker and the surrounding ones are in the form of necked discoids, an early design, and are not modern replacements.) It's possible that there could be earlier, unmarked graves, but they wouldn't be much older than Samuel's, as this valley was settled between 1833 and 1835.[69]

Town pride can perpetuate errors as well. Batesville (Independence Co.) boasts in promotional literature that it has the earliest cemetery in the state, but this, too, is an error.[70] The town's Pioneer Cemetery, formally established in 1826, doubtless contains burials made prior to this date as the first settlers arrived around 1810, and the town was partially laid out by 1821.[71] However, Jane Kinman's ledger-style marker is not proof of this, as her death date was 1848 and not, as the town claims, 1818. Hers, and other tombstones with death dates in the 1840s, are shallowly carved, and their delicate typeface means that fours are easily mistaken for ones.[72]

Families didn't always have access to professionally carved tombstones, and even the sturdiest stone is subject to breakage, outright destruction, or—in the case of riverside cemeteries—being washed away by high water. Add to this the practice of backdating tombstones and determining the state's oldest, original tombstone becomes problematic. Corning's city cemetery (Clay Co.) might

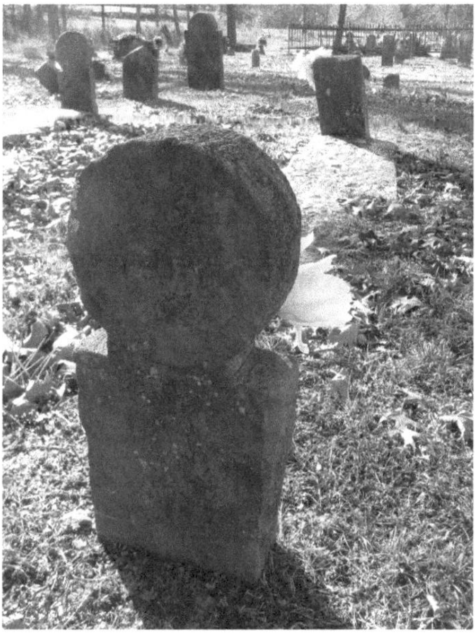

Fig 1.3. Necked discoids, a very old tablet shape, are found throughout the Ozarks. These examples date from 1837 through the 1850s. Whitehouse Cemetery (Washington Co.).

have claimed the title, if only the headstone in question could still be found. According to a town history, "Great oaks from little acorns grow, but it is strange indeed to think that the beautiful Corning cemetery sprang from a little Wart!" That would be E.C. Wart, "borned" in 1814 and "Dide" on July 24, 1815.[73] No trace of this child's marker can be found in recent times.

Although the death date is hard to see (the cemetery is surrounded by a locked iron fence), the Pyeatte-Mason Cemetery at Maumelle (Pulaski Co.) has a marker inscribed 1818. Found on Andrew Scott's box crypt, it is one of only two stones, out of the ten marked burials in this early cemetery, carved with a death date.[74] This leaves Fort Smith National Cemetery (Sebastian Co.) as runner-up for the contender of oldest headstone. In this case, it's a standard military-issue marker for army surgeon Thomas Russell, who died at the fort on August 24, 1819. His is "thought to be" the oldest burial there. However, the fort had been established for well over a year and a half before Russell died, during which time it was occupied by soldiers who were so ill while en route to the fort that they had to spend time recuperating at Arkansas Post before proceeding.[75] One source states that the graveyard was established in 1817 and "mostly unmarked,"[76] while English naturalist Thomas Nuttall, who met Russell at the fort a few months before Russell's death, wrote that he "now sleeps obscurely in unhallowed earth!"[77] The contents of this graveyard were moved to the National Cemetery in Fort Smith in 1867.[78]

THE STATE'S MOST UNUSUAL CEMETERIES

Singling out some graveyards for attention is as unfair as singling out one child for acclaim while ignoring its siblings. Any attempt to create a list of the state's oldest or grandest cemeteries quickly becomes complicated and almost inevitably leads to overlooking something of interest. Still, if any cemetery is unusual and belongs on a taphophile's bucket list, it's Mount Holly in Little Rock (Pulaski Co.) due to its history, the fame of its occupants, and the extravagance of its marble monuments. Though established in 1843, the grounds contain over sixty tombstones bearing much earlier death dates. Little Rock was settled in 1820, at which time families buried their dead on their own land or used a public burying ground located beneath what is, today, the Federal Building on the grounds of the state capitol. In 1834, the city council prohibited burial on private property and, as the city's original public graveyard was filling up, these earlier graves were exhumed and moved to the newly established Mount Holly Cemetery at 1200 Broadway.[79]

This "Westminster Abbey of Arkansas" holds the remains and, in some instances, the likenesses of illustrious statesmen, governors, and other notables. Still, the most arresting markers are those whose meanings are conveyed through the funereal symbolism of the mid-1800s to early 1900s, such as three-dimensional broken or pall-draped columns, infinity represented by a snake biting its own tail (known as an Ouroboros), and three-dimensional marble angels, cherubs, lambs, and doves.

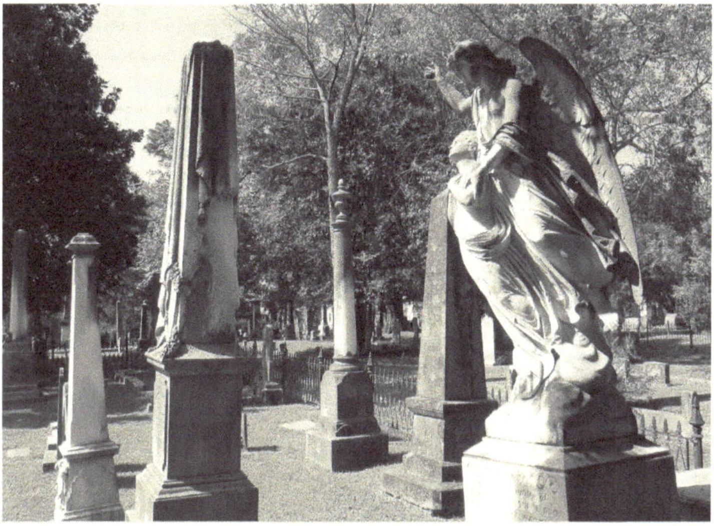

Fig 1.4. Known as the "Westminster Abbey of Arkansas" due to the notable Arkansans buried there, Mount Holly Cemetery houses elaborate markers and statues, such as Mary Watkins being lifted from her grave by an angel (at right). Little Rock (Pulaski Co.).

Though Mount Holly contains a few Black burials and, at one time, had a section reserved for Jewish ones (most of which were moved to Oakland and Fraternal Cemetery's secular Jewish section between 1874 and 1915), it does not give the appearance of being divided into ethnic or religious subsections. This is in contrast with several of the state's largest cemeteries that are, in reality, made up of several small cemeteries separated—or segregated—by race or religion. Little Rock's Oakland and Fraternal Cemetery contains the greatest number of burial grounds: Fraternal (which is Black), National, two Confederate, and two Jewish (Jewish Oakland and Agudath Achim) cemeteries, in addition to white Protestant burials, including several sections for infants.[80] This count, however, overlooks the original African American section inside of Oakland, abandoned when Fraternal was established across the road in 1888.[81]

Texarkana's Stateline Cemetery (Miller Co.) is another conglomerate of burial grounds. Its formal entrance gates face the road that is, literally, the state line between Arkansas and Texas. An interior fence and gate divide the white burials from Woodlawn No. 2, which contains two African American graveyards and a second white one. The Stateline side also includes Mt. Sinai Memorial Park, a Jewish cemetery delineated by plantings and a large Star of David.

ETHNIC COMMUNITIES AND THEIR CEMETERIES

Felton D. Freeman, at work on a PhD in sociology in 1948, wrote that foreigners were not exactly plentiful throughout the South, yet "an observer traveling over the state of Arkansas cannot fail . . . to note the considerably ethnic heterogeneity that is represented," especially in towns along the state's back roads. As evidence Freeman cited the communities of Marche (a Polish town with a French name), Gospoda, Tontitown, Ulm, Stuttgart, and Slovaktown.[82] One wonders what conclusions he would have drawn from the Arkansas towns named Congo, Egypt, Macedonia, Palestine, and Thebes.

Marche (Pulaski Co.) and Gospoda (Prairie Co.) have disappeared from state maps, but the rest still exist, and some are thriving. Stuttgart, one of two county seats of Arkansas County, and the tiny town of Ulm (Prairie Co.) were both founded by German Lutherans. Slovaktown, now known as Slovak (Prairie Co.), was created by Pennsylvania's Slovak Colonization Company in 1894.[83] Tontitown (Washington Co.) was settled by Italian Catholics who initially immigrated to work on plantations in the Arkansas Delta (Chicot Co.) in the 1890s but who relocated to northwest Arkansas in 1898 to escape unfair and harsh living and working conditions. One year later, the death of Pacifico Bastianelli led to the founding of Tontitown's St. Joseph's Cemetery.[84] (The Italians who stayed behind founded Hyner Cemetery in 1898.[85]) Despite Freeman's emphasis on place names, immigration can more easily be traced through the names of cemeteries, such as these in Prairie County: Czech National (south of Hazen), Slovak Catholic Cemetery (next to Saints Cyril and Methodius Church), and Slovak's Russian Orthodox Cemetery.

Internally these cemeteries are not noticeably different from the Lutheran and Catholic cemeteries found elsewhere, where Catholic iconography (rosaries, chalices, praying hands) predominates on tombstones, although modern markers are just as likely to contain emblems referencing the region's rice-growing and duck-hunting cultures. One exception is the Russian Orthodox cemetery, near Slovak, where the gateway arch and numerous grave markers display the Russian Orthodox cross. This emblem, the symbol of the Russian Orthodox Church, has three crossbars. Moving from top to bottom, they represent Pilate's inscription above Jesus's head (INRI, or "King of the Jews"), the beam on which the hands are nailed, and, at the bottom, the footrest that supported the crucified person's feet, portrayed in the emblem as a short, slanted crossbar.

JEWISH CEMETERIES

> Strange are the mysteries God employs.
> Yet we his love will trust;
> Though it should blight our dearest joys,
> And bruise us into dust.
>
> —SELIGMAN SEEMAN, 1834–1892; MINA SEEMAN, 1836–1893, BETH EL CEMETERY, HELENA (PHILLIPS CO.)

Abraham Block has the distinction of being the first person of the Jewish faith to settle in Arkansas, taking up residence in Washington (Hempstead Co.) as early as 1823, and on its tax rolls in 1825.[86] Block's wife and children joined him a few years later.[87] In 1828, their son Isaac died just two weeks before his eleventh birthday and was buried in the town cemetery (now known as Pioneer Cemetery), becoming the state's first documented Jewish burial. The next Jewish settlers arrived around 1830, after the territory's administrative center was moved from Arkansas Post to Little Rock.[88] The location of the state's first Jewish graveyard, established in Little Rock on a one-acre plot of land specially designated as a Hebrew burial ground, was lost during the Civil War.[89]

As Jews moved into other parts of Arkansas, they established synagogues and cemeteries, such as Jewish Rest Cemetery in Hot Springs

(Garland Co.), Temple Beth El Emeth's Jewish Rest Cemetery in Camden (Ouachita Co.), founded 1870, and Temple Beth El Cemetery in Helena (Phillips Co.), founded in 1875, which is actually the second Jewish cemetery in Helena. Graves in the first one were exhumed and moved into Temple Beth El the year it was founded.[90]

Some Jewish burial grounds are located within larger nondenominational cemeteries, such as Congregation Anshe Emeth Cemetery inside Pine Bluff's Bellwood Cemetery (Jefferson Co.) and, as mentioned earlier, Mt. Sinai inside Texarkana's State Line (Miller Co.), and two inside Little Rock's Oakland and Fraternal Cemetery (Pulaski Co.). Of these two in Little Rock, B'nai Israel was established first and includes Jewish burials disinterred from Mount Holly starting in 1874, with the Orthodox congregation of Agudath Achim creating an adjacent graveyard inside Oakland and Fraternal in 1902.[91] Jonesboro (Craighead Co.) also has two Jewish cemeteries: Temple Israel, meticulously maintained with nearly every grave outlined with a stone curb, known as a cradle, and nearby Mt. Sinai, an Orthodox burial site both inaccessible and abandoned, with only a half dozen headstones.

The two Jewish cemeteries inside Oakland, in Little Rock, contain interments from across the state, as not all synagogues maintained their own burial grounds. In some communities Jews used their local cemeteries. For example, the congregants of McGehee's Temple Meir Chayim, dedicated in 1949 and closed in 2016 (Desha Co.), buried their dead in family plots in the McGehee town cemetery, in Walnut Lake Cemetery near Dumas (Desha Co.), and in Bellwood Cemetery in Pine Bluff (Jefferson Co.).

Many of the oldest Jewish grave markers contain the same iconography found on Protestant ones, including lambs, doves, roses, lilies, clasping or pointing hands, sculpted books, urns, and marble infants. Rare, but also universal: bas-relief carvings of reaped sheaves of wheat and trees with broken, toppled trunks.

With the exception of the six-pointed Star of David, mortuary symbols unique to Judaism are quite rare in Arkansas and are sometimes misinterpreted. Ten-month-old Joseph Edward Iness's marker in Sand Hill Cemetery (died 1883, Newton Co.) is a unique piece of folk art that depicts a roosting dove, perched on what may be the handle of a shovel. Easily overlooked, at the base of this tablet, is a shallow carving of a seven-branch menorah.[92] This is not proof that an isolated corner

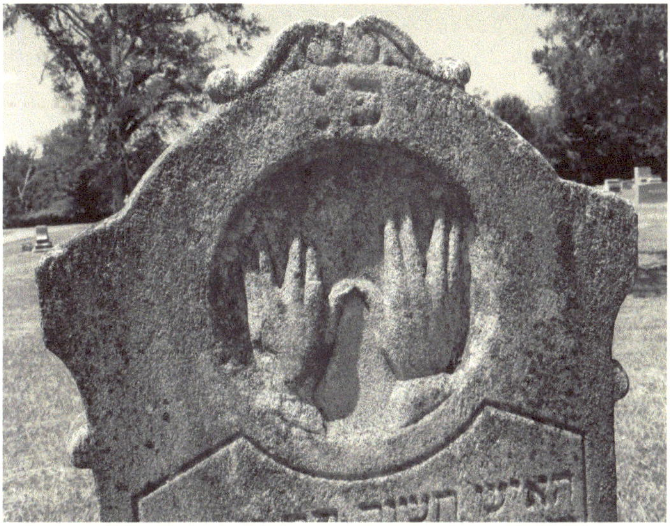

Fig 1.5. Sam Altschul's marker displays the kohanim hands, denoting men who are descendants of priests. Bellwood Cemetery, Pine Bluff (Jefferson Co.).

of Newton County was once home to a Jewish family, however, as traditionally this emblem is found *only* on women's markers.

In addition to finding Hebrew writing or a Star of David on a headstone, the most obvious way to identify a Jewish burial—although this custom is occasionally now found in Protestant cemeteries—is by the presence of small rocks, or pebbles, placed on the marker. "Judaism teaches that the guarantee of immortality to the deceased is how the dead are remembered by the living," writes Rabbi Joshua L. Segal. "Pebbles on a monument show other visitors that the individual buried on that site has been visited recently and has not been forgotten."[93]

The most attention-getting emblem, however, is known as the kohanim hands: two hands depicted with the middle and ring fingers splayed to form a V shape with thumbs and, sometimes, index fingers touching. This invariably reminds viewers of Leonard Nimoy's "Vulcan salute" from the *Star Trek* television show, which is not a coincidence as the actor acknowledged getting his inspiration for the gesture from this Jewish symbol. The emblem represents the priestly blessing and is found only on the headstones of men descended from priests. "Daughters of priests did not participate in offering the priestly blessing," Segal writes.[94]

According to Segal, "People with the last names 'Cohen, Kagan, Kahn, Kaplan and Katz' often have the hands of the priest on their monument,"[95] and in Arkansas examples are found on the headstones of Jacob Cohn (1820–1895) and Henry Cohn (1844–1904) in Jewish Rest in Hot Springs (Garland Co.). However, the headstones of Sam Altschul in Congregation Anshe Emeth in Pine Bluff (died 1878, Jefferson Co.) and Mendel Hopp in the Fort Smith Jewish Cemetery (died 1900, Sebastian Co.) also display the kohanim hands. "Jewish names are tendencies, not absolutes," Segal clarifies. "While names like Cohen, Katz, etc. are most likely to contain the hands, there are many others who claim priestly descent."[96]

Related to this is the symbol of the pitcher, found on graves of descendants of Levites, "historically the assistants to the priests," according to Segal. These are the men who washed the priest's hands before he gave the blessing. This, like the menorah, is gender-specific because, again, women did not participate. Two spousal headstones in Beth Jacob Cemetery in Fountain Lake (Garland Co.) have emblems of pitchers above the husbands' names and five-branch menorahs above the wives' names.[97]

There was no prohibition against Jews joining fraternal lodges, which is borne out by the variety of lodge emblems seen on Jewish headstones: Masons and the Eastern Star, Shriners, Odd Fellows, Knights of Pythias, Woodmen of the World, and Modern Woodmen of America. Jews also joined the B'nai B'rith, a benevolent Jewish fraternity founded in the United States in 1843, although the first of Arkansas's eight lodges was not established until 1866, in Pine Bluff (Jefferson Co.).[98] Two examples of this fraternity's emblem, a seven-branch menorah, are found in the Alexander plot inside Oakland and Fraternal (Pulaski Co.). Marx Hirsch's marker (1852–1878) in Jewish Rest in Camden (Ouachita Co.) contains an emblem that states his membership in the Elah Lodge of the International Order of B'nai B'rith, now called the B'nai B'rith International. But rather than using the menorah, this emblem has crossed feather quills—sometimes associated with court reporters or stenographers—along with the IOBB initials.[99]

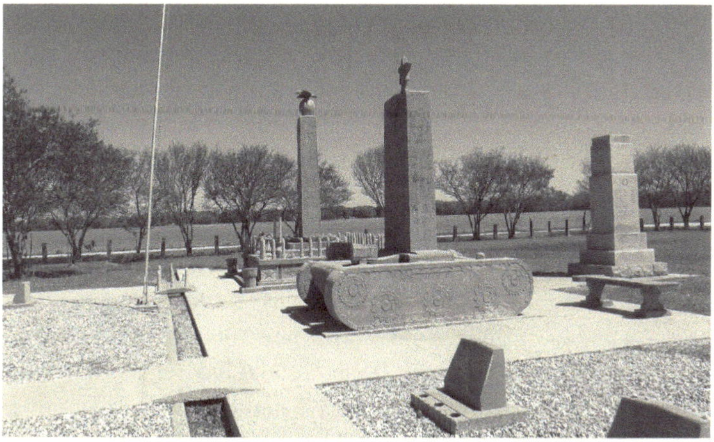

Fig 1.6. Japanese American citizens were detained at Rohwer Relocation Center for three years during World War II. In their cemetery, detainees created a concrete tank to honor the thirty men from Rohwer who died serving in the US Army, and an obelisk, covered in religious symbols, commemorating the twenty-four detainees buried there. Rohwer Relocation Center Cemetery (Desha Co.).

ROHWER RELOCATION CENTER AND CEMETERY

In October 1945, one month before the Rohwer Relocation Center (Desha Co.) was closed, Japanese Americans detained there put the finishing touches on the second of two immense concrete memorial monuments inside the camp's cemetery. Resembling a full-size military tank, complete with headlamps and caterpillar tracks, the monument honors thirty men from the camp who, as members of the US Fifth Army, 100 Battalion, 442 Regiment, were killed in battles in France, Italy, and Germany during World War II.[100] A modern granite marker repeats this list with the addition of Corporal Teruo Hozaki, killed in Italy.

The cemetery's other huge monument had been completed exactly one year earlier. It, like the tank, has a tall tablet rising from its center. This piece, created to honor those who were buried in the cemetery,[101] is covered in Japanese calligraphy and Buddhist religious imagery (including a lotus, crane, turtle, and rising sun), as well as employing military and patriotic emblems. Surrounding the stacked bases are representations of missiles, while the tablet is surmounted by a bald eagle perched atop a globe. Though it had been created a year before the site was shut down and its residents—forcibly sent there at the start of World War II—dispersed, the monument's creators anticipated the end. They inscribed the rear of the tablet with this wish, for when the time came: "May the people of Arkansas keep in beauty and reverence forever this ground where our bodies sleep."[102]

Sadly, the people of Arkansas did not. Within a short time the cemetery had become "nothing but a weed patch" or worse.[103] (In another account monuments could barely be seen over the brush, grass, and trees.[104]) In 1961, Japanese American members of the American Legion in Chicago joined forces with Desha County Boy Scouts and Future Farmers of America to clean up the cemetery.[105] It was rededicated in 1969,[106] perhaps after another cleanup, but it was not until 2010, with a $250,000 grant from the National Park Service, that the concrete monuments were professionally stabilized and restored. By that time the site had been placed on the National Register of Historic Places (in 1974), making it the sole remnant of an internment camp that had housed around 8,500 detainees during its operation from September 18, 1942, to November 30, 1945.[107]

In all, Rohwer Relocation Center and Jerome, the state's second internment camp for Japanese Americans (later used to hold German prisoners of war, situated in Drew and Chicot Counties) housed a combined total of around 16,000 detainees, 64 percent of whom were American citizens by birth, sent there from the West Coast. (Actor George Takei, incarcerated at Rohwer in 1942, when he was five years old, may now be its most famous detainee.) These were two of ten "relocation centers" built by the War Relocation Authority as part of an executive order signed by President Franklin D. Roosevelt in 1942 in response to the Japanese attack on Pearl Harbor. Rohwer was both the easternmost of the camps and the last one to close.[108] Its extreme temperatures, clay mud, primitive barracks-style living conditions, and ever-present mosquitos made it, according to one resident, "a living nightmare."[109]

Over the three years 168 detainees died at Rohwer and 76 at Jerome,[110] yet the sole cemetery has just twenty-four headstones—not counting one, outside the grounds, for the superintendent's dog (discussed in chapter 7). This is due to the fact that the residents

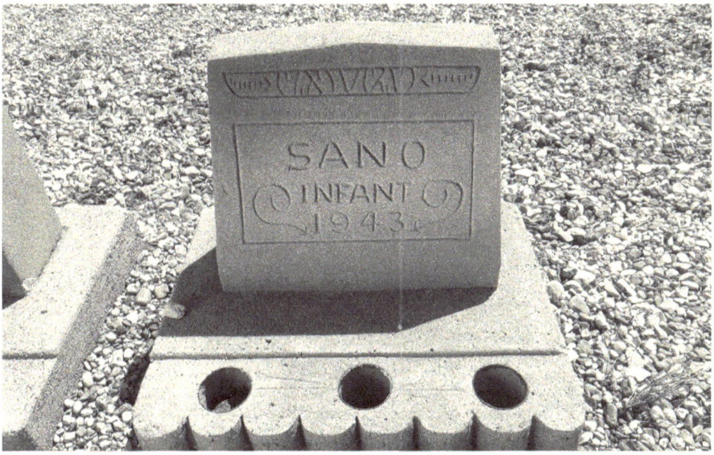

Fig 1.7. One of the twenty-four matching concrete grave markers made by detainees. Most bodies were cremated and families kept the ashes, but in these instances some bodies and cremains were interred. Rohwer Relocation Camp Cemetery (Desha Co.).

were predominantly Buddhist, a religion that favors cremation over burial. Then, too, the internees hoped to be released and would not have wanted to leave their dead behind. Bodies from both camps were transported to Memphis, Tennessee, for cremation under the auspices of the Dyer Funeral Home in the nearby town of McGehee. There is little information about this service, but one story survives. When Setsu Fukuda died at the Jerome camp in 1943, her ashes were returned to her daughter in a coffee can, which, when opened, contained a piece of paper identifying the cremains as "Jap Woman."[111]

Of the cemetery's twenty-four headstones, three mark the graves of unnamed infants identified only with surnames; three are for adult women. With the exception of one married man, the remaining seventeen graves are those of men whose death certificates list them as single, divorced, or widowed, with ages ranging from sixty to eighty-three. Their lack of relatives can be inferred from the California addresses given on their death certificates, which include "old folks home" and the Salvation Army. Five of these men were cremated, so presumably their cremains were then buried and given headstones.

One woman's story can be pieced together from information on her death certificate and from what is known of her family situation.

By the time she died from an advanced form of tuberculosis that may been responsible for her secondary cause of death, a miscarriage (recorded as an "Inevitable Abortion"), her only family member was her sister. Their mother had died in 1928, their father was assigned to a camp in another state, and their brother cannot be accounted for but may have been serving in the military. It is likely that her sister had no option except burial.

Books and memoirs about these camps often highlight the Japanese Americans' resourcefulness in creating beauty from found objects, and the cemetery exemplifies this. Here, concrete has been molded and shaped, patriotically painted (an American flag and the eagle both have color), or given delicate, traditional bas-relief decorations. Individual grave markers were made in a mold, the bases having three openings created by sinking tin cans into the wet concrete to make receptacles for plantings or bouquets. A photo taken in June 1944 shows the graveyard enclosed by a wood and wire fence with a picket gate. And echoing traditions practiced across the South, the ground appears to have been swept bare and each grave mounded with loose soil to create the appearance of a recent burial.

The memorial that expresses the wish that the graveyard be maintained also contains this prayer:

> To him who sleeps
> eternally here
> a descendant of
> glorious Yamato
> who came in his
> prime with hopes
> and ambitions
> heroic to battle
> the fortunes of
> life peace and bliss
> be yours.
>
> —1944

1. Evergreen Cemetery, Fayetteville (**Washington**)

2. Cherokee African American Cemetery (**Sebastian**)

3. Oak Ridge, aka Nebo Cemetery, Dardanelle (**Yell**)

4. De Ann Cemetery, Prescott (**Nevada**)

5. State Line Cemetery, Texarkana (**Miller**)

6. St. Mary's Cemetery, Bradley (**Lafayette**)

7. Mt. Willie Cemetery, Camden (**Ouachita**)

8. Hampton Springs Cemetery (**Dallas**)

9. Magnolia Cemetery, Helena (**Phillips**)

10. Scott Bond Cemetery, Forrest City (**St. Francis**)

11. George Berry Washington grave, Earle (**Crittenden**)

12. Gum Grove Cemetery, Newport (**Jackson**)

13. Grisso Cemetery (**Fulton**)

14. Oakland & Fraternal Cemetery, Little Rock (**Pulaski**)

15. Arkansas River | **16.** Mississippi River

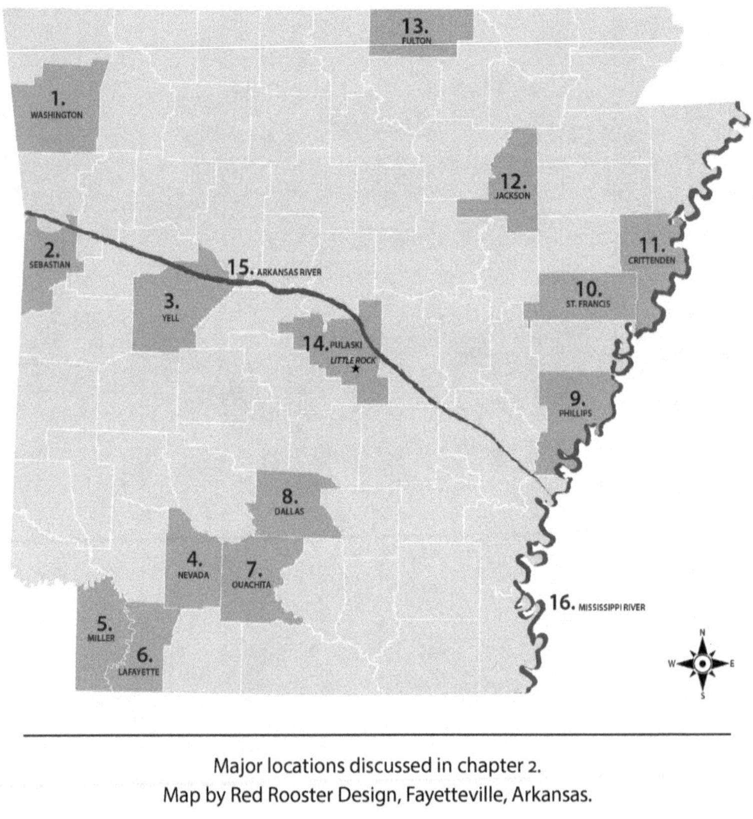

Major locations discussed in chapter 2.
Map by Red Rooster Design, Fayetteville, Arkansas.

Chapter 2

AFRICAN AMERICAN GRAVEYARDS AND GRAVE MARKERS

Hallelujah! tis done.
I believe in the Son.
I am saved by the blood
Of the Crucified One.[1]

—GEORGE BERRY WASHINGTON, 1864–1928, ARKANSAS HWY. 149 (CRITTENDEN CO.)

The corn growing in a small field near Earle (Crittenden Co.) is tall, but the marble angel standing on a mound at the back is even taller, giving the impression that she rises out of the green stalks. This angel, part celestial being, part mourning figure, is frozen in the act of dropping an open rose—the symbol of a full adult life—onto the grave of George Berry Washington.[2] The statue's marble pedestal, with its inscription stating that Washington was a minister and a Mason, has an empty niche that once held his portrait. Fortunately, the little ceramic photo was discovered in the dirt below the marker and is now on display at the Crittenden County Museum. It shows a smiling, mustachioed man in a suit and tie, its Windsor knot held in place with an oval pin.[3]

The sorrowful angel was purchased by Washington's daughters and his second wife as a tribute to the man who, born enslaved, had become one of Crittenden County's largest landowners by the time

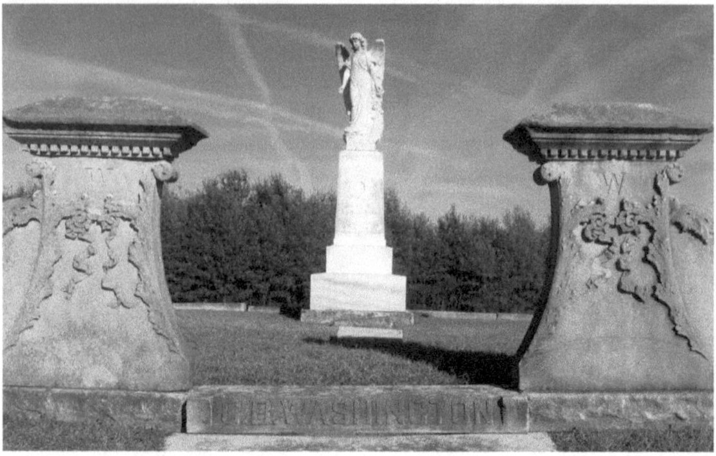

Fig 2.1. George Berry Washington (1864–1928) has an elaborate grave on a naturally occurring mound, all that remains of his 1,145-acre holdings, near Earle (Crittenden Co.).

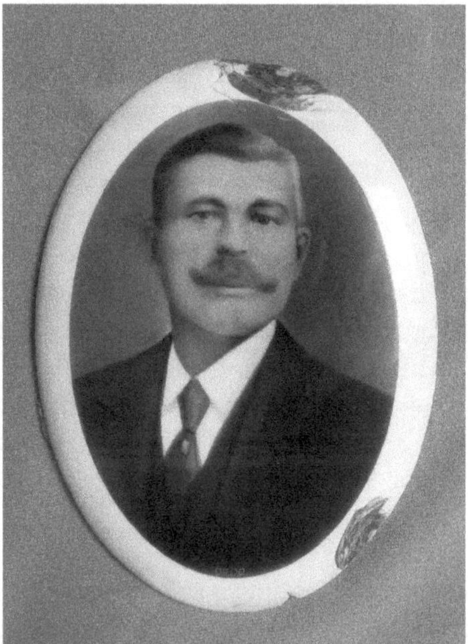

Fig 2.2. The photoceramic portrait of George Berry Washington, once attached to his marker, is now on display at the Crittenden County Museum at Earle.

he died in 1928 from acute gastritis, at age sixty-three. His grave is situated on top of a naturally formed knoll that could be mistaken for a Native American mound,[4] a logical conclusion given its proximity to the Parkin Mound, a Mississippian period (AD 1000–1541) American Indian village just five miles away as the crow flies. This small mound is all that's left of Washington's 1,145-acre holdings.

Washington's wealth had come from leasing out land under the sharecropping system, in addition to employing as many as one hundred farm laborers. A year after his death, however, his wife was forced to borrow almost $28,000 (the equivalent of well over $526,000 today[5]) in order to continue farming. Three years after that, at the height of the Great Depression, she defaulted on the loan and the property was sold. The grave, and its angel, are all that are left of Washington's plantation empire.[6]

Large statues of angels are not especially plentiful in Arkansas's white cemeteries and, except for small, commercially made concrete cherubs, are all but unknown in African American ones.[7] This makes Washington's sculpture an outlier, but one that would be perfectly at home among the showiest marble sculptures in a city cemetery. It lies at one end of the spectrum of funerary markers, with unmarked graves at the opposite end, and homemade and locally manufactured concrete markers somewhere in the middle. In addition, there are the professionally made stones supplied to members of various fraternal lodges. "The general poverty and oppression of the Black community did not permit many African-Americans the luxury of a fine tombstone," notes the National Register of Historic Places nominating form for De Ann Cemetery (Nevada Co.), founded in 1880.[8]

Magnolia Cemetery in Helena (Phillips Co.) is an exception. It contains a wide variety of grave markers while, at the same time, serving as a case study in how land was allotted to Blacks for their cemeteries. Here there is everything from homemade concrete tablets to expensive, professionally carved marble obelisks and draped urns, the largest and most detailed of which is W.H. Grey's tiered marker, which displays numerous emblems denoting his high Masonic rank and details his political accomplishments. The land throughout Magnolia Cemetery, however, has standing water after heavy rains and is flanked by a hillside too steep to easily accommodate burials.

Helena is in southeastern Arkansas, a region where a Black cemetery's neglected appearance could be attributed to a number of factors: cultural norms, a lack of funds with which to pay for upkeep, massive vandalism, and the sadly universal fact that Blacks' cemeteries were relegated to the lowest, swampiest land by whites, who buried their own dead on the highest, driest, and most scenic elevations. But there are other explanations for this lack of upkeep, which is common throughout the South. According to Vennie Deas-Moore, a South Carolina folklorist, Black families maintained their own family plots within cemeteries. "It isn't unusual to find an African-American grave completely overgrown, especially when burials are no longer taking place," she writes. But rather than being proof of neglect, "This . . . is done so the dead will not be disturbed."[9] Dr. Robert Miller, interviewed by Helena's Delta Cultural Center in 1999, voiced the same opinion that families were responsible for tending their own graves while acknowledging that not all of them did so.[10]

Carla Coleman, vice president and a founding member of Arkansas's Preservation of African American Cemeteries, explains another underlying cause. "Black people—we care, but it was always that you had a certain time to care for the cemeteries, and that care usually came during the fall," she says, adding that Mother's Day, Memorial Day, or some time in August were also traditional days for cemetery upkeep. "So, if you worked, whether it was in enslavement or sharecropping or work, that was the time you could go and attend to your gravesites." Money, says Coleman, was not allocated to pay cemetery caretakers.[11]

The disparity in cemetery upkeep was also the product of institutionalized racism. Little Rock's Fraternal Cemetery (later merged with Oakland and now officially called Oakland and Fraternal Historic Cemetery Park) is a case in point. Oakland Cemetery was founded in 1863 and was immediately used to bury the Civil War dead. Twenty-five years later, in 1888,[12] the Grand United Order of Odd Fellows, the Masons, and the Twelve Knights and Daughters of Tabor (all African American fraternal lodges) petitioned the city for burial grounds and were given fourteen acres.[13] This was named Fraternal Cemetery five years later. According to a study by Joe Neal, not only was two-thirds of Fraternal Cemetery affected whenever nearby Fourche Creek overflowed, "turning the countryside into an impassable swamp,"[14] but as recently as 1973 the cemetery was so overgrown and "wild-looking" that a B-grade movie filmed scenes there.[15]

This was the end product of decades of an unequal allocation of city money, according to Neal. Oakland, the white cemetery situated across the street from Fraternal, had wealthy clients who could afford burial plots, while Fraternal buried Black paupers and unclaimed "John Doe" bodies for free. "Jim Crow had a strange career in the graveyards," wrote Neal of the 1950s, a time when the two cemeteries were city-owned but Oakland had a $14,000 yearly budget and Fraternal received just $400. Over the next decade the Fraternal acreage was reduced by half as the city signed leases whose revenues went solely to Oakland. By 1962, Oakland was receiving over $10,000 per year from these leases, while Fraternal remained unfunded. "Seen in the light of these historical events, the weird apparition of Fraternal Cemetery in the 1970s becomes more comprehensible," Neal noted.[16]

GRAVES OF THE ENSLAVED

There is something about abandoned graveyards containing uncarved fieldstones that causes people to conclude that these must be "slave graves." Some such places have been labeled slave burial grounds based on no other evidence than the fact that the stones lack names and dates. While some of these places may, indeed, hold bodies of the enslaved, in the Ozarks prior to the Civil War, there were few professional carvers, and people marked graves with rocks, hoping to upgrade them to professionally carved markers as soon as possible.

There is very little documentation showing how the enslaved were buried, but according to Malinda Sutton, interviewed by the Works Progress Administration's Writers' Project in 1941, and who was Black (born in Arkansas in 1845), they "had no tombstones during slavery days,"[17] presumably referring to Black burials. In the 1930s, WPA workers (likely all white, many of whom recorded responses in "dialect") conducted interviews asking about people's lives under slavery, and 185 of these interviews contain information about Arkansas,

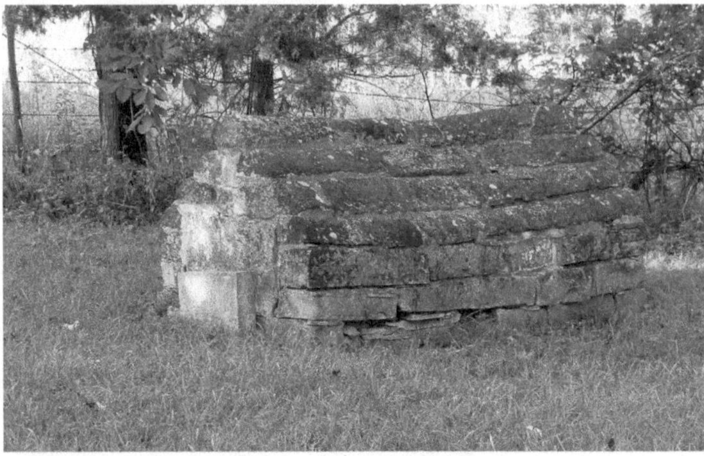

Fig 2.3. This small rock structure was built by an enslaved stone mason in 1857 over the grave of his brother. Grisso Cemetery (Fulton Co.). Photo courtesy of Vincent Anderson.

although very few mention graveyards and grave markers. Willis Winn said that although Blacks attended whites' burials and participated in the custom of dropping a handful of dirt into the open grave, Blacks were buried "anyway," adding, "Jest dig a ditch and civer them up."[18] Louis Davis said, "When a slave died, there wasn't no Christian burial, and there wasn't no ceremony of any kind."[19] John Bates appears to have answered this question twice, first equating such a burial with the disposal of dead livestock: "Jest digs a hole and rolls em in it and kivers em over wid dirt." He later elaborated that bodies were buried without any funeral.[20] The deliberate lack of respect at these burials likely extended to a refusal to mark the graves, although wooden markers, now lost, may have been used in some graveyards.

There is one notable exception, however: a stone box crypt with a pitched roof, found in Grisso Cemetery (Fulton Co.). Earl Harber recounted the story in 1975: "Jacob Grisso owned two slaves which were brothers. They were rock masons who were rented out by Mr. Grisso to build chimneys and to do other rock work. One of the brothers died of smallpox and was buried in the cemetery. The remaining brother, with the permission of Mr. Grisso, took a wagon and team of steers and built the monument which now covers the grave."[21] A concrete marker, placed there at a later date, is inscribed

"Grisso slave 1857" at one end of the structure, and there are two other in-ground concrete markers nearby inscribed "Slave" and "Allie the slave of Martin Harber 1859."[22]

CHEROKEE AFRICAN AMERICAN CEMETERY

Cemetery histories are difficult if not impossible to find, beyond the names and dates of the people buried there. It can be even harder to learn about ones that are rural and/or Black. Huntington's Cherokee African American Cemetery (Sebastian Co.) is a rare exception, thanks to research shared by sociologist and historian Jerry Harris Moore, whose family has, for generations, buried their dead in this graveyard.[23]

First, the name needs clarification. Though an online source says its unmarked stones "are thought to be the graves of people of Cherokee heritage,"[24] Moore says the name derives from Cherokee Creek, which originates in Oklahoma and runs north of the cemetery. "On the earliest maps the cemetery is known as Cherokee Chapel—which was a Black church that was organized before the Civil War, and burned down in 1894," Moore says. He adds that the cemetery has always been Black American.

According to Moore's research, the cemetery is on land originally owned by Elijah and Martha Wollage,[25] and the first two burials there were children Elijah fathered with Mariah, an enslaved woman who would ultimately bear ten children by him. Elijah, who died in 1870, left a will giving his property to wife Martha, after which the land passed to Mariah and her children. Mariah is buried in this cemetery, and very likely Elijah and Martha were as well, all three presumably in the section that is now underwater. This section flooded after the Frisco railroad tracks and their embankment were removed, which allowed Cherokee Creek to encroach on the cemetery. During a drought in the 1990s, Moore saw the outlines of graves in this area, but no headstones were visible.

The cemetery contains at least 102 identified burials, some of them marked with tablet-style sandstone markers made by Governor Knauls, a local coal miner who made tombstones on the side. Knauls created his final headstone to mark his own grave.[26] Moore explains why there is an iron cross next to the headstone of his great-great-grandfather Sam Martin (1850–1935), who was the manservant and bodyguard to the son of his white enslaver during the Civil War. The iron cross was placed there by the Sons of the Confederate Veterans in 2018 to commemorate Martin who, having survived the war, became a farmer, helped plot out Cherokee African American Cemetery, and later received a Confederate pension from the state.

SEGREGATION IN DEATH

The young, the old,
The rich and the high,
Shall mold unto dust,
And together shall lie.

—BIRD SHELTON, 1873–1902, WALNUT GROVE, NEWPORT (JACKSON CO.)

Perhaps unsurprisingly, this epitaph does not include "the Black and the white" among its list of intermingled remains. The verse is found in Walnut Grove Cemetery, Newport's white burying ground, located one short street away from Gum Grove Cemetery, which is African American. (See chapter 8 for an account of Caroline Dye, its most famous occupant.) Though these cemeteries are separate, in Arkansas—and elsewhere throughout the South—it is common to find adjoining Black and white graveyards divided by an unbroken length of chain-link fence, with no interior gate for passage between the two. (For that matter, even obituaries were segregated in Little Rock's *Arkansas Democrat* and *Arkansas Gazette* until the late 1950s and 1964, respectively.)

Segregation officially ended in 1964 with the signing of the Civil Rights Act and there are now fully integrated cemeteries, but Arkansas did not abandon the practice of dividing graveyards according to color. There were a few exceptions prior to 1964, as the races had long been buried side by side in potters' fields and prison and poor farm cemeteries.

It wasn't this way everywhere. The history of the Scott Bond Cemetery in Madison, just outside Forrest City (St. Francis Co.), illustrates changes in attitudes toward race and burial after the Civil War. According to Scott Bond's memoir, *From Slavery to Wealth*, published in 1917, the town's burying ground was a place where "white and colored for 50 years had buried promiscuously," which suggests that these graves were intermingled, or in close proximity.

This changed after it became known that the eighty-acre cemetery was owned by the Rock Island Railroad, which had the right to use the land for fill under railroad construction projects.[27] After Bond and a local minister took up a collection and personally surveyed the graveyard, the railroad deeded the property to the community and a three-man board of trustees was appointed. The trustees declared that the cemetery was now whites-only. Bond pointed out that Blacks, who had paid for the survey, were now fenced off from their own graves and lacked access to maintain them, but the trustees were unmoved. Bond then announced that he owned three acres adjacent to the existing graveyard and was going to deed this for use by the Black community. He described the ensuing reaction after he had a chance meeting with two of the trustees:

> They said they had thought over what I had said, about the piece of land I was going to give the colored people, and they had decided that the better way to do would be for me to deed that piece of land to the white people and they would give the old grave yard to the colored people. That if I gave the colored people the piece of land I spoke of the white people would have to always drive past the colored grave yard to get to the white people's grave yard.
>
> I told them I could not agree with them, because if it would be a disgrace to be buried with those now living it would be disgracing those that are already dead, and that it was not my object to disgrace anyone.[28]

The graveyard—originally called Madison Cemetery but today renamed the Scott Bond Cemetery—was then fenced and beautified. The graves of Bond and his entire family are marked by a single large obelisk, presumably placed there in 1933 after Bond was fatally gored by one of his bulls.[29]

This community graveyard is on high ground, but Black cemeteries were often situated on acreage prone to flooding. This is evident in the two oldest sections of Prescott's De Ann Cemetery (Nevada Co.). While it is not uncommon to find water covering graves in the Black section, the oldest white side is dry, perhaps because the ground may have been deliberately raised. A longtime resident remembered seeing a deep ditch (now filled in) separating the historic Black and white sections. "This ditch became a burying place for tramps and indigents of both races," according to the National Register of Historic Places nominating form. "It may have been the borrowing pit for dirt used to build up the west [white] end of the cemetery," with an informant likening the ditch area to "a kind of No Man's Land."[30]

SEGREGATION OF INDIVIDUALS

It's possible that somewhere there is a Black cemetery containing a single, white burial but, if so, it's unlikely that the deceased's race is spelled out on the headstone. The reverse is not true, however, when whites control the narrative, especially when they wanted to avoid anyone making assumptions about familial relationships within an otherwise all-white graveyard. Mariah Fancher, first enslaved by the Fancher family and then employed by them, is buried at a remove from other Fanchers in their family cemetery (1841–1901, Carroll Co.).[31] Her substantial and well-made tombstone includes the parenthetical (COLORED) in large letters separating her name from her birth and death dates.[32] This is similar to Tom Clements's marker in Mt. Zion Cemetery (1826–1916, Greene Co.), found at the end of a row of burials having the same surname.[33] Rev. Manen Clements brought enslaved people to Arkansas and, when freed, Tom Clements—a deeply religious man—stayed with the family and took care of the reverend's widow for nearly thirty years. His marker has "COLORED" in large, raised letters across its base.[34]

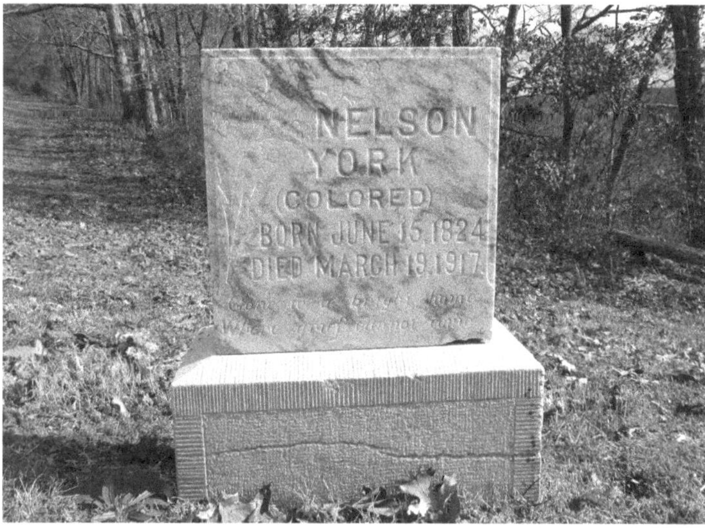

Fig 2.4. The word "colored" has sometimes been found on tombstones in white cemeteries, marking a Black burial. Nelson York (1824–1917), Lower Wharton Creek Cemetery (Madison Co.).

Without excusing racist behavior, it is possible that some whites thought they honored Blacks by burying them in proximity to their own graveyards or within their family plots. Such may have been the case with Jenny Madden (died 1903, Johnson Co.), whose stone, erected by Mrs. Arkansas Simpson next to her own family plot, contains a lengthy inscription in which Simpson talks about herself *in its entirety* while neglecting to give Madden's dates. She did, however, include the word "colored" as Madden appears to be the only Black burial in Brown Cemetery.[35]

One woman's story stands out in contrast to the rest: the burial of Adeline Blakeley (1850–1945) in Fayetteville's otherwise all-white Evergreen Cemetery (Washington Co.). According to one of her two obituaries, Blakeley "was the personal slave of Miss Elizabeth Parks, who married John Blakeley" in 1855. "Adeline took the Blakeley name at this time as was the custom."[36]

There is no truth to a local legend that Blakeley's body was brought to the cemetery in a sealed casket by the (white) Blakeley family using the ruse that Adeline was their aunt.[37] A descendant maintains that the burial was handled quickly and quietly to avoid local opposition, but the event was hardly a secret.[38] A Fayetteville newspaper reported that "a large crowd of white friends paid their last respects," gave the burial location, and listed six local businessmen who served as her pallbearers.[39] Two of these men were on the board of Evergreen Cemetery, as was Helen (Hudgins) Wiggans, Parks's granddaughter, who oversaw the burial. Blakeley's name and dates appear on the base of the family's shared plot marker, "next to Elizabeth Jane, her first mistress and longtime friend. She is the only black person buried in Evergreen Cemetery, interred with the family she served all of her life."[40]

THE LANGUAGE OF SEGREGATION

Tombstones made in an earlier era used language that may not have sounded racist at the time but certainly does now. Markers have been found for the enslaved that includes "Abbie, Campbell family slave, died circa 1860" (Searcy Co.)[41] and the following on headstones, all located in Crawford County: "Leanna / Colored girl of / Arnold O'Bryan / Aged 9 Ys";[42] "Negro Dan, former slave of James Edwards family, shot about 1870,"[43] and "Our little nurse Emily" in the family plot of Judge Jesse Turner.[44] None of these headstones dignify the enslaved person with a surname, several have death dates that were guessed at, and others contain no dates at all. Thanks to records kept by the sexton of Fairview Cemetery (Crawford Co.), we know that "little nurse Emily" was fifteen years old and died on August 31, 1862.[45]

One senses an attempt, by some whites, to pay tribute even though the language today is, at best, patronizing. Letty Horne, who took the surname of the family that had once enslaved her, is buried in White Church Cemetery (1792–1882, Prairie Co.) with the inscription: "Our father's and our own black mammy / With her tender care she nursed three generations of the family / We loved her."[46] The marker of "Aunt Kitty Sanford" (1833–1940) in Pine Bluff's Bellwood Cemetery (Jefferson Co.) reads: "Faithful slave servant / and friend to five / generations of the / Sanford, Lindsay and / Bocage families." In other instances, "faithful servant" is found on markers that were most likely paid for by whites.

These inscriptions are on what appear to be the original markers, but newer granite ones—modern creations erected on older burials—also

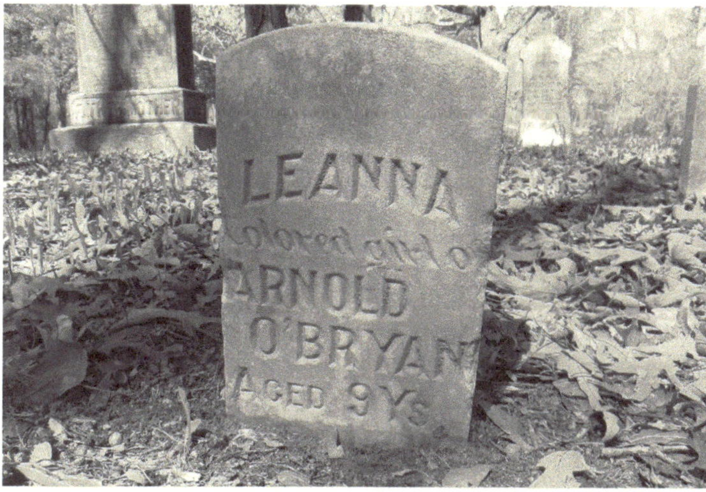

Fig 2.5. Leanna's marker is an example of the racist language found in inscriptions on graves of the enslaved. Peeveyhouse Cemetery (Crawford Co.).

display both racism and ignorance. In the late 1980s,[47] someone placed a marker on Bob Kidd's grave in Bean Cemetery (Washington Co.), a granite headstone inscribed, "Bob Kidd, 1824–1924, the slave of Tandy Kidd."[48] It doesn't take much research to discover that Robert Kidd was born in about 1842 and died in 1921, at about age seventy-nine, *not* age one hundred. He spent fifty-six of those years as a free man, a landowner who has a two-hundred-acre reservoir named in his honor. The burial location of Tandy Kidd, murdered in 1862, is unknown.[49]

It's hardly surprising that racism made its way onto headstones that were purchased by whites, because this language is also found in the obituaries of African Americans. This is illustrated by the following obituary for a man who, dying in 1903, had been enslaved for half of his lifetime, apparently the only thing pertinent to the obituary writer:

> Old Uncle Buck Evans, one of the oldest colored men in the county died at Batesville Wednesday at the age of 81 years. He was a former slave and was owned by Zachariah Saylors, one of the first settlers of this country. He was sold by Mr. Saylors to Perry Magness, then to Bill Magness, and was owned in succession by the following men: Ace Carpenter,

> Bill Meriwether and Tom Eaves. He was born on Uncle John Tomlinson's place near town and had lived in Big Bottom township all his life until a few months ago when he went to Batesville to live with a son.[50]

GRAVE MARKERS LARGE AND SMALL

Joe Neal's account of the early days of Little Rock's Fraternal Cemetery notes, "The earliest burials were the humble affairs of people born into slavery. Most of these first graves were never fitted with formal markers."[51] This is not surprising, as even Mount Holly, the capital's wealthiest white cemetery, used wooden headboards in its early years and those, too, did not survive.[52]

Some graves went unmarked because their headstones never made it to the purchasers. Tombstone salesmen solicited orders in Gregory (Woodruff Co.), which was on a railroad line. The headstones were delivered but "were used instead as pillars under houses. Those that are still in such positions cannot be read."[53] Two markers, lacking the year of death, were found near the site of a razed building, and another was found in the weeds near the Gregory train depot. This last example included a Black fraternal lodge emblem. These markers are not listed, online, in any of the county's cemeteries.

Related to the subject of mass-produced concrete markers (discussed in chapter 3) are ones made by local craftsmen, using commercial molds or homemade forms in which to shape tablets. Writing, inscribed while the concrete was still pliable, was done freehand or by pressing in, then removing, metal letters. Some carvers used stick-on letters, such as those found on mailboxes and house signs, owned professionally made stamps (doves, crosses, pointing hands, scrollwork), or repurposed metal decorative details of unknown origin that, when removed, left behind delicate and abstract shapes. Still other makers embedded ready-made cherub, angel faces, or ceramic figurines into the headstones' concrete surfaces.

Isaac Handley, a blind man working in the Brinkley area (Monroe Co.) up through the 1980s, was one such craftsman. A photo of

Handley shows him surrounded by examples of his work, all made from poured concrete in commercially made molds. A tablet-style marker, urns, and three-dimensional cherub statue seen in the photo have been found in cemeteries in numerous other counties, suggesting that Handley's molds were widely available.[54]

It is possible to identify some carvers based on distinctive symbols and decorative elements they applied to their concrete creations. Drew County contains over one hundred examples of markers, made up through the 1980s, embellished with an imprint of one or more four-petal flowers arranged along a leafy stalk. Though found predominately but not exclusively in Black cemeteries,[55] these are the work of Hubert Gumpert, a white craftsman whose markers are easily identifiable because, lacking a metal stamp with which to make a "2," he created one by placing a line at the base of a "9."[56]

Thanks to Evelyn Jackson Trammell's research, it is known who made over sixty unusual concrete headstones having a tripartite (three-prong) silhouette that has been called, locally, the "three point crown shape." According to Trammell's sources[57] William ("Willy") McGuire created these distinctive markers, almost all of which are found in St. Mary's Cemetery, a Black burying ground near Bradley (Lafayette Co.).[58] The markers' death dates range from 1926 to 1974.[59] McGuire used aluminum cookie cutters as molds to create decorative elements, packing concrete into the cutters and applying these shapes to the surfaces of markers and footstones. The molds, when removed, left behind raised shapes that bear the mark of the cutters' rippled edges and strap handles. He used stars and three of the four suits in a deck of cards: diamonds, hearts, and clubs.[60] Some are positioned sideways or upside down, and many bear traces of red paint. McGuire died around 1975 and is buried in St. Mary's Cemetery.[61]

A final marker category is that of repurposed objects, such as terracotta sewer tile, both shaped fragments and entire pieces. Woodlawn Cemetery No. 2 in Texarkana (Miller Co.) contains an upright piece of pristine ceramic pipe made by the San Antonio Sewer Pipe Works, and nearby are two metal water heaters marking graves inside a family plot.[62] Elsewhere on these grounds are homemade concrete markers embedded with seashells and shards of colored glass.

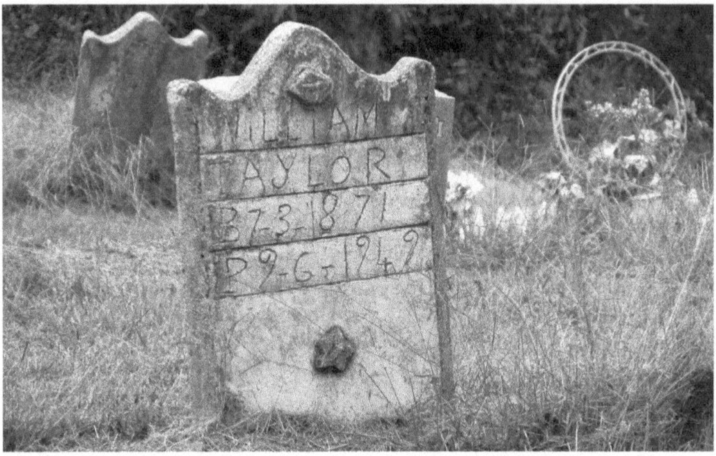

Fig 2.6. One of over sixty concrete tripartite markers made by William McGuire, using metal cookie cutters to create raised decorative details. St. Mary's Cemetery near Bradley (Lafayette Co.).

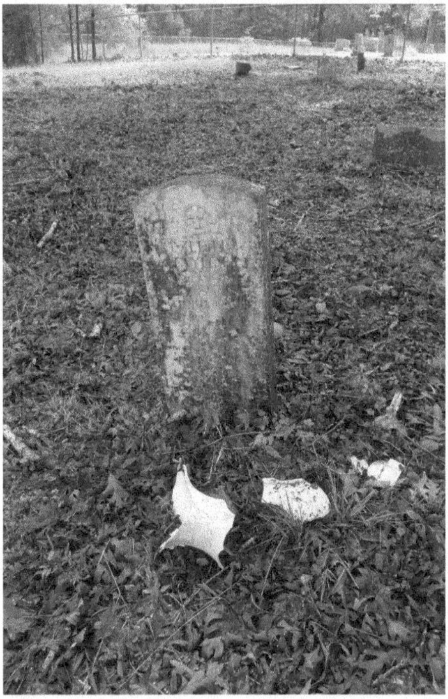

Fig 2.7. Broken glass and china, known as grave goods, on the grave of Ezekiel Taylor (died 1935), Hampton Springs Cemetery (Dallas Co.).

GRAVE GOODS AND OTHER OFFERINGS

Southern folklore literature has a lot to say about "grave goods," items left on graves by the living. Though today the term has come to mean anything decorative (toys, solar lights, flags), in the past such items were likely to have included broken dishes and other possessions once used by the deceased. This custom was not strictly an African American one, as it was practiced in a few white cemeteries, such as Corning's city cemetery (Clay Co.). Here there were once graves "adorned with dishes, china or glass or any object that seemed useful for a lasting remembrance on the grave of a departed loved one,"[63] although these pieces are not found there today and may simply have been intended to hold floral offerings. Similar objects have been documented on Black graves, such as Clemmie Farmer's (died 1925, Nevada Co.), photographed in 1954, which once held a collection of broken plates, cups, and at least one oil lamp. Nothing remains on Farmer's grave today, not even the mounded earth that once supported the row of objects.[64]

The best surviving collection of grave goods is found in Hampton Springs Cemetery (Dallas Co.). In 1982, when the Black section was nominated for inclusion on the National Register of Historic Places, the nomination form stated that the graves were marked "in . . . the traditional Afro-American method which has African antecedents," going on to call this "the only known resource in the county to have traditional Afro-American influences."[65] A ceramic pipe and a kerosene lamp were mentioned, used in lieu of headstones, with pipe (presumably a commercial drainage pipe) and petrified wood used to mark the foot of some graves.

"Grave offerings" seen in Hampton Springs included "mussel shells and broken glass and ceramic jars, bottles, plates and pitchers." The nomination form included a photo showing a grave whose entire length was covered in crockery.[66] A visit made to Hampton Springs in 2022 did not turn up mussel shells, the kerosene lamp, or bottles, but two graves were marked with petrified wood and three with the broken ends of glazed ceramic sewer pipe (one embossed with the manufacturer's name, Double Strength Pipe of Texarkana). Only one grave still had a collection of grave goods. The military marker of Ezekiel Taylor (died 1935)[67] was surrounded by pieces of pitchers and glazed ceramic mixing bowls, broken in half.

It's relevant that the bowls and pitchers were broken. According to a study of Afro-American decorative arts, "There is a discernible pattern in the types of objects left on graves. Most are containers, and most can be broken in such a way that they still retain their form." This breakage was not done to keep the items from being stolen (after all, even coins may be among the collection of items left on graves) but from a remembered custom. "Graveyard goods are a statement of homage; their function is to keep a tempestuous soul at rest. Far from being heaps of junk, funeral offerings are sanctified testimonies, material messages of the living intended to placate the potential fury of the deceased."[68]

CLOCK SYMBOLISM

Designs on tombstones fall into three categories—symbolic, literal, or decorative—and an understanding of symbolism can help us learn more about the deceased. Take clocks, for example. The original emblem used by the Benevolent and Protective Order of Elks is an elk's head whose antlers encircle a clock, its hands set at 11:00, the Elks' sacred hour. Their clock symbol serves as a type of memento mori, a reminder that the end is drawing near.

Actual clocks—or drawings of clocks—have occasionally been found on headstones, and those in Black cemeteries have their hands set to show the time of death. Mount Willie Cemetery near Camden (Ouachita Co.) contains two examples, both actual timepieces embedded in concrete headstones, each marking the grave of a minister. The hands of the Apollo brand timepiece set into Frank Hares's marker point to 10:00 and, for good measure, the words "10 O'clock" are written in the concrete on either side. Rev. Hares died on February 19, 1963, with no birth date given. The second example marks the grave of Rev. Adolph Murry (1901–1955), where the somewhat obscured hands on a Westclox brand Big Ben alarm clock appear to stand at 5:00.

Other examples have been found in Lee County, scratched onto homemade concrete markers. In Pilgrim Cemetery, Louis Pointer (1874–1964) has a marker whose large clock face has its hands faintly pointing to 3:00, while Morning Star Cemetery, now lost in the woods near Bear Creek Lake, contains two examples. The clock on Lucy

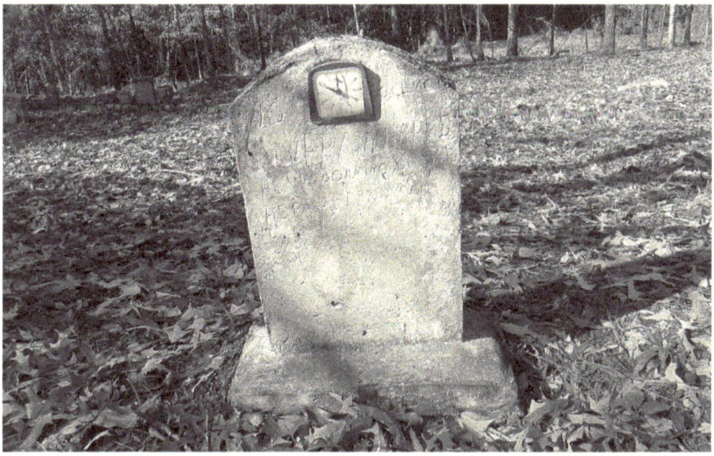

Fig 2.8. A clock, its hands set at the time of death, is embedded in the grave marker of Rev. Frank Hares (died 1963). Mount Willie Cemetery, near Camden (Ouachita Co.).

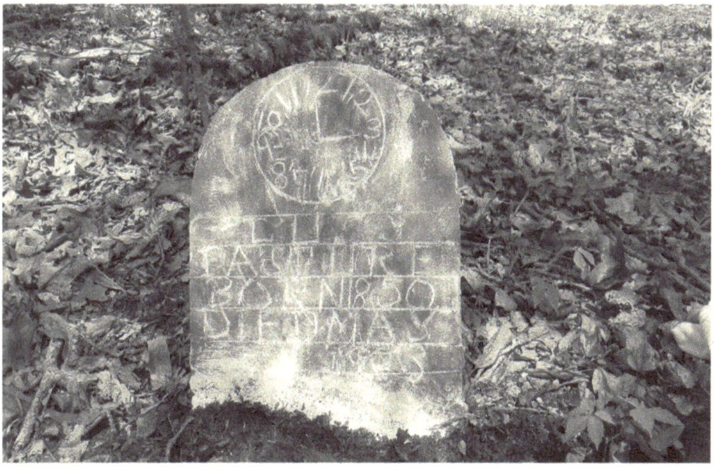

Fig 2.9. A clock, scratched into a concrete marker, with its hands presumably set at the time of death. Morning Star Cemetery (Lee Co.).

Pasture's grave (1850–1923) appears to be set to five minutes to 3:00 (although the hands are almost identical in length), while Johnnie Benford's clock reads 6:15 or, just as possibly, 3:30.[69] All of the markers in this cemetery are homemade, and several have "1965" scratched in them, perhaps the year that they were created.[70] (It should be noted that the remains of clocks have also been found in white cemeteries.[71])

In addition to the clocks, Morning Star Cemetery contains a single elaborate—and enigmatic—concrete marker. Encircled by decorative concrete posts, a round-topped marker (also bearing the 1965 date) marks a grave identified only as H.B., with this inscription:

> SOME DAY
> GONE OVER
> THE RIVER
> NEAVERRE
> FORGOTTEN
> WHEAR THE
> TREES ARE
> BLOOMING

The marker is set in a concrete base that is flush with the ground, on whose upper surface are scratched the enigmatic words: "Berry 3 feet in surper grave."

FRATERNAL LODGE EMBLEMS ON TOMBSTONES

Fraternal lodge symbolism—especially the Freemasons' compass and square—is found in practically all cemeteries, but African American ones tend to display a greater number, and variety, of these types of emblems. Fraternalism, in the form of Freemasonry, came to this country from England in 1733; in 1775, fifteen Blacks (including the free-born Prince Hall) were initiated into one of the British Army's Masonic lodges. Denied a charter to found a Masonic Lodge in this country, in 1791, these members created the African Grand Lodge of Massachusetts, later renaming it the Prince Hall Grand Lodge.[72] The first Black Masonic lodge in Arkansas was founded in Helena (Phillips Co.) in 1869 by Rev. Moses A. Dickson and together with the next two such Black lodges to be created (in Little Rock and Fort Smith) formed the Most Worshipful Grand Lodge (Colored) of Free and Accepted Masons, which erected a Masonic temple in Pine Bluff.[73]

Masonic emblems far outnumber those of any other lodges in white cemeteries, though not necessarily in Black ones. Perhaps this is because, unlike various Black lodges, the Masons did not provide tombstones for their members. Masonic lodges also had the greatest staying power, surviving the Depression and other events that caused smaller organizations to lose membership. But the Masons were just one of thousands of different fraternal organizations that once flourished in this country. (Women's lodges also used the term "fraternal.") Ironically, despite the various lodges' creeds emphasizing brotherhood and fellowship, they denied membership to Blacks, who formed highly popular and successful lodges of their own.

During fraternalism's heyday, between the end of the Civil War and the Depression, millions of people in this country received tangible benefits through their lodges. Some of these organizations, also called secret, benevolent, mutual benefit, and life insurance societies (each term having a slightly different connotation, but not synonymous with burial societies) founded hospitals or paid for medical treatments, provided assistance when traveling, established orphanages and widows' homes, and offered life insurance and various death benefits, although most fraternal lodges did not provide tombstones. According to one study, "In the 1920s, an estimated thirty million people, nearly half of the entire population of the United States, belonged to at least one secret order or fraternal benefit society."[74]

These social welfare benefits were of tremendous importance in an era before the creation of such federal entitlement programs as Social Security, unemployment, Medicaid, and Medicare. Prior to the availability of these safety nets, the only recourse for distressed widows, orphans, the elderly, and the indigent was going to the county poor farm—usually grim, dangerous, and socially stigmatizing places. The peace of mind experienced by a lodge member is nicely summed up by the emblem and motto on Ellis H. Shumate's marker (died 1906, White Co.),[75] which shows a wolf slinking away from a house as a bonneted woman brandishes her lodge membership paperwork. Inscribed around the edge of this scene: "The Fraternal Home keeps the wolf from the door."

The creed of the Odd Fellows (later renamed the Independent Order of Odd Fellows, or the IOOF; the Black affiliate is the Grand United Order of Odd Fellows, or GUOOF) includes the injunction to bury the dead, and to this end some IOOF lodges established public

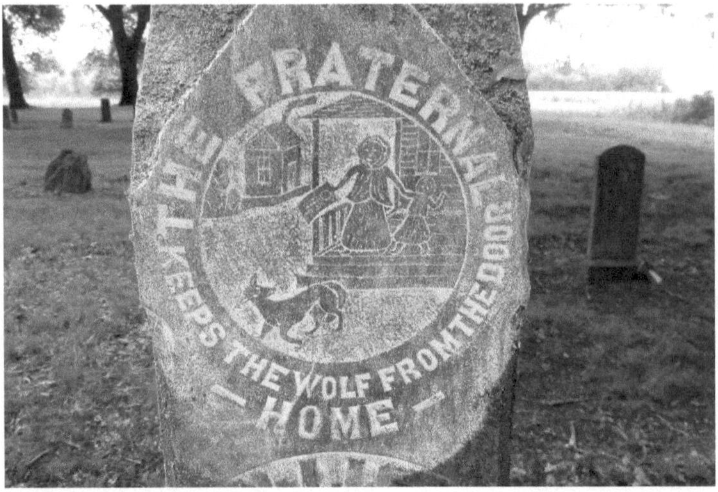

Fig 2.10. The emblem on Ellis Shumate's marker (1886–1906) shows a bonneted woman brandishing her lodge paperwork at a wolf, illustrating the security conferred by lodge membership. Old Dogwood Cemetery (White Co.).

cemeteries. These were almost always whites-only, but one exception is the IOOF cemetery in Eureka Springs (Carroll Co.), now deeded over to the town. There, Blacks are buried throughout the grounds, despite the local legend that they were consigned to a "Black section" next to the entrance gate.

It would be hard to overstate the importance and popularity of fraternalism and fraternal lodges. Newspapers would publish the times and meeting locations of these "secret societies," and cities prided themselves on the number of their lodges. Newport, the county seat of Jackson County (population seven thousand to eight thousand between 1870 and 1900) had the following Black lodges: Colored United Sons and Daughters of Friendship and Cooperative Union, International Order of the Twelve Knights and Daughters of Tabor, Israelites Cooperative, Protective and Beneficial Association, Knights of Pythias, Modern Order of Magians (a Black insurance benefit society founded in Newport in 1919 and bought out by another Black-owned insurance company in 1931),[76] Odd Fellows, Royal Circle of Friends, and both a Masonic lodge and a chapter of the Order of the Eastern Star, for women.[77]

Because different lodges offered different benefits, adults often carried multiple memberships, and thus some tombstones display multiple emblems. Oak Ridge, a.k.a. Nebo, Cemetery near Dardanelle (Yell Co.) exemplifies a community with numerous active lodges, as eleven different emblems are found on tombstones there, including two juvenile members of the Royal Circle of Friends, or RCF (identified on their stones as JUV No. 68). The columnar marker of Sophia Batson (died 1923) contains four emblems: the RCF lion, an Eastern Star, "D 333 T" (the women's symbol for the Twelve Knights and Daughters of Tabor), and a triangle containing initials M-I-L and the Latin motto "*Fortuna Audaces Iuvat*" (Fortune favors the brave), for a lodge whose identity is unknown.

All fraternal lodges, both Black and white, lost members during the Depression when high unemployment made it impossible for people to pay their dues and insurance premiums. While some of the smaller white lodges survived, most of the Black ones did not. According to a study of these societies, "This gloomy picture contrasted with those of previous depressions. During hard times in the past, workers had kept their dues current through strategies such as drawing from savings, borrowing money, or turning to kin networks. In some cases they had persuaded their lodges to carry them on the rolls."[78] Such strategies were not possible in the grim 1930s.

What follows is an overview of the most popular Black lodges that provided tombstones to their members as a death benefit. These distinctive stones are found in African American cemeteries across Arkansas and, in many cases, nationwide.

MOSAIC TEMPLARS OF AMERICA (MTA)

This mutual aid organization was founded in Little Rock in 1882 by John Edward Bush and Chester W. Keatts, both of whom started life enslaved. The MTA's goal was to provide burial insurance to Blacks; in 1913, it started providing tombstones as well. ("Mosaic" refers to the Biblical Moses.) The MTA's origin story was once so well known that an encyclopedia of notable African Americans needed only to remark, "Suffice it to say here that the need of a poor woman, begging

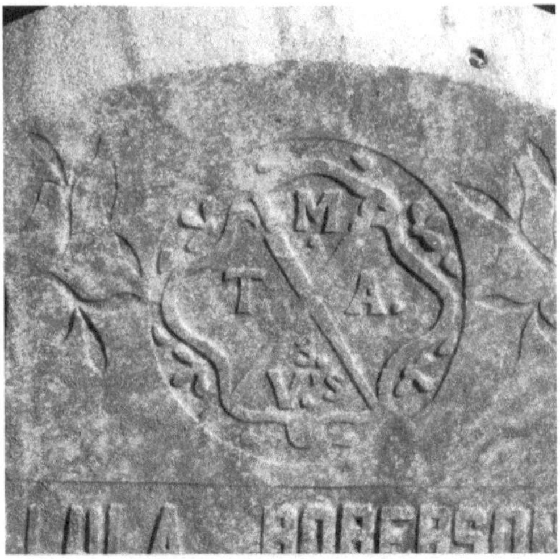

Fig 2.11. Mosaic Templars of America (MTA), founded in 1882 in Little Rock, Arkansas. Emblem on the grave of Lula Roberson (died 1920), Robinson Cemetery (Faulkner Co.).

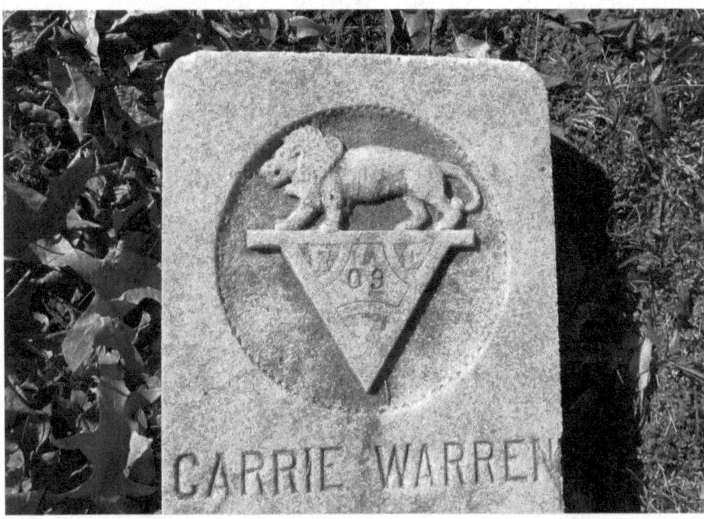

Fig 2.12. Royal Circle of Friends, founded in 1909 in Helena, Arkansas. Emblem on the grave of Carrie Warren (died 1912), Gum Grove Cemetery, Newport (Jackson Co.).

for help to bury her husband, the contempt of a white man and the chagrin of Mr. Bush at the whole situation started this organization."[79]

In addition to its insurance business, at the height of its popularity in the 1920s, the MTA also operated a building and loan association, a hospital and affiliated nursing school, and a newspaper. Its membership, estimated at over one hundred thousand, spanned twenty-six states and extended into South America. According to inscriptions on tombstones, men met in temples; women met in chambers. The organization went into receivership in 1930.[80]

Their marble markers, identical for both sexes, have a shallow carving depicting crossed shepherds' crooks encircled by a snake biting its own tail (an Ouroboros, or symbol of eternity) and "3 V's" for the Latin motto *Veni, Vidi, Veci* ("I came, I saw, I conquered").[81] The mausoleum of founder John Bush (1856–1916) contains an especially deep carving of the emblem, situated above its door, in Little Rock's Oakland and Fraternal Cemetery; Chester W. Keatts is buried nearby, his marker bearing a simplified emblem.

THE SUPREME ROYAL CIRCLE OF FRIENDS OF THE WORLD (RCF)

Founded in Helena (Phillips Co.) by Dr. Richard A. Williams to provide insurance, hospital coverage, and burial expenses to its members, Williams served as the Supreme Royal Circle of Friends' supreme president from the time of its inception in 1909 until his death in 1944. The lodge moved its headquarters to Chicago in 1918 and survived the Depression but filed for bankruptcy in 1947.[82]

The organization treated men and women equally; both sexes met in circles and were provided with identical marble headstones. The majority of these are upright columnar markers with the emblem carved on the beveled top surface: a lion, facing left, stands atop a triangle in which the RCF initials, in the corners, surround "09" for the lodge's founding year.

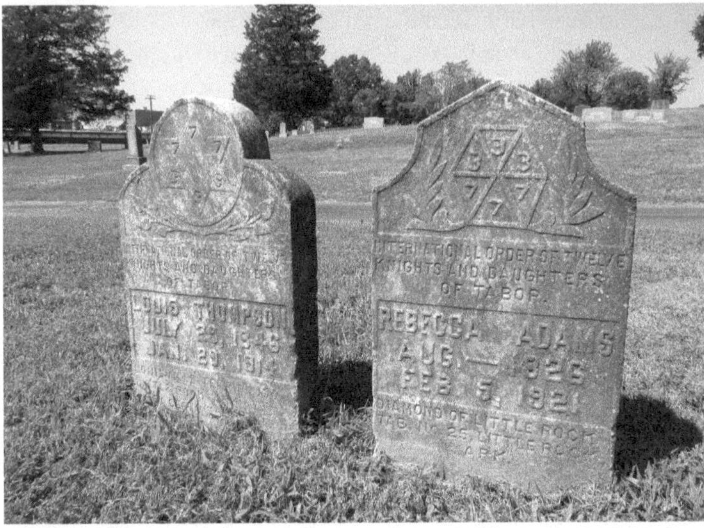

Fig 2.13. International Order of Twelve Knights and Daughters of Tabor, reorganized as a benevolent society in 1872 in Missouri. Louis Thompson (1846–1914), on left, has the emblem of the men's lodge (7s over 3s); Rebecca Adams (1826–1921), on right, has the emblem of the women's lodge (3s over 7s). Oakland and Fraternal Cemetery, Little Rock (Pulaski Co.).

INTERNATIONAL ORDER OF TWELVE KNIGHTS AND DAUGHTERS OF TABOR

The order grew out of an African American antislavery society, formed in 1846, reorganized in Missouri in 1872 as a benevolent society, and in receivership in 1930. A study of Black fraternal organizations concluded, "Women played a much more prominent role in African American fraternalism than they did in white fraternalism."[83] This is evident among the Taborians, who believed in treating men and women as equals,[84] with men meeting in temples and women in tabernacles.

Women's tombstones, found far oftener than men's, have a hexagon at the top, bisected to hold three 3s above three 7s. Men's markers are topped with a circle, inside of which is a six-pointed star whose points display three 7s above three 3s, although these are abbreviated on some tombstones to just "333" or "777" to make room for the logos of other lodges. No full explanation for the significance of these numbers has been found, but many lodges had sacred—and secret—numbers.

PARALLEL LODGES

Denied the charters that would have allowed them to establish Masonic, Odd Fellows, and Knights of Pythias lodges, Blacks formed fraternal lodges that paralleled these, using the same names and, for the most part, the same emblems on their tombstones. Identical to the stones of their white counterparts, Prince Hall Masons' tombstones display the compass and square, and the women's lodge, the Eastern Star, uses the same five-pointed star.

The Grand United Order of Odd Fellows was formed in this country in 1842 after Peter Ogden, an American freeman who was already a member in England, was denied membership by New York City's white Odd Fellows lodge. Ogden returned to England and received a charter there.[85] The first Arkansas lodge was established in 1876.

The GUOOF uses the same three links of chain and the Friendship, Love, Truth (F-L-T) motto, but the organization's full set of initials is not always included on headstones. The main difference is the women's lodge, which does not use the same name as the white lodge, Daughters of Rebekah, or its dove and crescent moon emblem. Instead, it is called the Household of Ruth (founded nationally in 1857) and uses a single sheaf of wheat, or two crossed sheaves, as its emblem.

The traditional Knights of Pythias logo of a helmet, raven, and crossed axes is unchanged. The women's lodge, however, instead of being known as the Pythian Sisters, is called the Grand Court Order of Calanthe (or the Court of Calanthe). Its emblem, a hand holding a rose, is easily mistaken for a standard funerary symbol.

Though neither the Woodmen of the World nor the Modern Woodmen of America (famous for placing tree trunk–shaped markers on members' graves) admitted African Americans, the American Woodmen—initially a white benevolent society founded in 1901 but which became Black-owned in 1910—gave its members stone tree trunk grave markers.[86] Other forestry-themed Black lodges include the Woodmen of Union, in existence in Hot Springs (Garland Co.) through the early 1930s,[87] and the Supreme Camp of Colored Woodmen in Marianna (Lee Co.), which was investigated in 1914 for failing to pay thirty-six death claims going back over a period of three years.[88]

Though the Benevolent and Protective Order of Elks (BPOE) was whites-only when it was founded in Kentucky in 1868, it had a Black counterpart, the Improved Benevolent and Protective Order of the Elks, but there do not seem to have been any such Black lodges in Arkansas. Perhaps any would-be founders recognized the irony of forming an Elks lodge as this organization was originally a social club for white minstrels, men who assumed racist makeup, clothing, and dialect to satirize Blacks onstage. The organization's original name, the "Jolly Corks," may have referred to their members' practice of using burnt cork to blacken their faces.[89]

OTHER LODGES

An unknown number of lodges, both Black and white, have existed in Arkansas. Some lasted only briefly; most did not provide members with headstones. One that did was the United Brothers of Friendship (founded in Kentucky in 1861, reaching Arkansas by 1905), which used an equilateral triangle with the initials UBF in the corners; the women's lodge, the Sisters of the Mysterious Ten, inverted the triangle and placed SMT around its perimeter. These headstones are found very infrequently.

Though hardly comprehensive, it is possible to compile a list of former Black lodges from a variety of published sources. In addition to the ones in Newport, listed above, these include St. Joseph's Aid of the Universe, American Charitable Homestead Society of the Western Thinkers of the United States,[90] the Supreme Council of Shepherds,[91] Independent Order of Immaculates, American Knights of Freedom, Ancient Order of Egyptians,[92] and the Grand United Order of Blackmen of America.[93] A list of African American fraternal societies and insurance providers, in 1923, included several of the lodges mentioned above, as well as the Imperial Council of the Jugamos, Independent Order of Daniel, Great Southern Fraternal Union, United Brothers of African Race, United Friends of America, and the United Order of Good Samaritans.[94]

Archaeologist Edward Palmer kept a journal while he traveled through eastern Arkansas, documenting Native American mounds, and it yields one more lodge to add to this list, along with a brief description of its pageantry. He wrote of Osceola (Mississippi Co.) in 1882: "The Colored people have a society known as Knights of wise men, they paraded at night with music and regalia—swords of wood silvered over[,] each one with [a] lantern.[95]

1. Harris Cemetery, Cotton Town (**Yell**)

2. Coop Prairie Cemetery (**Scott**)

3. Cherry Hill Cemetery (**Polk**)

4. Southwest Arkansas Regional Archives, Washington (**Hempstead**)

5. Mt. Olive Cemetery (**Nevada**)

6. Oakland Cemetery, Camden (**Ouachita**)

7. Lakeport Plantation (**Chicot**)

8. Kentucky Cemetery (**Saline**)

9. Zion Lutheran Cemetery, Ulm (**Prairie**)

10. Linwood Cemetery, Paragould (**Geene**)

11. Foster Cemetery, Scotland (**Van Buren**)

12. Hasty Cemetery, Mossville Washington Monument "quarry" (**Newton**)

13. Rowland Cemetery, Valley Springs (**Boone**)

14. Mount Holly Cemetery, Little Rock (**Pulaski**)

15. Arkansas River | **16.** Mississippi River

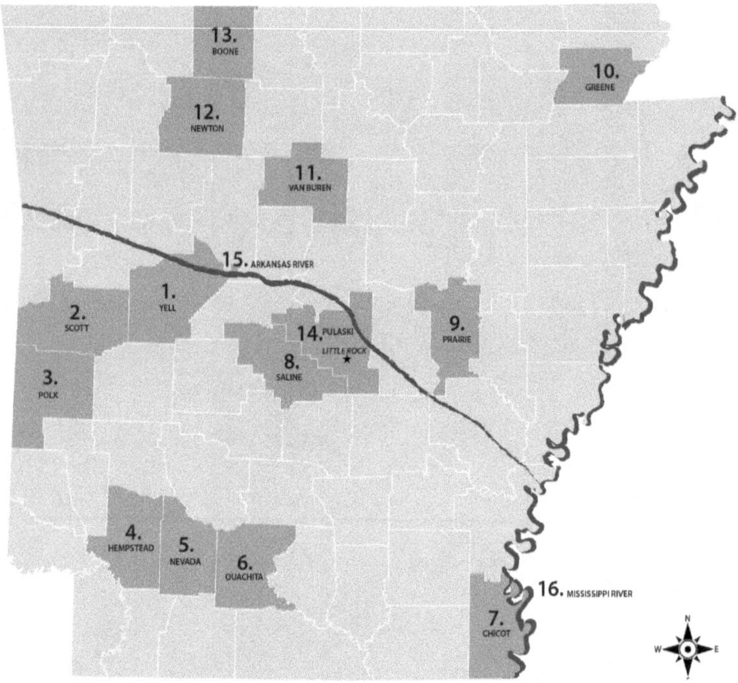

Major locations discussed in chapter 3.
Map by Red Rooster Design, Fayetteville, Arkansas.

Chapter 3

GRAVE MARKERS AND MORTUARY STRUCTURES

Peacefully lay us down to rest,
Place the turf—kindly on our breast.
Sweet is the slumber beneath the sod,
While the soul is resting with God.
—Peacefully sleeping.

—WILLIAM J. WILLIAMS, 1853–1930; LOVINA WILLIAMS, 1862–1944, BRADLEY CEMETERY (VAN BUREN CO.)

The object sticking out of the ground in Harris Cemetery in Cotton Town (Yell Co.) doesn't look like a grave marker—or a murder weapon. It is merely a knobbed length of heavy metal pipe, but could it be the object wielded by Carrie Hopkins when she "crashed in" her husband's skull on the morning of April 5, 1921?[1]

The Hopkins household had steadily increased in size in the years leading up to this killing. Under one roof were Luther, a tenant farmer, wife Carrie, three young children from Luther's first marriage, and one from Carrie's. The couple went on to have two children of their own; at some point Carrie's orphaned half sister Effie Blair joined this family. Luther began to sexually molest Effie when she was a teenager, which the neighbors eventually found out about. They demanded that

Luther stop or face prosecution but neither their threats nor his wife's repeated arguments convinced him to change his behavior.

Early on the morning of April 5, Luther preyed on Effie again, and again Carrie fought with her husband when he returned to their bed. But this time, unlike previously, Luther pulled out a gun and vowed to kill his wife. Carrie left the room, found a cut-off section of a Model T Ford axle, returned to the bedroom, and slammed the heavy piece of metal into the back of Luther's head. Her second blow left him dead. A coroner's jury exonerated her, ruling that her act was justifiable homicide, which enabled Carrie to collect her husband's life insurance. By one account Luther was buried the same day he died,[2] and for whatever reason, the axle was used to mark his grave.[3]

According to a newspaper account, "Sentiment in the neighborhood is said to be strongly in favor of the wife."[4] Everyone's lives improved: The children received educations, Effie married in 1922, and Carrie remarried a year after that, making it a happy ending for everyone except Luther.[5] Still, questions linger: Was his killing premeditated? After all, the only other people in the house that morning were Effie and an infant. Where were the five older children, ranging in age from four to sixteen? Then, too, how could a tenant farmer with eight dependents afford a life insurance policy?

A final question: Is this piece of metal *really* the murder weapon? The fifteen-pound, plaster-coated pipe in Harris Cemetery looks like it could be an axle,[6] but Robert Case Jr., who grew up next to Harris Cemetery and whose father, born in 1923, grew up hearing about the killing, said that the real murder weapon was stolen sometime in the late 1990s. Case, who has seen the actual axle, described it as having a large gear attached to one end. "Those gates from around the fenced graves were stolen by people gathering up any kind of iron to sell for scrap iron," he said of a period when the cemetery was not maintained, speculating that the axle could have been stolen at the same time.[7]

The length of pipe in Harris Cemetery, while presumably not the actual murder weapon, is still on someone's grave and belongs in the category of "found objects," where disparate items—such as clay sewer pipe or pieces of metal farm machinery—are used in lieu of a tombstone. A sub-category includes homemade concrete markers, found in both Black and white cemeteries, decorated with such things as pressed-in shells, beads, glass chips, marbles, toys, or bathroom tiles. Sometimes these materials are both pretty and regional, such as large quartz crystals found decorating both headstones and graves in Garland and Hot Spring Counties, where crystals occur naturally.

Another grave marker killed someone, though under very different circumstances. In 2018, a young boy climbed a very realistic stone tree trunk, a Woodmen of the World marker. This stone tree had become unlevel, and the unsecured marker slid off its base, crushing the child. Ironically, this lethal marker is on the grave of W. L. Lewsaw (1882–1909), whose epitaph says he ". . . lived a quiet and peaceable life."[8]

It is a cliché that everything is subject to fashion, and grave markers are no exception. The materials from which markers are made, and the designs, symbols, and poetry that embellish them, change as people's tastes change, as new materials come into use, and as carving technology improves. Whether through necessity, frugality, or lack of other materials, the state's earliest markers were created from wood, but as stone came into use, the preferred material was sandstone, along with limestone and marble (defined by the monument industry as any stone that can be polished), before transitioning to the granite that is still popular today. Even something as basic as a marker's shape is subject to regional variations, brought here from other states. For example, necked discoids—flat tablets cut out in the shape of a head, neck, and shoulders and resembling an upright human torso—are found primarily in rural graveyards in the Ozarks.[9]

This chapter will look at the wide assortment of materials used to create grave markers, as well as at grave covers and other symbolic structures built on top of burials, or constructed to house human remains. The term "grave cover" is used here to denote any shape or substance placed on top of an interment and, generally, made the length and width of the grave space, separate from a tombstone. Vaults, though technically burial chambers built in the ground to house casketed remains, have come to mean any structure that houses a coffin. While this has become interchangeable with "crypt," a crypt is a burial chamber built beneath a church, something not found in Arkansas. Here, however, the term "false crypt" denotes an empty stone box or coffin built on top of a grave.

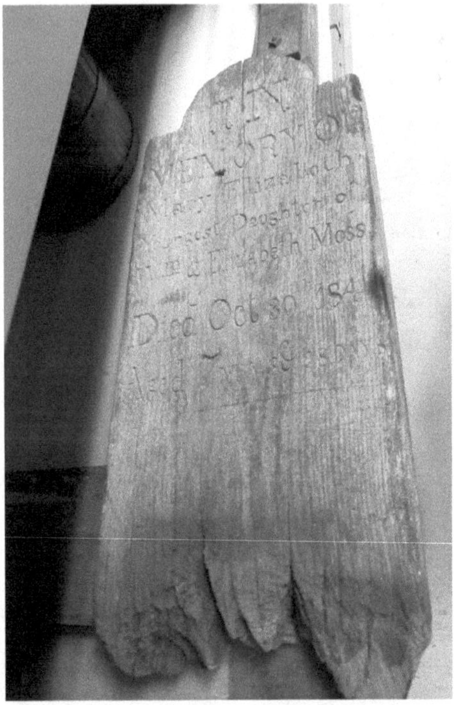

Fig 3.1. Wooden headboard of Mary Elizabeth Moss (died 1847), in the collection of the Southwest Arkansas Regional Archives. Found near Pioneer Cemetery, Historic Washington State Park (Hempstead Co.).

WOODEN MARKERS

When the state's older residents were interviewed by the Works Progress Administration's Writers' Project in the 1940s, few respondents made it as far as question number forty-six, which asked about early tombstone inscriptions. Of those who did, several stated that there were no tombstones in the early days.[10]

The word tomb*stone* misleads, because the state's earliest markers were carved from wood and are more properly termed "headboards." The oldest surviving example is housed in an archive at Washington, now Historic Washington State Park (Hempstead Co.), a town originating in the 1820s and fully functional by the 1850s.[11] This headboard was carved from Bois D'arc, also known as Osage orange (*Maclura* *pomifera*), a wood that resists rot, and marked the grave of seven-year-old Mary Elizabeth Moss, who died in 1847.[12] Found near Pioneer Cemetery, this board did not mark its oldest burial, as the cemetery was used as early as 1825.[13]

In the town's early years, families may have preferred such wooden markers, carved to imitate round-topped slates, or they may have lacked access to imported marble. Several marble tablets with death dates spanning 1840 to 1867 (possibly carved years later and back-dated) contain their makers' signatures, showing that professionally carved marble was shipped in from Shreveport and New Orleans, Louisiana, Memphis, Tennessee, and Patterson, New Jersey.

Little Rock's Mount Holly cemetery (founded 1843) also used wooden headboards during its earliest years, though these may have been intended as placeholders until the family could purchase a permanent marker. A letter to the *Arkansas Gazette* in 1875 deplored conditions at the cemetery, such as the sexton's practice of regularly burning the grounds to remove brush, an act that destroyed "temporary head-boards of graves, old and new" along with the identities of the graves' occupants.[14] Families may have lacked the money to mark the very oldest graves and "suitable stone was not found in quantity nearby,"[15] but the city's first professional carvers arrived in 1840, and in 1852, Scottish partners Joseph Clark and James Tunnah established a monument shop in Little Rock.[16] Elsewhere in the state, county histories contain references to early cemeteries having wooden headboards, and remnants of round-top wooden markers can still be found in Van Buren County.[17]

Lastly, not all wooden markers are what they appear to be. Petrified wood, found on graves across Arkansas, comes from fossilized (or mineralized) tree trunks. Clay County is known for its reserves of this material and the county's eastern district courthouse at Piggott has a permanent display of large pieces, but the greatest concentration of petrified wood grave markers is found in the southwest quadrant of the state. Chunks of petrified wood mark graves (including African American ones) or are cemented together to create tablet-style markers (Huckabee Cemetery, Hempstead Co.); sometimes entire logs are used (Sylvania Cemetery, Lonoke Co.). It's likely that these stones were chosen for their appearance, rather than harking back to earlier times when grave markers were made from wood.

STONE

The block of stone that Arkansas sent to the nation's capital in 1849 as the state's contribution to the Washington Monument came from an outcrop in what is now Newton County.[18] Perhaps because of its connection to the monument, or because the fine-grained Mississippian limestone is a dusty rose color, stone from this "quarry" was highly prized by tombstone carvers well into the 1900s. The site was destroyed in the 1920s when Scenic Route 7 was constructed. Another forgotten quarry with a presidential claim to fame is the one at Cartney (Baxter Co.), the source of the "Arkansas red marble" used to create the massive sarcophagus inside Abraham Lincoln's remodeled and expanded tomb in Springfield, Illinois, in 1929.[19]

Despite having local sources, city-dwellers often preferred something grander. Even when carvers advertised access to imported marble, or established permanent businesses in their cities, the wealthy continued to exercise their option of ordering monuments from out of state, or even from Italy. Though itinerant carvers had to use whatever stone they could quarry locally, established monument shops had access to marble by the mid-1800s. The earliest on record is Joseph Clark of Little Rock, who advertised "Marble or Stone" monuments in 1850,[20] while in 1856, James Jennings of Camden (Ouachita Co.) advertised Italian marble,[21] and S.W. Meyers of Helena (Phillips Co.) promoted his stock of white marble.[22]

GRAVE COVERS MADE OF DIRT AND STONE

Prior to the Civil War there were few professional stone carvers working outside of the larger cities, but not all families wanted tablets, preferring instead to create grave coverings in a variety of styles—especially in the Ozarks. The white settlers coming into the Arkansas Ozarks (comprising all or portions of twenty-two counties, roughly the upper third of the state) brought with them burial traditions from their states of origin, or the states through which they migrated en route to the Ozarks. The greatest number of settlers came from Tennessee, so it is no surprise that these structures are also found there, as well as in Appalachia as a whole.[23]

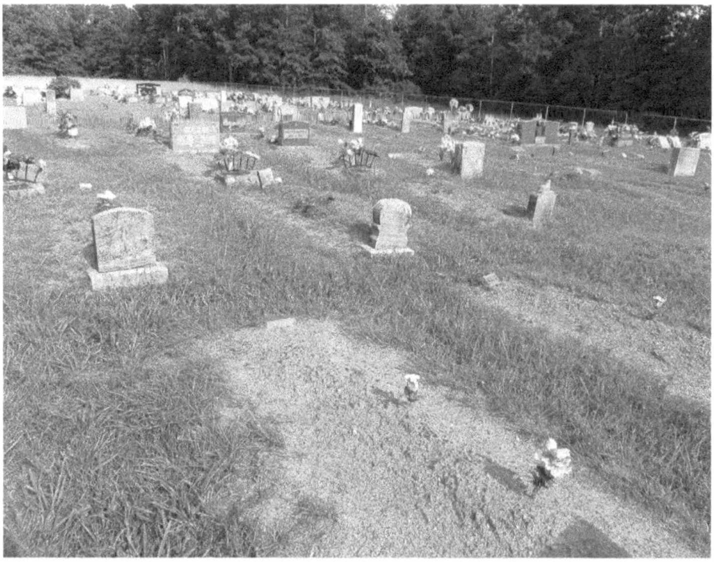

Fig 3.2. Scraping and mounding, the practice of adding fresh dirt on top of all graves, keeps each burial looking like a recent one. Mossville Cemetery (Newton Co.).

Think not of me as in the ground
For this is only an earthly mound
For I am far above the Sky;
Where Joy and Pleasure never die.

—LUCINDA WEAVER, 1837–1898, HOLMES (BOONE CO.)[24]

The most basic grave cover is made by piling up loose dirt to create a mound that spans the length and width of the grave and replenishing and re-mounding this pile as it wears away. Such mounds make each grave look like a recent one—in other words, a memento mori, a reminder of recent death intended to inspire the living to treat each day as if it could be their last. Scraping and mounding is no longer practiced throughout entire cemeteries (Newton County's Mossville Cemetery is an exception) but still exists within individual families' plots, where graves may be mounded with loose dirt, sand, gravel, or even concrete shaped to permanently represent a mound.

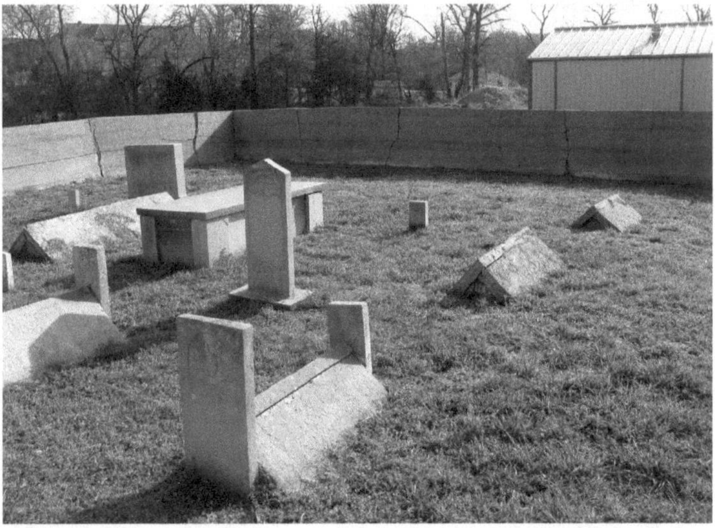

Fig 3.3. Comb graves (resembling pup tents) and box tombs, a.k.a. false crypts, are Ozark burial traditions. These examples have death dates spanning 1858–1868, in Rowland Cemetery, Valley Springs (Boone Co.).

Many grave covers were elaborate stone constructions that were time consuming to create, which should put to rest the notion that they were intended to repel marauding animals or human grave robbers. There was a taboo against completing any part of the traditional labor-intensive burial process before death occurred, and this included digging the grave or making the tombstone or other marker. Lacking access to embalming or even ice, burial almost always took place within twenty-four hours of the death, so such structures could not have been completed immediately, when threats to the body would be greatest. Furthermore, a grave needed time to settle before placing a heavy stone structure on top of it. One final argument: coffin lids were tightly nailed down after the final viewing of the body, so a digging animal might have exposed the box but would not have been able to open it.

The stone grave covers most commonly found in the oldest Ozarks graveyards are combs, box crypts, slot and tab tombs, and grave houses. A comb is made up of two rectangular stone slabs that lean inward, sometimes held in place by triangular endcaps, and resemble little pup tents. (For this reason they have also been called "tent graves.")

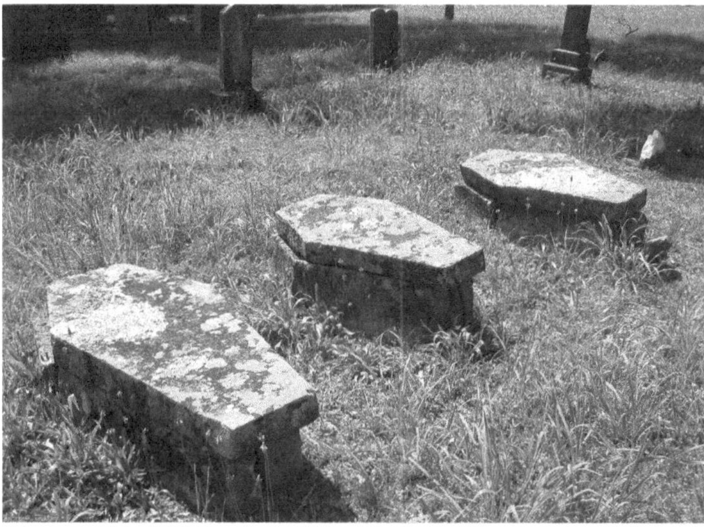

Fig 3.4. Coffin-shaped false crypts, a style of grave covering found throughout the Ozarks. Though realistic, these did not house bodies but were meant as reminders of the coffin and of death. Brashears Cemetery (Madison Co.).

Richard C. Finch, a geologist who has made a study of these grave coverings, has documented over five hundred Tennessee cemeteries containing combs and as of this writing identified twenty cemeteries in eleven Arkansas counties having them, most of these in the northwest corner of the state, but several outside the Ozarks. Not all combs have inscriptions with names and dates.[25] According to Finch, "None of the dated combs pre-date the early combs of Tennessee, and none post-date the late combs of Tennessee. One can speculate from this limited sample that, while the custom of comb graves never became a dominant practice in Arkansas, it was almost certainly imported from Tennessee."[26]

Another type of grave cover is the box crypt or false crypt, an empty structure built on top of a grave in the form of a rectangular box or one having a hexagonal coffin-shaped "lid" resting on a rectangular base. (Realistic hexagonal coffins were also created from solid blocks of stone, sometimes having overhanging lids mimicking actual coffin lids.) Related to this is the slot and tab tomb, a stone box with two holes cut in the lid, into which are slotted a headstone and footstone. Such empty shapes were representative of the coffin or casket and were not created to house bodies above ground. However, this cannot be ruled out everywhere as at least one above-ground stone box, shown to the author in 2018, does hold the remnants of a child's iron casket.[27]

Some of the variations on these styles include combs constructed on top of box crypts (Holmes Cemetery, Boone Co.); two-tiered box crypts, each stacked pair atop a single burial (Canaan Cemetery, Searcy Co.); and stacked stone covers, also called ashlar cairns, made up of cut blocks or slabs of stone that have been laid up like building stone. Armstrong-Collins Cemetery (Newton Co.) contains a long row of tiered ledger stones where large ovals of stone (ledgers) are placed on tiered stacks of stone bases. These have been referred to online as "wolf stones" but, due to their size and similarity, were likely all made at the same time.

CONCRETE

Up until 1900 most stone carvers signed the tombstones they made, so their businesses' locations and partnerships are easy to track. Practically nothing, however, is known about the men who created, but did not sign, concrete grave markers. (These are hereafter referred to as tombstones, with their creators—presumed to all be men—referred to as carvers.) It's easy to see why the medium was so popular. Concrete, an aggregate of sand or gravel mixed with cement in liquid form, is cheap and readily available and can be molded and imprinted relatively easily, thus making it ideal for creating low-cost tombstones.

M. Ruth Little, in a 1998 study of North Carolina headstones, divides concrete markers into three categories: commercially made mass-produced ones, ones made in limited quantities in commercial molds by local craftsmen, and folk art markers made in homemade molds. Little notes that these markers, somewhat deceptively, often appear to mark a cemetery's oldest graves when, in reality, many were placed there starting in the 1920s on graves originally marked with uncarved fieldstones or long-since decayed wooden headboards.[28]

Commercially made tablet-style concrete headstones are found in practically all cemeteries across Arkansas. More than one factory produced these tablets, evidenced by the differences in marker shapes and the execution of symbols, such as one company's two easily recognizable motifs: an anchor and ivy, and a broken branch with a dangling bud. Between the 1890s and the 1920s, newspapers across the country ran articles about "cement tombstone" factories that were about to be built or patents for the technology needed to create these markers, though it's unclear how much of this came to fruition.

In 1919, Little Rock's *Daily Arkansas Gazette* announced that both a bargain and a new business could be had in Forrest City (St. Francis Co.), where several boxcars of unsold concrete tombstones had been dumped beside a city street. Though these markers were ordered in advance, apparently buyers changed their minds once the tablets arrived. This, the article suggested, was an opportunity for a "wide awake, bustling young man . . . to enter the second-hand tombstone business."[29]

While it's hard to understand how markers ordered by specific customers could be reused, it's possible that these were blank markers and that the deceased's name and dates were to be added later. Ian W. Brown, a professor of anthropology at the University of Alabama, and his student Joseph Hicks studied comparable concrete markers in Tuscaloosa County, Alabama.[30] Their theory, according to Brown, is that "all of these are prefabricated cement markers, superbly crafted. A thin veneer of cement was added to the outside when a person died, and the inscription was added by carefully stamping, when the cement was in a leather-hard condition."[31]

Forrest City is only twenty-five miles from Brinkley, home of the National Cement Monument Works in 1919, which is likely where those abandoned tombstones originated. Perhaps in response to this wasted inventory, the following year the factory relocated to Memphis, Tennessee, where it billed itself as "the only concrete tombstone factory in the United States."[32]

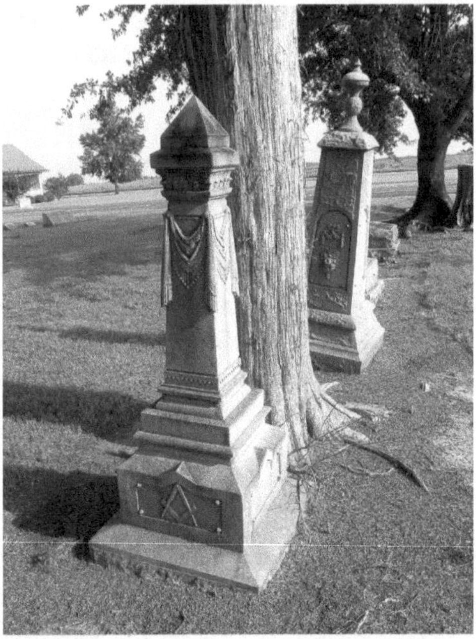

Fig 3.5. Zinc, a.k.a. white bronze, markers showing two of the monumental styles that were cast so that inscription panels, containing names, dates, mortuary symbols, and fraternal lodge emblems, could be bolted on. Zion Lutheran Cemetery, near Ulm (Prairie Co.).

METAL MARKERS

An unblemished blue-gray monument really stands out amid a sea of conventional tombstones. Such markers, marketed as "white bronze," were actually cast from pure zinc in a wide variety of sizes and shapes, including ones intentionally mimicking twigs, logs, and rough-cut stone. Though individual examples are found across Arkansas, the greatest concentrations tend to be in city cemeteries, indicating the presence of a local dealer, aided by railroad lines for easy shipping.

These markers were the product of the Monumental Bronze Company of Bridgeport, Connecticut, founded in 1874, which eventually had subsidiaries and foundries in other states, including Detroit, Michigan, and Chicago, Illinois. A client would pick out a monument style from a catalog, choose additional symbols if space allowed (options included a wheat sheaf and sickle, a woman clinging to the cross, a supine body on a barge, and emblems denoting fraternal lodge affiliations), and supply the deceased's name and dates. Some families included epitaphs, birth location, a marriage date, or even the deceased's favorite hymn or dying words. The company would then cast inscription panels, bolt them into openings in the marker, and ship it to the buyer. As long as the zinc industry flourished, new inscription panels, cast with names and dates, could be swapped out for blank panels as family members died.[33]

"Age will not impair their beauty," the Monumental Bronze Company said of its products, which was accurate.[34] These markers never require cleaning. Lichens and moss do not grow on zinc, the metal is impervious to weather, pollution, and discoloration, and the cast lettering remains crisply legible a century or more later. The only real drawback to zinc is that the weight of the metal causes monuments to pop apart at the seams, which can lead to structural deterioration. It's not uncommon to find an obelisk or other upright shape with a hole where an inscription panel once was, which has given rise to the urban legend that these markers were used by bootleggers, during Prohibition, to stash alcohol.[35]

In 1914, at the start of the first World War, the Monumental Bronze Co. suspended casting grave markers, and by the time World War I ended so, too, had the fad for zinc. The company did not create new markers after 1914 but continued to cast inscription panels for existing monuments until finally going bankrupt during the Depression in 1939.[36]

Most of the markers found in Arkansas are from the cheaper pages of the company's catalog, but a few big-ticket monuments stand out. An immense obelisk marks the grave of Lafayette Gregg (died 1891, Washington Co.),[37] which, though badly vandalized, was restored by having its topmost element recast by sculptor Hank Kaminsky in 2004.[38] Hollywood Cemetery (Hot Springs, Garland Co.), Calvary (Little Rock, Pulaski Co.), and Shady Grove (Clarendon, Monroe Co.) contain life-sized statues of Faith, portrayed as a robed female figure holding an open book under her left arm. Stylistically the statues are slightly different, not to mention that Shady Grove's statue is missing her upraised right hand, which was shot off by a vandal and never restored.[39] On a much smaller scale, a few three-dimensional zinc lambs have been found in Arkansas cemeteries, ones whose heavy-lidded eyes and diminutive size give them the appearance of children's toys.

Another type of commercial zinc marker, made from zinc sheet metal, is much rarer than Monumental Bronze's castings. From the late 1890s through the early 1910s, the Warsaw Zinc Works in Warsaw, Missouri, produced several styles of grave markers, identifiable by an attached tag inscribed with W.Z.W. and a patent date.[40] These hollow structures deteriorated easily, and very few have been found intact in Arkansas. Some include a unique feature: a hinged metal cover that protects a photo of the deceased as long as the glass's gasket remains intact (the Warsaw town cemetery contains several examples). Though damaged, Mary Ollie Whitlow's zinc marker in the Wesley Cemetery (died 1900, Madison Co.), may be the state's best-preserved example, as eleven-year-old Mary's face is still visible when the protective metal panel is lifted.[41]

Round-top iron markers are found across Arkansas, likely the product of a mail-order company. A tiny iron footstone, slightly larger than a slice of bread, seems to have been included, but not many of these survive. The heavy tablets have the patent date "March 22, '87" cast at the bottom, and customers could choose from various symbols at the top: lambs, doves, angels, buds, clasping hands—emblems traditionally used by stone carvers. At the center of the marker is a raised square, into which was placed a piece of paper with the deceased's name and dates (often gilded), then covered with a protective pane of glass.[42]

Though these iron markers are found across Arkansas, another style of iron marker—one with a little hinged door—seems to have been sold only in the Ozarks. The best preserved and most elaborate example is in Hall Cemetery (Searcy Co.), though in none of the extant examples are the names and dates still legible. The maker's name, cast in raised lettering, is easy to make out: A. Russell Monument, pat. 1894.[43] Another type of metal marker, a highly decorative cross, often with a metal crucifix, is found solely in Catholic cemeteries.

GLASS AND CERAMIC MARKERS

Not all markers are impervious to weather and vandalism. Some—such as glass headstones—seem to positively invite their own destruction. Only one professionally made example has been found—a thick, etched pane of glass bolted into a zinc marker[44]—but two homemade versions are still standing in Bodcaw's Corinth Cemetery (Nevada Co.). After Ophelia Cleopatra Whitten Caldwell died in childbirth on May 9, 1899, and her infant died three months later, someone painted their names and dates on pieces of glass, reinforced the edges with metal strips, and erected the panes over their graves.[45]

Clay is nearly as fragile and subject to damage as glass, but it is also cheap, readily available, and easily lettered. A few glazed ceramic markers have been found in Scott and Sebastian Counties, believed to be the work of John H. Caldwell (1846–1935), a Mansfield farmer, jeweler, hardware dealer, and undertaker. Caldwell, who was also a third-generation potter, manufactured pottery in Sebastian County before establishing his other businesses and drew on this knowledge to create glazed ceramic markers for his poorer clients.[46]

Assuming that the six examples found by this author are Caldwell's work,[47] the earliest (1905 death date) is the most elaborate, with the deceased's name and dates molded in raised, blue-glazed letters. The remaining examples are generic white glazed boxes with holes on the top surface where a metal inscription plate (many now missing) could be attached. In addition to these six boxes there are two infants' markers in a wholly different style and glaze color.[48] Caldwell's obituary states that he produced "his invention" for a few years before his retirement,[49] so the small sample may be due to very few markers having been made, the fact that they're easily broken, or the possibility that families eventually replaced them with stone markers.

It is possible that potter John Welch made ceramic grave markers in Dallas County in the mid- to late 1800s. Historic Arkansas Museum in Little Rock has a small salt-glazed stoneware tombstone in its collection, believed to have been made by Welch to advertise the type of marker he could create, but no full-size versions are known to exist.[50]

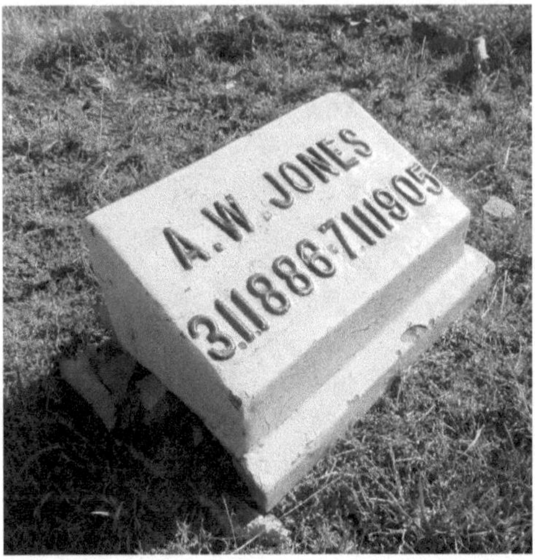

Fig 3.6. Glazed ceramic grave marker attributed to John Caldwell, an undertaker and third-generation potter who made ceramic grave markers for his clients. Coop Prairie Cemetery (Scott Co.).

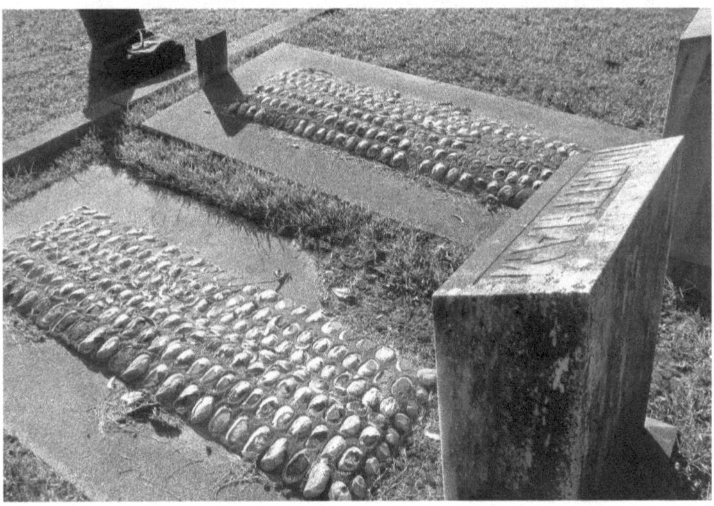

Fig 3.7. Shell-covered mounds cover the graves of siblings Claude Dixon (1904–1940) and Alice Wortham (1894–1924). Mount Olive Cemetery (Nevada Co).

Commercially produced ceramic markers are even rarer in Arkansas than Caldwell's work, and even less is known about them. These hollow markers, molded in the shapes of conventional monuments, are a type of vitrified terracotta and were glazed in colors resembling various shades of granite. As of this writing nothing can be proven about the manufacturer of these markers, but the majority of them have death dates spanning the early 1900s through the late 1920s. The factory appears to have closed down during the Depression. In Arkansas three examples have been found near the Missouri line[51] and two near the Oklahoma line,[52] which suggests that these monuments were sold by dealers outside of Arkansas.

GRAVE COVERS: SHELLS

> Death thou art another birth
> Freeing the spirit from the clods of earth.
>
> —LEMUEL J. PADGET, 1857–1886, OZONE (JOHNSON CO.)

Shells show up in graveyards all the time. For instance, large marble scallop shells serve as backdrops that protect three-dimensional carvings of sleeping infants and, occasionally, lambs. Such shells may be functional, ornamental, or symbolic, as some symbolism guidebooks suggest that they represent baptism, a journey, or birth and resurrection,[53] or even reference the Christian custom, in the Middle Ages, of wearing a scallop shell to signify having made a religious pilgrimage.[54]

Actual shells are another matter, but whether they were used symbolically or merely decoratively is unknown. A photo taken in 1924 in Pine Grove Cemetery (Independence Co.) shows a half dozen grave mounds outlined with shells, though none remain today.[55] Most of the shells that have survived, in situ, did so because they were cemented down. These include conch shells, used singly atop markers or plot curbing, and mussel shells that completely cover permanent concrete grave mounds in Polk, Nevada, and Union Counties in southwestern Arkansas. Graves in these three counties are covered with

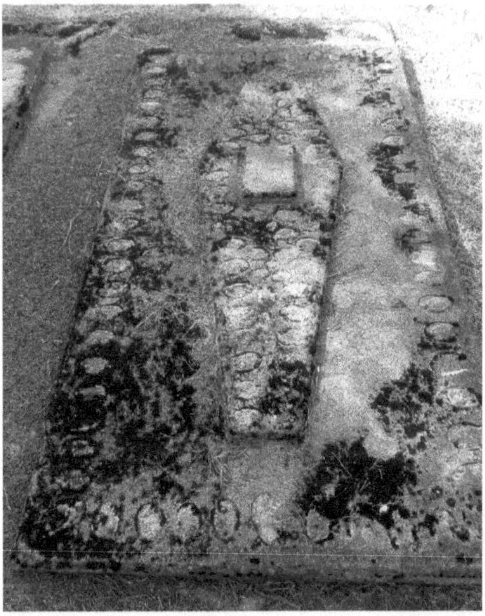

Fig 3.8. Cherry Hill Cemetery (Polk Co.) has nine graves covered in shell mounds, arranged in the shape of hexagonal coffin lids.

a rectangular concrete pad, atop which is a mounded, oval shape imitating a scraped and mounded grave. A source states that in Mount Moriah Cemetery (Nevada Co.), one family "bleached to perfect whiteness enough mussel shells of uniform size to embed in rows in concrete over graves of two of their loved ones," giving the graves "a perpetually clean, simple and handsome appearance."[56] In the intervening years, many of these shells shattered or crumbled, and now only fragments are found clinging to the concrete mounds. Mt. Olive Cemetery (also in Nevada Co.) contains four identical examples.

Cherry Hill Cemetery (Polk Co.) has nine hexagonal coffin-shaped grave covers, on which nothing is left but outlines of the once-embedded shells. It's hard to be certain when this custom started because, in cases of paired grave covers, both may have been created following the second spouse's death, but the practice ended in the 1950s.[57]

These examples feature permanent, intact shells, but punched-out mussel shells, as holey as Swiss cheese, were also used decoratively.[58] Scott Akridge, a White County Historical Society board member, says this was common practice along the White River. "Holes were punched in the shells to knock out the buttons," he says. Then the discarded shells "were piled outside [the button factories] free for the taking. Shells were used to outline graves or even piled directly over the graves in a thick bed. . . . Of course, over time grass grew through the shells, making the shell-outlined, or shell-covered, graves almost impossible to find today."[59] These remnants were also used in African American cemeteries. A photo taken around 1917 in the now-inaccessible Black Cemetery (Sharp Co.) shows a grave completely covered in punched-out shells that came from the Black Rock button factory, beside the Black River.[60]

A memoir, not specific to Arkansas, says that broken dishes, household items, and shells placed on Black graves are "echoes of early traditions in West Africa and the eighteenth- and nineteenth-century enslaved Africans in America," and that such items represent the break between the living and the dead.[61] Another study of African American traditions puts shells in the same category as grave goods, "usually white, whether they are china, porcelain, enamel ware, bleached sea shells," etc., suggesting that all of the items found on grave mounds have some connection to water. "Sea shells have obvious water associations. When placed on top of the grave they create an image of a river bottom, the environment in African belief under which the realm of the dead is located."[62]

BRICK VAULTS

When two-year-old Cable Johnson died in 1867, his coffin was placed inside a round-topped brick vault behind his family's home on their Lakeport cotton plantation (Chicot Co.). This was unusual, because prior to this, Lycurgus and Lydia Johnson had sent the bodies of their three other children back to Kentucky for burial.[63] Perhaps the Johnsons intended the same for son Cable, because his vault was specially constructed with removable sides, but when his parents eventually moved back to Kentucky, they left his body behind.[64]

Another brick vault with an interesting history, located in Kentucky Cemetery (Saline Co.), houses the remains of Harriet Staner, who was

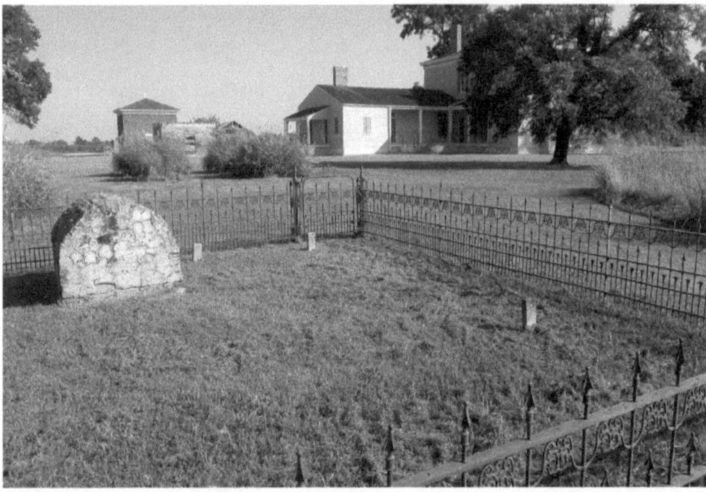

Fig 3.9. Two-year-old Cable Johnson (died 1867) was placed in a brick vault, with removable sides, behind the family's home, but his parents did not take his body with them when they left Arkansas. Lakeport Plantation family cemetery (Chicot Co.).

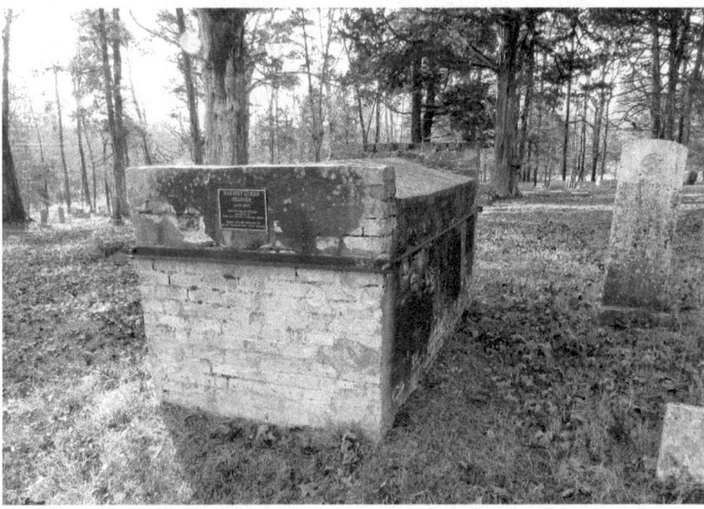

Fig 3.10. Murder victim Harriet Staner (1840–1877) is in an above-ground brick vault; a modern plaque states that her murder resulted in the county's last legal hanging. Kentucky Cemetery (Saline Co.).

murdered by her nephew in 1877. A modern plaque is attached to one end and gives her name as Harriet Glenn Stainer, stating that her murder "resulted in Saline County's last legal hanging." In fact, it was the county's only legal one,[65] though an enslaved Black man had been lynched in 1854. On January 24, 1877, Tom Staner beat his aunt, then her neighbor Parlee Taylor,[66] to death with an iron poker and stole money and jewelry. Jailed on suspicion of having committed the crime, Staner eventually confessed, attempted to escape by burning down the jail, and was hanged (or, as a Little Rock newspaper put it, "Dances the Aerial Quickstep") that November.[67]

Above-ground brick vaults, or ones half-buried in the ground and having domed brick roofs, are found across Arkansas, mainly in white cemeteries. Hill Cemetery, which is African American, and Mount Carmel, which is white, both located at Eudora (Chicot Co.), contain almost identical brick crypts with rounded tops and raised ends, both having death dates in the early 1900s. According to Woodruff County cemetery records, "It was the custom of the more affluent citizens who lived before and during the Civil War to line their graves with bricks, extending a foot or so above the ground."[68]

These vaults were constructed to house the coffin, a way of protecting it in an era before the invention of in-ground metal or concrete burial vaults. False crypts (empty, rectangular boxes built on top of in-ground burials) were sometimes constructed from brick and topped with a stone ledger carved with the deceased's name and dates.

GRAVE HOUSES

The grave house is a roofed structure built over one or more in-ground burials. This makes it neither a mausoleum nor a crypt but, rather, an empty structure—sometimes an elaborate one—that has no obvious function. Judging by references in obituaries and memoirs, and from early photos, these structures were once a common feature of cemeteries across the Ozarks, though they have now almost entirely disappeared. These were not exclusive to the Ozarks, however, as houses have also been found elsewhere around the state, mostly in the southwestern quadrant.[69] Grave houses have also been built in recent times, both traditional styles and ones that look like carports, with metal uprights and open sides.

In some cases, houses are replacements for ones that stood there originally: The house of Cleveland Jacobs, nine months old (died 1889, Grant Co.),[70] has a brass plaque giving its history, while a plaque on Lula Lorraine Williams's little house (died 1916, Calhoun Co.) states that it is a replica of the original one.[71] In Foster Cemetery (Van Buren Co.), a welded metal cage-like structure protects the grave of eighteen-year-old Calvin Whitfield, who bled to death following an accident. According to a local history, "There was snow on the ground when they buried him, and William [Whitfield] couldn't stand the thought of the snow being on his son's grave, so he built a little house over the grave to protect it. This has been over 100 years ago and some of the Whitfield descendants have replaced and repaired this little house several times so as to keep it as it was built," but at some point family members apparently decided to re-create the house from more permanent materials.[72]

Houses are still built occasionally. Graves Cemetery (Logan Co.) once had a variety of older examples, perhaps prompting the Graves family to construct a new one in 1999.[73] A house constructed from welded rebar covers the grave of Vietnam veteran Terry Lee Williams (1947–1968) in Oak Ridge Cemetery at Dardanelle (Yell Co.), and a modern structure protects Brendan Carter's grave (2009–2015) in Free Union Cemetery (Union Co.); both are African American.

Practically none of the surviving grave houses are alike, and they differ from one another in size, design, and construction materials. Some have a stone foundation, called a pen, topped with wooden uprights and a conical shingle or metal roof, while others incorporate wood, brick, and metal structurally and may or may not include a carved tombstone. Some resemble garden gazebos with lattice or picket fence siding, while others are low sheds with peaked, corrugated roofs, almost resembling comb graves. They are as diverse as the people who made them.

Who did make them, and why? Historians have noted a concentration of these structures in middle Tennessee—the state of origin of so many Arkansans living in the Ozarks—but they have been found throughout the South, including in Alabama, Georgia, Kentucky, Louisiana, and Texas. Though there is no definitive explanation for why

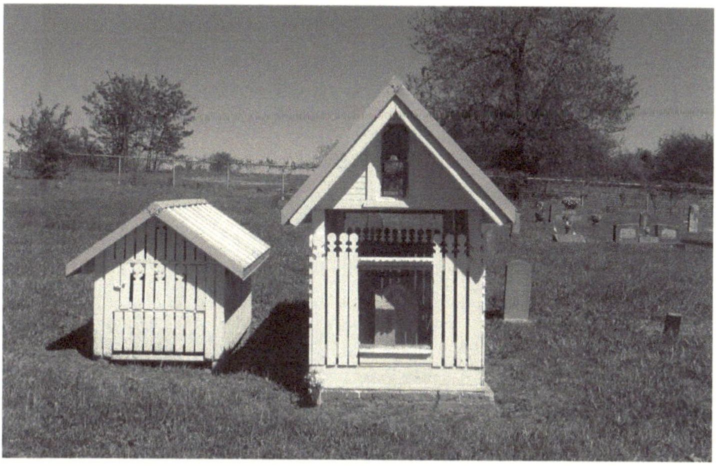

Fig 3.11. The best-documented grave houses in the Ozarks are the two William Newton Christian built over the graves of his two young grandsons, around 1915. The Agee descendants have done repeated restorations to the houses over the years. Agee Cemetery, a.k.a. Hasty Cemetery (Newton Co.).

they were built, the reason given most often was to keep inclement weather—especially rain—out of the grave. Other rationales are that a dying person requested one, or that a structure provides protection from digging animals.[74] This last explanation is the least likely because, just as with massive stone constructions, a house could not have been started before the death occurred and would take a considerable amount of time to build after it, even if work began immediately.[75]

Of the state's surviving houses, the best documented and best-preserved examples are the two constructed over the graves of the Agee children, at Hasty (Newton Co.). These were built by William Newton Christian for his grandsons, an unnamed infant (death date unknown) and two-year-old Guffrey Agee (died 1914). Guffrey's house incorporates several mortuary traditions: a concrete cover over the grave, beveled in a manner similar to a comb (perhaps to shed water before the house could be built), and a tombstone anchoring one end, the work of local carver William Maberry.[76] Both houses once sported a two-tone paint job, with the top portion of their elaborate picket fence siding carved to resemble a necked discoid shape. Christian, who died five years after his grandchildren, created these buildings using only simple hand tools.[77]

A FAMILY VAULT

Confederate soldier Marvel Rhyne had time on his hands when he was stationed at Camden (Ouachita Co.) in November 1863, so he amused himself by visiting the town graveyard. There Rhyne was impressed by marble monuments he estimated as having cost over a thousand dollars (the equivalent of over $25,000 today), but "the most magnificent thing" he saw was the Hill family's burial chamber. He described the brick structure as having been dug into a hillside and resembling a store front, complete with an iron door in the middle. He wrote to his wife, "Inside, different valts [vaults] was made so as to chamber each member of the family, which the[y] placed in a fine coffin, and placed in the vault, where their friends can go and see them at their leisure."[78]

This vault was created in 1856 by James Decatur Hill for his family's use. It initially housed the bodies of his two daughters, infant Olive Ione (died 1847) and one-and-a-half-year-old Margaret Olive (died 1855), whose names are carved on a large marble tablet built into an arched niche to the left of the entrance. It's not known why James and wife Emmaline, who died in 1861 and 1864, respectively, have conventional in-ground burials, and tombstones, a short distance from the vault, but a later visitor described the chamber as holding a number of coffins, so it may have been full by the time they died.[79]

Rhyne wasn't the only person to peer into the Hill burial chamber. A history of the cemetery, published in 1910, says of the cemetery's two vaults, "A gruesome pastime has been afforded many who loitered in the grounds by peering into their gloomy, untenanted apertures."[80] This type of entertainment wasn't unique to the 1800s either. The concrete block mausoleum created by J.E. Matthews in Corning to house the remains of "Little Jim," his toddler son (died 1905, Clay Co.), was similarly compelling. "The iron door to the crypt had a round medallion type window which provided a view of the coffin. Though fully aware of a nightmare to follow, gazing in at the moldy coffin was an irresistible urge on Sunday afternoon visits to the graveyard."[81] The mausoleum was later demolished, and all that remains today is the "Praying Samuel"–style statue, now decapitated, that once graced its roof.[82]

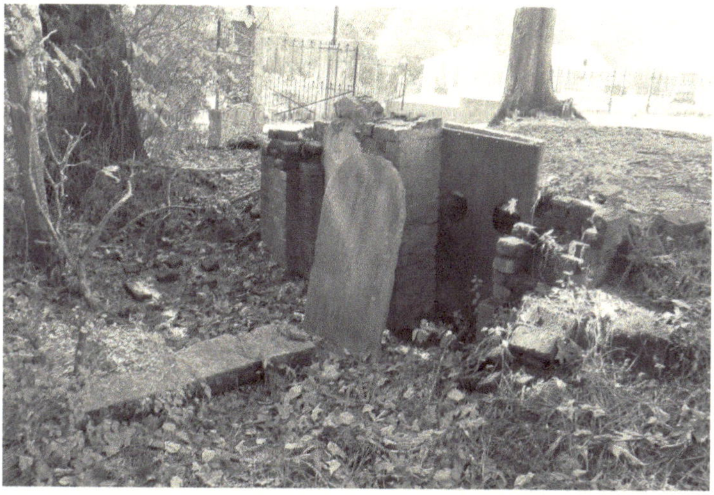

Fig 3.12. All that remains the James Decatur Hill family vault, or burial chamber, constructed in 1856. Oakland Cemetery, Camden (Ouachita Co.).

It's unknown what the other burial vault in Camden's Oakland Cemetery looked like, as it no longer exists, but the Hills' burial chamber contains an illustration showing how it looked when all of its elements were intact. Camden tombstone carver James Jennings, a business associate of James Hill, created two round-topped marble tablets, originally built into the vault on either side of its center door. At the top of the sisters' shared marker he carved a detailed illustration showing the front of the vault with its door, the two arched tablets, and a brick walkway flanked by weeping willows. This verifies Rhyne's description that the vault's front looked like "a city front" because clearly it once had a raised brick façade resembling an early store building's false front.

The vault's appearance today is a far cry from Jennings's delicate and detailed illustration. Over 160 years have passed since it was built, and massive storms, hillside erosion, and the passage of time have caused immense deterioration. The interior has filled with soil and the false front is no longer erect, though the iron door still anchors one side of the structure. Although Jennings continued to work as a stone carver in Camden, the second marble tablet was never inscribed, so there is no way to know who else is interred within.

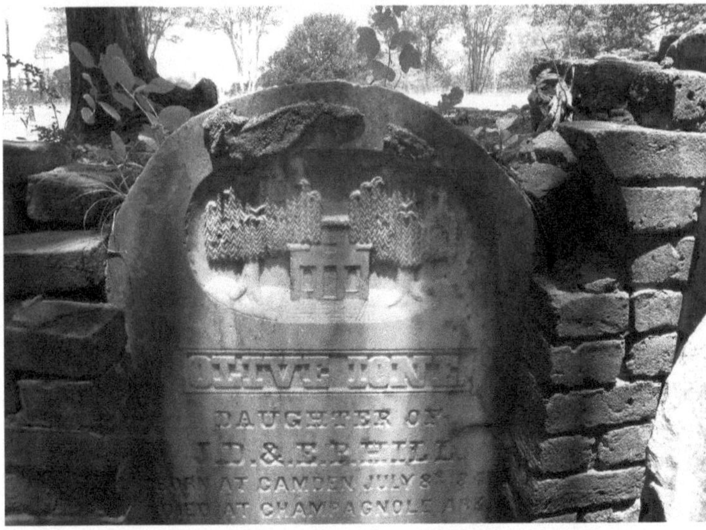

Fig 3.13. Close-up of the carving on the front of the Hill vault, depicting the structure when it was newly built, made by Camden tombstone carver James Jennings. Photo by B. Craig Stinson, used with permission.

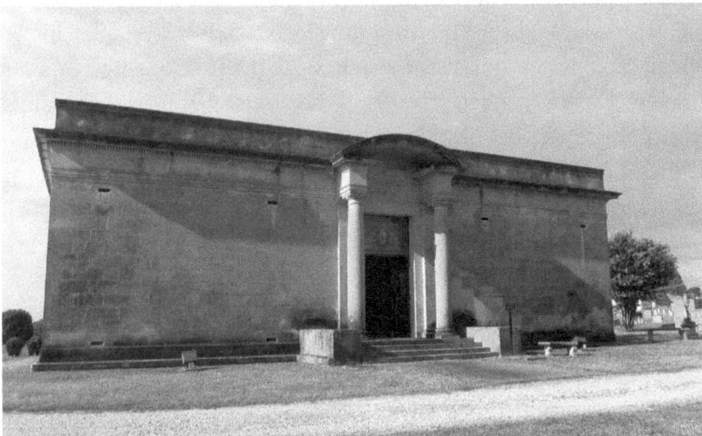

Fig 3.14. Paragould's community mausoleum houses the body of gangster Frank "Jelly" Nash (1887–1933), killed, along with four FBI agents, by gangsters attempting to free him from custody. Linwood Cemetery (Greene Co.).

It's possible that the vault was constructed to hold bodies until they could be sent back to the family burying ground in Maine. There, Yarmouth's Hillside Cemetery has two immense stone "billboard" style grave markers (the stone version of wooden grave boards, with an inscription panel suspended, horizontally, from stone posts). One was created by J.D. Hill's brother-in-law and business partner Cyrus Sargent, on which he recorded that his wife, Mary Margaret Hill, had died in Champagnole, Arkansas, in 1852, with her "remains removed" to Maine in 1853.[83] The body of Mary and J.D. Hill's brother, Alexander Greenwood Hill, had already been shipped back to Maine in 1848, nearly a year after he was killed in the explosion of the steamboat *Edna* near Columbia, Louisiana. Hillside Cemetery may also contain the bodies of two other Hill children, brought there from Arkansas and Louisiana.

Transporting a corpse in the era before embalming was available raises some questions. Though metal burial capsules were in existence, the most intriguing conjecture is that they were shipped back immersed in alcohol, as an 1843 Yarmouth burial record mentions a body coming back from the West Indies "in spirits."[84]

A CITY MAUSOLEUM'S INFAMOUS OCCUPANT

There was a period in the early 1900s when cities created community mausoleums, large buildings designed to house caskets in individual niches. Though relatively rare in Arkansas, there are large mausoleums in Little Rock's Mount Holly and Oakland and Fraternal Cemeteries (Pulaski Co.), Morrilton's Elmwood Cemetery (Conway Co.), Oak Hill in Siloam Springs (Benton Co.), and Linwood Cemetery in Paragould (Greene Co.).

This last example in Linwood Cemetery is well maintained and on the National Register of Historic Places, though all 160 of its niches have long been filled. Inside, in a marble-lined transept off the main entrance, marble faceplates cover the casketed remains of the Nash family, including their most infamous member, gangster Frank "Jelly" Nash (1887–1933). His nickname supposedly came about in childhood, but a more plausible explanation has to do with his fondness for using nitroglycerine jelly to crack open bank safes.

Nash's long and colorful career included murder, train robbery, and numerous prison escapes, but this came to an end after FBI agents learned that he was living in Hot Springs, Arkansas, a city favored by members of organized crime for recreation and relaxation. Nash was arrested in Hot Springs on June 16, 1933, and the following day agents took him by train to Kansas City. Someone leaked word of their destination, and armed men (reputedly including Charles "Pretty Boy" Floyd) were waiting outside the train station when Nash and the agents arrived. The gang, in attempting to free Nash, shot and killed him along with four FBI agents.[85]

Nash's sister, Alice Nash Long, claimed his body and planned an opulent funeral for him in Paragould on June 21. This attracted a lot of attention. A long line of black cars conveyed Nash's colleagues in organized crime to the mausoleum, and according to local lore there was a détente between law enforcement and these visitors for the duration of their stay. Apparently, there was some question about whether Nash had really died. "Locals still tell of hearing that after the funeral, two men emerged from a black car parked in the distance and demanded of local officials to see the body just entombed to verify that it was Nash's."[86]

1. Sacred Heart Cemetery, Hartman
Yale Cemetery **(Johnson)**

2. Hamby Cemetery, Booneville **(Logan)**

3. Hampton City Cemetery **(Calhoun)**

4. Hill Family Cemetery **(Franklin)**

5. Mount Holly Cemetery, Little Rock **(Pulaski)**

6. Greenwood Cemetery, Hot Springs **(Garland)**

7. Butlerville Cemetery
Whiteley Cemetery, Cabot **(Lonoke)**

8. Hazen City Cemetery **(Prairie)**

9. Grissard Cemetery, El Paso **(White)**

10. Hite Cemetery, Biggers
Masonic Cemetery, Pocahontas **(Randolph)**

11. Agnos Cemetery **(Fulton)**

12. Mountain Home City Cemetery **(Baxter)**

13. McFerrin Cemetery, Compton **(Newton)**

14. IOOF Cemetery, Eureka Springs **(Carroll)**

15. Arkansas River | **16.** Mississippi River

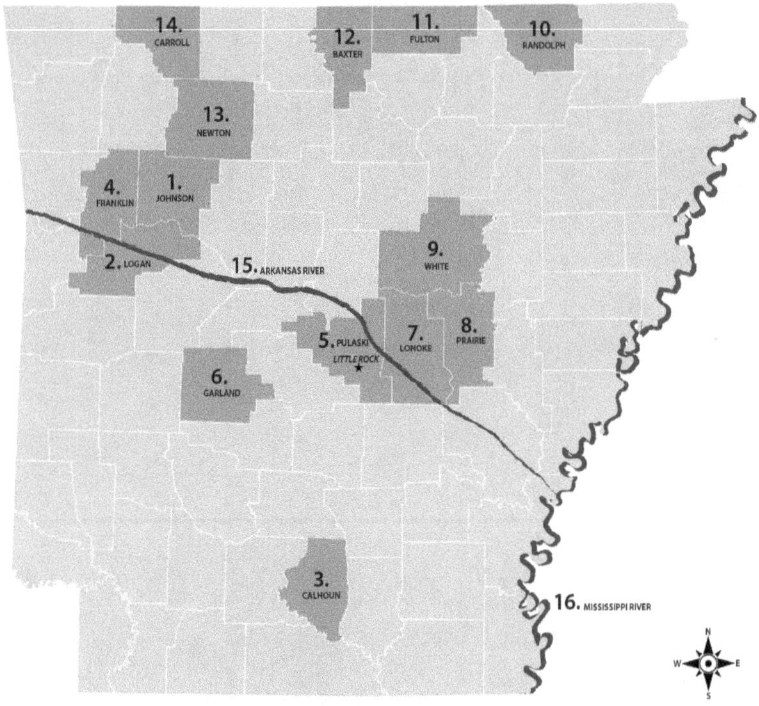

Major locations discussed in chapter 4.
Map by Red Rooster Design, Fayetteville, Arkansas.

Chapter 4

TOMBSTONE INSCRIPTIONS

Be this alone his epitaph
Whose life has closed its span,
Beneath this stone a brother sleeps
Who loved his fellow man.

—CHARLES BEASLEY, 1877–1912, WHITE OAK CEMETERY (WASHINGTON CO.)

Seven-year-old Johnnie Hite's tombstone (died 1880, Randolph Co.)[1] shows the profile of a curly-haired boy, his arms embracing the neck of a slightly older girl, with his cheek pressed against hers and his lips pursed in a kiss. This deep bas-relief was carved by Baker and Braun, a West Plains, Missouri, monument company whose signature has been found on other stones that use unusual iconography. (Examples include a woman, borne upward by an angel, looking back at her own corpse laid out on a bed,[2] and a bird on a branch gazing at a dead bird on the ground.[3]) It's not little Johnny's portrait that makes this stone so startling, however, but its inscription: "One babe was laid in earth before he died / another now slumbers at his side."

This sounds like a child was buried alive, and cursory research into the Hite family does not immediately dispel this. Genealogy files in the Regional Library at Pocahontas contain a letter raising the possibility that Siamese twins had been born to another member of the Hite family. Twin births tend to run in families, which suggests a horrifying possibility: Did one baby die and, thus dooming its twin, somehow cause both to be buried while one was . . . still alive?

The reality is that conjoined twins—unsubstantiated hearsay—have nothing to do with Johnnie's story. The Hites' first child, a daughter, died at birth in 1872,[4] a year and a half before Johnnie was born, so his epitaph simply reflects the death of this baby sibling before "he" (Johnnie) died. The carving represents the reunion in heaven between a little boy and his older sister, who is depicted at the age she would have attained. As for the baby that "slumbers" on Johnnie's other side, that would be an unnamed infant (born and died on August 23, 1895), the child of Johnnie's surviving brother, Harry.[5]

EPITAPHS

Cemetery-lovers tend to get chills when they discover the epitaph "Stranger smile not as you pass by / As you are now, so once was I / As I am now you too shall be / Prepare for death and follow me." This is not a one-of-a-kind macabre warning, however, as the verse is found across the United States and abroad, with death dates in the 1800s up through the present day. It is simply a reminder to the living to get their affairs in order. Occasionally the verse was altered to heighten its impact, especially on the young. Fifteen-year-old Mary Johnson's epitaph (died 1859, Clark Co.) is targeted at her peers: "Remember girls as you pass by / As you are now so once was I, / As I am now so you must be / Prepare in youth to follow me."[6]

Not all epitaphs should be taken literally, such as Rev. Stephen Carlile's, which suggests that he was killed in an Indian War (died 1860, White Co.).[7] Rather, this verse comes from a poem, later turned into a hymn, that was written to commemorate a deceased minister. (In the original version, the last line ends with "felt no fear."[8])

> The voice at midnight came,
> He started up to hear;
> A mortal arrow pierced his frame.
> He fell but felt no pain.[9]

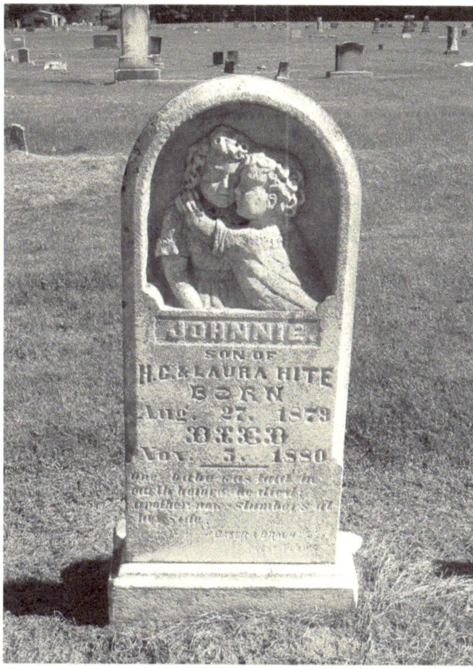

Fig 4.1. Johnnie Hite (1873–1880) is shown embracing his older sister, who died before he was born. Hite Cemetery (Randolph Co.).

Cemeteries are also places to find one-line inscriptions, some of them inexplicable: "Revenge is my motto" on the murdered John McKinney's grave (died 1869, Washington Co.);[10] "A lying in his grave" on the stone of Marion C. Shaddox (died 1884, Newton Co.);[11] or the irrefutable "We know not the hour" on a plot set aside for railroad workers in Little Rock's Oakland and Fraternal Cemetery (Pulaski Co.). What is one to make of fifteen-year-old Malanthan Carver's inscription in isolated Morris Cemetery (died 1888, Newton Co.): "Pa I have missed that awful fire"?[12] Is there really a headstone in Franklin County that lacks the deceased's name and dates, but reveals that "He choked on a Turkey bone"?[13]

Sometimes finding the word "murdered" on a stone raises more questions than it answers. For example, "Innocently murdered,"[14] "Excusably murdered,"[15] and "Killed on Mill Creek through mistake."[16] J.W. Meal (died 1868, Desha Co.) has an inscription that describes his killing but does not reveal why he is buried in Cincinnati, Ohio: "Killed on his plantation in Ark. while writeing [sic] at his desk by an unknown assassin March 23, 1868."[17]

Occasionally an inscription provides unexpected details, such as the fact that John D. Holt (died 1884, Newton Co.) "Weighed 190 lbs."[18] or that schoolteacher Mary Beller Russell (died 1902, Boone Co.) "Never struck her children."[19] Family tensions are evident on C.A. Carter's tombstone (died 1888, White Co.), which was, the inscription reveals, "Bought by the minor heir." [20] The widowed and remarried daughter-in-law who commissioned Nancy Cooper's marker (Carroll Co.) had no idea of her former mother-in-law's age but was likely encouraged by tombstone carver Nick Miller to inscribe both guesses, 102 or 110, on her headstone.[21] In fact, Cooper was either 85 or 92 when she died in 1892.[22]

Hazen's cemetery (Prairie Co.) contains an intriguing inscription on the marker of Samuel Erwin (died 1907). It asserts, "I was dying with 2 ounces of lead under my brain." Erwin was struck in the head with a minié ball (a conical lead bullet) during the Civil War battle of Chickamauga in 1863, and while the conventional wisdom is that such objects generally plowed straight through flesh and bone,[23] in Erwin's case the bullet remained lodged in his brain. It caused him to suffer constant pain over the next four decades, until February 1904, "by which time it [the bullet] had worked its way down to the roof of his mouth and was removed. The wound, however, failed to heal, and gave him much pain," leading to his death from erysipelas (a skin disease) three years later.[24]

Now and then a story emerges by doing a little subtraction, such as the fact that Allice L. Williams, *wife of* William Williams, was one week away from turning twelve when she died (1882, Washington Co.).[25] Sarah E. Lynch's original headstone in Hampton's town cemetery (died 1901, Calhoun Co.) states that she survived the Mountain Meadows Massacre,[26] but it is the modern metal marker, nearby, that tells the story. Sarah was "a member of a wagon train from northwest Arkansas destined for California that was attacked by Mormon Militiamen and Indian allies at Mountain Meadows, Utah (near Cedar City) on September 7–11, 1857 where approximately 121 people were massacred." Sarah Dunlap was just over a year old at the time of these murders. Capt. James Lynch and the US Army retrieved the surviving children two years later, and he married Sarah thirty-four years after that, when he was seventy-four and she was thirty-eight. He still outlived her by nine years.

Even lengthy epitaphs may only hint at dire events, such as the words found on Louis Elle's marker in the Jewish section of Texarkana's State Line cemetery (died 1894, Miller Co.): "Would that some supreme power had stayed the hand, who in that evil hour, robbed us of our dear husband and father, and left us in this world alone to wander." The hand in question belonged to a policeman who, from two hundred yards away, shot at a vicious dog but missed, hitting and killing Elle instead.[27]

NAMES AND NAUGHTINESS

Some graveyards have names that range from the puzzlingly descriptive: Red Door, Bucksnort, Convenience, Burnt Schoolhouse, Eight Mile, and Big Flat;[28] to the devout: Humble Hope, Bold Pilgrim, God's Little Half-Acre;[29] to the morbidly evocative: Dark Hollow, Dark Corner, Silent Grove, Shadowlawn, Strangers' Home.[30] Without intending any disrespect, humans have unusual names too. Children's names—or the lack thereof—can be informative, such as the heartbreaking "Silent Babe" ("Born Nov. 13, 1887" with no death date given, Pope Co.),[31] "Un-named Moss," who died at two months of age (1896, Faulkner Co.),[32] or the two-and-a-half-year-old "To be named in Heaven" Johnson (died 1880, Marion Co.),[33] not the only time "named in heaven" has been found on a headstone.[34] The unnamed didn't always die young, but surviving childhood didn't guarantee a name either: The 1910 Census lists forty-nine-year-old Infant Bea, married and the head of a household (Lonoke Co.), although no tombstone has been found for him.[35]

Sometimes names are poetic or evocative, such as adults Rose Budd (died 1915, Washington Co.),[36] Darling Love (1881, Pope Co.),[37] and Green Fields (1967, Madison Co.).[38] Other names are unusual to modern sensibilities: Wash Pigg (1942, Sebastian Co.),[39] Vestal Virgin (1945, Greene Co.),[40] Lemon Good (1926, Conway Co.),[41] Spicey Byrd (1955,

Faulkner),[42] while some sound like characters out of fiction: Palestine Teegarden (1938, Boone Co.)[43] and Pleasant Cowhorn (1911, Randolph Co.).[44] Sometimes it's just the first name that stands out: Glespy, Erple, and Mamil, for example, all found in the same cemetery,[45] while women's first names, like Gladness and Mourning, suggest there was a story behind their naming.[46] This author's personal favorite: Goode Pickler, "His memory is sweet" (died 1932, Columbia Co.).[47]

Modern markers yield an entirely different type of inscription, mocking death or cracking jokes, including the popular line, found on headstones everywhere: "I told you I was sick." Sometimes humor results from missing punctuation, such as "Rest in peace from your loving family."[48] An intentional joke is found on Tony Griffin Sherrod's marker in Conway's Oak Grove (died 2010, Faulkner Co.): "Died while fending off a great white shark during a triathlon." According to Sherrod's obituary he died of colon cancer, but it's true that he was a triathlete.

The words "bullshit"[49] and "asshole" have been found on modern markers, along with risqué one-liners referring to couples' sex lives. Deliberate jokes are entertaining now, but future cemetery visitors may be mystified by inscriptions such as "Just Google it,"[50] "Follow me on Facebook!"[51] and "He did not like his phone."[52] That last one-liner is found in Alabam Cemetery (Madison Co.), not far from the tombstone that yields this gem:

> Here's to the bull that roams the woods,
> Who does the cows and heifers good.
> If it wasn't for his big red rod,
> We wouldn't have any beef by God.[53]

STONES THAT TELL A COMPLETE STORY

It's too bad that nothing is known about the life of fourteen-year-old Robert Marsh, but his tombstone illustrates his death in words and a picture (died 1878, Lonoke Co.).[54] According to the inscription, Robert "died from accidental gun shot," then adds this unique detail: "was found by the barking of his faithful dogs, Jack and Bulger." Above the

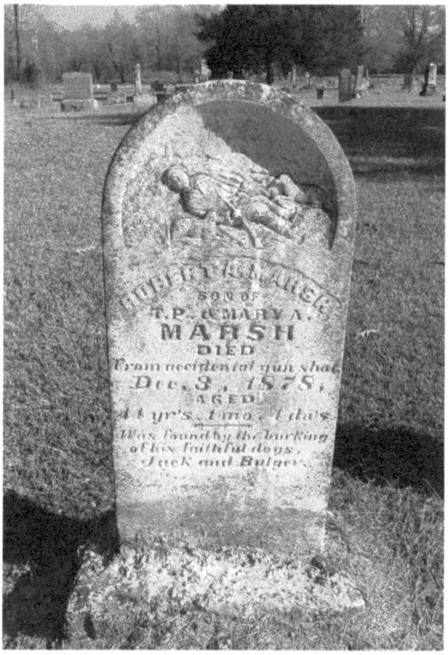

Fig 4.2. The tombstone of Robert Marsh, killed in an accident in 1878, shows his body and his dogs. Butlerville Cemetery (Lonoke Co.).

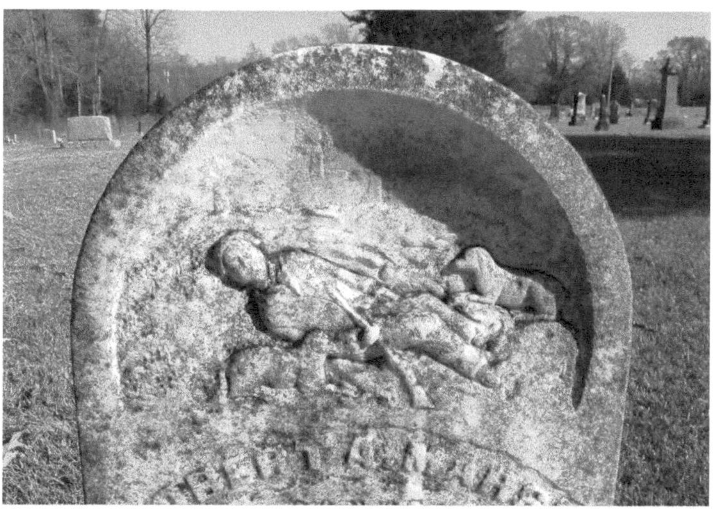

Fig 4.3. Close-up of Robert Marsh's stone, showing his dogs guarding his body, in Butlerville Cemetery (Lonoke Co.).

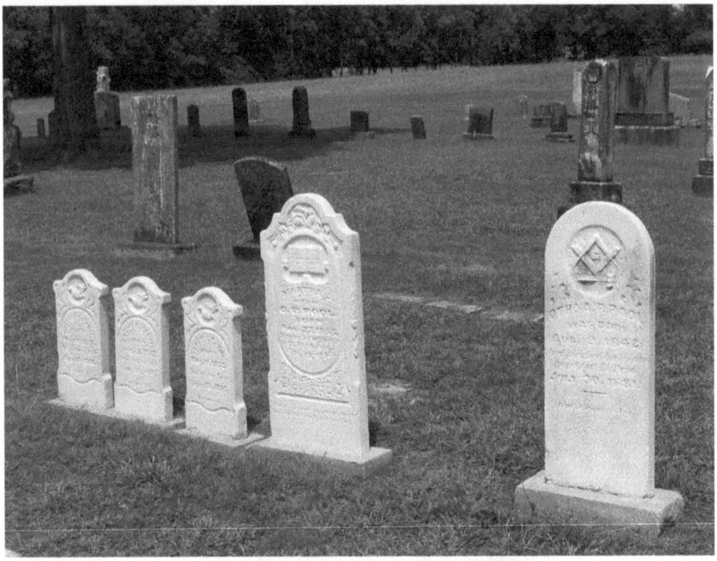

Fig 4.4. Martha Pool and three of her children have stones reading, "Perished in the storm" in 1880. Father Otho Pool, on the right, died by suicide a year later. Grissard Cemetery, El Paso (White Co.).

inscription is a detailed carving of Robert lying on the ground, his right hand clutching the barrel of his gun, pointed toward his head. His two dogs nestle against him, guarding his body, while in the background, faintly visible, are forested hills and grape vines.

Another story is found just twenty-five miles from Robert Marsh's grave, in Grissard Cemetery at El Paso (White Co.). This one can be pieced together from a collection of headstones: three small tablets, each decorated with a dove, and one adult-sized stone. All four of these markers contain the inscription "Perished in the storm," the words "God knows why," and the shared death date: April 18, 1880. William Pool, age six, Caleb, not quite three years old, Elbert, four months old, and their mother, Martha, were all killed by a massive storm that struck the town of El Paso. Seconds before their house was torn apart, husband Otho picked up the couple's five-year-old daughter, and the pair was blown into a crater left by an uprooted tree. Otho was badly injured, but the two survived.[55]

The story ends at the fifth tombstone in the row, set slightly apart from the others. Fifteen months later, Otho Pool, who never fully

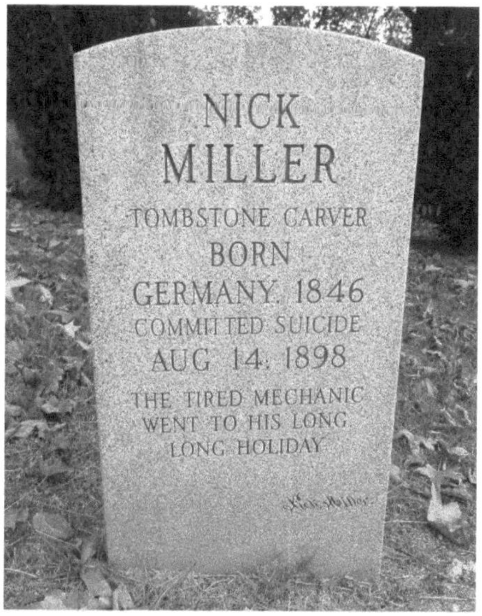

Fig 4.5. Tombstone carver Nick Miller committed suicide in 1898, and his grave went unmarked for well over a century. His modern marker includes the epitaph he requested in his suicide note. Berryville city cemetery (Carroll Co.).

recovered from the trauma inflicted by the storm, went into his dry goods store, lay down on the counter, and shot himself in the chest with a revolver. Then he cocked the gun again and shot himself through the head.[56] Inscribed "Perished by his own hands at El Paso," his is the only known original tombstone to include suicide as a cause of death and it, too, repeats the refrain, "God knows why."

The headstone of tombstone carver Nick Miller in Berryville (died 1898, Carroll Co.)[57] also has "committed suicide" on it, but this is a modern creation. Miller's grave went unmarked for more than a century, until a local historical society had a tablet-style headstone made and inscribed with the epitaph he requested in his suicide note: "The tired mechanic went to his long long holiday." Because Miller encouraged his clients to include unusual information on the headstones they commissioned from him, and because he had long been open about his intention to kill himself when his alcoholism got out of hand, his cause of death was included on his stone along with his signature.[58]

STRANGERS IN A STRANGE LAND

I was carried far from home
But could not escape death.

—JOHN M. MARTIN, 1850–1904, PALESTINE CEMETERY (BRADLEY CO.)

Dying far from one's home and family heightened an already sad event, something mentioned on certain tombstones. The sister of Connecticut native Edward Platt, who died in Little Rock in 1850, chose a puzzlingly contradictory epitaph: "Although he died among strangers, he was surrounded by friends in the hour of his death,"[59] while the parents of Massachusetts native Joseph Waite, who died of tuberculosis (1844, Yell Co.), chose "Far from friends and home—he met his final doom" for their son's stone.[60] (The term "stranger" is used by some city cemeteries to denote the outsiders who died in their midst.)

Another sad story, told in blank verse, is found on the ledger covering the grave of John Acheson, in Pocahontas's Masonic Cemetery (died 1833, Randolph Co.). Acheson came to Arkansas from Washington, Pennsylvania, in 1831, hoping to make enough money to get his formerly wealthy father out of debt. To do so, he joined Thomas Drew, the owner of both land and slaves (later to become the state's third governor) in a business partnership as a merchant and mill owner. "Tell Mother she must not be so uneasy about me," he wrote home in February 1833, just before leaving Arkansas on a trip to New Orleans.

Cholera was "raging" along the Mississippi River ports in the summer of 1833, and New Orleans was heavily affected.[61] Perhaps Acheson contracted this disease, though when he died five months later newspaper notices attributed his death to congestive fever or bilious fever (both related to, or the byproducts of, malaria). He was just twenty-six years old when he died on July 4, his obituary calling him "a stranger in a distant land, cut off from the attentions and sympathies of his relations."[62]

Mary Acheson grieved deeply for her firstborn. Despite her family's continued poverty, she commissioned a large tombstone, "the cost of which was met by her own self-denial," and had it shipped to Arkansas.[63] The words she chose are her personal expression of a mother's grief, combined with just a hint of disdain for the strangers—presumably the Drew family—who cared for her son at the very end.[64]

> For him no sister wept; no wife or mother
> In bended sorrow hung around
> His shrouded form, or stood
> Beside the deep, damp vault that held her own
> "Yet in a strange land, strangers wept—
> Strangers to him" who guessed not
> Half his worth—[65]

INFANTS' EPITAPHS

> In the cold moist earth we laid him
> When the forest cast the leaf,
> And we wept that one so lovely,
> Should have a life so brief.

—ISAIAH MORRIS, DIED DECEMBER 10, 1865, AGED THIRTY-SIX HOURS, WALNUT GROVE, NEWPORT (JACKSON CO.)

Consolation verses were meant to help parents reconcile themselves to the deaths of their children. "Never will know sin" is one attempt, on the grave of five-year-old Bobby Hanks in Cane Hill (died 1907, Washington Co.),[66] and "God blesses in an early death / And takes the infant unto himself" for an unnamed Willis child, stillborn in 1892, at Pricetown (Johnson Co.), or a shorter version of this, "Blessed are the early dead," on the marker of Denver Burdine, who lived just two months (died 1918, Newton Co.).[67] In some versions the child is happy, or relieved, to die; another variation is that the child *chose* to exit a sinful world, as is found on one-and-a-half-year-old Alfred Swagerty's marker (died 1867, Johnson Co.):[68]

He came to this world to see
A sample of our miseries
He turned his little head aside
Disgusted by the sight and died.[69]

Some parents were comforted by the thought that God loved their child more than they did, or that he needed their child to round out an incomplete set of angels, musicians, singers, or flowers in a heavenly choir or garden.[70] One variation is that the child had come to earth as an angel or cherub and was merely returning. There was comfort to be had from the belief that their child was too pure for earth, or simply better off in heaven. "Rest, little one, a mother's tears may fall, / But not for worlds would she her child recall."[71]

While this may seem like cold comfort, many parents rationalized their children's deaths as an incentive to live better lives (being baptized, attending church, reading their Bibles) so that they could be reunited in the next world. "Follow me to Paradise" is one expression of this or, more explicitly, "Those lovely babes so pure and sweet, / Are now watching at Heaven's gate, / And may it guide the parents feet, / Into the path that is narrow and straight."[72] The parents of ten-month-old Mansel Bryant (died 1914, Boone Co.) chose a verse ending with this justification: "Bright eyed darling, the light of our home / Was taken so early to welcome us come."[73]

Children's epitaphs sometimes provide harrowing details: "Here we lay our precious child / Who lived to weep but not to smile. / Whose life was lived in one short hour— / Too pure and tender for a long life flower" (died 1911, Boone Co.),[74] or this: "I will lay my head on my mother's breast / She will watch as I sink to my last long rest."[75] One wonders what caused the death of eleven-year-old John Justice (died 1901, Logan Co.) that led to his parents choosing the inscription "Happy now is little John / Far away from pain & weeping."[76] Carl G. Inklebarger's short life (May–June 1901, Franklin Co.) is summed up in this inscription: "He came, wept, smiled and died."[77]

Children's dying words are found less often than those of adults, but are usually more poignant, such as the plea of five-year-old J.H. Williams: "Mama get me well, the Dr. won't," and the inscription continues, in the voice of Williams's mother, that she couldn't get her child well (died 1899, Franklin Co.).[78] While most obituary verses are fairly standard, occasionally parents, like J.C. and Ama Reed (undated, Washington Co.),[79] wrote original epitaphs containing unexpected information:

> Here our babies lie six in a row,
> The little ones are now in Heaven
> The Bible tells us so
> The first to go was Oscar C.
> The last to go was Jennie B.
> The rest not named but never forgotten.

Though such epitaphs helped grieving parents come to terms with their devastating losses, practically none attempted to console families over the death of an old person. ("A hoary head is a crown of Glory" is a rare exception.[80]) A few inscriptions stressed the inevitability of death for all ages, such as "Death's fiat, 'dust to dust,' sooner or later goes forth to everyone . . ." (1894, Woodruff Co.).[81] This is the opposite of the sentiment that gives comfort to mourners today and that has been found on countless granite markers: "God only takes the best."

INFANTS' BURIAL PLACEMENT

Evidence of high maternal and infant mortality is all too easily found in the oldest sections of cemeteries. More unusual, however, is a record of where the baby is buried in relation to a parent. When noted, this is often in the mother's arms, or by her side, but there are exceptions. The stone of Mary Carlton (died 1901, Newton Co.) notes that her two-month-old infant "lies sleeping at her feet,"[82] while the grave of Nancy Redman (died 1861, Jackson Co.) contains "also her three infants, two by her side & one in her arms."[83]

The inscription on one multiple burial (died 1887, Little River Co.) is unusual because it is found on the father's original marker: "Two of my children are with me at rest, / One at my side and the other just west."[84] Of all of these references the most disturbing are those that hint at a mother "taking" the life of her infant, though this is likely just poetic language. Examples include Sarah Carlton (died 1885, Newton Co.),[85] who "also took her infant babe with her" and Nin A. Gray (died 1879, Washington Co.) who "gave her life for her child; and took it with her."[86]

CAUSES OF DEATH

On beds of affliction
—he lingered not long;
When the Death angel come [sic]
—so mighty and strong
In the cold arms of death
—he gently laid down.

—ARTHUR CARPENTER, 1880–1900, DENVER CEMETERY (CARROLL CO.)

Given the epidemics of smallpox, cholera, yellow fever, influenza, and even measles that decimated communities, it's surprising how seldom older tombstones mention illness as a cause of death, although a few hint at it. The concrete marker of Sarah Gibson (died 1900, Logan Co.) provides a few clues: "No scorching fever or cruel pain / Can ever hurt my darling again";[87] Hassie Morrison (died 1919) has a verse describing her death: "The weakening pulse, the shortning breath / The last faint fluttering sigh . . ."[88] while Rush Batterton's enigmatic "Perfect through sufferings" (died 1920, Garland Co.) makes sense if you know that he died from appendicitis.[89]

Antinette Blackwell's epitaph has been partially obscured by a smear of concrete, but enough can be read to reveal her cause of death. Blackwell was thirty-four (died 1885, Clark Co.), and perhaps her husband chose this verse, from a poem written by William Cullen Bryant. The poem is titled "Consumption" (another name for tuberculosis), which is, presumably, how Blackwell died:

Light winds, wandering through groves of bloom
Detach the delicate blossoms from the tree;
Close thy sweet eyes calmly and without pain;
And we will trust in God to see thee yet again.[90]

A specific illness is named on the sandstone marker of Commodore Perry Wilson (his given name, not a naval rank). Wilson, aged twenty-two, was working as a clerk aboard a mail steamboat when he died in 1849. His body was brought back to Mount Holly (Pulaski Co.) for burial beneath a tombstone reading, "died of Cholera." Another rare reference to disease is found in Augusta Memorial Park (Woodruff Co.) on the grave of Meredith Wilkerson (died 1854, four days shy of his fifteenth birthday). His lengthy inscription, presumably written by his schoolmates, refers to "our young and interesting friend" who died of pneumonia, which "hurried him to that bourne from whence none return." Still, Wilkerson had enough time to repent turning his back on his religious upbringing and to request that his friends and family meet him in heaven.[91]

Death from disease may have been so much the norm that, although mentioned in obituaries, it simply wasn't worth putting on a tombstone. But when the cause of death was something out of the ordinary, families wanted the world to know. There are numerous tombstones with "Drowned," several of which give the name of the river in which it happened. Also common: "Killed by a train" and "Struck by lightning"—or even more specific—Pearl Oxford's marker, "Struck by lightning while plowing corn" (died 1903, Boone Co.).[92] William Lang was "Killed by a falling tree" (died 1914, Franklin Co.),[93] Charles Russo "Died accidentally under a motor truck" (died 1919, Jefferson Co.),[94] while Edmond C. Christy has the most unusual but, unfortunately, untraceable cause of all: "Died from aeroplane fall" (1917, Jonesboro, Craighead Co.).[95]

Children's lives were possibly even more dangerous than those of adults, as their gravestone inscriptions show. All we know about two-and-a-half-year-old Jefferson Pierce is that he was "Killed by accident" (died 1900, Newton Co.),[96] but Lilly V. Howerton's cause of death was surprisingly common in the 1800s: "Accidentally burned to death" (died 1885, Carroll Co.).[97] Other unusual causes include four-year-old Demoss Dillahunty (died 1888, Mississippi Co.),[98] who was "Kill'd by a stick of wood rolling over him," and Lula Crossland's marker, "Killed Aug. 3, 1928, by car driven by unknown man" (Fort Chaffee, Sebastian Co.).[99] According to their shared headstone, seven-year-old Bessie Hobbs and her nearly four-year-old brother Hugh were "Killed by Explosion of a boiler" on March 20, 1884. A newspaper account states that the engine in a nearby steam mill exploded (Woodruff Co.), killing Hugh from shrapnel and Bessie from "concussion caused by the shock."[100] The children's father was injured in the blast but survived; their mother was ill and bedridden after having recently given birth, making the Hobbs children's epitaph relevant to all four family members: "In the midst of life we are in death."

News stories and obituaries offer ample proof that life in the 1800s and early 1900s was dangerous, and certain jobs were especially so, such as coal mining, sawmill, and railroad work. Deaths among these professions often included mutilations and dismemberments. (See chapter 8 for more on amputations.) Despite this, references to work-related deaths are rare on tombstones. One exception is found in Coal Hill (Johnson Co.), where the superintendent of the coal mines paid for John Rutherford's marker after he was "accidentally burnt by an explosion of gas on the 19 of July and died on the 23 day of July 1891."[101]

Another work-related death was that of sixteen-year-old William Lafayette Cecil, who left an isolated Newton County farm and traveled sixty-five miles to Fayetteville (Washington Co.) to train as a city electrician. As with Rutherford's death, when Cecil was electrocuted on the job, his supervisor paid for the large marker that gives the young man's cause of death: "Killed by a live wire at Fayetteville, Ark." (1905, Newton Co.).[102] Perhaps it is merely a coincidence that young Cecil had recently testified at a trial involving his employer and that his death was caused by negligence for which no one was held accountable.[103]

DEATH IN SERVICE TO OTHERS

A wartime death is a heroic one, whether it occurs saving the life of a fellow soldier or fighting to save an entire country. Such information is found on cenotaphs (memorial stones), or on graves of bodies repatriated from overseas cemeteries in the years following both world wars. It's common for these markers to include an epitaph about how the deceased died for a noble cause ("The war to end all wars") or to quote John 15:13, "Greater love hath no man than this, that a man lay down his life for his friends."

Two tombstones tell of teenaged girls who sacrificed themselves to save other children. One spring evening in Little Rock in 1905, little Charlie Carlin ran onto the tracks in front of an oncoming streetcar. His thirteen-year-old African American nanny, Catherine Lawson, reached him just in time and was able to grab him up in her arms and throw him clear of the car before she was dragged beneath its wheels. Badly mangled, she died shortly after an operation to amputate her leg.[104]

Charlie's parents, who were white, paid for Lawson's elaborate burial, complete with a white casket and a white hearse (the color denoting youth and innocence) and attended Lawson's funeral. Little Rock's sheriff immediately began raising money for a tombstone for Lawson, personally donating $10, the largest amount received.[105] Little Rock newspapers gave daily tallies of the amount raised, but although $136 was pledged, ultimately organizers realized only $100 in cash for a marker and a burial plot. Lawson's body was exhumed and moved to Oakland and Fraternal Cemetery in Little Rock (Pulaski Co.), where a towering, urn-topped obelisk was erected, inscribed: "Erected by white people to the memory of Catherine Lawson who sacrificed her life at the age of 13 years in saving the life of a white child (she was nursing) from being killed by a street car in this city on May 21, 1905."

Shortly after the tragedy, a newspaper suggested that Lawson was worthy of posthumously receiving an award from the Carnegie Hero Commission (today called a Carnegie Medal of Honor).[106] Despite the logic of this, no such prize was given. However, before the year ended, Charlie Carlin's father brought suit against the Little Rock

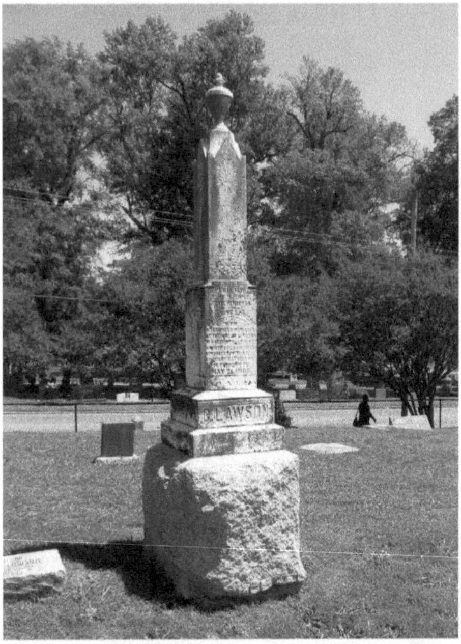

Fig 4.6. Catharine Lawson, protecting the child she was caring for, was killed by a streetcar in Little Rock in 1905. Her marker tells the story of her heroism. Oakland and Fraternal Cemetery, Little Rock (Pulaski Co.).

Railway and Electric Company and received $500 in compensation for his son's minor injuries, described after the event as "scarcely an abrasion."[107] S.P. Vaughter, running for reelection as Pulaski County coroner, also profited from Lawson's death when he campaigned on his successful efforts to get fenders put on local street cars. Despite this, less than a year later, eight-year-old Willie Trager was killed by a streetcar, "the second child that has been killed in the same way at Little Rock during the last few days."[108]

Another Arkansas teenager—who was white—did receive a posthumous Carnegie Medal for saving the life of a child. The tombstone of fourteen-year-old orphan Francis Spanke (died 1914, Johnson Co.)[109] states that she "died attempting to save the life of Marie R. Oberle from being run over by a train, at Clarksville, Ark." A

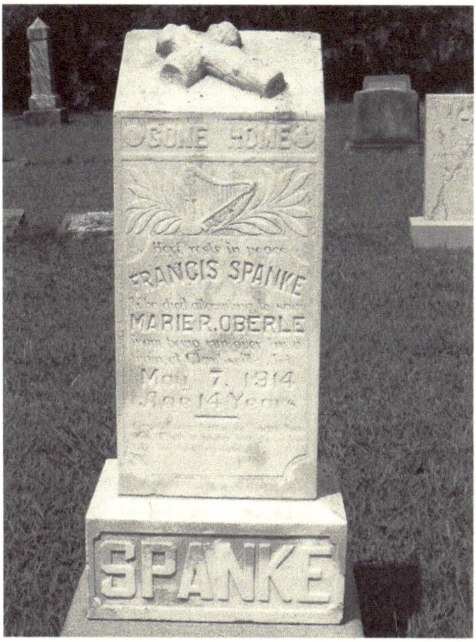

Fig 4.7. Francis Spanke's stone tells how she died saving Marie Oberle from being hit by a train in 1914. Sacred Heart Cemetery, near Hartman (Johnson Co.).

newspaper account tells how eleven-year-old Oberle stumbled and fell on a railroad bridge just as a train approached. "Miss Spanke ran back on to the bridge, helped up her companion and they were off the track and trying to get down the path when the cowcatcher caught them, tumbling the smaller girl down the path and striking Miss Spanke and throwing her several yards," which fractured her skull and resulted in her death.[110] Oberle, though injured, eventually recovered.

An application was made for a Carnegie medal. Though eyewitness accounts differed as to whether Spanke could or could not have saved herself instead of helping Oberle, a silver medal and a $200 death benefit were awarded to the widowed Louise Spanke, foster mother of the deceased girl.[111] (Despite the surname on her tombstone, Francis was never formally adopted.)[112]

KILLED, MURDERED, ASSASSINATED

Of all of causes of death found on tombstones, murder may be the most common, especially during or just after the Civil War. Zeblon Jetton was "innocently murdered by his political enemies for claiming his Southern principles" (died 1865, Johnson Co.),[113] while "G.W. Biggerstaff was cruelly murdered Jan. 4, 1868" (single grave near Spadra, Johnson Co.). Jake Bogard supposedly spit in the face of a captured Federal prisoner and the man returned later to exact a lethal revenge. The inscription on Bogard's tombstone (Lonoke Co.)[114] says that he was "waylaied [sic] and shot on the 6th of Dec. 1863" and goes on to entreat, "Oh God may thy Judgement prove severe upon those who murdered the Beloved one that lies here."[115]

The headstone of John L. Davenport in Pleasant Grove Cemetery (Scott Co.) comes close to naming his killers: "Assassinated by the Waldron Ring Feb. 6, 1878."[116] This happened during the Waldron War, "a decade-long period of violence that began during the Reconstruction era and was characterized by arson, general lawlessness, personal and political feuds, electoral misconduct and violence,"[117] including several murders. These events reached their peak with Davenport's murder, for which several prominent citizens stood trial but were acquitted. Perhaps Davenport's family had to content themselves by naming the Waldron ring as his killers.

Sometimes families knew and hinted at a murderer's name. A family member witnessed bushwhackers shoot Spencer Horner and torture and shoot his son William Riley Horner on August 2, 1864, though William didn't die for several days. "Killed by parties well known to his family," is inscribed on William's marker in the now inaccessible Horner family cemetery (Franklin Co.).[118] The family of Leonard Sims knew who killed their son in Oklahoma (died 1901, Crawford Co.)[119] but chose to inscribe that he "was murdered by a traitor and coward, whose name is not worthy to appear here," which is identical to what's written on outlaw Jesse James's granite marker (died 1883, Clay Co., Missouri).[120] Not worthy, perhaps, but also not unknown: gambler Charley McKnight was acquitted of Sims's shooting, which also killed a bystander.[121]

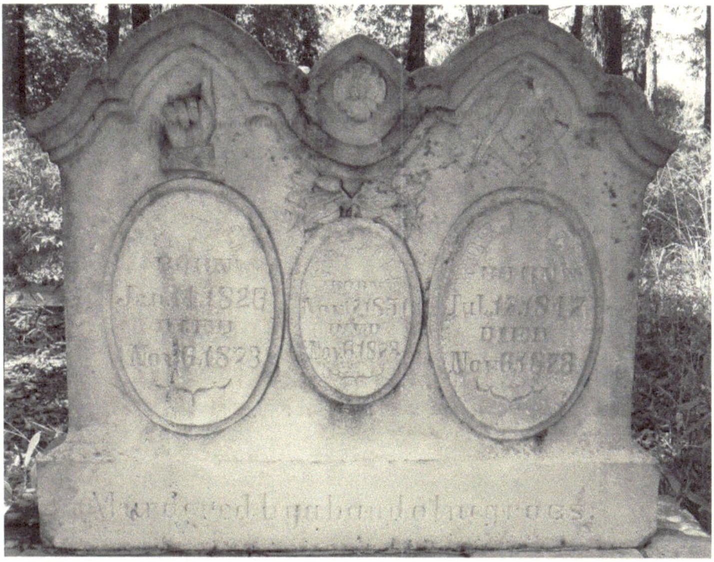

Fig 4.8. Three members of the Eagle family share an 1878 death date. Despite differing versions of events, their family chose the inscription, "Murdered by a band of negroes." Whitley Cemetery, at Cabot (Lonoke Co.).

Anton Wallace Anderson's epitaph provides an added detail about his killing (died 1899, Franklin Co.):[122]

> Remember friends when this you see
> Here lies the last remains of me,
> But yet while in the prime of life
> The victim of an assassin's knife.

In this case, the word "assassin" is a bit fanciful. Anderson's brother got into a fight at a dance, and both were stabbed—Anderson fatally—when he came to his brother's aid.[123]

The words, "Murdered by a band of negroes" is emblazoned across an elaborate marker for three members of the Eagle family in Whitley Cemetery (Lonoke Co.). Above this inscription are the names of father and son George and William H. Eagle and George's nephew Robert Eagle, all having the same death date: November 6, 1873.

These men, along with several friends, were bear hunting when their dogs became lost. As they were searching for the dogs, two of the party came across two Black men on horseback, carrying four hogs. The men fled when ordered to give the source of the hogs, and the hunters took the hogs to the nearby home of Squire Sullivan. He identified them as being his property and, as there was no local law enforcement, Sullivan gave Robert Eagle a writ for the arrest of the two thieves, and Robert then deputized the rest of the hunting party.[124]

What happened next depends on who is telling the story. Dock Gray, the only uninjured member of the posse, stated that when the posse arrived at the thieves' house Robert Eagle displayed the writ and announced that they were there to arrest the hog thieves. In response, armed Blacks replied that "five hundred or a thousand men couldn't arrest any of them" and opened fire as the posse dismounted "to save themselves." The injured James Sullivan told a similar story. Gray was able to get back to Lonoke and alert the sheriff, who returned and retrieved the bodies.[125]

Black participants told a very different story, including that the Eagles had fired first. The newspaper disputed this. There was evidence of bullets fired from both directions, but the paper called it "remarkable that none of the negroes were hurt, for the Eagles were considered among the best shots in the county."[126] At a grand jury hearing later that month, eight Black men and one woman testified that members of the posse rode up and, after swearing at them and vowing to kill them, fired first. (One man admitted that they'd rehearsed giving the same testimony.[127]) It is not known what happened to these suspects, although four years later one was killed by a mob.[128]

The Eagles' marker doesn't give the names, only the race, of their killers. Murderers' names were sometimes carved on their victims' tombstones when justice was not done, which explains this marker in Bozarth Cemetery (1871, Benton Co.): "In memory of J.M. Lefors who was murdered by F.A. Sanders." Relatives offered a $400 reward for Sanders's capture, describing him as a hangdog, hump-shouldered "inveterate smoker" wearing an overcoat with a fox collar, but despite this vivid description the reward seems to have gone unclaimed.[129]

Other stones that name a killer include Sylvanus Hinds's marker (died 1863, Madison Co.),[130] stating that he "came to his death by being willfully murdered on June 13 by his cousin John Hinds."[131] Sylvanus died of blood loss on June 27, two weeks after John struck him in the neck with the sharp blade of a grain cradle. John moved with his wife and family across the border to Missouri, out of reach of the law.[132] A small headstone, tucked away in the isolated Youngblood cemetery, states that Hattie Youngblood (died 1906, Boone Co.) was "murdered by Frankey Seel," who also avoided prosecution by quickly leaving town. Accounts differ as to whether the teenaged girls were close friends or rivals for the same young man's affections.[133] Then there's Spencer Kennedy's granite marker in Mountain Home (died 1947, Baxter Co.), which states that Kennedy was "Murdered in cold blood by Newman Harrison better known as Rip Fee Marshal of Yellville." (Harrison was the city marshal, and it is unclear why he had an alias.[134]) Kennedy and his two brothers were drunk and disorderly in a Yellville café, and they attacked Harrison when he tried to arrest them. In the melee, Kennedy was shot in the abdomen, the café owner in the leg, and Harrison (who was later exonerated) required medical treatment for injuries inflicted by the brothers.[135]

It's a pity that nothing remains of Henry Conway's "marble shaft" in Scull Cemetery (Arkansas Co.). His lengthy inscription, written by his brother James S. Conway, the future first governor of Arkansas, reportedly included the information that Henry was "unfortunately mortally wounded in a duel with Robert Crittenden on the 29th of October, and died 9th of November, 1827."[136]

Deny Hill's large tombstone in her family's cemetery,[137] signed by its maker, Benjamin Farley, is easily the most informative one in this category (died 1871, Franklin Co.) as it gives her murderers' names and their motive. Thus we know that, "bill Chinouth & Joe forbush / Murdered this lovely / Child and hid her in / The creek to get / The Family out to / Look so they mite / Rob & Steal." (Transcribed exactly as carved.)

Newspapers provided the full, horrifying details of how the men raped and murdered Deny then submerged the three-year-old's body in a creek; she was almost unrecognizable when finally found. The men were quickly apprehended; they confessed and were en route to jail when they attempted to escape and were shot by the posse guarding them. (A privately told but unverified version of events states that

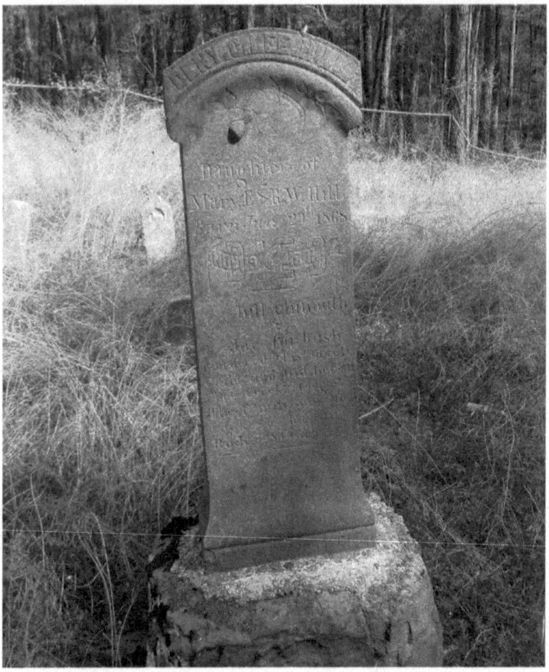

Fig 4.9. Deny Hill, murdered in 1871, has a tombstone naming her killers and giving their motive. Hill family cemetery (Franklin Co.).

the two murderers were executed at "Hanging Rocks," where bodies could be hanged from a crossbeam placed across two immense, upright stone slabs.) Deny's father surely wanted to see his daughter's killers publicly hanged but had to content himself with having their full names carved on her tombstone.[138]

A final example, though it does not name a murderer, is found on Obed Hill's tombstone in Yale cemetery (died 1918, Johnson Co.), just down the road from the Richard Hill family cemetery where Deny is buried. The inscription states that Obed and three others "were murdered by a bank robber at Camp Funston, Kan., Jan. 11, 1918," an army base training soldiers to fight in World War I. He was thirty years old.

Hill had worked as a teller for only a short time when Capt. Lewis Whisler entered the camp's bank after hours and forced cashier Kearney Wornell, at gunpoint, to tie up the others. Whisler then used a hatchet and hacked these four men (one of them a visitor) to death, and badly wounded Wornell. Whisler returned to his barracks with $62,800 of the bank's money, which he hid in a wall. After it was announced that all officers would have their fingerprints taken, Whisler wrote a suicide note in which he explained his motive: "I have been thinking of committing suicide for a long time but I have never had a good reason. Yesterday I went out and made myself a reason." Then he shot himself twice in the head with his service rifle.[139]

Without arguing the merits of one death over another, exactly two months after the murderous rampage, the country's first case of influenza occurred at Camp Funston, quickly killing forty-eight soldiers in a week's time and sickening hundreds of others.[140] Ultimately, deaths from the influenza epidemic would outnumber the deaths from World War I casualties. Hill, who had expected to be called up for military service, may have been doomed to a short life no matter what. He left an insurance policy in his youngest sister's name, but she did not continue her education as Obed had wished. Perhaps the money paid for his massive tombstone, which includes a poem signed "Obed." The verse urges that love and friendship be expressed during a person's lifetime, concluding, "Why should good words ne'er be said / Of a friend till he is dead."

UNRELIABLE NARRATORS

> Say nothing but good of the dead.
>
> —DR. E.O. GRIGSBY, 1832–1899, ODD FELLOWS CEMETERY (NEAR MCCRORY, WOODRUFF CO.)

Whether from custom, courtesy, or superstition, it is said to be wrong to speak ill of the dead, and this extends to the deceased's epitaph. Extreme modesty, however, *is* allowed. Eighty-year-old Burnett Denney's epitaph states, "He has gone to join his many relations that outstripped him" (died 1888, Madison Co.),[141] while Benjamin Turner Clement (died 1913, Pike Co.) has a longer inscription, likely chosen by his son, that is even more explicit:

How loved, how honored once,
avails thee not,
To whom related, or by whom begot;
A heap of dust alone remains of thee,
'Tis all thou art, and all the proud shall be.

Clement was born in Virginia; his father, a wealthy physician, enslaved sixteen persons prior to the Civil War. Clement was both a merchant and a postmaster in Arkansas, and according to the long inscription on the back of his stone in Kirby Cemetery, he died in his son's arms. These epitaphs might be considered "humble bragging," but in recent times some people, when picking out their own headstones, have chosen (presumably) self-deprecating one-liners, such as "Feared or hated by most" and "I thought I was too mean to die."[142]

When the deceased wasn't a saint, relatives sometimes scrambled to do a bit of character rehabilitation on the tombstone. The elaborate marker of Solon Borland Blackburn, who died in New Orleans in 1876 and was brought to Little Rock for burial in Mount Holly Cemetery, is a case in point. Thanks to Ronald Fuller's painstaking transcription of the solid blocks of text that cover the front of Blackburn's monument, we know that the twenty-four-year-old was affectionate and obedient in childhood, brave, kindhearted, noble, and generous as an adult, "the very soul of honor and worth."

This is somewhat at odds with newspaper accounts of Blackburn's death by suicide. Two years earlier he had received a letter from his fiancée telling him that "until his habits improved he was discarded." Rather than mending his dissipated ways, it appears that Blackburn brooded over the rejection and kept right on drinking. On December 17, he penciled what was either a request or a taunt, "try and forget me," at the bottom of her letter,[143] then shot himself in the head with a dueling pistol, which he had rented at a firing range. Accounts differ as to whether he was intoxicated at the time.[144]

A tombstone inscription is intended to commemorate, not condemn, the deceased, but occasionally one hints that there is more to a story. When William and Robert ("Chock") Hamby were killed near Paris (1881, Logan Co.),[145] their relatives put two Bible verses on the brothers' shared monument, verses that contain the words "persecute"

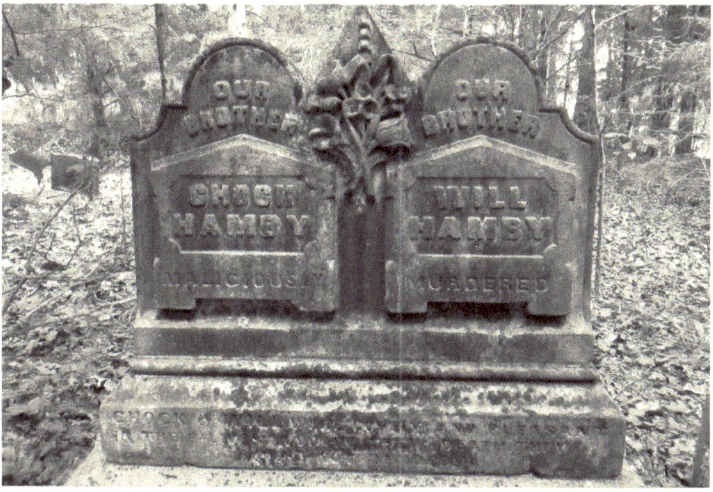

Fig 4.10. Chock and Will Hamby's shared marker states that they were "Maliciously murdered" in 1881, but the brothers were complicit in their own killing. Hamby Cemetery, outside Booneville (Logan Co.).

and "persecuted."[146] Another inscription states that the boys "were lovely and pleasant in their lives." They were also, their tombstone insists, "Maliciously murdered."

But were they *any* of these things? Contemporary newspaper accounts tell a very different story. Earlier, the Hambys' friends William Jetton and Jesse "Bun" Fuller had assaulted Leander and Emmett Logan, Black men, who swore out a warrant.[147] Jetton and Fuller went into hiding to avoid arrest, and on September 10, 1881, they asked to borrow the Hambys' guns in order to kill the Logans. The Hambys handed over their guns, knowing exactly how their friends planned to use them.

Jetton and Fuller lay in wait by the banks of the Petit Jean River, but the Logans (possibly having been tipped off) returned home by a different route.[148] Meanwhile, the Hamby brothers delayed their return from town until, they estimated, the deed had been done, then rode home via the river road expecting to see the dead bodies. But as they rode up, the assassins mistook them for the long-awaited Logans and fired on them, killing Robert on the spot.[149] William, wounded, managed to stay on his horse for nearly a mile before he fainted, fell, and was dragged for a long distance, dying a few hours later.[150]

The Logans were questioned about the crime and then released. Jetton and Fuller were arrested and indicted for murder—Fuller claimed that Jetton had fired the fatal shots. The two managed to dig their way out of the Paris jail (Logan Co.) and escape. Despite a reward offered by the governor, Jetton was never found, but five years later Fuller returned to Paris, turned himself in, and was tried for Robert's murder.[151] Perhaps his lawyer was convincing in his argument that the jury not be shown his client's signed confession because Fuller was acquitted.[152]

Nearly a century later the *Booneville Democrat* looked back at this crime in an article that altered a few key details (such as that the Hambys wanted the Logans killed and paid two assassins to do it) but mostly agreed with the newspaper accounts of 1881.[153] This angered descendants of the Hamby family. Their version of events bore zero resemblance to 1881 reportage but, conveniently, was impossible to verify because, they claimed, all proof of their assertions had burned up in a hotel fire. Nevertheless, the newspaper published an abject retraction, blaming their earlier reportage on "a fictitious community legend."[154]

One final example of an unreliable inscription is found on the truncated obelisk of Johnnie Poynter (1894, Carroll Co.), hanged on Judge Isaac Parker's Fort Smith scaffold for having brutally murdered his two traveling companions in 1891. Somewhat surprisingly, given these facts, the stone contains two Bible verses: "He healeth the broken in heart, and bindeth up their wounds," and "Greater love hath no man than this, that a man lay down his life for his friends."[155]

Poynter—who had a history of being rescued from various "scrapes" by his father—claimed that he had accidentally killed the two men while trying to stop them from killing one another. Their heads had been bashed in with an ax (found nearby); when located, Poynter was wearing one victim's pants and carrying his watch, and he had sold their horses and wagon, details that helped doom him to hang.[156] Judge Parker summed up Poynter as having "exhibited a state of more depravity seldom seen in one so young,"[157] and after his execution a newspaper said that he had always been heartless, cruel, cold-blooded, and brutal, as well as a bully and a coward, adding, "He, when quite a boy, bound a companion and then attempted to burn him."[158]

LAST WORDS

My wife as she lay
Mid friends who round her hover,
Aroused once more to feebly say,
"Thank God I'm almost over."

—ELIZA J. LOWREY, 1818–1889, LOWREY-RYE CEMETERY (SEBASTIAN CO.)[159]

When it came time to choose an epitaph, families could select a verse from monument dealers' books or from hymnals, the Bible, collections of mourning poetry, or the inscriptions on other tombstones. Very occasionally, they wrote their own. Sometimes these choices are mystifying. It's hard to know what to make of the following verses on the stone of Charles Edward Moore, who worked as a bartender aboard a riverboat and was shot by a passenger in a dispute over a bar tab[160] (died 1870, Ouachita Co.):[161]

I give thee to thy native dust,
Thou loved and honored form;
I murmur not for God is just,
And I, am but a worm.

I kneel upon thy grave while prayer
Bursts from my aching heart,
O Savior reunite us where
We will never part.

Moore's epitaph, while not original,[162] is certainly unusual, especially considering that families tended to opt for the same few verses over and over again. "A precious one from us has gone, a voice we loved is still . . ." begins one very popular epitaph that runs to two verses, while children's deaths were often commemorated with either "Budded on earth to bloom in heaven," or "Weep not, papa and mama for me / For I am waiting in heaven for thee."

Given such repetitiveness it comes as a welcome relief to discover something out of the ordinary, such as the dying person's last words. These are easy to identify if the inscription states, "His dying words" or "Her last audible statement." Even without such identifiers, "Meet me in heaven" is the phrase most often uttered by the dying, although injunctions to relatives to live good lives (so everyone can meet in heaven) are found often. Though normally sad, on occasion some final utterances can be inspiring, predictive, entertaining, or even unintentionally funny. Rev. Alexander Stevenson (died 1875, White Co.)[163] surely gave comfort by saying, "This can't be death—I feel too good," while Belle Wilson Williams (1911, Madison Co.),[164] after reassuring her mourners that she had been well cared for, ended with, "I have this written for fear the other children will not get here in time, and this will be such a comfort to them to read." S.Y. Collier (1913, Carroll Co.)[165] predicted his own death, saying, "I will pass away tonight."[166]

Given that the dying person was very likely suffering, it's surprising how rarely last words reveal distress. Twenty-one-year-old Lydia Dickerson (1861, Washington Co.)[167] died asking her mother whether she had sinned.[168] Ira Marvin was more resigned. "If the good Lord don't want me to get well, I don't want to get well," he said *twice* when dying (1903, Boone Co.).[169]

Occasionally someone doled out advice on his or her deathbed, or had something ominous to say, such as Uriah Rackley (1902, Sevier Co.): "Weep not for me but weep for yourself."[170] Mary Bourland's final words of wisdom to her elderly husband fill the front of her marker in Ozark's Highland Cemetery (1910, Franklin Co.), informing him that she would not recover ("and you will go soon"), then urging him to stay on in their home because "you do not want to live with young folks," advice that he took. Somewhat more startling is John Simmie Evans's advice to his brothers (died 1894, Fulton Co.),[171] "Shun bad company and the dance," then telling his mother that they would "meet at the Judgement." (John's mother predeceased him seven years earlier, presumably following childbirth, so perhaps he was addressing a stepmother.) In addition to this inscription, the words "Wait at the gate till I come" are inscribed at the top of his stone, which may also have been part of his dying remarks.

John's sister Polly died three years later and was buried beside him. Hers is the family's most elaborate marker, featuring a three-dimensional carving of a small disembodied hand clutching at a stack of books. Below her name and dates is an inscription that begins, "Brother Simeon in a dream I thought you came for me, reached your hand [to me and I] reached mine to you," but the marker is broken above the line that would have revealed what happened next.[172]

Some families turned their loved ones' last words into poetry, perhaps in the belief that an epitaph ought to rhyme. Tombstone carver Marcus Lafayette Kelly did this when creating his wife Sarah's marker (died 1890, Benton Co.).[173] One side of the marker is headlined "A request," followed by these instructions to her children:

> My darling little children,
> Take heed to what I say,
> For I am on my dying bed,
> And soon must pass away.
> I have loved you in your infancy,
> And you've loved me quite well,
> If you by acts in future years,
> Your love for me would tell,
> Always be industrious,
> And do your duty well.

On another side of the marker Sarah tells her husband not to grieve for her, reassuring him that "you have loved me well as an affectionate wife." (This praise is suspect, considering that Kelly was unkind to the many women he subsequently married and to the children he sired by them.) Another husband, William Reed, created a shared marker with his wife Jeannetta Ann (died 1912, Montgomery Co.)[174] that includes a poem rhyming her dying words:

> Still Jesus is faithful to me,
> He pities the pains I now feel;
> I shall not stay out his decree,
> Farewell, my dear husband, said she;

Now from your kind bosom I leap,
With Jesus my bridegroom to be;
My flesh in the tomb then shall sleep[.]

It probably should not come as a surprise that a professional comedian died telling a joke. Minstrel Billy Rice, despite a long and successful career as a performer, died penniless in Hot Springs (1902, Garland Co.). According to his tombstone his final words were, "Well boys, I've told my last joke, now I'll go way back on the end and sit down." It took a year to raise money for Rice's marker, by which time his actual joke was long forgotten, but when he died newspapers had reported that it was, "Well boys, I am down to my last white chip, and the Almighty has coppered that," then announcing that he was going back to the end seat.

This makes sense in the context of the minstrel show—a wildly popular nineteenth-century entertainment in which white men donned blackface makeup, wigs, and costumes to do viciously cruel impersonations of African Americans. The shows began with these minstrels, many carrying instruments, filing onto the stage and sitting down, in a semicircle, to face the audience. "End men," the shows' comedians and actors, occupied the two end seats and were called forward by the master of ceremonies when it was their time to perform. When his act was finished the end man returned to his seat.

Rice's "joke" may have had to do with God turning his single white chip (the lowest value among poker chips) into a penny, and that his life—just like his act—was finished. He said his final words before lapsing into a uremic coma, surrounded by friends who had raised the money to get him to Hot Springs, a popular spa destination whose spring water had a reputation for healing. Rice's body, unburied for ten days, nearly ended up in a potters' field graveyard but, just in time, his friends found the money for a plot in Greenwood Cemetery. He was escorted there by these friends, a minister, and "four professional ladies who had known Rice in his palmy days."[175] Over a year later his marker, paid for in full by a fellow minstrel, was erected, and the cemetery's African American sexton was given five dollars to keep violets planted on the grave.[176]

For all I have to give to God
are just my thoughts of you
and though you never know or care
perhaps the angels do.

—MRS. W.G. (PERNINA ANN) CAMPBELL, 1841–1926, HOGUE CEMETERY (ASHLEY CO.)

1. Rogers City Cemetery **(Benton)**

2. Brock Cemetery, Victor
Atkins City Cemetery **(Pope)**

3. Looper Cemetery **(Scott)**

4. De Ann Cemetery, Prescott **(Nevada)**

5. Wilson Cemetery, Lewisville **(Lafayette)**

6. Flat Creek Cemetery **(Ashley)**

7. Mt. Tabor Cemetery **(Drew)**

8. The New Cemetery, Rison **(Cleveland)**

9. Oakland Cemetery, Fordyce **(Dallas)**

10. Maple Hill Cemetery, Helena **(Phillips)**

11. Lonoke City Cemetery **(Lonoke)**

12. Calvary Cemetery, Little Rock
Mount Holly Cemetery, Little Rock
Oakland & Fraternal Cemetery, Little Rock
(Pulaski)

13. Fakes Cemetery **(Woodruff)**

14. Beebe City Cemetery **(White)**

15. Jonesboro Memorial Park, Jonesboro **(Craighead)**

16. Oak Bowery **(Faulkner)**

17. Bruno Cemetery **(Marion)**

18. Arkansas River | **19.** Mississippi River

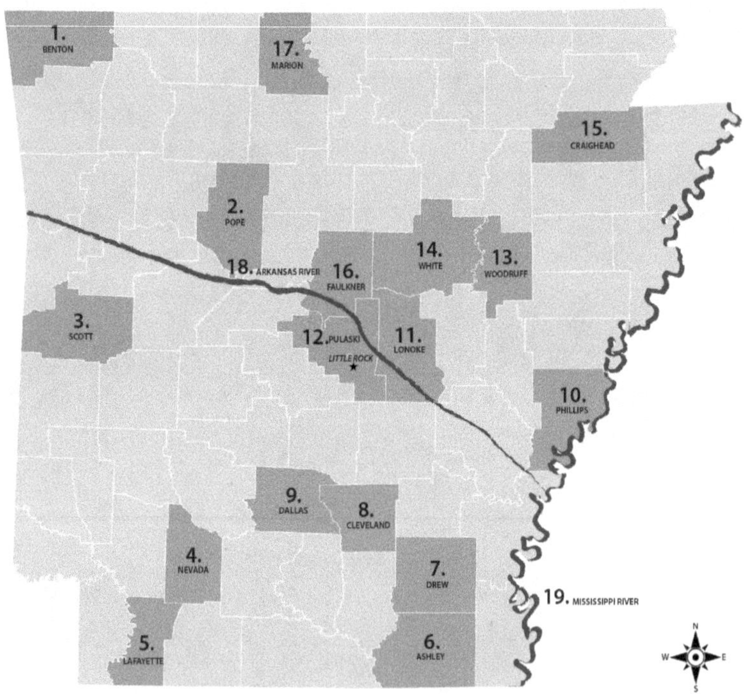

Major locations discussed in chapter 5.
Map by Red Rooster Design, Fayetteville, Arkansas.

Chapter 5

PORTRAITS AND PERSONALITIES

To the past go more dead faces
Every year;
Come no new ones in their places
Every year;
Everywhere the sad eyes meet us
In the coming dusk they greet us
Every year.

—ABEL GOOLSBY, 1857–1903, DUNCAN CEMETERY, WALDRON (SCOTT CO.)[1]

The feeling that one is being watched, in a graveyard, could come from an overactive imagination or from the belief that there are hidden security cameras, which there sometimes are. But usually someone *is* visibly watching, in the form of a marble statue, bust, or cameo whose sightless eyes, nonetheless, stare right at us. Then, too, some grave markers contain photographs on ceramic tablets showing what the deceased looked like in life—or after death. Modern markers are even starting to include selfies.

Not every stone face is a portrait, of course. In the 1800s, monument companies sold generic child- and adult-sized female statues, praying cherubs, and winged angels, all representations of the family's grief. Some are in grieving postures, others take the form of "petal-droppers" whose outstretched arms are frozen in the act of

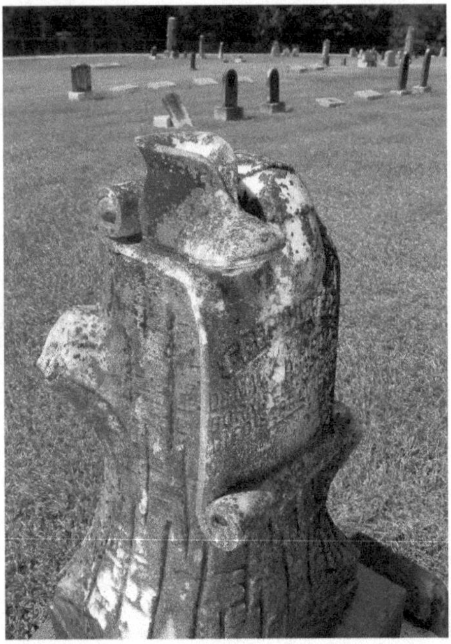

Fig 5.1. Children were sometimes memorialized with carvings of small shoes, socks, and hats. The tombstone of Eric Homer Pitts (1894–1895) shows upturned boots and scrunched-up socks. Flat Creek (Ashley Co.).

dropping blossoms of remembrance on graves, as exemplified by the statue on George Berry Washington's grave (died 1928, Woodruff Co.), described in chapter 2.

Though odd to modern sensibilities, it was once popular to commemorate the dead with stone representations of their possessions, such as the "vacant chair" that symbolizes the loved one who no longer occupies it. Oakland and Fraternal, in Little Rock, has a grave covered by a stone slab that, with covers thrown aside, represents a stylized bed,[2] Augusta Memorial Park Cemetery (Woodruff Co.) has a full-sized marble bed pillow,[3] while the graves of numerous children have been memorialized with dimensional carvings of small straw hats, buttoned boots, cast-off stockings, and, occasionally, toys.

Even more unsettling are the three-dimensional carvings of infants shown as either dead or sleeping beneath overarching scallop shells,

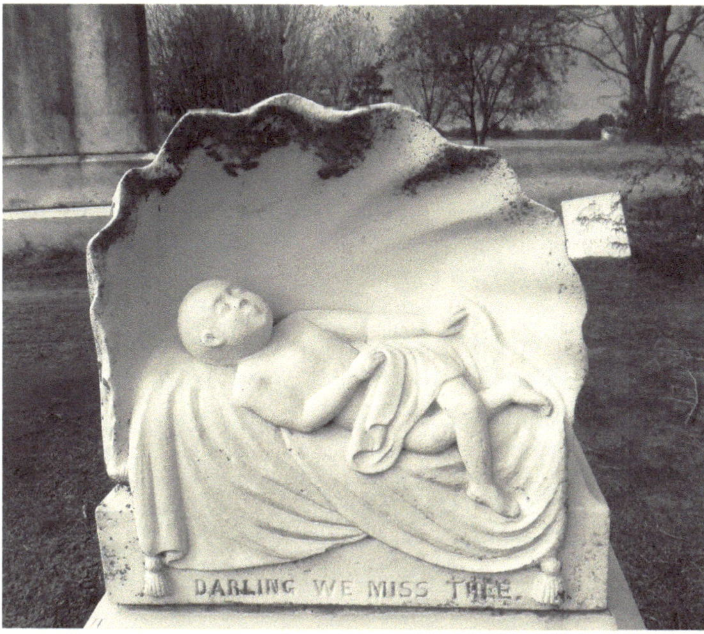

Fig 5.2. Marble children, sometimes posed inside scallop shells, were not intended as portraits. Edwina Fakes (September 23, 1890–July 23, 1891), Fakes Cemetery (Woodruff Co.).

though these are not literal likenesses of the deceased. Families seeking a stone portrait needed both money and access to a skilled carver, and such likenesses are rare, especially for children. It's more common to find them for adult males, and Little Rock's Mount Holly Cemetery houses the state's best collection, including wealthy Little Rock residents Dr. Craven Peyton (died 1872), James H. Hornibrook (died 1890), Sydney J. Johnson (died 1899), Daniel G. Fones (died 1912), and Leon Le Fevre (died 1892).

Not far from Mount Holly is the Catholic Calvary Cemetery, home to two markers containing portraits. Local monument dealer W.L. Funston received a reported $1,500 commission to create a towering column of white marble, topped with a winged angel holding both a scroll and the remnant of a trumpet.[4] "Trust in the Lord" is inscribed beneath her feet and, below that, a carved portrait of the deceased. This is Angelo Marre, framed by a wreath of laurels (representing "victory, eternity, immortality, and chastity") and oak leaves

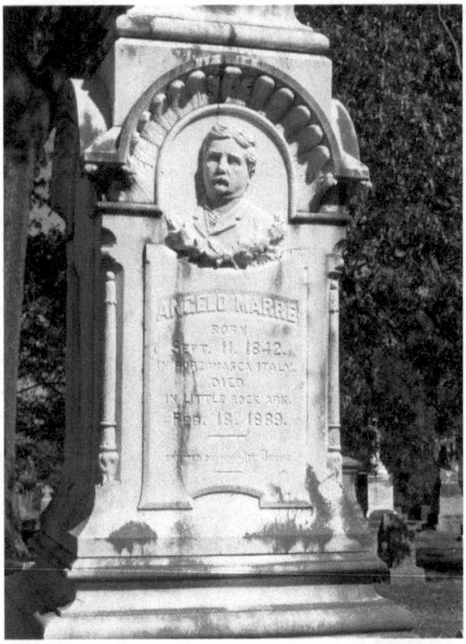

Fig 5.3. Angelo Marre (1842–1889) has his portrait on an elaborate marker, topped with an angel holding a wreath of laurels. Calvary Cemetery, Little Rock (Pulaski Co.).

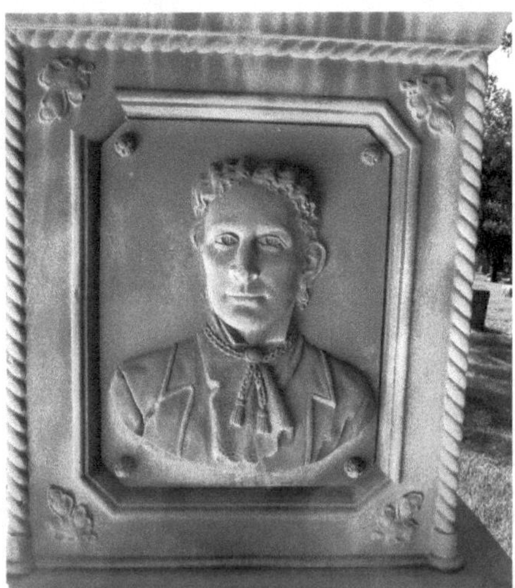

Fig 5.4. The marker for Rosa Kupferle (1842–1885) is unusual in that it includes her portrait, cast in zinc. Calvary Cemetery, Little Rock (Pulaski Co.).

(representing "strength, endurance, eternity, honor, liberty, hospitality, faith, and virtue").[5] The inscription tells us only that Marre was born in Borzonasca, Italy, in 1842, died in Little Rock in 1889, and that the monument was erected by Jennie, his wife.

What it doesn't tell us is that Marre was acquitted of killing a man in Memphis, then implicated in a counterfeiting scheme for which he spent four years in the Tennessee penitentiary. Upon coming to Little Rock, he opened a saloon, gambling hall, and billiard parlor before going into local politics. The *Arkansas Gazette* did not sugarcoat Marre's biography, publishing all of these details one day after his death and concluding that the deceased "was one of the queerest compounds in the mysterious storehouse of human nature," citing his violent temper and method of resolving "personal difficulties" using his physical strength and gladiator-like build.[6] Two weeks later another newspaper went even further, calling him "the noted whisky dealer, and one of the most prominent manipulators of dirty politics in Arkansas."[7] To be fair, both newspapers also mentioned his good qualities, one stating that he had "in large measure recovered" from his earlier reputation,[8] and another asking readers to "draw the veil of charity over his follies."[9] Marre died of blood poisoning following three operations on his foot—the initial one to amputate an infected big toe—all performed without anesthesia.[10]

Women's portraits are rare in Arkansas cemeteries, and Calvary contains a remarkably detailed example. The grave of Rosa Kupferle (died 1885) is marked with a towering zinc monument, topped with a statue of Faith. The base displays Kupferle's bas-relief portrait that depicts her wearing a patterned scarf, tasseled necklace, and pierced earrings. Though this clearly portrays a real person, women's graves are more often embellished with petal-droppers or allegorical statuary (representing Faith, Hope, or Charity) while men are memorialized with their actual likenesses. Generic representations of women extended to their epitaphs, too, such as the underwhelming, "She was—but words are wanting to say what; think what a wife should be—she was that."[11] The husband of Aurelia Smith put even less thought into eulogizing his wife when he chose to say on her tombstone, "If you would know her worth, ask her Relatives, Friends and Neighbors" which is difficult as she died in 1877 (Oaklawn, Independence Co.).

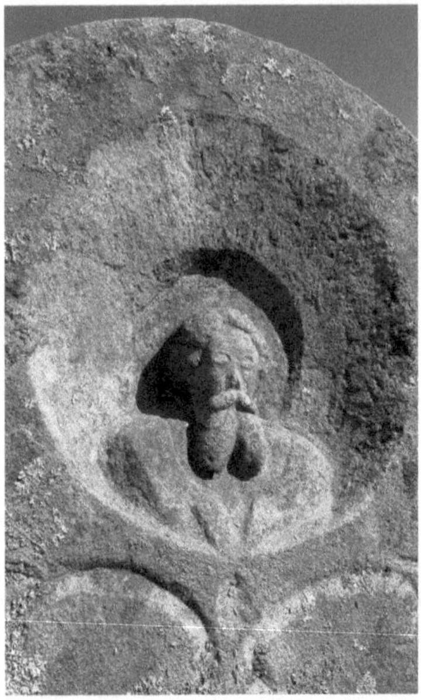

Fig 5.5. Though primitive, this portrait of Daniel Looper (died 1883?) shows his curly hair and parted beard. Looper Cemetery (Scott Co.).

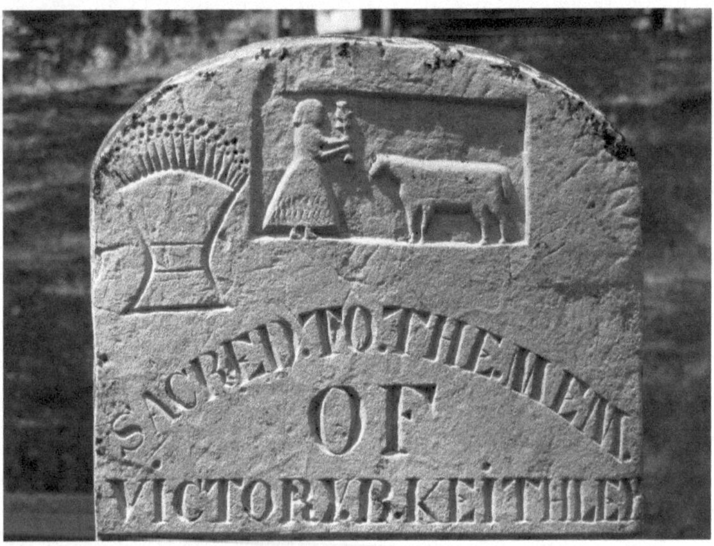

Fig 5.6. Seven-year-old Victory Keithley (died 1875) is portrayed on a headstone carved by her father. Brock Cemetery, Victor (Pope Co.).

Behold this grave it doth embrace
A virtuous wife, with Rachel's comely face,
With Martha's care, and Mary's better part.

—SARAH M. STANFORD, APRIL 4, 1852–FEBRUARY 8, 1884, GAR CREEK (FRANKLIN CO.)[12]

THE PRIMITIVE

Even carvers with rudimentary skills sometimes attempted portraiture. Scattered through various Scott County cemeteries are sandstone markers, seemingly the work of a single carver (U. Putasky or Pulasku),[13] whose rough-hewn iconography is bracketed by surprisingly delicate vine and leaf designs. His most striking creation is the small but distinctive portrait he carved in Looper Cemetery, from which we know that Joseph Daniel Looper (about 1815–1883?) wore a mustache and a full beard that was parted up the middle, his face framed by curly hair. This carver also created a thumb-sized face of an infant peering from an immense oval frame, in nearby Pleasant Grove Cemetery, for three-day-old George Pennington (died 1882).

Victory Keithley was two months away from her eighth birthday when she became sick and died during her family's relocation from Southern Missouri to Arkansas (1875, Pope Co.). She was buried in Brock cemetery, at Victor, and the family traveled on to their destination in Yell County, but her father returned later and erected a marker on his daughter's grave. In keeping with Ozark tradition he used solid blocks of stone to create a coffin-shaped grave covering and inserted a tombstone in one end, a stone he is believed to have also carved. A panel at the top of the marker depicts a sheaf of wheat (normally the symbol of a full, adult life) next to a bas-relief tableau: a girl, wearing a patterned skirt, uses both hands to extend a flower to what appears to be a sheep. With so many unusual details, including the child's short hair and little boots, it would be reasonable to assume that this is a father's portrait of his child.[14]

Another primitive carving contains a hint that it is a portrait. The obelisk on seven-year-old Annie Hooker's grave (died 1882, Benton Co.) displays a round-cheeked face with staring, pupil-less eyes. Though unsigned, the inscription matches the typography used by

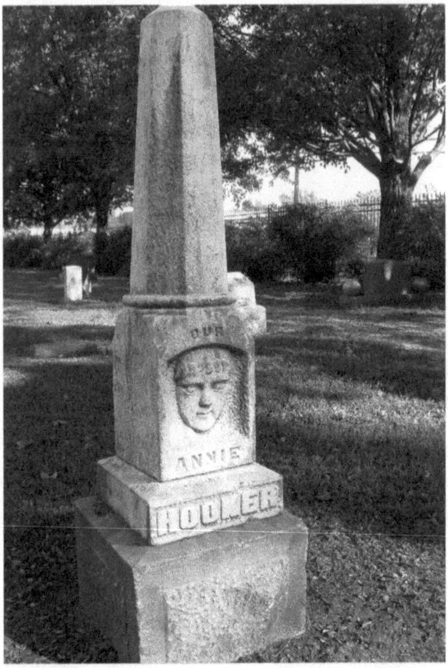

Fig 5.7. The face on Annie Hooker's marker (1875–1882) could be a portrait carved by Isom Daniel or his daughter Lucy. Rogers Cemetery (Benton Co.)

Isom and Lucy Daniel, a father and daughter who opened a monument shop in neighboring Washington County in 1883.

The Daniel family moved from Kentucky to the Arkansas Ozarks in 1871, where Isom Daniel farmed and produced tablet-style tombstones not far from the Looper and Pennington markers. The Daniels did not sign their work, but Isom Daniel was known to have worked for Lilly Bros., in Fort Smith, whose business name he apparently carved on a few markers. (The lower case "g" and "i" are, like a person's handwriting, one key to identifying a carver's work.[15]) The Daniels moved to Fort Smith (Sebastian Co.) for their children's education, then to Springdale (Washington Co.). By the time she turned twenty, in 1885, Lucy had acquired enough carving skill from her father to polish and letter tombstones and to take over the management of their monument shop.[16]

Lacking a maker's mark, or signature, it is impossible to know who made Hooker's marker, but very likely Lucy and her father collaborated on it. Lucy is known to have produced one sculptural work, a statue honoring reconciliation between the men who fought on both sides of the Civil War. The monument was unveiled at the Pea Ridge battlefield in 1899 (Benton Co.) during a reunion of veterans from both sides of the conflict. The face of this statue, a large, primitive female figure, resembles Annie's with its almond-shaped eyes and high forehead. But Annie's portrait contains one thing that Lucy's "Spirit of Liberty" statue does not: bangs across her forehead. It's a telling detail.

Thanks to the 1880 Census it's known that Anna Harris, Annie Hooker's Pennsylvania-born grandmother, lived with the Hooker family in Jacksonport (Jackson Co.),[17] and that she was a milliner, a profession ruled by fashion. In the 1870s, and well into the 1880s, bangs were a fashionable hairstyle for women but, unlike the plain fringe worn today, in this era bangs were created by curling individual bundles of hair to form a row of curls across the forehead, a time-consuming process.

Perhaps seven-year-old Annie wore her hair this stylishly, or perhaps she merely yearned to do so. Ironically, the woman who most likely carved these exacting little stone spirals had no time, personally, for this hairstyle. When profiled in a trade journal in 1895, Lucy Daniel said she was doing such good business (by then, in Exeter, Missouri) that, "I don't wear bangs, [I] have not time to fool with such things."[18] And she never did, based on photos taken throughout her long life.

THE PROFESSIONAL

Itinerant carvers moved around Arkansas after the Civil War, creating backdated tombstones for deaths that had occurred over the previous decades, when most people lacked access to professionally carved stones. Most of these carvers produced simple tablets, and unless families had photographs from which to work, it's unlikely that any carver could have captured the deceased's appearance, nor would families have wanted to pay for the extra work such an endeavor

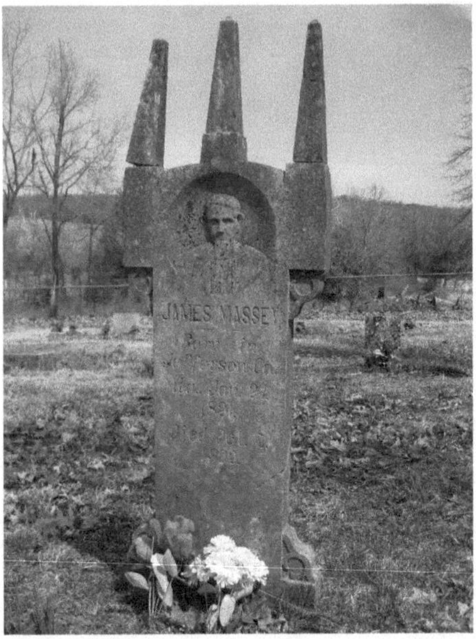

Fig 5.8. The bas-relief portrait of James Massey (1821–1902) was carved by his son-in-law DeCalb Plumlee, a professional tombstone carver. Bruno Cemetery (Marion Co.)

entailed. One professional carver, however, made unique markers for his father and father-in-law—acts of love independent of being paid.

DeCalb, or "Dee K.," Plumlee (1855–1935) was a prolific carver whose headstones can be found in Newton, Boone, and Marion Counties in the Arkansas Ozarks. His work is easily recognizable due to his precise lettering style, combined with dove, lamb, and clasping hands motifs so simply done that they seem to be, simultaneously, both folk art *and* modern art.[19]

Plumlee carved a three-dimensional bust of his father, Civil War veteran William Plumlee (died 1904, Newton Co.), set atop a conventional tablet and flanked by two small, three-dimensional obelisks. It's not known when the carving was created, but Plumlee almost certainly worked from the photo of his father[20] that shows him wearing the same jacket, vest, and collared shirt as he does in the bust, his hair side-parted and combed neatly away from his forehead.[21]

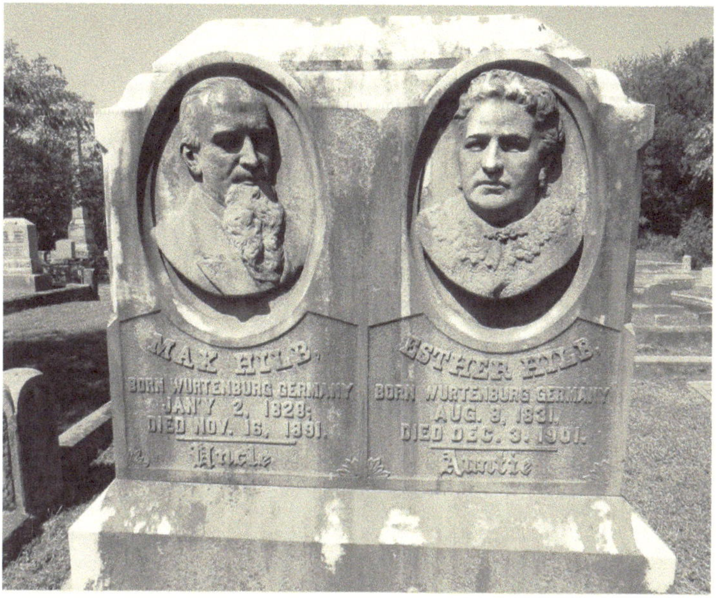

Fig 5.9. Spouses Max Hilb (1828–1891) and Esther Hilb (1831–1901) are portrayed in matching ovals in one of the Jewish cemeteries inside Oakland and Fraternal Cemetery, Little Rock (Pulaski Co.).

Plumlee also created something similar to mark the grave of his father-in-law, James Massey, in Bruno Cemetery (died 1902, Marion Co.). This portrait, a deep bas-relief carving at the top of a tablet, is flanked and crowned by three small obelisks. No photo has been found of Massey but, given the man's pendulous ears, deep-set eyes, and emphatically downturned mouth, the unflattering nature of the portrayal suggests that it was likely an accurate one.

PAIRS

One place where women are represented equally—though still found infrequently—is on grave markers they share with their husbands. German-born Max (1821–1891) and Esther (1821–1901) Hilb stare out of carved portraits on their marker, both portrayed in old age. Max, a wealthy liquor merchant, was initially buried in Mount Holly's Jewish

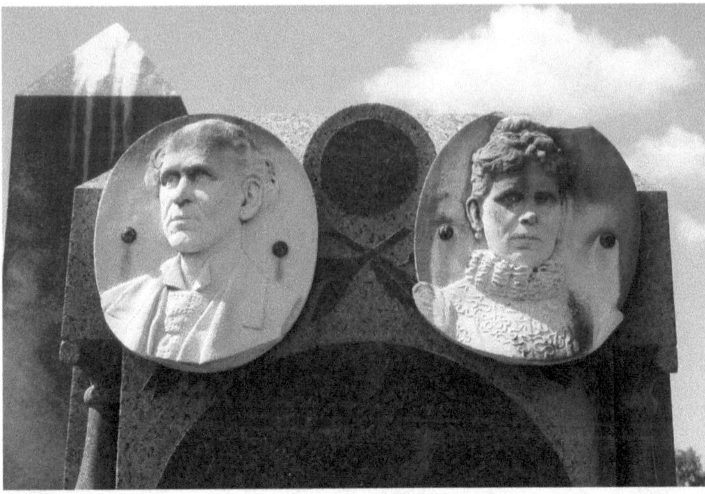

Fig 5.10. Cassius and Margaret Leigh's shared marker has attached marble portraits and a long diatribe, on the back, written by Margaret. Wilson Cemetery, Lewisville (Lafayette Co.).

section. Many of these burials were moved to Oakland and Fraternal Cemetery's Jewish section (Pulaski Co.)[22] over a forty-year period, and it is possible that Esther had Max's grave moved there, or that this was done at the time of her death. Their marker was made by Morriss Brothers, of Memphis, Tennessee.[23]

Cassius Leigh (1825–1893) and wife Margaret (1835–1916) have white marble cameos bolted to their massive granite marker in Lewisville's Wilson Cemetery (Lafayette Co.) but, unlike the companionable composition of the Hilbs' portraits, Cassius turns away from his wife, who stares impassively from her oval. Margaret outlived her husband by two decades and presumably erected this marker after the years it took her to resolve numerous lawsuits,[24] but if so, the passage of time did little to diminish her need to settle some scores, which she did on the back of the granite monument.

Cassius Leigh was a single man, a wealthy lawyer and landowner, whose household in 1870 was made up of a Black domestic servant and her children, listed as farm laborers.[25] On the 1880 Census, however, Cassius, now fifty years old and retired from the law, was a boarder in the household of the widowed Margaret McClendon and her adult son, William. Despite William's chaperonage, their living arrangement was unconventional for the times. This was a farming community, no other households took in lodgers, and Margaret was a wealthy woman—her first husband had been the son of Lafayette County's biggest slaveholder and landowner.[26]

Six years later, Margaret and Cassius married; seven years after that, he died. The back of the Leighs' marker contains this intriguing inscription:

Quietly resting

> Where—notes and accounts never go out of date—no mortgages required—no false swearing allowed—false friends—dishonest people and thy kin people can not rob thee or me of our rights.
>
> Peace to thy memory—love and honor to thy name—farewell my darling pet.
>
> Your wife.

Margaret had much to be upset about. Despite his long career as an attorney, Cassius died without having made a will to protect his reported $30,000 estate,[27] roughly $1 million in today's money. Margaret became the administrator of her husband's estate, hiring a lawyer to represent her in the lawsuits that began to roll in. She won some, lost some, but her biggest challenge came the year Cassius died, when she had to fight off his relatives who sought a share of his fortune. Ten "heirs at law" initiated a lawsuit at the county court and received permission to take their case to the Arkansas Supreme Court, though apparently it was never heard there. The following year the court heard a different, unrelated case having to do with Cassius's estate. This time Margaret lost and had to pay the plaintiff over $1,500 plus interest.[28]

Another shared grave marker also involves strained family relations. William Graham Hayes and Libbie Lucille Brownlee faced the adamant disapproval of the bride's father. Dr. John Brownlee, a physician in Burnet, Texas, may have thought that his sixteen-year-old

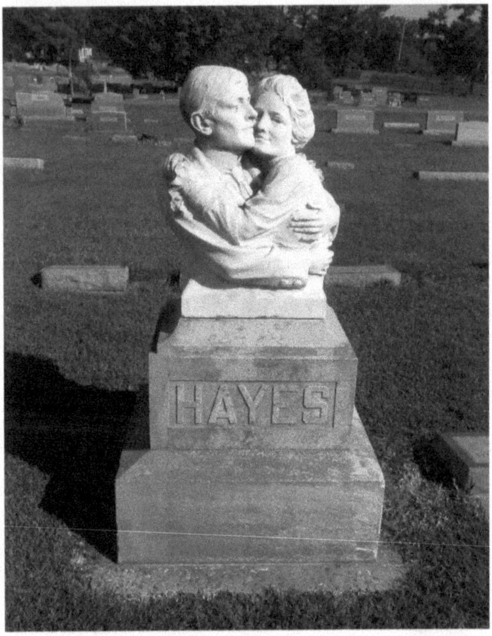

Fig 5.11. Libbie (1881–1913) and William Hayes (1879–1952) embrace in a sculpture carved in Italy from a photograph taken by William. De Ann Cemetery, Prescott (Nevada Co.).

daughter was too young for marriage, or that eighteen-year-old William Hayes, a Methodist minister's son and an aspiring photographer, wasn't worthy of her. After the couple eloped in 1898, Dr. Brownlee carried out his threat to disown his daughter, leaving her just one dollar in his will.

By the 1900 Census, William and Libbie and newborn son William were living in Morrilton (Conway Co.), where William was a photographer. It was here that he likely took the self-portrait (found on an ancestry website) in which he wears a distinctive high-collared shirt and large necktie. Then he presumably put on a jacket and had another picture taken, one that shows him wrapping Libbie in an embrace and leaning in for a kiss. She rests her hands on his shoulders, gazing out toward the viewer with a reserved smile, a public representation of a private moment.

It was such a photograph that William would send to Italy a decade or so later, to be turned into a pair of joined, life-sized sculptures to place on Libbie's grave in Prescott's De Ann Cemetery (Nevada Co.). Heart disease ran in Libbie's family—her father was found dead in bed of an apparent heart attack in 1909, and all four of Libbie's adult sons would die from coronary complications. Libbie's mother had died giving birth to her, and Libbie died eight days after the birth of her fourth son, Candler, in 1913. The cause was said to be from a heart attack. She was thirty-two.

William Hayes married two more times, and throughout his long life he worked at a variety of jobs, including running a steam laundry and selling insurance. He died in 1952 from a blood clot to the coronary artery (similar to a heart attack)[29] and is buried next to Libbie beneath the embracing marble busts he commissioned.[30]

STATUES

Atop his thirty-foot pedestal, Henry Pomeroy Coolidge has a commanding view of Helena's Maple Hill Cemetery (Phillips Co.). Depending on the direction of the light, Coolidge's face looks either solemn or peevish, but his sartorial style is unambiguous: He dressed like the wealthy merchant he was. Coolidge, born in Maine in 1812 and orphaned at a young age, worked his way up in life, marrying New Orleans native Elizabeth Jane Legier in 1832. After a few moves the couple settled, almost by accident, in 1842 in Helena, where Coolidge built a large mercantile business, the supercenter of its day. He sold everything from fabric to home furnishings, from groceries to gun powder. One surprising omission in an era when furniture dealers also laid out the dead was that he didn't sell coffins. Perhaps he had seen too much death, as the base of his statue lists the names and dates of his six children who died in infancy, with only two others surviving to adulthood. (Mayo and Newman, undertakers and furniture dealers, were located next door to the Coolidge company and carried a full line of coffins, caskets, and metallic burial cases, so perhaps Coolidge chose not to compete in this area.[31])

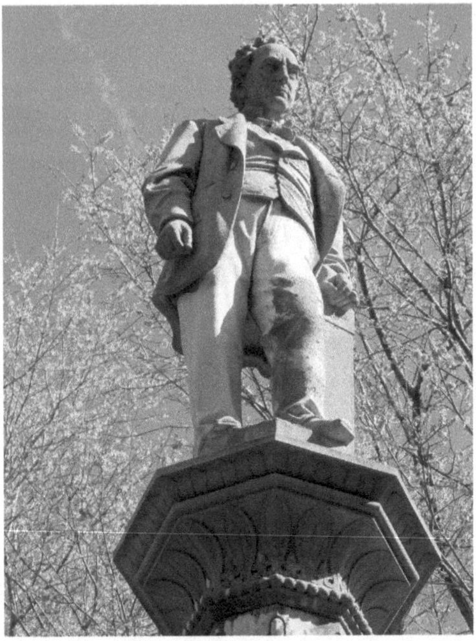

Fig 5.12. Henry Pomeroy Coolidge (1812–1872) looks down from a tall pedestal in Helena's Maple Hill Cemetery (Phillips Co.).

Upon Coolidge's death in 1872, son Charles Royal commissioned the statue of his father, carved in Italy at a reported cost of $6,000—the equivalent, today, of the equivalent, today, of $158,000.[32] This probably didn't make a dent in the family fortune, reported on the 1870 Census as $70,000 in real estate plus an $80,000 personal estate,[33] making them multimillionaires by today's standards. The statue's base is signed M. Muldoon & Co., a Memphis, Tennessee company.

This was the firm of Michael McDonald Muldoon, an Irishman, and French-born Charles Bullett. The company was founded in Louisville, Kentucky, in the mid-1850s[34] and later established branches in St. Louis, Missouri, New Orleans, Louisiana, and Memphis, Tennessee.[35] Their advertisements promoted both Italian marble and the fact that sculptor Charles Bullett worked out of Carrara, Italy.[36] It is unlikely that Bullett carved Coolidge's statue, however, as he reportedly injured his carving arm through overuse and had retired from sculpting shortly before his death in October 1873.

Still, it's tempting to think that Bullett might have had a hand in designing Coolidge's full-length likeness, complete with jeweled finger ring, square-toed boots, and a waistcoat that strains, a bit, across the man's abdomen, because the sculptor was known to have made some *very* realistic statues. The life-sized statue of Wade Hampton Bolton in Elmwood Cemetery (Memphis, Tennessee) illustrates this. Bolton, a cotton and slave trader, killed—supposedly in self-defense—by a business partner in 1869, is portrayed with one hand resting on a cane and his other hand, with fingers crossed, tucked behind his back. His vest is crookedly buttoned and one shoelace hangs untied, a sculpture so lifelike that it reportedly caused his wife to faint the first time she saw it.[37] The Muldoon firm's originality is also evidenced in the same cemetery, by their statue of Henry Montgomery (1827–1887), depicting Montgomery in mid-sentence just before he dropped dead of a heart attack.

> O God! it is a fearful thing
> To see the human soul take wing.
>
> —EDWARD PLATT, (ABOUT) 1827–FEBRUARY 23, 1850, MOUNT HOLLY CEMETERY, LITTLE ROCK (PULASKI CO.)

If there were a prize for the most arresting mortuary sculpture in Arkansas, it would go to the one standing over the grave of twenty-three-year-old Mary Watkins in Mount Holly Cemetery (died 1878, Pulaski Co.). It portrays a young woman loosely wrapped in a winding sheet, with her arms crossed over her chest in the posture of a laid-out body. Though in all other respects prepared for the tomb, the young woman's eyes are open, she is alert, and she is supported by a winged angel who directs her gaze upward toward her heavenly destination. This image, more commonly found as a bas-relief carving and always depicting a female (or an infant), is said to represent the ascending soul, not a resurrecting body, although Mary's statue certainly appears otherwise.

There is good reason to believe that this tableau, dated 1880 (two years after Mary's death) came from the Memphis firm of Anderson,

Venn & Co. Mary's father, Arkansas Supreme Court Chief Justice George C. Watkins and his brother-in-law, physician Craven Peyton, died exactly one month apart in 1872, and their elaborately detailed markers were both created by Anderson, Venn & Co.[38] (Peyton's includes his bas-relief portrait under the heading, "The Good Doctor.") These deaths orphaned Mary and widowed her maternal aunt Cara Peyton, who adopted Mary, the first of many relatives she would help. It would have been logical for Peyton to use the same carving company a mere six years later when commissioning a statue to commemorate her niece's death.

But *is* the figure that is being dragged from its grave a portrait of Mary? Similar statuary groups, found in city cemeteries in other states as well as London, England,[39] show the same configuration, but the faces of the deceased are different in each example. This may be the result of the various sculptors' own interpretations of the design or a reflection of their carving abilities. Lacking a portrait of Mary, it's hard to be certain. Artist J.W. Banks's crayon and watercolor sketch of Mary was exhibited one month after her death, but this portrait is now unaccounted for.[40] Still, the statue has a face with a sweet expression, surrounded by curly hair, and Mary's obituary praised her "rare beauty" of both mind and body.[41]

If this is a likeness of Mary, her statue is in good company because Mount Holly also contains life-sized statues of sisters Pearl (died 1886 at age six) and Martha (died in 1887 at age four and a half) Basham. Legend has it that these statues were sent back to Italy to be re-carved when the Basham parents weren't satisfied with the daughters' likenesses.[42] Another statue in Mount Holly shows a tiny, helmeted fireman perched atop a slanted roof, the nozzle of a firehose clutched in his hands. This marks the grave of Henry Brookin (1852–1891), who was en route to a call when he fell from the fire truck and was run over by it. (An inscription on the base reads: "He was killed while responding to an alarm of fire.") Though the statue shows a mustachioed man—fitting Brookin's description—it is very similar to commercially made statues that commemorate firemen, found in other parts of the country.[43]

It's impossible to give a definitive list of all statues and portraits found across Arkansas, but several should be mentioned, such as

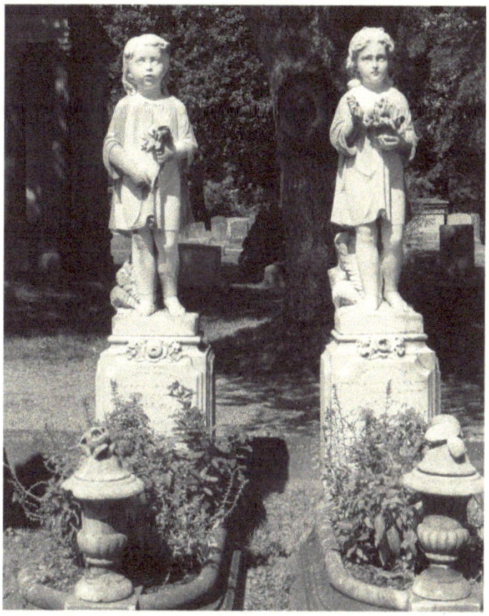

Fig 5.13. Statues of sisters Martha Basham, on left (died 1887) and Pearl Basham, on right (died 1886) were vandalized in 2016 but expertly restored. Mount Holly, Little Rock (Pulaski Co.).

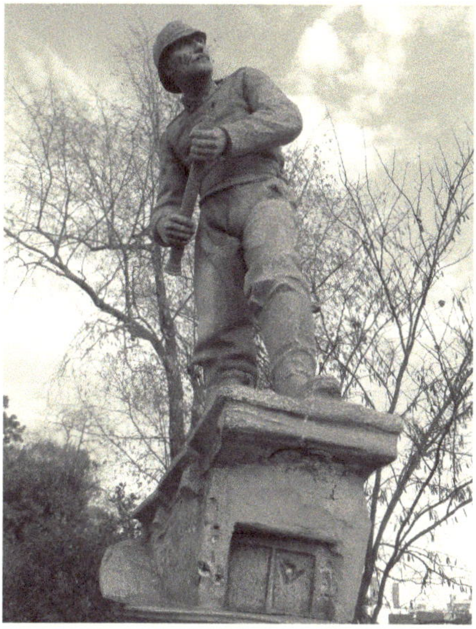

Fig 5.14. A tiny sculpture shows Henry Brookin (1852–1891) fighting fire atop a slanted roof, though he was killed en route to a fire. Mount Holly, Little Rock (Pulaski Co.).

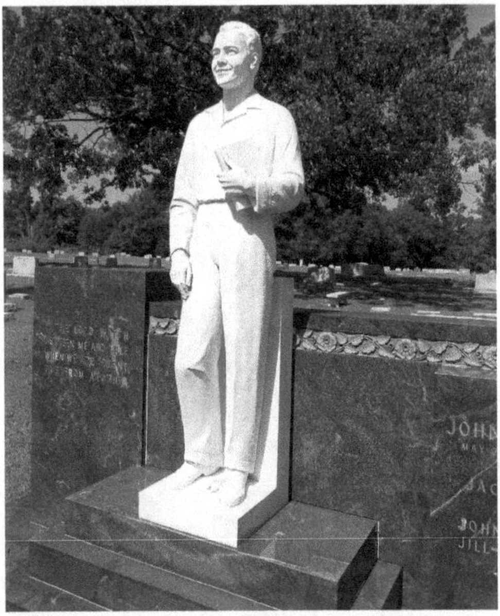

Fig 5.15. Dr. John H. Kilgore (1927–1964), who died in a car crash, is immortalized with a life-sized marble statue. Oakland Cemetery, Fordyce (Dallas Co.).

the life-sized statue of Rev. John F. Carr (1834–1906) in Pine Bluff's Bellwood Cemetery (Jefferson Co.). His adjacent headstone notes, "He went about doing good." Other examples include the life-sized marble statue of Dr. John Kilgore in Fordyce's Oakland Memorial (Dallas Co.). Dr. Kilgore was killed in 1964 in an automobile wreck minutes after his wife got out of the car "because she said her husband was driving too fast."[44]

Then there's the massive bronze female bust in Lonoke's city cemetery, memorializing James Lloyd, who was accidentally killed while on a hunting trip (1923, Lonoke Co.). Lloyd's widow, Mayme (Chapline) Black went to New York to pose for the sculptor, and the finished work was placed on her husband's grave two years after his death.[45] An especially sad example is on Maud Scarlett Duffie's grave, in Atkins's town cemetery (Pope Co.), though it may not be a portrait. A sorrowful woman gazes down at a robust and smiling infant in her arms, representing the death of both Duffie and her baby, following childbirth, in 1904.[46]

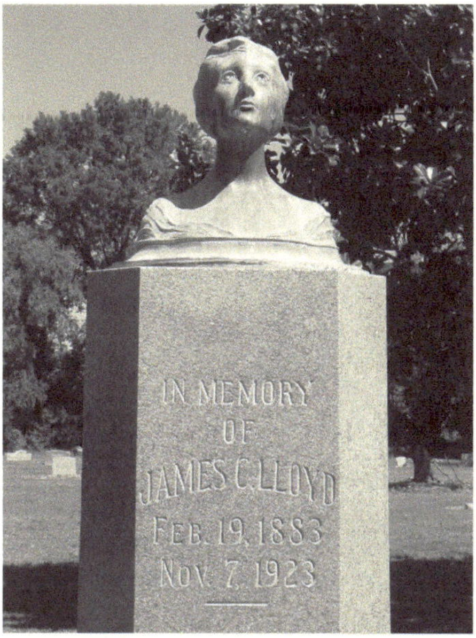

Fig 5.16. Mayme (Chapline) Black Lloyd modeled for the bronze portrait atop the grave of her husband, James Lloyd, killed in 1923. Lonoke city cemetery (Lonoke Co.).

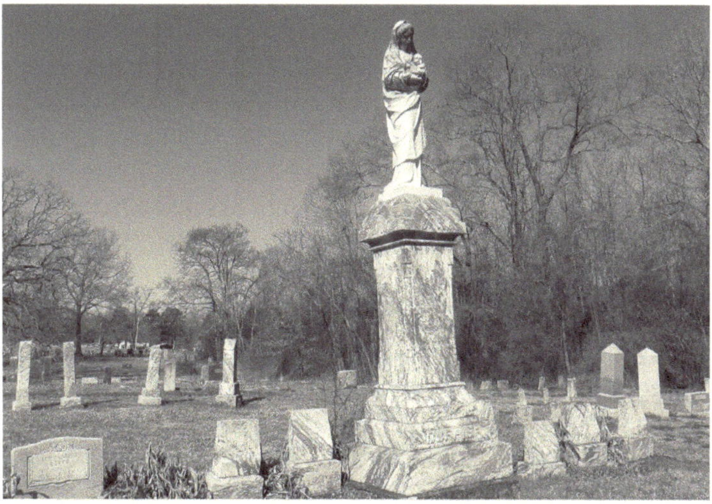

Fig 5.17. Maud Duffie and her infant died in childbirth. The two are depicted on their shared marker. Atkins city cemetery (Pope Co.).

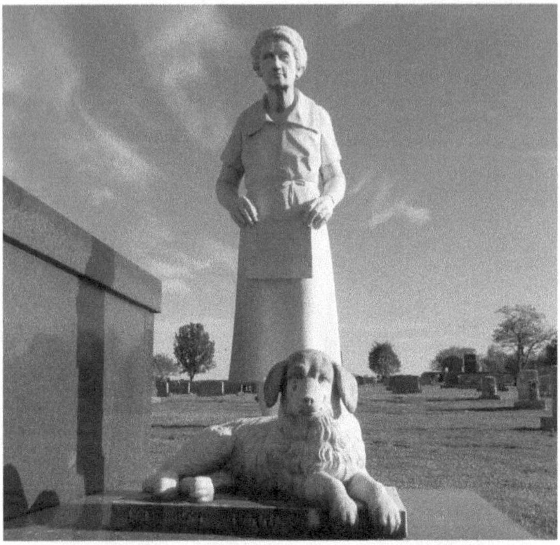

Fig 5.18. Thelma Holford (1906–1989) had statues of herself and her dog Bunny carved in Italy and chose some lively language to adorn her box crypt. Jonesboro Memorial Park Cemetery (Craighead Co.).

None of these convey the deceased's forceful personality quite like the portraiture found in Jonesboro Memorial Park Cemetery (Craighead Co.). Thelma Holford, a noted Jonesboro eccentric, had life-sized sculptures of herself and her dog Bunny positioned next to her above-ground vault. Despite an urban legend that Thelma had herself encased in plaster, the truth is that she went to the Jonesboro Monument Company and commissioned these statues. Employees took numerous measurements and photos to send to Italy. Plaster models of the statue pair were sent back to Holford for her approval, prior to doing the carving. She found no fault with her own likeness, clad in a house dress and sensible shoes, holding a small sign reading, "Don't be afraid to stand alone." However, the model of Bunny did not please her. "You've made my dog look like an elephant," she reportedly said, and the work had to be redone to her satisfaction.

These carvings provide visual proof of Holford's unusual personality, as do the inscriptions she chose to place on the ends of her vault. Below Holford's name and dates (1906–1989) is her daily prayer: "God help me keep my long nose out of other people's business and give me twenty-six hours each day to mind my own."

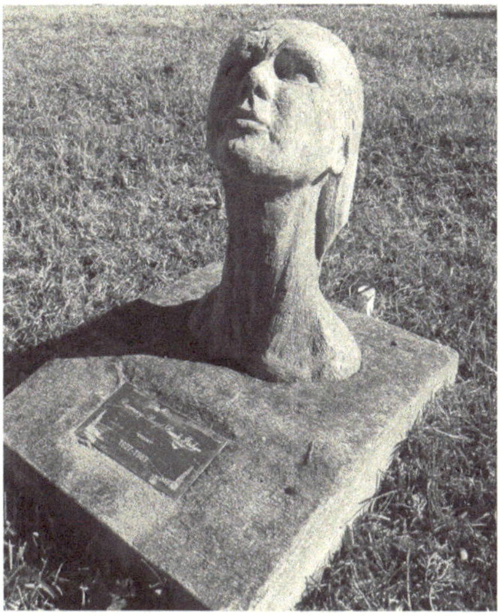

Fig 5.19. Rosemary Beryl Snook ("Snooky") Fisher was an artist and a ceramicist who may have made the bust that adorns her grave. Beebe town cemetery (White Co.).

As if that weren't enough, the opposite end of the box contains her claim to fame, followed by her personal adages: "World's first awning woman—Selling, Mfg., Installing Since—1934." "Made everything but an appetite. Mended everything but a broken heart."

It's unclear what the last sentence refers to, as Holford was divorced and, from local accounts, had a rather abrasive personality. Perhaps it's a reference to her own broken heart.

A teenaged vandal knocked down Holford's statue in 2010, breaking the marble in two places. Again, Jonesboro Monument Company stepped in, repairing the statue and returning it to its base by 2012. In addition to these sculptures, Holford left behind money to establish a pet cemetery, which was created next door to the monument company but is no longer in business. Bunny as well as Holford's many other beloved dogs were buried on her home property long before this cemetery was established.

A final example of what may be a portrait is a head, atop a long neck, that rises out of Rosemary Beryl Snook ("Snooky") Fisher's grave marker in Beebe's town cemetery (White Co.). Rosemary Snook met George Edward Fisher, her future husband, when the two attended art school in

Bournemouth, England, during World War II. George Fisher went on to become a well-known political cartoonist for the *Arkansas Gazette* who, in the same way that celebrity caricaturist Al Hirschfeld hid his daughter Nina's name in his drawings, tucked the name "Snooky" into each of his cartoons starting in 1976.[47] Rosemary died in 1983, George in 2003. The grave marker's upraised, staring face may be a piece that Rosemary, a professional artist and ceramicist, made.[48] Snooky fans on Facebook claim to recognize her likeness in the work, leading to jokes about this marker being, quite literally, a head stone.

PHOTOCERAMICS

Glance around any modern cemetery and there will almost certainly be photos on headstones, either laser engravings or actual, attached photographs specifically created for use on monuments. Through these little windows we view the dead during some of their happiest moments in life: holding up a freshly caught fish, cuddling a dog or a grandchild, sitting astride a motorcycle, slicing a wedding cake. Some of these are studio portraits; others are candid photos that give us glimpses of the deceased's possessions, such as refrigerator magnets, wind chimes, musical instruments, and sports trophies.

The complicated process of permanently transferring a photograph to a ceramic or metal disk was invented by two Frenchmen in 1854 and almost immediately touted in this country as something that would help the living with their grief when visiting the grave. The process was said to be permanent, and in many cases it was, but it's not hard to find examples of older photoceramics that are fading away. Early manufacturers sometimes touched up the photo with black ink, darkening pupils or outlining hair or a hat and, as the original photo fades from view over time, the inked-in additions remain. The disks are also prone to detaching, breaking, vandalism, and outright theft, leaving many markers with empty oval niches that were once filled with portraits.

There are very few extremely old photoceramics in Arkansas cemeteries, due either to a lack of funds to pay for the photograph or a lack of access to this technology. Photoceramics are found in greatest

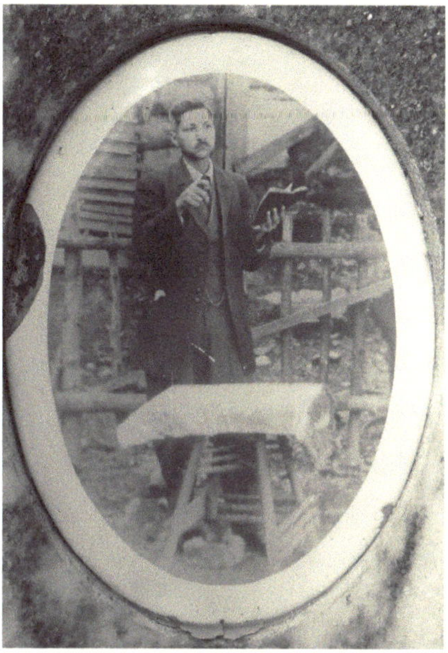

Fig 5.20. Though older photoceramics are not often found in Black cemeteries, this rare exception shows Thomas W. Rogers (1875–1918) preaching. New Cemetery (Cleveland Co.).

concentrations in Catholic and/or immigrant cemeteries; occasionally multiple examples will be found within one family's burial plot. Athens Cemetery (Howard Co.) boasts an unusually large collection: eleven intact photos, with death dates spanning 1908 to 1928. In contrast, African American cemeteries boast high numbers of modern photoceramics but almost no older ones. A rare and detailed example is found on the grave of Thomas W. Rogers (1875–1918) in the New Cemetery (Cleveland Co.), depicting him preaching outdoors, an open book in one hand.

In rare instances families chose a postmortem photo (taken after the person's death) to put on the tombstone. Of the ten earliest examples found so far in Arkansas, the oldest has a 1924 death date and the rest of the ones of children are from the 1940s through the end of the 1950s. Very likely these were the only pictures ever taken of these children, especially in the case of stillbirths, and all are posed in their caskets. This practice has been revived in recent times, and

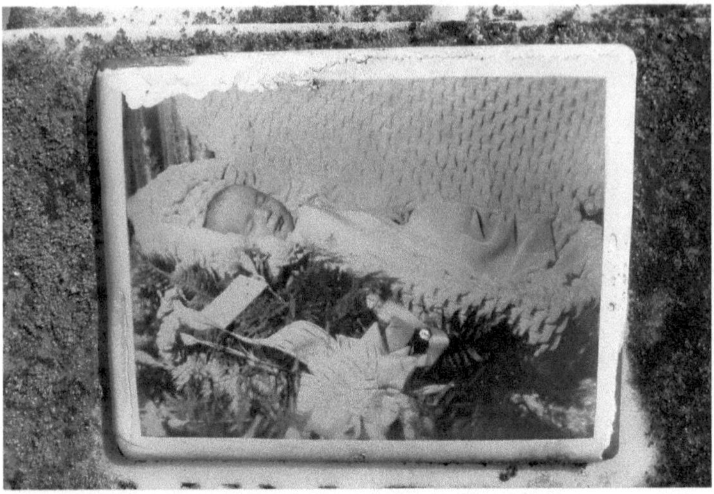

Fig 5.21. Postmortem photoceramics are scarce in Arkansas; most depict infants such as three-month-old Benjamin Franklin Butler III. Oak Bowery (Faulkner Co.).

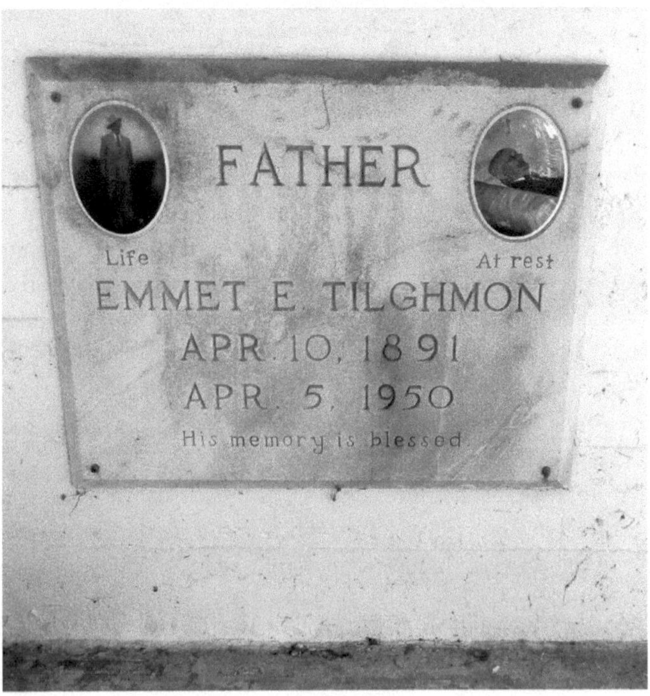

Fig 5.22. One of three members of the Tilghmon family who are pictured on the grave marker, both in life and after death. Mt. Tabor Cemetery (Drew Co.).

it isn't unusual to find modern granite markers containing photos of deceased infants, some with evidence of birth trauma.

The photos found inside the Tilghmon family's grave house in Mt. Tabor Cemetery (Drew Co.) are an exception to the generalization about infant postmortems. Inside this house, above each of the three inground burials, are marble plaques containing two photos apiece. These show the three family members in life and "at rest." Mother Ida Bell Tilghmon died January 15, 1933; daughter Kittie, age eighteen, died just three days later, from both lobar pneumonia and the flu. It's possible that their funerals were held together because both "at rest" photos were taken on a sunny day, with the women's matching caskets posed in front of the same picket fence. Father Emmet Tilghmon died in 1950 and he, too, is shown in an open casket.

Seeing an actual image of the deceased, in the graveyard, helped the living grieve their losses. That, at least, was an argument put forth by the Montgomery Ward company in its 1929 monument catalog. They offered "the portrait eternal" (photoceramics) cemented onto the headstones they sold. This, their advertising claimed, "endows the resting place of the dead with a living personality." Respectful too. "With the familiar face looking out at you, it seems as though with your visit there you have indeed paid the intended homage of respect and remembrance to one who has gone."[49]

> Go to thy heavenly rest, 'twere better thus,
> to dwell forever with the just,
> than here with us.
>
> —GRAY H. ATKINSON, 1825–1873, OAK GROVE, A.K.A. WHITE CHURCH CEMETERY (LINCOLN CO.)

1. Nichols Family Cemetery, I-40 Rest Stop **(Franklin)**

2. Petit Jean State Park, Morrilton **(Conway)**

3. Hendrix College, Conway **(Faulkner)**

***4.** Rose Hill Cemetery, Texarkana **(Bowie County, Texas)**

5. Historic Washington State Park, Washington **(Hempstead)**

6. Conway Cemetery Historic State Park, Bradley **(Lafayette)**

7. Lakeport Plantation, Lake Village **(Chicot)**

8. John Patterson historical marker, Marianna **(Lee)**

9. Unknown child's grave, Judsonia **(White)**

10. Parkin Archeological State Park, Parkin **(Cross)**

11. Blytheville Courthouse Lawn
Wilson Town Center
Herman Davis State Park, Manila
(Mississippi)

12. Crowley's Ridge State Park, Walcott **(Greene)**

13. Davidsonville Historic State Park, Pocahontas **(Randolph)**

14. Great Passion Play, Eureka Springs **(Carroll)**

15. Arkansas River | **16.** Mississippi River

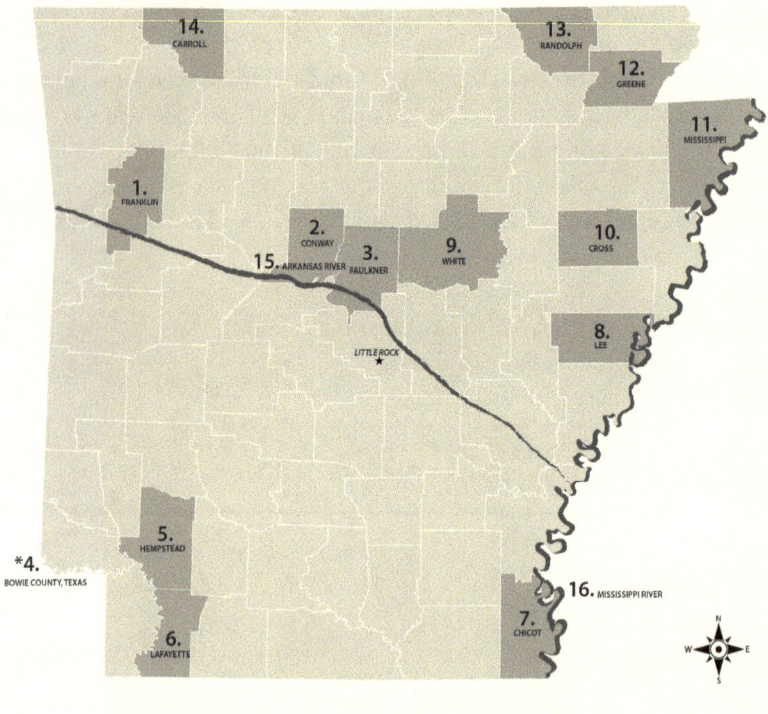

Major locations discussed in chapter 6.
Map by Red Rooster Design, Fayetteville, Arkansas.

Chapter 6

PRIVATE GRAVES IN PUBLIC PLACES

In the grave yard softly sleeping
Where the flowers gently wave
Lies the one we love so dearly
In her silent lonely grave.

Peaceful be your sleep dear Frances,
It is sweet to breathe your name
In life we loved you dearly,
In death we do the same.

—FRANCES ARLINE WHITE, 1919–1935, OAKLAWN CEMETERY, BATESVILLE (INDEPENDENCE CO.)

Not all graveyards are public ones, with names spelled out above elaborate gates. Prior to the Civil War it was customary for families to bury on their own land, whether that meant rural acreage or behind houses in town. Over time many of these individual graves were exhumed and moved into formal cemeteries being established in towns and cities, but sometimes only the headstones were relocated.

For this reason, many early burial grounds have been lost, but there are also instances where land surrounding a cemetery was later purchased and put to another use. Today, these little graveyards show up in unexpected places: at the intersection of two county roads, or behind a college stadium.[1] Other examples include Lewisville's Courthouse Cemetery, with the Steel family's graves in the lawn of the Lafayette County Courthouse,[2] or the graves of William B. Dumas, founder of the city of Dumas (Desha Co.), and his son Arthur, buried in front of what is now the entrance to Gill Gym at the city's junior high school.[3]

Andrew Marvell wrote, "The grave's a fine and private place,"[4] but what follows is a guide to some of the state's graves and graveyards that are now anything but private.

CEMETERIES IN STATE PARKS

Crowley's Ridge State Park (Greene Co.): Shiloh, also known as Pioneer Cemetery, the tiny burial ground of the Benjamin Crowley family, is now completely surrounded by the park's amenities. If it ever had legible tombstones, none remain, though a plain block is inscribed, "Resting place of settlers of Crowley's Ridge." The eponymous first settler is memorialized by a flat-topped tower of native stone, in which is embedded a plaque reading, "Benjamin Crowley, 1758–1842 / The man for whom Crowley's Ridge is named."

The park, constructed in the 1930s by the Civilian Conservation Corps, is located twelve miles west of Paragould, on the site of the Crowley family's original homestead. However, a visitor would be hard-pressed to learn the significance of this family from onsite signage and park literature.

Davidsonville Historic State Park (Randolph Co.): A park visitor expecting to see one of the state's earliest communities would be forgiven for being confused. Davidsonville's origins may date back to an 1804 French settlement, with the town platted around 1815, part of the Missouri Territory. It once boasted of having the state's first post office and brick courthouse, among other achievements, but today little is known about this planned community, which died out in the 1830s after commerce shifted to larger towns.[5] (A dramatic, though largely discounted, version is that passengers from a New Orleans steamboat infected the residents with cholera or yellow fever, decimating the population. Survivors fled, and "nearby farmers" burned the town to remove any remaining contagion.[6]) The park has constructed steel beam "ghost structures" (their term) to show the outlines of two key buildings that once stood there.

Two cemeteries exist within the park. Philips-Reeves, just off what was once the town square, has scattered tombstones for the Cox, Scott, and Moore families with death dates starting in the late 1890s. Scott Cemetery, the older of the two burial grounds, is reached by hiking the Scott Cemetery Trail. In addition to a few markers, it supposedly has unmarked graves dating back to the founding of Davidsonville.

Parkin Archaeological State Park (Cross Co.): This park's stated purpose is to "preserve, collect, research, and interpret the site and its associated American Indian culture," with emphasis on AD 1200–1600.[7] However, because the Northern Ohio Cooperage and Lumber Company operated a sawmill on the site from the early 1900s until 1946, there is a workers' cemetery at one end of the modern walking path that skirts the Parkin mound.

Signage at the site notes that members of the Sawdust Hill community used this land for burials from 1909 to 1927, with many stones now missing; some graves were moved when a cemetery was established nearby. Tombstones are widely scattered and several bear the emblems of fraternal lodges that provided headstones for their members: Woodmen of the World (for men) and the Woodmen Circle (which insured women), both of which were whites-only, and the Supreme Royal Circle of Friends, an African American lodge.

Petit Jean State Park (Conway Co.): The park is named for a fictitious French heroine who, legend has it, followed her aristocratic lover to this country in the late 1700s during the French exploration of the New World. A single grave on a natural bench of land below the park's observation deck supposedly holds the remains of this woman, Adrienne Dumont, who disguised herself as a boy (called "Petit Jean" or Little John) in order to accompany—yet somehow remain undetected by—Cheves, her fiancé, on his voyage to America.[8]

Here is Frank W. Allsopp's version of the tale, from his collection of "romantic" Arkansas folklore. He writes that the couple sailed up

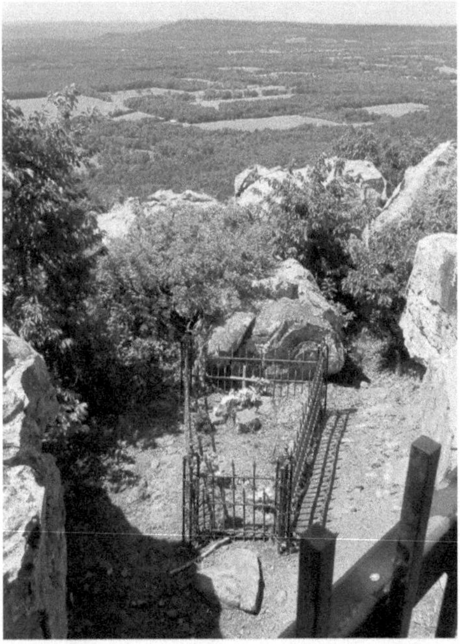

Fig 6.1. The grave of the romantic, but improbable, heroine Petit Jean, situated on a bench of land at Petit Jean State Park (Conway Co.).

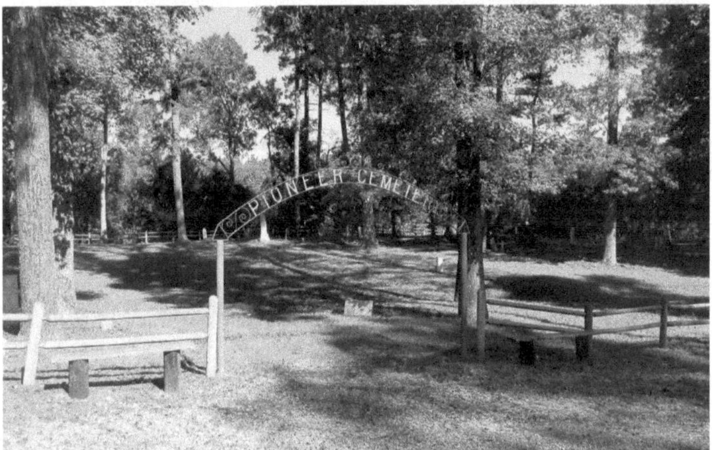

Fig 6.2. The entrance to Pioneer Cemetery, inside Historic Washington State Park (Hempstead Co.), which has both white and Black sections.

the Mississippi River to the Arkansas River, where "they found the Indians friendly, the country beautiful, and the climate delightful," and they decided to settle down. "The Indians adored Petit Jean, and regarded her as a being from another world. They brought her offerings of fruit and flowers, and strove in every way to express their love." However, when Cheves decided to return to France to get his fiancée, Petit Jean became ill and, on her deathbed, revealed her secret identity to her unobservant lover. She died in his arms after telling him to bury her on the mountain, which he did.[9]

None of this actually happened, of course, but there *was* a "Little John" who, even Allsopp admits, was likely a short-statured Frenchman. This man, or possibly a different Petit Jean, far from being beloved by the Indians was, in fact, killed by them.[10] According to historian Morris S. Arnold, in 1733, eleven French hunters went missing and were presumed to have been killed by the Osage. But "it turned out that the Osages had killed only two persons, a slave and a Frenchman named Petit Jean," whom they had mistaken for an Indian, someone also identified as a tramp. (Arnold notes that Petit Jean "was a common nickname in eighteenth-century Louisiana."[11])

Though it's impossible to say who is buried in this grave, legend has it that it's Dumont's, now protected by a trapezoidal iron fence that serves to contain the coins tossed down by visitors. Numerous early versions of this tale exist,[12] as does a legend from the 1920s that says a ghostly voice can be heard calling, "Poor Petit Jean!" near the grave.[13]

Historic Washington State Park (Hempstead Co.): It is thought that Pioneer Cemetery, whose earliest recorded burial was in 1825, was established at the time the county seat was created at Washington, part of a congressional land grant. The grounds' front half holds European American burials (many more are believed to be outside the modern fence), and the rear portion is an African American cemetery.[14]

Just outside the park is the Washington Presbyterian Cemetery, founded in the late 1850s, and lovers of ornate carvings, funerary symbolism, and flowery epitaphs are advised to visit both graveyards. Pioneer Cemetery contains numerous delicately detailed markers, one signed by Crane & Co. of Patterson, New Jersey, and the grave's occupant is thought to have been from New Jersey.[15] W. Hecox and Co.

of Shreveport, Louisiana, and T. Maydwell of Memphis also signed stones in this cemetery. Another interesting tablet is that of Ephraim Mirick, who died in 1874. At the top of his marker is a raised carving of perfectly balanced scales, which, although sometimes used to represent the legal profession, here refer to Mirick's role as a merchant, who, with another man, established the first store in town. His epitaph: "An honest man."[16]

The African American section contains far fewer carved stones, most of these with death dates after 1900, several of which were provided by Black fraternal lodges. Two of the earliest marked graves are those of "Aunt" Lotty Block (presumed to have been enslaved by the Abraham or David Block family), which lacks dates, and Lucrettia Booker (died 1866), who may have been the daughter of an emancipated African American family, "so it is possible that the right side of Pioneer Cemetery, or some other portion, was used from the very beginning to bury Washington's African-American residents."[17]

CEMETERIES THAT *ARE* STATE PARKS

Conway Cemetery Historic State Park, Bradley (Lafayette Co.): James Sevier Conway, Arkansas's first governor, chose a site south of his cotton plantation for a family burial ground. Wealth was no safeguard against death, and the Conways lost five of their ten children at young ages. The first burials here were Mary Elizabeth, age twelve, and James Sevier, age seven, who died two weeks apart in 1845. Three-year-old daughter Sarah Juliette died the next year, and Governor James Sevier Conway, whose urn-topped column is the cemetery's most impressive marker, died in 1855, followed by a four-year-old son just seven months later. There is also a headstone for an unnamed infant.

The eleven-acre park, half an acre of which is occupied by the cemetery, was placed in the Arkansas State Park System in 1984. The name "park" is a bit of a misnomer as there are no facilities other than for some signage, and visitors will likely have the place to themselves. It is an isolated and lovely piece of land. A short distance away, two Herdon family graves are located inside a chain enclosure.

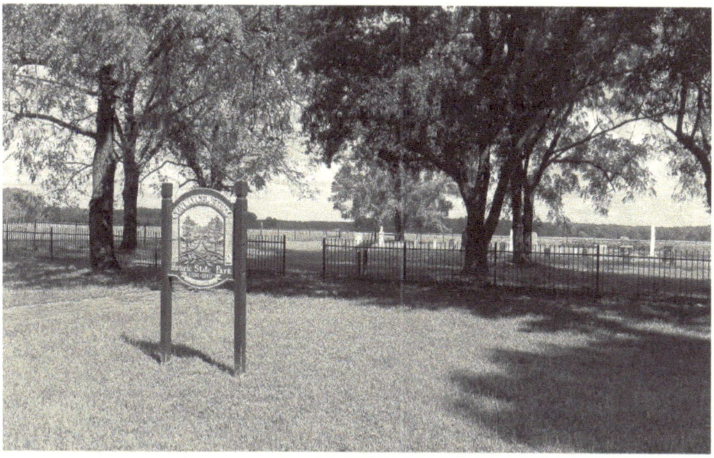

Fig 6.3. The family cemetery of James Sevier Conway (1796–1855), the first governor of Arkansas, is now Conway Cemetery Historic State Park, at Bradley (Lafayette Co.).

Herman Davis State Park, Manila (Mississippi Co.): Herman Davis was not an obvious candidate for the army the first time he faced a World War I draft board.[18] He was described as shy, short, and prematurely gray. He also was married, a father, and had only a fourth-grade education. Despite the army's initial rejection, he was inducted in 1918, at age thirty, and trained as a scout. The survival skills he had acquired through daily necessity over his lifetime—most notably proficiency with a gun—served him in good stead. By the time he was honorably discharged, a year later, he had been awarded the Distinguished Service Cross, while France gave him three military medals: the Croix de Guerre with Palm, the Croix de Guerre with Gilt Star, and the French Medaille Militaire, all of which he stored in a tackle box and none of which he willingly talked about.

Davis risked his life in France on numerous occasions to take out enemy machine guns, including killing fifteen occupants of a machine gun nest and, on a separate occasion, eleven fleeing soldiers. While on patrol he was exposed to poison gas multiple times. He died in a Memphis military hospital, on January 5, 1923, of chronic pulmonary tuberculosis, which the medical officer in charge deemed to have originated "Probably in Military Service."[19]

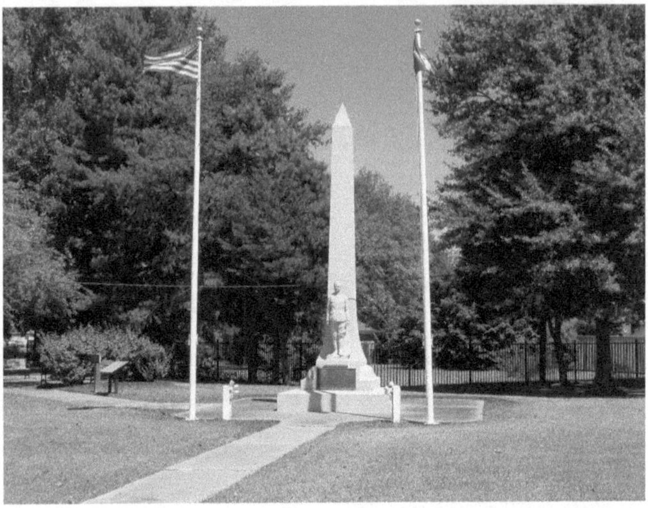

Fig 6.4. Herman Davis (1888–1923), an army scout and sharpshooter decorated for World War I heroism, is buried in Arkansas's smallest state park, founded in his honor. Herman Davis State Park, Manila (Mississippi Co.).

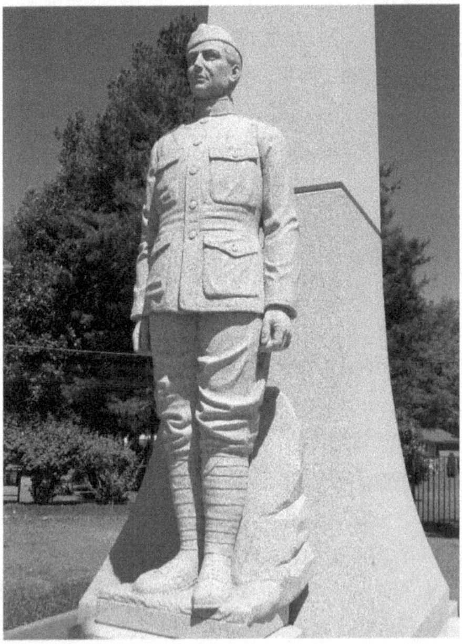

Fig 6.5. Close-up of the granite statue of Herman Davis, created after the first one was decapitated by a vandal. Herman Davis State Park, Manila (Mississippi Co.).

Almost immediately, plans were made to honor the man proclaimed as the state's most distinguished "son in action" during the war. Schoolchildren were asked to send pennies to pay for a monument, and by November 1924 a massive granite obelisk had been shipped from Barre, Vermont, to what would become the Herman Davis Memorial at Manila. A separate statue of Davis, carved from marble in Carrara, Italy, and said to have cost $5,000, was not delivered for another year, at which time Davis was exhumed from a church cemetery and reburied below the towering obelisk.[20]

The site was designated a state park in 1953, which, at less than one acre, makes it the smallest state park in Arkansas. In 1967, the life-sized statue of Davis was vandalized and the head stolen, possibly due to a rumor that it contained diamonds. (The head, but apparently not the culprit, was eventually found.) Once again money was raised through donations, and a new statue, this one made from granite and costing around $3,000, was put in place of the original marble one.[21] This statue came from Barre, Vermont, to match the granite obelisk behind it.

Anyone interested in Davis's memorial should also visit the grave of **Otis Henry (Rose Hill Cemetery, Texarkana, Bowie County, Texas).** This highly unusual burial plot is not, technically, in Arkansas, but it is less than a mile from the Arkansas-Texas state line that divides the city into Miller County, Arkansas, and Bowie County, Texas. As in Davis's case, the grave contains a life-sized statue of a soldier in uniform but, unlike Davis, this is not a portrait. Rather, it has elements of the famous Viquesney statues, known as "The Spirit of the American Doughboy."[22]

Otis Henry's fate is inscribed in abbreviated fashion on the front of the statue's base, then in full on the reverse side of the marker: He was a corporal in the 359th Infantry, 90th Division, Co. H., and gassed one kilometer southeast of the village of Vincey, France, dying October 6, 1918.[23] Below the soldier's pedestal stands a life-sized statue of Henry wearing a suit and bow tie. He is flanked by an angel holding a wreath and upended torch, and a mourning figure holding a spray of lilies. The second figure has been vandalized, so it is unknown what else she once held, but carved below her feet are the words, "Remember, Remember."

This statuary group was commissioned by Susan Tate Wilder to mark the grave of her only child.[24] In 1917, Otis Henry was twenty-two

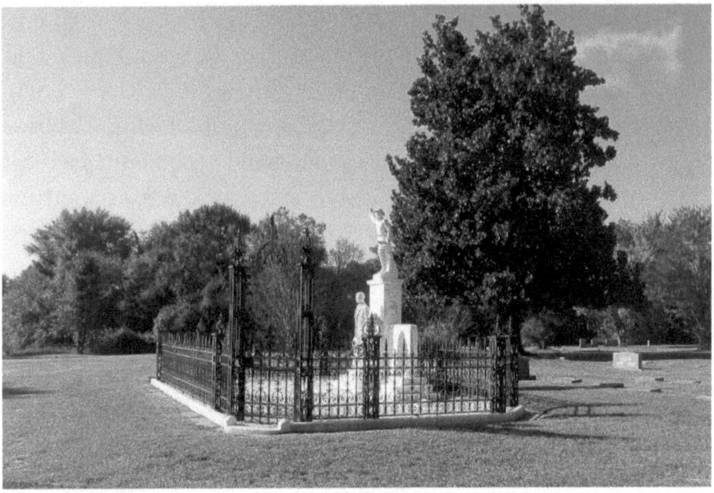

Fig 6.6. Otis Henry (1843–1918) died from exposure to gas in World War I, and his elaborate gravesite, with statuary grouping, was commissioned by his mother. Rose Hill Cemetery, the Texas side of Texarkana (Bowie County, Texas).

and working in a soda fountain in Louisiana when he registered for the draft. Local lore says he was planning to be a schoolteacher, which could explain why he was sculpted wearing a suit and tie. Wilder, who died in 1941, is identified as "His mother" on the marble slab marker she shares with Otis, the entire mortuary assemblage surrounded by an ornate iron fence that has an electric light fixture above its entrance.

SINGLES, DOUBLES, AND FAMILIES

Capt. W.W. Martin, Hendrix College (Faulkner Co.): William Wyle Martin, a former captain in the Confederate army, though not yet extremely wealthy pledged $10,000 of his own money to help Hendrix College realize its goal of relocating from Altus to Conway. This inspired his wealthier friends to make their own generous donations, enabling the college's move in 1890. Ultimately Martin's financial contributions to Hendrix totaled around $75,000, which included personally paying teachers' salaries during a period when this was needed to keep the school afloat financially.[25]

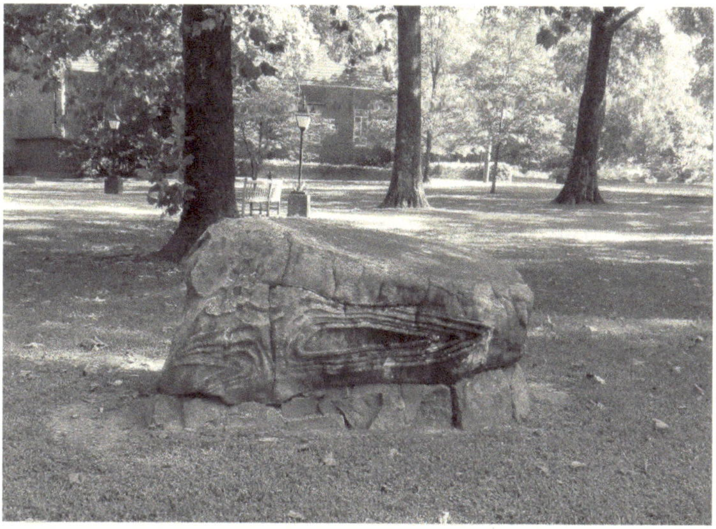

Fig 6.7. Capt. W.W. Martin, an early financial supporter, was reburied on the Hendrix College campus beneath a five-ton boulder. Conway (Faulkner Co.).

Perhaps in light of his philanthropy and the many public offices he had held, in 1911, Martin was one of a select number chosen to take part in "Arkansas on Wheels," a public relations trip, by train, to promote Arkansas in northern and eastern states. The group visited the grave of former president William McKinley in Canton, Ohio, where Martin placed a wreath on the grave. He acknowledged the irony of the gesture given that, during the Civil War, "once my company clashed bayonets with his [McKinley's] men" but added, "I now revere his memory." The weather was inclement, and Martin caught a cold that developed into pneumonia, leading to his death on December 10, 1911, shortly after he returned to Arkansas.[26]

Martin had set aside a burial plot in Martinville—a town renamed in his honor in 1887[27]—and was interred there in accordance with his wishes.[28] Eight years later Hendrix College had Martin's body exhumed and brought to Conway, reburying him in the southwest corner of the campus and naming a new dormitory in his honor at the same time.[29] Perhaps they also moved his tombstone, but it is gone now, as in 1937 his grave was marked with a five-ton boulder having deep, concentric ring formations (known as Liesegang banding) on its sides.[30] An attached bronze plaque details his many roles, including citizen, philanthropist, churchman, pioneer, and leader of men.

Lakeport Plantation, Lake Village (Chicot Co.): Lycurgus and Lydia Johnson's 1859 plantation, and Arkansas's only surviving antebellum mansion beside the Mississippi River, is now owned and operated by Arkansas State University and open to the public. Behind the plantation home is a small fenced cemetery containing a brick crypt and evidence that as many as five Johnson children and grandchildren are buried there, though only some of their marble tombstones have been found. Somewhat oddly, the unmarked fifth occupant is grandchild John Peak Johnson, who died at thirteen months old in Iowa in 1888 and whose body was sent to Lakeport Plantation for burial.[31] (The round-topped brick vault, in which son Cable Johnson was buried, is discussed in chapter 3.)

The plantation's large corn and cotton crops were possible due to the forced labor of 155 enslaved people.[32] Old Lakeport Cemetery, their burying ground, is located in the middle of a field and is not easy to find, but directions may be obtained at the plantation's visitor center.

Edgar Harold Lloyd, Blytheville Courthouse Lawn (Mississippi Co.): A large monument containing a deep bas-relief portrait marks the grave of World War II hero Edgar Harold Lloyd in front of the courthouse in Blytheville (one of two county seats of Mississippi County). Lloyd, a first lieutenant with the US Army infantry, was posthumously awarded the Medal of Honor for wartime valor near Pompey, France, on September 14, 1944. The citation for the Medal of Honor says he "leaped to his feet and led his men on a run into the raking fire, shouting encouragement to them. He jumped into the first enemy machine-gun position, knocked out the gunner with his fist, dropped a grenade, and jumped out before it exploded." He destroyed five machine gun nests in this way and thus "inspired his men to overrun the enemy positions and accomplish the objective in the face of seemingly insurmountable odds."[33]

Two months later, Lloyd was killed in action near Limey, France, on November 16, 1944, at age twenty-two. In 1948, his body was brought back from France and interred beside the courthouse, his

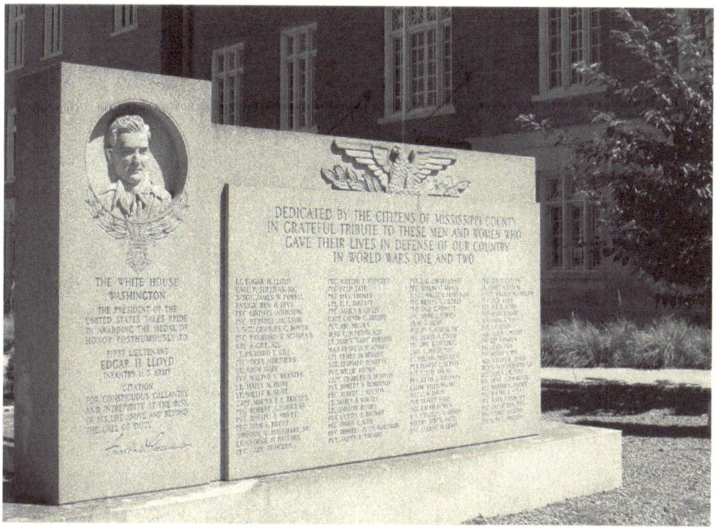

Fig 6.8. World War II hero Edgar Harold Lloyd (1922–1944) is buried in front of the Blytheville courthouse (Mississippi Co.).

grave covered by a ledger situated behind the granite marker that bears his portrait and the names of the other Mississippi County men killed in this war.[34]

Gerald L.K. and Elna Smith, Eureka Springs (Carroll Co.): Visitors to the Great Passion Play might be surprised to see an above-ground burial vault next to the path that encircles the immense statue known as Christ of the Ozarks. The red granite box holds the bodies of the attraction's founder and his wife, who died in 1976 and 1981, respectively. Founded in 1964 by Gerald Lyman Kenneth Smith, an evangelical minister, the grounds of the Passion Play also contain a Bible museum, a recreation of the Holy Land, and an outdoor theater, where live reenactments of the life and death of Jesus are presented each summer.

Though the Smiths' tomb is situated beneath the statue's outstretched left hand, it may be observed that the sorrowful, six-story-high Jesus turns his back on the grave of a man famous for his hatred of Jews, African Americans, and other minorities. Smith proudly spewed his venom in well-publicized books, speeches, and a self-published magazine.[35] An added irony is that the Christ statue, completed

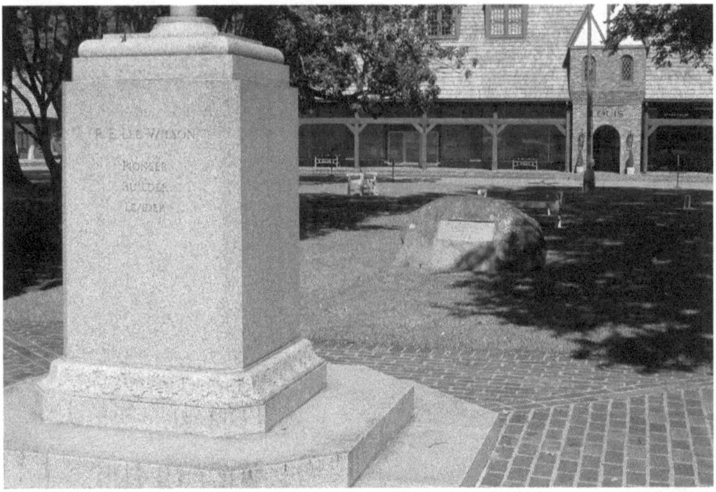

Fig 6.9. Robert E. Lee (R.E.L.) Wilson and wife Elizabeth Wilson, founders of the town of Wilson, are buried beneath a boulder in the town center (Mississippi Co.).

in 1966, was sculpted by Emmet Sullivan, who claimed to have worked on Mount Rushmore. Sullivan's true calling, however, was sculpting immense dinosaur statues for various tourist attractions in South Dakota and one in Beaver, Arkansas.

Robert Edward Lee (R.E.L.) and Elizabeth Wilson, founders of Wilson (Mississippi Co.): It's no accident that the town center in Wilson, named for its founder, resembles a quaint English village. Wilson's son and his wife were inspired by the Tudor architecture they saw on their honeymoon in England and built their Arkansas home in this style in the 1920s. The town, created to match, was designed in a style incorporating red brick, carved stone, copper detailing, and windows with leaded panes.[36]

Town founder and family patriarch Robert Edward Lee Wilson started life orphaned and in poverty but overcame these obstacles to build up an empire, from a logging and sawmill industry to a farming operation, and, in the process, created a complete company town. He died on September 27, 1933, at age sixty-eight, the result of amoebic dysentery contracted while visiting the 1933–1934 Chicago World's Fair. Though his obituary states that he was buried in the nearby town of Bassett,[37] today he and wife Elizabeth, who died in 1943, are buried beneath a shared boulder in the center of the village green.[38]

GRAVES BY THE SIDE OF THE ROAD

John Patterson historical marker (Lee Co.): Although his assertion cannot be proven, Patterson (born sometime between 1790 and 1800) claimed to be the first white child born in Arkansas. His favorite riddle is detailed on a historical marker beside Highway 44, east of Marianna, along with its answers:

> I was born in a kingdom—Spain
> Reared in an empire—France
> Attained manhood in a territory.
> Am now a citizen of a state
> And have never been 100 miles
> From where I was born.

This plaque is the nearest thing Patterson has to a tombstone. He died in 1886 and was buried in an unmarked grave somewhere in the vicinity of the marker.[39]

Nichols Family Cemetery (Franklin Co.): Pull into the rest stop beside I-40, westbound between Mulberry and Ozark, and a small burial plot can be seen inside a chain-link fence. There, stone curbing delineates the graves of three siblings, the children of William and Catharine Nichols: sisters Carrie, age nineteen, and Ollie, twenty-four, and their brother Robert, twenty-five. All three stones give their death date as 1899. According to information at the rest stop kiosk, the three died of typhoid fever near what was then the Nicholses' home place. The state later acquired the land.

Unknown child's grave between mile markers 50 and 51, US 67 N/167 (White Co.): Wedged between the highway and the on-ramp coming from Judsonia is a single grave inside a chain-link fence. A modern bronze marker states: "The unknown baby girl. In death she belongs to all of us." Visitors poke artificial flowers and stuffed animals in the fence, tipped off to its location by tourism sites that play up the pathos of the memorial.

Who was this unnamed child? Online sources call this the Cousins Cemetery, and in 1986 the county's historical society wrote that a local woman had attended the baby's funeral (at an unknown date).[40]

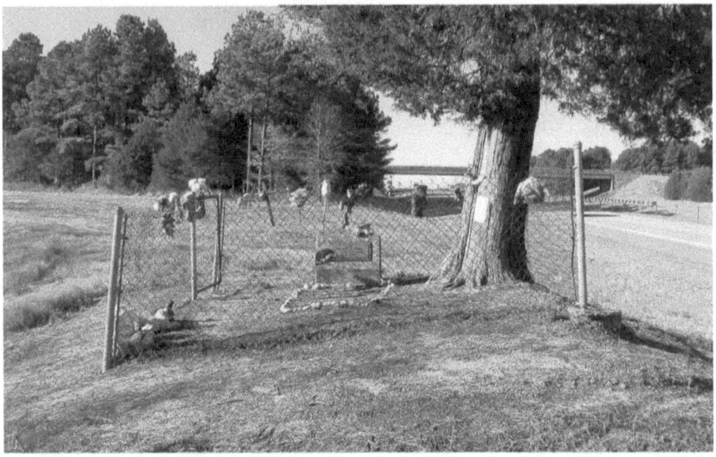

Fig 6.10. Visitors leave stuffed animals and other toys on the grave of this unknown child, buried beside US 67 N/167 (White Co.).

Supposedly the child died when her high chair toppled over and she was mortally cut on a large knife or, in a different version, by a fork.[41] Nothing is known about the child, but it practically goes without saying that urban legends and paranormal sites assert that the grave is haunted and that the child was a revered Indian princess. Further embellishment of this legend states that she died despite her tribe's efforts to carry her to a white doctor in a fruitless attempt to save her.[42]

OTHER EXAMPLES

There are many graves in public places, for example, the resting place of William Lewis Lovely (1750–1817), who became an Indian agent for the Western Cherokees in 1813. Though the actual location of his and wife Persis's graves is unknown, a state historical marker and a boulder with an attached metal military marker give the appearance of a graveyard, found at the center of an RV campsite inside Lake Dardanelle State Park (Pope Co.).

The Ingram family's unmarked graves are also encircled by paved roads (near Lowell, Benton Co.).[43] According to a modern plaque, the site is believed to hold at least nine burials, including "Unknown man of Quantrill" and "Negro slave (circa 1869—murdered)." But by far the most arresting occupant is Rev. James M. Ingram (about 1826–September 4, 1870), a captain in the Confederate cavalry. The plaque tells his story: "Years after the war ended, as a self-taught minister he went to preach at a church and was murdered—shot in the back by 19 year old John M. Stone. During the Civil War, John Dudley Stone (John M.'s father) was a Union soldier killed by Ingram in retaliation for Stone having killed some Confederate soldiers in a cave along White River. Young John M. witnessed his father's wartime killing and vowed revenge someday against Ingram."

A final example, though this "burial" is only occasionally seen by the public, is the ornate copper urn containing the cremated remains of bacteriologist Moses Tran Clegg (1876–1918). Credited with isolating and growing the first leprosy bacilli in a laboratory, a necessary step toward finding a cure for the then-incurable disfiguring disease, Clegg died of kidney disease in Hawaii shortly before his forty-second birthday. In-ground burials were prohibited in Hawaii, so Clegg's widow had him cremated, sealed in an urn, and shipped back to Arkansas, where he had been born and raised. His father, a doctor, oversaw the Arkansas Medical Society's gift of the urn to the Arkansas History Commission, where it remains in the Arkansas State Archive in Little Rock.[44] Over the years it has occasionally been put on display and may also be viewed by appointment.

1. St. Boniface Church Cemetery, Bigelow **(Perry)**

2. Greenwood Cemetery,
Hot Springs
Hollywood Cemetery, Hot Springs
(Garland)

3. Rohwer Relocation Camp Cemetery **(Desha)**

4. Maple Hill Cemetery, Helena **(Phillips)**

5. Lonoke City Cemetery **(Lonoke)**

6. Rhea grave, Walnut Ridge **(Lawrence)**

7. Woodland Heights Cemetery, Rector **(Clay)**

8. Crescent Hotel lawn, Eureka Springs **(Carroll)**

9. Arkansas River | **10.** Mississippi River

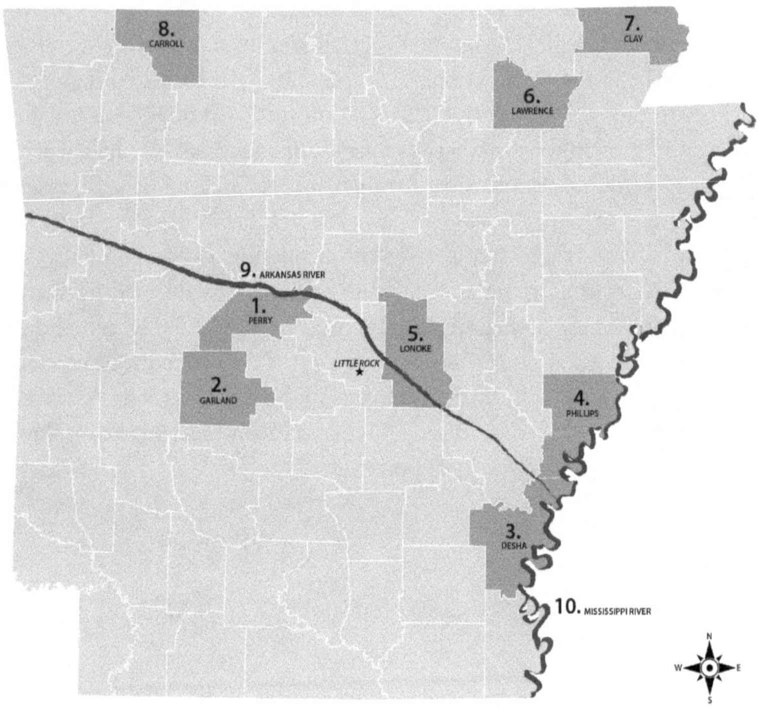

Major locations discussed in chapter 7.
Map by Red Rooster Design, Fayetteville, Arkansas.

Chapter 7

ANIMALS—ON AND IN GRAVES

And there asleep in her lowly bed,
Where winter & summer so softly spread
Their white & their green all over the dead,
We leave her with him, who keepeth his own
Whether living above, or under a stone.
And his angels will guard her there sleeping alone.

—MARY JANE MOULDEN, 1829–1890, STRAIN CEMETERY (WASHINGTON CO.)

Pedro the Irish setter has been sitting on his pedestal in Helena's Maple Hill Cemetery for just over 130 years as of this writing. The word "Waiting" is carved below his paws, while "Fidelity" is lettered on the back of the base. In other words: faithfully waiting, perhaps for the return of his owner, Dr. Emile Overton Moore, who is buried below the life-sized sculpture of the dog.

We know nothing about Pedro other than his name, which is found in raised letters on his collar, but we know a lot about the doctor. Moore was a prominent physician in Helena (Phillips Co.), yet something very dark is suggested by the two lengthy inscriptions on the marker's base. Luckily, a fully dimensional tale can be assembled from newspaper accounts of the events that led up to his death, and beyond.

Let's start with the tantalizing inscriptions on the two bases stacked beneath the vigilant Pedro. (Sometime before 1962 a new polished red granite base was inserted between the dog's statue and the marker's

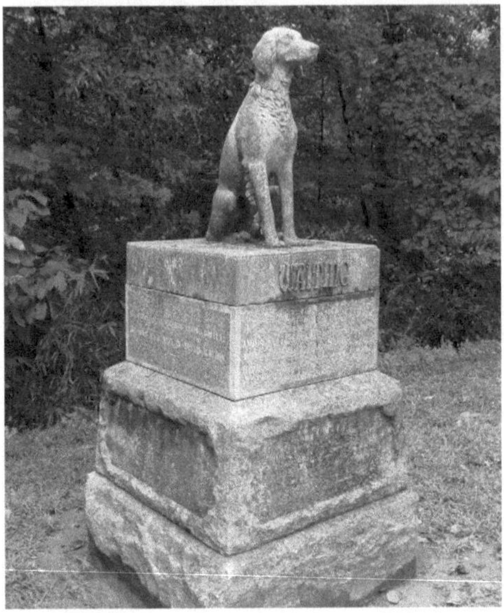

Fig 7.1. Pedro, an Irish setter, guards the grave of Dr. Emile Overton Moore, killed by a fellow doctor in 1893. Maple Hill Cemetery, Helena (Phillips Co.).

original base.[1] Each contains the same inscription.) Here we read that Moore was born in 1854 and "murdered" on February 16, 1893. This cause of death is again referred to in one of the two epitaphs:

> He possessed marked individuality. He was incapable of dissimulation. His errors were the errors of a man, and they stood out in bold contrast with the time-serving, two-faced hypocrites who conspired to have him murdered.
>
> "Let us remember that after midnight cometh morn."

The second inscription reads like a funeral sermon: "He is now beyond the reach of blame or praise. And love will hope and faith will trust that he has felt the joy that is felt where there are no tears and no graves."

This fulsome and forgiving language hides the ugly truth that Helena residents, though perhaps respecting Dr. Moore as a physician and surgeon, feared him as a person. Following his death, newspapers described him as a dangerous man, both "violent and revengeful,"[2] and "a terror to the community when drinking."[3] He was known to carry a gun and had been implicated in several previous "scrapes" that terrorized his town.[4] One of these had taken place ten years earlier, when Moore argued with an elderly patient, called him a liar, and shot him twice in the bowels with a double-barreled shotgun.[5] Though acquitted of this killing, feelings against the doctor were strong enough to create talk that he might be lynched.[6]

His fellow physicians were surely aware of their colleague's reputation because Dr. Charles Shinault also went about armed—at least he did so the day he made a house call to treat a patient with a broken limb. The patient's family, seeking a doctor, sent for both Dr. Moore and Dr. Shinault, though another version of events says that Shinault was called after Moore failed to show up. As Shinault prepared to set the broken bone, Moore arrived and quickly became angry and threatening. The two doctors stepped outside on the porch, away from the patient, and engaged in a heated argument. Swearing at his rival, Moore started to unbutton his coat, and Shinault, expecting him to draw a gun, pulled out his own gun and shot Moore in the head, killing him on the spot. This was not the first time the two had had professional difficulties.[7]

Shinault turned himself in to authorities and voluntarily remained in jail until the funeral had concluded, to allow Moore's family time to hire a lawyer and gather witnesses.[8] Moore's estranged wife Jennie Wright Moore and their son John, age eleven, and daughter Catherine, age four,[9] arrived from Nashville, Tennessee, for the funeral. One week later Shinault was acquitted of the charge of murder, having convincingly pleaded self-defense.

The story doesn't end there, however. Moore had a life insurance policy worth $5,000, a policy that the insurance company initially declined to honor on the grounds that Moore had violated the contract and incurred his own death when he broke the law by fighting.[10] Furthermore, Moore had recently changed the policy's beneficiary from his two young children to local schoolteacher Minnie Robertson. Moore and his wife were separated, but accounts differ as to whether they had divorced; either way, Robertson claimed she was Moore's fiancée and that the policy was his early wedding gift to her.[11]

The case was fought in Little Rock,[12] then again in federal court in St. Louis, which, three years after Moore's death, ruled in favor of Robertson. A Little Rock newspaper headline blared the shocking outcome: "Won by a woman"[13] to announce that she had received a verdict for $5,902—worth roughly $226,000 today. Despite this victory, she had to go back to court to force the insurance company to finally pay her.

Who sought to exonerate Dr. Moore with those enigmatic epitaphs, and who chose Pedro's statue? Unless Minnie Robertson used some of the insurance money to honor her fiancé, the grave marker was most likely purchased by Moore's wealthy parents, John and Martha Moore. Their son's unsigned canine statue is situated behind the Moore parents' large obelisk, which was signed by Morriss Brothers, a Memphis firm. The Moores' epitaphs are philosophical in nature: "We are creatures of circumstance and our faith is a matter of intellect and education" is carved above John's name and dates, and "Every cradle asks us whence / and every coffin whither" below Martha's name.

Pedro's statue has generated numerous urban legends. Versions include the family dog witnessing the killing, guarding Moore's body, attending his funeral, or refusing to leave the grave until his own eventual death and burial near his master, with the statue made to honor both man and dog.[14] Another story involves a jealous husband shooting Moore and his dog, while paranormal books and websites assert that a dog's ghostly pants and howls can be heard near the gravesite. (Nicely coincidental, though entirely unrelated, is a large clay brick containing two paw prints, found in the paving of a family plot downhill from the Moore graves.)

Whether or not a ghost dog remains on duty, there is a final twist to the story. Two days before the murder, Dr. Moore had an unsettling dream, which he recounted to his sister, who, in turn, told to a newspaper after her brother's death. In the dream he arrived at a patient's home to perform surgery and found another doctor in attendance; following an argument Moore's rival pulled out a gun and shot the doctor below the left eye. The dream proved to be eerily prophetic, as Shinault's bullet inflicted "a huge bullet wound . . . immediately under his left eye."[15]

It must have been socially awkward to continue to practice medicine in the same town as Moore's brother, Dr. Frierson Moore, but Dr.

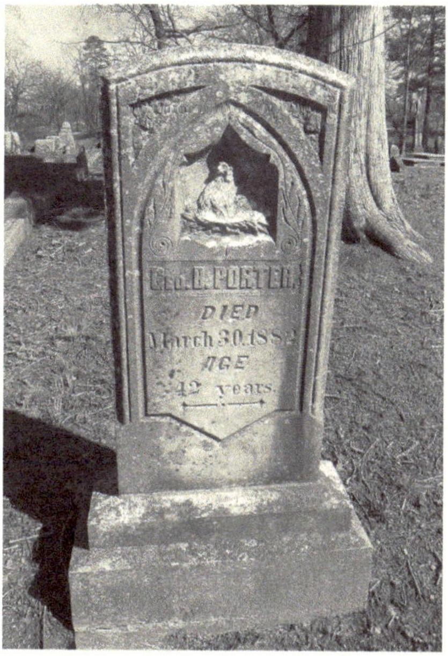

Fig 7.2. This spaniel carving, its meaning unclear, marks the grave of George Porter (died 1882), who came to Hot Springs to open either a spa or a bordello. Greenwood Cemetery, Hot Springs (Garland Co.).

Shinault's actions damaged neither his reputation nor his fortunes. He married the following year, was elected president of the Arkansas Medical Society in 1902 at age thirty-five, and enjoyed a long career in medicine in both Helena and Little Rock. He died in 1926 and was buried in Helena's Maple Hill cemetery in a family plot quite some distance away from that of the Moore family.

Pedro, with his slightly slouched posture and identifying collar, may be a portrait of an actual dog, but traditionally canine statuary is symbolic and represents loyalty, vigilance, and watchfulness.[16] A grieving dog may symbolize a family's loss when positioned on or near a child's grave, but it is rare to find a dog carving, of any kind, in Arkansas cemeteries. One exception is a deep bas-relief carving of a spaniel on George Porter's marble tablet in Greenwood Cemetery in Hot Springs (died 1882, Garland Co.). Porter died unexpectedly, shortly after he arrived in that city with an interest in "conducting

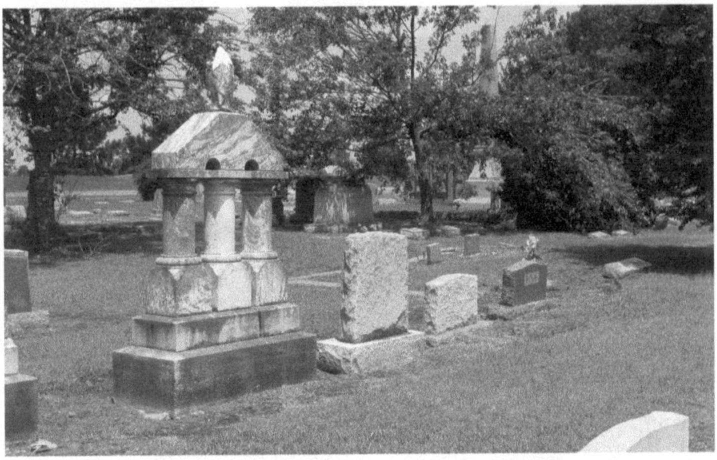

Fig 7.3. Three Booe men, buried beneath a shared three-column marker (on the left), is close to the Eagle family's large obelisk (visible through the trees on the right). The Eagles killed the Booes in 1898. Lonoke city cemetery (Lonoke Co.).

a fashionable bagnio."[17] A bagnio can be either a spa—which would be logical in a city that promoted its healing thermal waters—or a brothel (also something known in Hot Springs). Based on context when the word was used elsewhere by this newspaper, the latter definition seems to have been intended.

MURDERERS AND THEIR VICTIMS, TOGETHER FOR ETERNITY

A graveyard containing a killer and the man he killed is hardly unique to Chenault and Moore. In Lonoke's city cemetery (Lonoke Co.) the Eagle family's massive obelisk is practically close enough to shade the graves of the three Booes, father W.K. and his two sons, gunned down by members of the Eagle family, which must have made Decoration Day awkward for all descendants. Despite friends' attempts to reconcile the two families over an earlier incident, a shootout among the well-armed participants left the three Booe men dead on April 25, 1898, as they exited the local railroad station. The five Eagle men were acquitted, their lawyers arguing that the Booes were violent and dangerous men, intent on starting a duel.[18] Only son Charles Booe's name on the shared marker has a death date,[19] but all three deaths are commemorated by a single epitaph: "Neither can they die any more for they are equal unto the angels."[20]

The Eagles, all related to James P. Eagle, former governor of Arkansas (from 1889 to 1893), may have been entirely innocent or simply too well connected to convict. In addition to the three Eagles killed in 1873 (discussed in chapter 4), the family seems to have had a propensity for violence. In 1891, Charlie Eagle, one of the governor's nephews, emptied his revolver into his sleeping stepfather, E.F. Solomon, after learning that Solomon had been "outraging" (sexually molesting) his stepdaughter, Charlie's sister.[21] Presumably, Charlie was acquitted. Two more acts of violence occurred in 1903. Another of the governor's nephews, Little Rock bartender Pat Eagle, shot and killed Charles Walker, who was Black ("it was not proved that the negro had a weapon, but after he was killed an open knife was found beside him") and a judge ruled that Eagle had acted in self-defense.[22] Later that same year, John Wait and an unnamed orphan boy, both Black, burned to death in a building owned by the Eagles.[23]

Rector's Woodland Heights Cemetery (Clay Co.) contains another example of predator and prey buried within sight of one another. In this instance the killer's and the victim's deaths are separated by nearly one year, and their graves by just 190 feet. Even their epitaphs are similar. Killer Martin Van Buren Vowell's tall, urn-topped column is inscribed, "Erected by his friends and neighbors who did what they could for him," while victim William Lovejoy's stone column reads, "Erected by his friends." Themes of love, loss, and mourning are also expressed in both men's epitaphs.

Their story has been published in various venues, always with the same plotline: Vowell, Rector's city marshal, arrested Lovejoy and thus set off years of animosity between the men. Though it's not known what prompted Lovejoy's arrest and eventual release, he was known to have killed nearly a dozen men by employing a peculiar trick. He would pretend to have been shot and fall to the ground, face down, hiding a gun beneath his body. When his opponent rolled him over he would miraculously revive, and shoot to kill.[24]

On August 12, 1903, Lovejoy ambushed Vowell and his children on their way to church. After the men exchanged shots Lovejoy tried his usual tactic, but Vowell was familiar with this trick and, rather than rolling Lovejoy over, killed him by shooting him twice in the back with a shotgun, then in the back of the head with a pistol—none of which counts as self-defense. After two trials (the judge dismissed the first jury after they refused his instructions to return an indictment in the first degree),[25] Vowell was sentenced to hang.[26] Despite receiving a petition with one thousand signatures asking that Vowell's sentence be commuted to life in prison, and despite reportedly having pardoned eight hundred convicts during his first three years in office,[27] Governor Jeff Davis declined to take action and the sentence was carried out in Paragould on June 9, 1904.

It turns out that this is not as straightforward as it first appears. In addition to the petition asking for clemency for Vowell, Gov. Davis also received "a remonstrance"—a petition bearing 1,200 signatures requesting that he *not* overturn the death sentence. The governor set the record straight two months later in a speech he gave at Hardy, Arkansas. In it he noted that despite being deluged by requests for clemency from ex-Confederate soldiers, he had inside knowledge about Vowell's past, told to him by a Confederate veteran who knew something that they did not: Vowell, too, was a brutal and cold-blooded murderer.

". . . While on the scaffold this old man [the Confederate veteran] made a statement to numerous citizens who witnessed the execution that Mart Vowell killed his [the veteran's] brother in Tennessee, shot him through the head, and that his brother's brains spattered in his face and that he came all the way to Arkansas to see him hung." Not only that, but Davis knew of two other murders that Vowell had committed, including one told to him by the mother of a boy shot by Vowell, an act so horrific that Davis refused to listen to the details.[28]

A MAN AND HIS HORSE

A popular website devoted to strange and quirky tourist destinations recommends seeing the grave of a man who was killed on—and buried with—his horse. According to a cherished urban legend, John A. Rhea and the horse on which he was riding were struck by a train near Walnut Ridge (1893, Lawrence Co.), and man and beast were buried

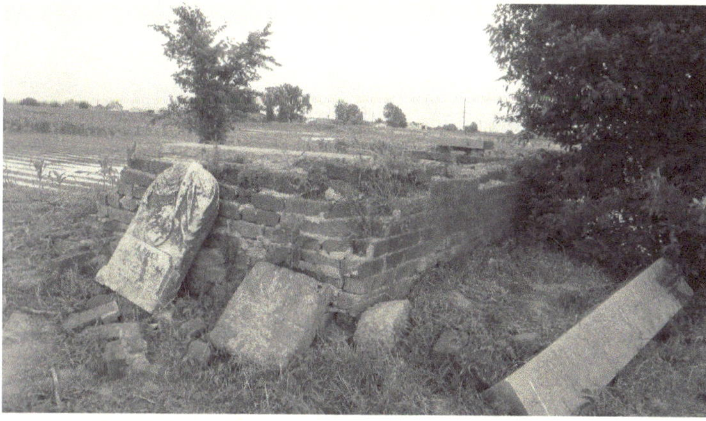

Fig 7.4. John A. Rhea's brick vault stands alone in a field near Walnut Ridge (Lawrence Co.) where, folklore has it, he was buried with his horse.

in the same solitary grave.[29] Rhea's tombstone makes no mention of this unusual death and burial, which isn't surprising as there is no real proof that it occurred.

Still, Rhea's massive brick burial chamber, constructed atop a small mound at the edge of a field, appears considerably larger than would be needed to hold a single casket. Rhea's probate papers at the Lawrence County courthouse include a lengthy itemization of the labor and materials needed to construct this burial vault. The list includes charges for nine thousand bricks and six loads of sand, as well as cement, lime, and the services of two brick masons. Oh, and a charge of one hundred dollars for "one horse known as Gray John, sold about July 7, '92."

This does not prove, of course, that Rhea, the owner of a livery stable in Walnut Ridge, was killed on horseback. His probate file includes a hefty eighty-dollar charge from the physician who stopped seeing his regular patients in order to comply with Rhea's "urgent request" to take care of him, day and night, for the duration of his final illness, which lasted just over a week.[30] A local merchant charged Rhea's estate thirteen dollars for wines, liqueurs, ice, and lunches "during his sickness," which rules out death by train.

The *Daily Arkansas Gazette*, in Little Rock, published a short death notice, saying that the wealthy Rhea was "identified with every progressive movement in this town."[31] What's strange is that this praise came less than a decade after Rhea stabbed James Bottoms in the neck with a penknife during a barroom fight. Bottoms died a week later, and Rhea disappeared and reportedly hid out in Mexico. The governor offered a $200 reward for his arrest and conviction but apparently it went unclaimed,[32] and two months later Rhea was back in Walnut Ridge, where he appeared "in broad daylight, with a double-barreled shot-gun and defied arrest."[33]

Research into Rhea has brought other peripheral deaths to light. Rhea was married to Elizabeth ("Lizzie") Cooper, a woman who, anecdotally, held grudges and settled scores. Though a Walnut Ridge newspaper editor described her as a "big-hearted, charitable woman with a sweet disposition and pardonable pride of a true southern woman" in 1912, when she was in her fifties,[34] just two months after her husband's death, Mrs. Rhea was implicated in the fire that destroyed two city blocks of Walnut Ridge and killed two adults and an infant. According to the man who confessed to the crime, Mrs. Rhea had offered him two suits of clothing if he'd set fire to the Star Hotel after the hotel's owner ordered her to move out.[35]

The year 1910 was an especially bad one for Lizzie Rhea—now Mrs. Burel and the proprietor, with her third husband, of the Rhea Hotel. Shots fired from the Rhea Hotel killed Alf and Isham Bagley, a son and father who were embroiled in a feud. Lizzie Burel's brother would later provide the testimony that got her indicted as an accessory to Isham Bagley's murder, though apparently she was never prosecuted.[36] Earlier that same year her hotel was the scene of another death when a traveling salesman, weighing 260 pounds, was found dead inside a wall after the heavy bed on which he was sleeping (known as a Murphy bed) folded up, trapping and smothering him to death, despite his frantic efforts to escape.[37]

Lizzie Rhea Burel later claimed to have worked her way up from extreme poverty to affluence, and though a fire destroyed Rhea Hotel in 1914, she was later described as one of the richest women in the county. She died in 1925, but though her first husband's brick crypt appears commodious and was perhaps constructed to house both of their bodies, she was buried in the town cemetery beneath a small, plain marker.

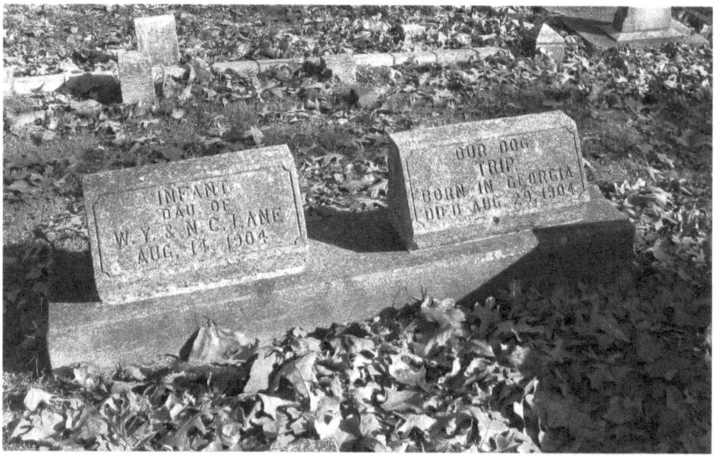

Fig 7.5. Two weeks after the Lanes' unnamed infant daughter died, their dog Trip died and was given a matching tombstone. Greenwood Cemetery, Hot Springs (Garland Co.).

A horse story that *can* be substantiated is that of Mitchell Vernon Herzberger and his horse Joelee. The two share a granite tombstone *and* a death date (December 31, 2013), although dying on the same day was just a coincidence. The horse died on a Wyoming ranch in the morning, and Herzberger died of cancer later that same day, in a Colorado hospital. Supposedly he regained consciousness and told family that he was going to ride out of the hospital on Joelee, not knowing that the horse had just predeceased him. The two were cremated and now share a grave in Georgia Cemetery (Benton Co.), their epitaph reading, "Riding together forever."[38]

ANIMAL BURIALS

Even cemeteries that forbid pets sometimes contain them anyway, according to groundskeepers who have found evidence of surreptitious burials. Other families openly share their plots with their pets. The Rector family put up a headstone for "Ouachita our pet, 1930–1940" in Hot Springs' Hollywood Cemetery (Garland Co.), and across town Greenwood Cemetery also contains a dog's headstone. The Lane family's unnamed infant daughter died in August 1904,

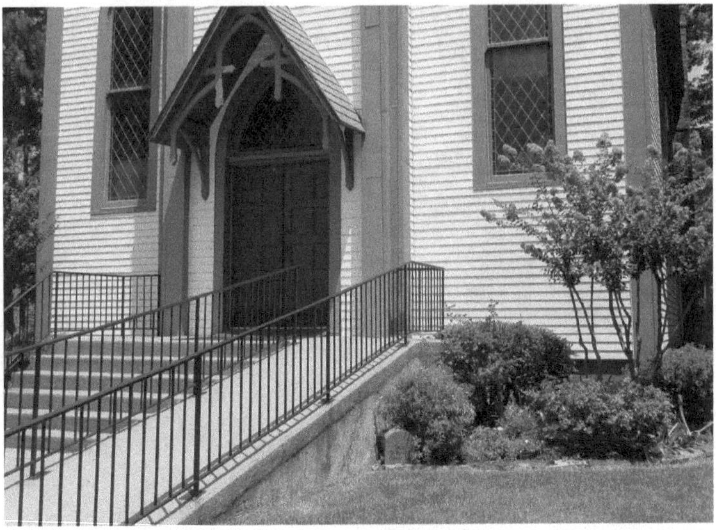

Fig 7.6. Sheba, St. Boniface Church's "greeter dog," is buried to the right of the church steps (Perry Co.).

then, two weeks later, "Our dog Trip, born in Georgia" died and the family placed matching markers, with death dates, in their plot in Greenwood to commemorate both losses.[39] Russellville's Oakland Cemetery (Pope Co.) reportedly has several marked pet burials, including "Mouchee" buried in one corner of the Jenkins family plot.

Aldridge Cemetery (Cleburne Co.) has homemade concrete markers for German shorthair pointers Sam (1986–1998) and Katie (1986–2003), buried at the feet of John Robert Reedy (1943–1997) in the Reedy family plot, while the owner of the land containing Cross Cemetery (Lawrence Co.) erected a beautiful headstone for Sultan De Ripper (1953–1968) at the end of the row of humans' headstones. It's not hard to find other likely pet burials, small markers with names like "Muffy" and "Taz" tucked between headstones in a family plot, identities sometimes verified by the inclusion of a pawprint emblem.

Not all marked graves are for pets—some are for working animals. Sheba was the "St. Boniface Greeter Dog," according to the inscription on her granite marker. She was noted for her habit of howling along each time the church bells were rung for mass. Sheba was killed by a car in 2005, and a parishioner made her marker, complete with a

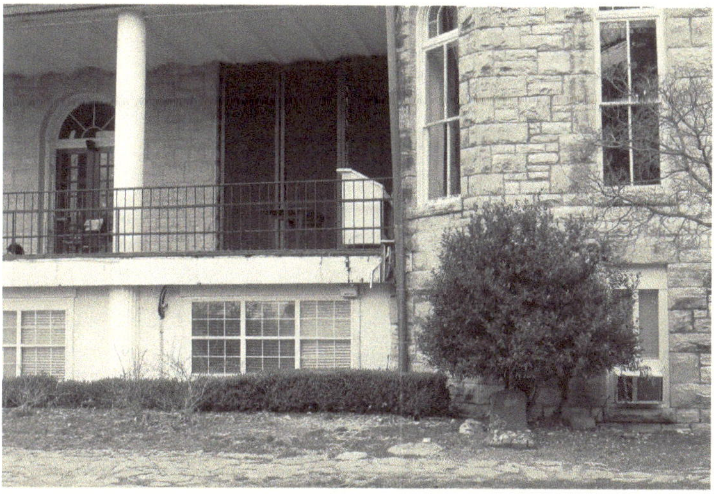

Fig 7.7. The Crescent Hotel's resident cat, Morris (1973–1994), was buried with full honors in the hotel garden. His picture and a laudatory poem are displayed in the hotel lobby, Eureka Springs (Carroll Co.).

small drawing of the black lab,[40] located to next to the entrance to St. Boniface Church at Bigelow (Perry Co.).

The cemetery adjacent to the church contains the graves, and granite marker, of four members of the McNulty family, all of whom have the same December 26, 1987, death date. Below the names and dates is the inscription, "Felled by the sword of an assassin they are now safe in the arms of our Lord." The reference to the sword should not be taken literally. Shiela (Simmons) McNulty and husband Dennis were shot, and children Sylvia Gail, age seven, and Michael, nearly two, were strangled by Shiela's father, Ronald Gene Simmons, along with ten other family members and two members of the public near Dover, Arkansas.[41] A ledger marker in Briggsdale, Colorado, commemorates the fourteen members of the Simmons family without saying where all of them are buried, but another five of the victims are in the Smith-Morgan Cemetery (Cleveland Co.), while the killer, executed by lethal injection in 1990, is buried beneath a military marker in Lincoln Memorial Lawn Cemetery (Lincoln Co.).

The Crescent Hotel in Eureka Springs (Carroll Co.) once had a "working cat," which is not a term one hears very often. Morris, an orange tabby, prowled the corridors of the Crescent Hotel for two

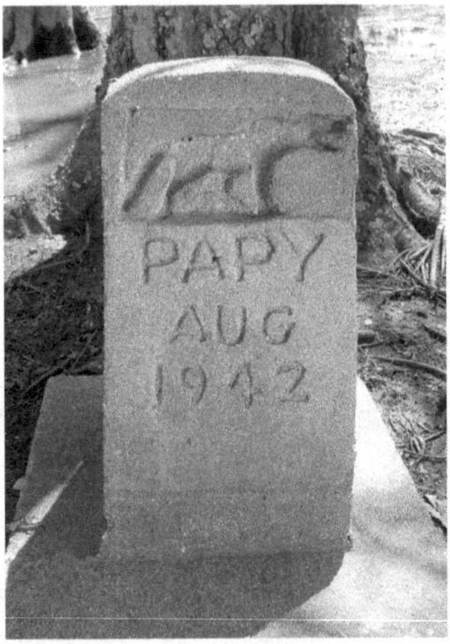

Fig 7.8. The headstone of "Papy" is found well outside the boundary of the Rohwer Relocation Center's cemetery (Desha Co.) and is believed to mark the grave of a camp overseer's dog.

decades before dying at age twenty-one, in 1994. Over fifty people attended Morris's funeral and burial in the hotel garden, where he was laid to rest in a velvet-lined walnut casket. (According to one account, a witness in an idling tour bus mistook the event for an infant's burial.[42]) Though the grave is in the hotel's formal garden, the hotel's then-owner had the cat's specially made tombstone moved to a less obvious location at the edge of the grounds. These days the hotel promotes its resident ghosts through psychic conventions and ghost-hunting tours and claims that the spirit of the friendly cat still prowls the halls.[43]

Then there is the enigmatic headstone for "Papy" with a simple death date of August 1942. This little concrete marker is found in a grove of trees far beyond the burials at the Rohwer Relocation Center's cemetery outside McGehee (Desha Co.). The marker's material and workmanship is similar to that found on the internees' headstones, although it, unlike the humans' markers, has no built-in containers for flowers and is decorated with the crude outline of what appears to be a dog, believed to be a pet of a camp overseer.[44] The internment camp was still under construction in August, ahead of the detainees' arrival in September, so perhaps it was made later, when markers were being made for human interments. And while Rohwer historians believe this to be a pet's grave, at the time that the camp cemetery was enumerated, in 1968 or 1969, the grave was identified as "Papy (Hobo—an American)."[45]

A final and possibly apocryphal animal burial story has to do with a group of gypsies who camped beside a creek in Evansville (1894, Washington Co.). With them were two bears trained to do tricks and to wrestle anyone willing to place a bet on the outcome of a match. Some of the gypsies left to make a trip to Fayetteville, leaving the bears chained to a tree. While they were gone a massive storm blew in, causing the creek to rise rapidly. After water levels fell, eight of the travelers' bodies were recovered and buried in nearby Vineyard Cemetery. A separate grave, outside the cemetery's boundaries, held the drowned bruins, buried beneath a large stone with the word "Bears" carved on it. This stone was supposedly seen in the 1930s.[46]

PET CEMETERIES

Graveyards dedicated to the burial of dogs and cats are a fairly recent development in Arkansas, and there aren't many. As mentioned in chapter 5, in 1989, Thelma Holford left money to establish the Thelma Holford Memorial Pet Cemetery in Jonesboro (Craighead Co.), now closed. Hot Springs (Garland Co.) has Pet Lawn, located in Crestview Memorial Park, and Bentonville's Rest Haven Pet Cemetery, situated behind Dodson Cemetery (Benton Co.), is paved with dozens of in-ground markers.

East Memorial Gardens in Texarkana (Miller Co.) has a dedicated area near the cemetery entrance for the burial of law enforcement K-9s. There, bronze plaques mark the graves of Zorg, Zeus, Bruno, Amigo, and nearly a dozen other dogs, giving their names, dates, and the names of their handlers. The markers also tell where the dogs worked, the majority having served the Texarkana, Arkansas, and Texarkana, Texas, police departments, as well as other towns, counties, and one fire department.

In the regular pet cemeteries, inscriptions almost always assign the family surname to the cat or dog and occasionally give a religious affiliation (including a Star of David) as well as verses normally found on humans' markers, expressing love and loss. Some markers give added details about the animal's life, such as "Momma's 22.5 lb. baby" and "To me, you were more than just a puppy, you were my son." Or this, on a cat's grave, "I came, I purred, I conquered."

1. Friendship Cemetery, Springdale (**Washington**)

2. Fairview Cemetery, Van Buren (**Crawford**)

3. Greenwood Cemetery, Hot Springs (**Garland**)

4. Mt. Calvary Cemetery, Mena (**Polk**)

5. Oak Ridge Cemetery, Malvern (**Hot Spring**)

6. De Ann Cemetery, Prescott (**Nevada**)

7. McFarland Cemetery, Banks (**Bradley**)

8. St. Joseph's Cemetery, Pine Bluff (**Jefferson**)

9. Easton Cemetery (**Woodruff**)

10. Vandale Cemetery (**Cross**)

11. Gum Grove Cemetery, Newport
Walnut Grove Cemetery, Newport (**Jackson**)

12. Ermen Cemetery, Osceola (**Mississippi**)

13. Hale Cemetery (**Boone**)

14. Arkansas River | **15.** Mississippi River
16. White River

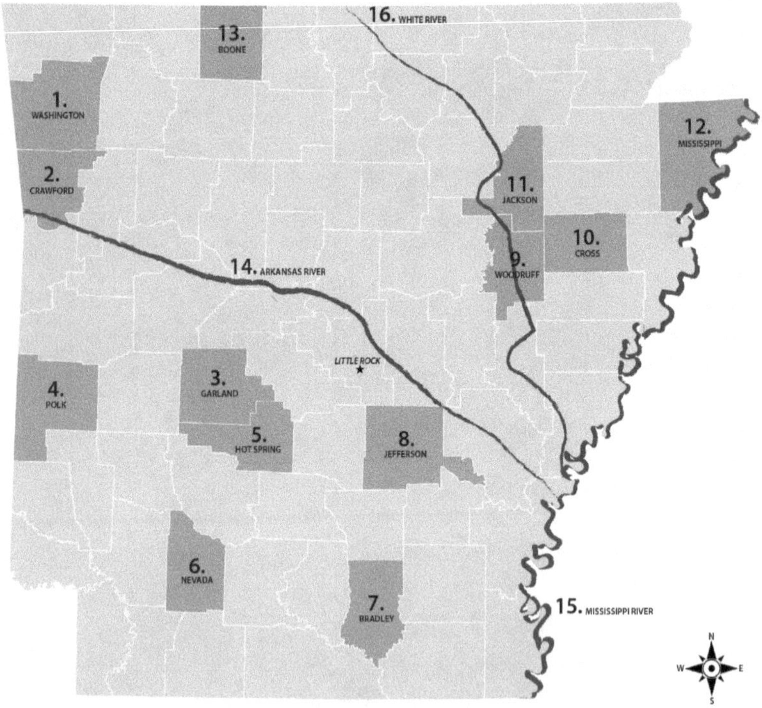

Major locations discussed in chapter 8.
Map by Red Rooster Design, Fayetteville, Arkansas.

Chapter 8

SEERS, CIRCUS FOLK, ECCENTRICS, AND GRAVEYARD ODDITIES

Array'd in glorious grace,
Shall these vile bodies shine,
And ev'ry shape and ev'ry face,
Be heav'nly and divine.

JEREMIAH PATE, 1794–1858
—PIONEER CEMETERY, HISTORIC WASHINGTON STATE PARK (HEMPSTEAD CO.)

William DeHorn and Caroline Dye were born with clairvoyant abilities. Neither seer charged for advice on love, finding lost objects, or solving problems, but both accepted cash donations via the mail as well as from clients who showed up at their doors seeking guidance. There are many parallels between the lives of these two African Americans who lived fewer than thirty miles apart, but only DeHorn's tombstone reveals his special talent.

DeHorn, who was either seventy-two or eighty-one when he died of pneumonia on November 24, 1944,[1] has a large concrete tablet in Easton Cemetery, at the edge of a field outside McCrory (Woodruff Co.). It is inscribed: "Here lies a man with special God given power

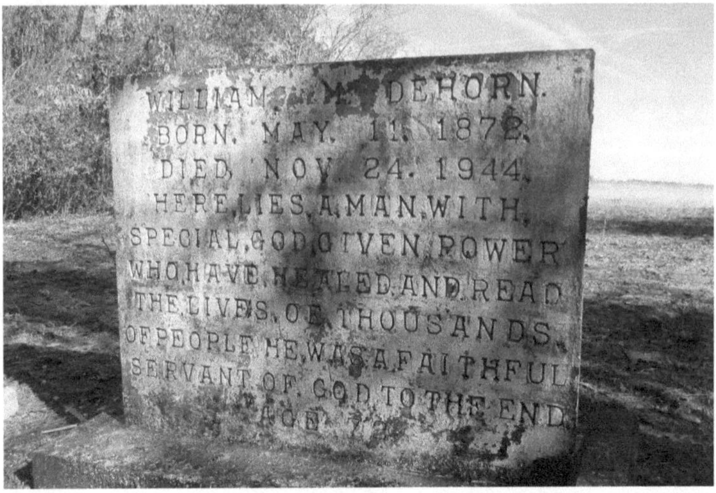

Fig 8.1. The concrete marker of seer William DeHorn (1872–1944) mentions his "special God-given power." Easton Cemetery near McCrory (Woodruff Co.).

who have healed and read the lives of thousands of people. He was a faithful servant of God to the end."

Growing up in McCrory, J.E. Browning witnessed DeHorn's abilities firsthand. He recounted stories in which the seer would tell clients to leave immediately in order to be in the right place at the right time to find money or a missing person. In one dramatic account, when the Woodruff County sheriff sought help locating the body of a man who drowned in the White River, DeHorn told him to go to a certain location on the river and search protruding tree roots. "The sheriff told us that this would be highly unlikely because the root-wad was upstream from where the boy was known to have fallen in," Browning wrote, yet ultimately this is where the body was found.[2]

Browning, acknowledging that DeHorn used his own money to build a church, said he never pastored one and was called "Reverend" as a term of respect. However, the 1930 Census identifies him as a pastor of a church, and on the 1940 Census he is listed as both a preacher and a fortune teller.[3]

Given the many parallels between their lives, it would be interesting to know if DeHorn knew Caroline Dye, the more famous of the two. She was born enslaved in South Carolina and had married and moved to Jackson County, Arkansas, by the time of the 1870 Census, while Dehorn was born in Newport, the county seat of Jackson County, in about 1863, to parents who were also born there.[4]

Both DeHorn and Dye received such large volumes of mail that they required assistance from paid secretaries, Dye because she was illiterate. (Despite this, several books—including one on palmistry—were among her possessions when she died.) Dye wasn't just famous locally, she was mentioned in several songs of the period and made national news for certain predictions as well as for the size of her estate following her death. Her executor had to ask the probate court to increase its legally sanctioned fees to pay appraisers to travel to four locations, as Dye owned several farms and two houses packed with possessions. There they inventoried well over one thousand items of clothing and household goods, everything from corset covers to cuff buttons, from pillows to pin trays, as well as large quantities of groceries.[5]

Both seers were civic minded. In addition to building a church, DeHorn organized a brass band, built a building for its members to practice in, and hired a Memphis band instructor, while the patriotic Dye purchased liberty bonds and war saving stamps ($1,000 of these, the maximum allowable), as well as raising money for "other war work funds."[6] She also took in people in need. Various censuses list orphans and wards among her household, which in 1880 also included two unrelated adults who were "not of sound mind at times" but each of whom, the census-taker noted, "lives as one of the family."[7]

Their visiting Black clientele likely had trouble finding food and lodging, so the two created restaurants on their properties, and Dye also ran a boardinghouse, which explains the large number of household linens and groceries in her probate inventory. Their wealth was obvious. DeHorn carried two bulging wallets, dressed well, and drove a new car; at the time of Dye's death it was reported that over $12,000 in cash (roughly the equivalent of a quarter-million dollars today), was found hidden in her house, in addition to what she had in the bank.[8] On top of standard charges for embalming and funeral directing, the itemized bill for Dye's funeral expenses included a $675 coffin covered in silver-gray silk plush, a silk burial dress and shoes, special gloves for the pallbearers to wear, and the hiring of numerous cars and buggies, for a total of $970, an unheard-of amount in 1918.[9]

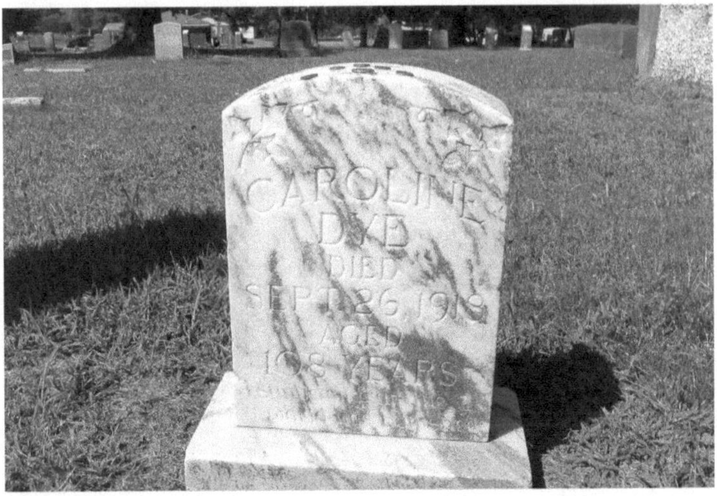

Fig 8.2. Seer Carolyn Dye was either seventy or seventy-five when she died in 1918. Gum Grove Cemetery, Newport (Jackson Co.).

These clairvoyants used similar methods when divining the future. DeHorn would place his hands on his head and close his eyes in order to visualize an answer, and Dye—despite W.C. Handy's blues song about her claiming, "She reads your fortune, and her cards don't lie"[10]—used the cards merely to help her concentrate. More often, she merely covered her face with her hands when giving a reading."[11]

One difference between them has to do with how and where they are buried. The tombstone of DeHorn, who died in 1944 from bronchial pneumonia, is difficult to find due to its isolation, where it has been damaged by people using it as a base when shooting at beer bottles. Caroline Dye died on September 26, 1918, in Newport from what her obituary said was acute indigestion,[12] and is buried in Gum Grove, Newport's African American cemetery (Jackson Co.). Her tombstone gives her age as 106 years, which is wildly inaccurate.[13] Though she claimed to have been eighteen at the start of the Civil War (making her birth year 1843), the 1900 Census recorded her birth as May of 1848, meaning that she was either 70 or 75 when she died. She rests beside Mart Dye, her husband of over 40 years, where visitors sometimes leave dimes on the base of her modest marble headstone.

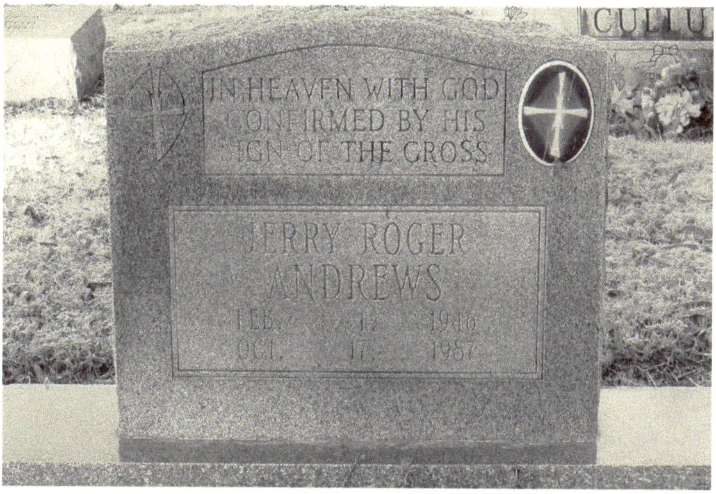

Fig 8.3. The headstone of Jerry Roger Andrews (1946–1987) shows two versions of the mystical cross that was seen inside his home after he died. Vanndale Cemetery (Cross Co.).

MIRACLES

Epitaphs routinely express the hope that the deceased's soul is safely in heaven, but now and then a tombstone offers proof. For example, after fifteen-year-old Henry Mayes died of a spider bite (1898, Boone Co.) what happened next is spelled out across the base of his tombstone in White Church cemetery: "In answer to the prayers of his mother, a voice said weep not, he rests in peace."[14]

The modern granite marker found in Vanndale's town cemetery for Jerry Roger Andrews (died 1987, Cross Co.) is even more explicit: "In heaven with God confirmed by His sign of the cross." The cross in question is illustrated on the stone both in a line drawing and in a photo. After Andrews was killed in a one-car accident, his widow, Darlene, saw a cross reflected on an inside pane of her front door and took it as a sign that her husband, who did not attend church on a regular basis, "has made things right with the Lord."[15] Over four thousand people flocked to the Andrews home over a ten-day period to see the cross or, sometimes, multiple or colored ones, when the door was held at just the right angle.[16]

SARACEN: THE MYTHS, MISTAKES, AND MULTIPLE BURIALS

There are several reasons why a body might be subjected to multiple burials, exhumations, and reburials. Among these are patriotism (moving a forgotten hero from an obscure to a prominent cemetery), the desire of trustees of a new cemetery to attract visitors and customers, or the belief that the deceased may have wanted burial in a different location.[17] Some or even all of these explanations are relevant to the story of Saracen, a supposed leader of the Quapaw tribe whose headstone in Pine Bluff's St. Joseph Cemetery (Jefferson Co.) lauds him as "Friend of the Missionaries / Rescuer of captive children." It marks his third resting place.

According to legend, Saracen was a Quapaw leader who rescued two children kidnapped by the Chickasaw tribe sometime in the late 1800s. Acting alone, he entered the Chickasaw camp at night, gave a war cry, and, in the ensuing confusion, scooped up the children, leapt into his canoe, and paddled them to safety. "Unfortunately there is no documentary evidence which guarantees the authenticity of the legend," writes Burney McClurkan, "but we can assume there is some truth to it or it would not have persisted or been so widely accepted."[18] More likely, writes historian Morris S. Arnold, the legend originated in an 1824 account of a Quapaw chief throwing a spear into a group of Native Americans (possibly Creek), frightening them and thus saving the child of the commandant of the Arkansas Post. "By 1895, the story had changed somewhat, but according to it a Quapaw, now identified as Saracen, is credited with having rescued two children, this time from Chickasaws."[19]

Saracen is a word used in the Middle Ages to identify a Muslim, but in his case it was a corruption of the surname of Francois Sarazin, his French father. Saracen has an entry in the Arkansas Encyclopedia disputing his widely published 1832 death date.[20] According to Arnold it was more likely to have been 1840. Nor was he a tribal chief in any real sense, as territorial governor George Izard "made Saracen an honorary chief and that other Quapaws considered Saracen to be 'a simple individual only.'"[21]

Saracen was buried in "Old Town Cemetery" in what later became downtown Pine Bluff, and his grave was apparently overlooked when

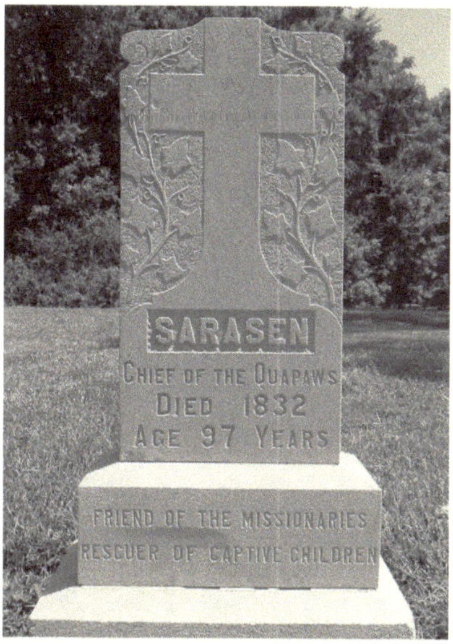

Fig 8.4. Saracen's tombstone lauds him as "Rescuer of captive children." St. Joseph's Cemetery, Pine Bluff (Jefferson Co.). It marks his third burial.

the graves were exhumed and moved to the city's Bellwood Cemetery, founded in 1860. Two bodies were discovered in 1883 during excavations for a commercial building, with one body described as "the remains of some Indian chief, probably that of the famed chief Sarasen."[22] Apparently that was sufficient authentication to get him moved to Bellwood.

Records kept by St. Joseph's cemetery show that the body was moved, yet again, in 1905 due to the supposition that Saracen had converted to Catholicism at some point in his life. Unlike the previous tenuous attribution, this time a Bellwood caretaker "swore under oath . . . that the grave in question was indeed that of Saracen."[23] At this time a large marker was installed, spelling his name as "Sarasen," and carved with a cross, ivy, and the laudatory inscription. If only his story, which appears from time to time in collections of Arkansas legends, was verifiably true.

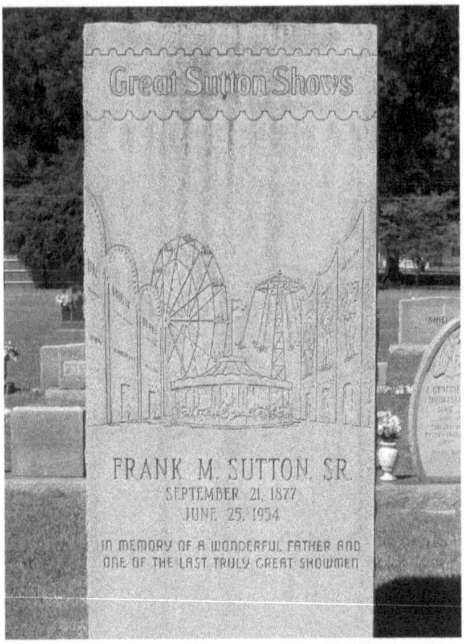

Fig 8.5. Circus-owner Frank Sutton Sr. (1877–1954) has a marker showing a circus midway and sideshows. Ermen Cemetery, Osceola (Mississippi Co.).

CIRCUS AND SIDESHOW PERFORMERS

Numerous small family-owned circuses once spent the winter months in Hugo, Oklahoma, before going back out on tour. Performers, animal trainers, and carnival workers who died there, or while traveling, would be buried in "Showmen's Rest," a specially designated corner of Hugo's Mount Olivet Cemetery. Arkansas also has a Showmen's Rest, although it does not contain comparably colorful markers. Inside Hot Springs' Memorial Gardens (Garland Co.) is a monolithic marker carved with a tall sword, in whose shadow rest dozens of former carnival workers. Ronald Fuller, who grew up in Hot Springs and whose mother, a professional singer and musician, played the piano at the city's Showmen's Club in the 1960s, remembers the era. "These were the people who ran food concessions and games, the carnival barkers and vendors. Carnivals and fairs came through, some had tent shows, others were one-carousel deals that wintered in Hot Springs, which has a temperate climate. There were very few after the 1960s."[24]

Though this is not a burial ground filled with lion tamers, several circus and sideshow performers have graves in various parts of Arkansas. The most detailed of these tombstones belongs to Frank Sutton Sr. (1877–1954), buried in Osceola's Ermen Cemetery (Mississippi Co.). Sutton wintered his circus in Osceola, and his epitaph hails him as "one of the last truly great showmen."

If only Sutton's marker revealed more about his career and death. The business originated in 1895 when Sutton's father, Levi, acquired a two-tailed horse and started charging people to see it. This led to the founding of a carnival, renamed the "Great Sutton Shows" in 1901, that claimed to be "the oldest singularly owned, continuously operated carnival in the United States." In 1954, Frank Sr. was found shot to death in his office in Louisiana, a crime that went unsolved.[25]

A detailed illustration on Sutton's large granite marker depicts carnival rides flanked by a circus midway whose attractions are illustrated above their individual labeled entrances: a tall man ("Thin"), a scantily clad woman ("Beauty"), and a heavy person ("Fat"). Today it seems almost unimaginable to pay to gawk at human beings, but "sideshow freaks" were a big attraction at these events. Representatives of each of the three categories depicted on Sutton's grave marker are buried in Arkansas, starting with James Grover Tarver, a man who was over eight feet tall and worked for Ringling Bros. and Barnum & Bailey Circus. He lived on his Arkansas farm when the circus wasn't touring, and he died there at age seventy-two in 1958. His grave is marked by an inconspicuous, in-ground bronze tablet in Marion's Crittenden Memorial Park (Crittenden Co.). His unusual height is revealed by his epitaph ("The Texas Giant") and the fact that his oversized casket was so long that it extended beyond the end of his plot and into the next row of graves, necessitating a gap between two burials.

The category of scantily clad women is represented by Forrestina Bradley Campbell (1891–1973), known familiarly as "White River Red," a red-haired trapeze artist whose life was colorful even by circus standards. After giving up trapeze work, supposedly following an injury, she lived in a common-law marriage with Jack Campbell and the two ran a store and gas station in Washington County. After Jack Campbell was shot and killed in 1935, his wife took to wearing men's clothing, selling firewood by the truckload, and living beside

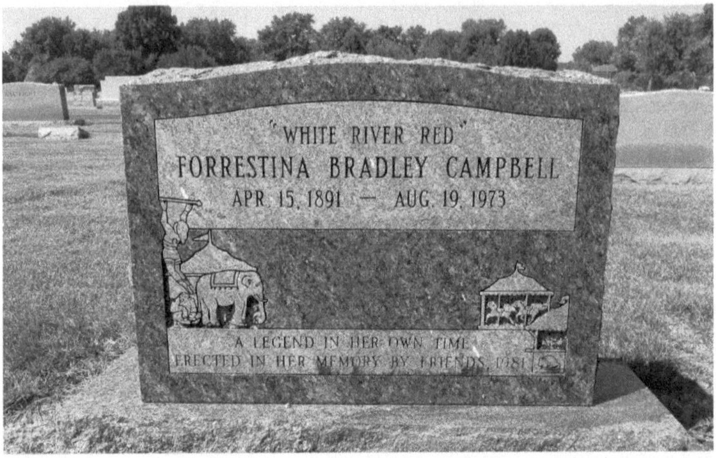

Fig 8.6. Circus and carnival emblems embellish the marker of Forrestina Bradley Campbell (1891–1973) and include her pet rat. Friendship Cemetery, Springdale (Washington Co.).

the White River. She did, that is, when not traveling the carnival and county fair circuit in Arkansas, Missouri, and Oklahoma with her pet rat.[26] According to Jim Tackett, "She had a game of chance in which you bet on which hole the rat would run into,"[27] while Phillip Steele recalled Campbell's hands as "scarred and bleeding from rat bites."[28]

When interviewed in 1950, Campbell had no financial worries; she owned a large tract of land and spent her summers traveling with carnivals, operating rides and concessions.[29] However, by 1969 she was unable to pay her taxes, and in 1971 she was declared "incompetent" and placed in Fayetteville City Hospital's nursing home, whereupon her possessions were sold at a public sale to pay for her support. She died in 1973 and was buried in Springdale's Friendship Cemetery (Washington Co.). In 1981, her friends raised enough money for a red granite headstone loaded with circus motifs, including a big top, a carousel, an elephant, a concession stand, a baboon, and a tiny carving of a rat.[30]

Of all these motifs it is the baboon that prompts one last story about the woman whose headstone hailed her as "a legend in her own time." According to Rolland Endsley, the manager of a local Freeze-n-Store Cold Storage plant, Campbell owned a large baboon. When it died she asked Endsley to provide temporary storage for the carcass. Campbell retrieved the baboon later that summer, placed it on ice in a trailer, and started driving to Tulsa, Oklahoma, to take it to a taxidermist. The truck broke down en route, the ice melted, the baboon began to decompose in the summer heat, and Campbell "gave up her idea of mounting her baboon friend and buried the animal alongside Highway 412."[31]

Carnival sideshows exhibited extremes: the very tall, the very short, and the very fat. Teamster Lee Trickey, born in Wisconsin in 1870, worked hard to keep his weight in check, but ultimately he could make more money touring with carnivals, where he was billed as "The Half-ton Man," "The human Leviathan,"[32] and "The biggest man in the world."[33] At his heaviest he was said to tip the scales at just over 700 pounds, but most articles say he weighed around 650 pounds, or the oddly specific 619 pounds reported at the time of his death.[34] When a Minneapolis "dime museum" exhibited him in its third-floor Curio Hall in 1897, a safe-moving company was hired to hoist Trickey in through an upper window because the stairs couldn't withstand his weight. (For that matter, Trickey's own legs could barely support him.) This trapped him there for the duration of his contract, but he proved to be so popular an attraction that his "term of imprisonment" was extended an extra week.[35]

His was a sad and difficult life, lived under the mocking gaze of the paying public. Periodically Trickey would resume work as a farmer and a teamster to provide for himself and his wife, but in 1903, she successfully sued him for divorce on the grounds of non-support. A newspaper writer mused, "How so fat a man could support himself, let alone a wife, was a mystery to the people who crowded the court room."[36] Trickey went back on tour, becoming one of the Cosmopolitan Carnival Company's "chief attractions." The company was performing in Newport, Arkansas, in November 1903 when Trickey died of inflammatory rheumatism, which was believed to have affected his heart.

A Newport undertaker embalmed the body, reportedly using seventeen quarts of embalming fluid to do so (given his estimated weight, the amount could well have been closer to seventeen *gallons*),[37] in the belief that family back home in Wisconsin would send for him. Instead, Trickey's stepfather replied, in what a newspaper called a "cold-blooded and laconic" telegram, "You have had the use of him,

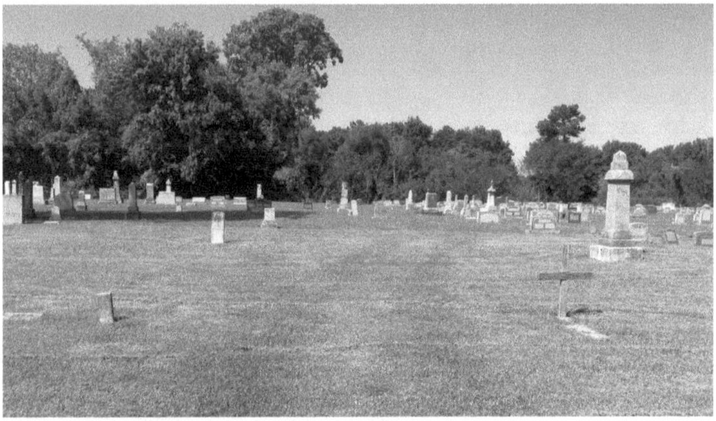

Fig 8.7. Lee Trickey (1870–1903), a circus fat man, died in Newport and was buried in an unmarked grave somewhere in this open area of Walnut Grove Cemetery (Jackson Co.).

now bury him."[38] And so they did, in a specially constructed six-foot by three-foot coffin. According to Newport's weekly newspaper, he was conveyed to Walnut Grove Cemetery "upon one of the large cotton dray wagons and was lowered to its last resting place by a big derrick, the windlass of which was handled by two stout negroes. The strain upon the ropes from their heavy burden could be seen in the manner they cut into the woodwork of the box."[39] It was the last time the public would gather to stare and point at him.

The carnival moved on, leaving Lee Trickey behind in an unmarked grave. At least it was in the city cemetery and not its potters' field.[40]

"Little Dixie" was another popular sideshow attraction laid to rest without a headstone. Billed as the world's smallest horse, the four-year-old, fifty-pound little animal died of indigestion in Prescott (1910, Nevada Co.) while on display as part of a traveling carnival. Dixie's equine parents were of normal size, which is a common feature among such accounts. Tarver's parents were said to be of average height, while Lee Trickey reportedly consumed no more food than a normal, or even small, adult would eat. Despite Dixie's well-attended funeral, complete with burial in a box covered in the stars and stripes,[41] and reports that money was being raised to purchase a headstone,[42] the exact location of the horse's grave in the De Ann Cemetery's potters' field is unmarked and unknown.

A final example of a circus death is found in Mena's Mt. Calvary Cemetery (Polk Co.). There a simple granite block marks the grave of Maria de Campa, "Killed by circus lion, 1942–1951." According to newspaper accounts, the Campa Brothers' circus had just performed in Mena when Maria, the nine-year-old granddaughter of an animal trainer, entered an unlocked cage and was clawed by a lion. (A different version of events states that the chained lion dragged Maria under a vehicle and mauled her.) A doctor who happened to be on hand treated her and got her to the local hospital,[43] but she died shortly afterward from blood loss. Her death certificate gives her cause of death as hemorrhage due to "cat bites (Lion)."[44]

Maria's grandmother stayed behind in Mena with Maria's body, pending instructions from the girl's mother, who had just returned to Mexico. The circus left town, but just a few hours later, while heading east through mountainous territory, a truck overturned and released a variety of animals, including leopards, bears, "and the child-killing lion."[45] Local hunters and law enforcement formed posses, one leopard was shot, and some of the animals were recaptured, but nothing more was written about the lion and its whereabouts.

It has been claimed that the cause of death on Maria's marker is unique. Quite likely this is true for Arkansas, but Elmwood Cemetery in Charlotte, North Carolina, contains a marker for sixty-five-year-old Charlie Houck on which is found the inscription, "Killed by a lion Jan. 9, 1930, with the Melville Ress Show."[46] It is questionable whether Maria's marker was put in place immediately after she died, thus putting it in the category of "genealogy stone," a back-dated tombstone containing details unlikely to have been included at the time of death. Such a practice is illustrated by markers erected by the Izard County Cemetery Preservation Association. Since its founding in 2005 the association has marked over a thousand previously unmarked graves,[47] and some of these modern stones include unusual and unexpected details, for example, "Typhoid epidemic took life of wife and five children"[48] and, on the Masters family's marker, "5 daughters of Jesse & Margaret d. [died] same day of medicine (poisonous) adm. [administered] by a local Dr."[49]

A related subject is that of rodeo riders' grave markers, and Arkansas contains several examples. These are usually young men whose

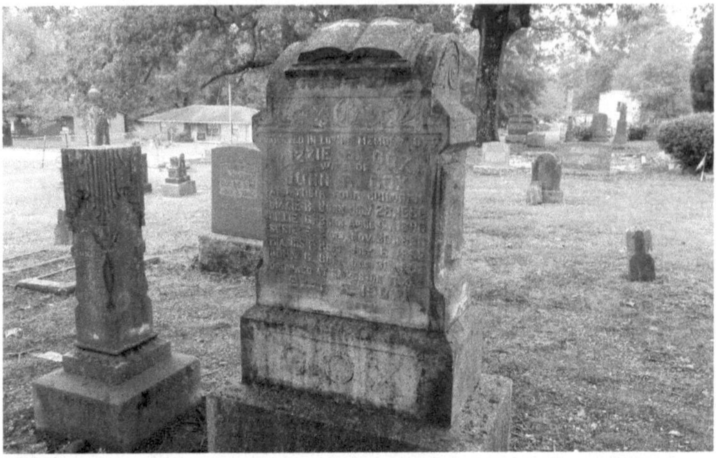

Fig 8.8. The cenotaph for Lizzie Cox and her four children, who were swept away in the Galveston flood of 1900 and their bodies never recovered. Oak Ridge Cemetery, Malvern (Hot Spring Co.).

tombstones contain referential epitaphs ("Entrance fees paid") or show artwork of them atop bucking bulls. An interesting addition to this category is the granite marker of rodeo clown Roger Larry Mawson (1933–2003, Sebastian Co.),[50] which contains two photos of Mawson, one wearing a cowboy hat, and one in clown makeup.

STONES WITHOUT BODIES, BODIES WITHOUT STONES, BURIALS THAT RAISE QUESTIONS

Not all tombstones mark actual burials. Ones that commemorate a burial that took place elsewhere, if burial occurred at all, are known as cenotaphs. Malvern's Oak Ridge Cemetery (Hot Spring Co.) contains an example, a large monument that appears to mark the graves of Lizzie Cox and her four young children yet occupies a space barely large enough to hold a single burial. In fact, no bodies are buried there, and the stone explains why: "Drowned at Galveston, Texas," followed by a single death date, September 8, 1900.

This occurred during the Great Storm of 1900, a hurricane whose storm surge inundated the city and drowned or swept away an estimated eight thousand people, making it the deadliest Atlantic hurricane recorded in this country. (Other estimates put the death toll at six thousand to twelve thousand fatalities.) John Cox, a railroad conductor, survived and though initially his wife and four children were listed among the survivors,[51] eventually she and five children (likely including the addition of niece Katie May Adams) were reported among the lost.[52] Robert M. Smith, his wife, and four of their five children also perished in this storm, but only he is named on a cenotaph in Little Rock's Mount Holly Cemetery, in its Masonic section, due to his having been the Free and Accepted Masons' grand master of Arkansas in 1898. Smith's epitaph reads, "Lost in Galveston Flood September 8, 1900."

John Weaver's tombstone inscription is clear about the absence of his body. Although this stone is located in Ozark, Missouri, for a death that occurred in Memphis, Tennessee, Weaver's body ended up somewhere in Arkansas. The marble tablet gives complete details and two dates for John Weaver, who died at Memphis on March 2, 1854. The reverse side of the tablet explains: "Erected at this place as the spot selected by him for his BURIAL who now lies in White River Ark. from the burning of the CAROLINE Mar. 5, 1854."

Weaver, in Memphis on business during one of that city's episodic cholera epidemics, caught the disease and died. Cholera is contagious and embalming was unknown,[53] so his body was sealed in a metal coffin and placed aboard the steamboat *Caroline* for transport back to Missouri for burial. About twenty miles north of the mouth of the White River the boat caught fire and quickly sank. Forty-five people drowned and, though the ship's safe was later raised, Weaver's coffin and one other were never found. Weaver's cenotaph, in the Weaver Cemetery, was originally placed at a right angle to the other family tombstones, something said to be symbolic of a death at sea, but has now been aligned with other stones in the row.

McFarland Cemetery at Banks (Bradley Co.) contains two graves, and two inscribed grave markers, but it's not known who is buried where. In 1913, Sam White and A. B. Stevans exchanged fatal pistol shots after Stevans refused to pay for his room and board at White's hotel, claiming he was owed money by the hotel's co-owner.[54] Their graves, side by side, went unmarked until 1997, when granddaughters of one of the men were shown the locations and they created inscribed

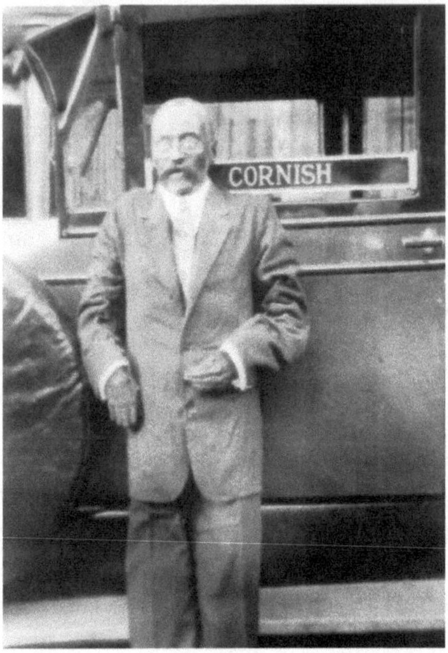

Fig 8.9. The embalmed body of "Old Mike" remained unburied for sixty-four years but is now in De Ann Cemetery, Prescott (Nevada Co.). Image provided by the Nevada County Depot Museum, Prescott, Arkansas.

metal plates set into concrete markers. Not knowing which body was in which grave, each plate states, "Died in a gun duel 3-22-1913," adding "Unknown which graves belongs to which, Whitey or Shorty."[55]

THE UNBURIED

In March 1911 a man, possibly intent on committing suicide, was struck and killed by a freight train near Prescott (Nevada Co.). Undertaker J.D. Cornish retrieved the body, which was tentatively identified as W.C. Heber. This was based on finding this surname written inside the man's shirt collar and the initials on a monogramed handkerchief. No one came looking for him, so Heber was buried in Prescott's De Ann Cemetery in an unmarked grave.[56]

Five months later another unidentified male body was found, this one in Prescott's town park. After a coroner's jury ruled that the man "came to his death by unknown means" (later supposition was that he died from a heart attack), the body was, again, taken charge of by Cornish. But rather than burying this unknown man, Cornish rigidly embalmed him, dressed him in a suit and tie, and propped him up in an open coffin. Supposedly this was done in the hope that someone would come forward and identify him. This didn't happen, despite his having such identifying features as elaborate dental work, a scar, and a distinctive tattoo of a woman standing on a pedestal.[57]

Undertaker Cornish eventually named the body "Old Mike."[58] The corpse became a Prescott personality and a tourist attraction, visited by people searching for missing relatives and by young people seeking a morbid thrill. As time passed Mike's skin darkened and his eye sockets deteriorated and were filled with not especially realistic wide-open artificial eyes. Not only did he receive visitors, children sometimes danced with him[59] and adults performed other disrespectful activities with the corpse.

Mike remained in residence at the Cornish funeral home until employee Henry Shakelford began agitating for a proper burial. In 1975, the state's attorney general compelled Cornish Funeral Home to relinquish the remains, which had now gone unburied for sixty-four years. Shakelford arranged for a grave space in De Ann cemetery and, following a private graveside service, Mike was finally buried. His grave was marked with a funeral home temporary marker embedded in concrete, but decades later someone purchased a small granite marker for him. On it, below the single name "Mike," is an engraving of a pencil and the words "Died Aug. 21, 1911," and "Buried May 12, 1975."

Money may have been the reason why the two bodies were treated differently, as Cornish found twenty dollars hidden in the lining of Heber's coat, enough to pay basic funeral expenses. Mike, a crippled transient who visited Prescott every month to peddle pencils, pins, thread, and other notions, had only eighty cents and a silver spoon on his person.[60] Given that he traveled a regular circuit between Prescott and surrounding cities, it's hard to imagine that *no* one knew his name. In fact, the coroner's jury that convened to examine his corpse very nearly learned it. Witness McElrath told the jury that he had seen the man in Little Rock's police court ten days earlier, in the company of a Pat McFarland, both charged with drunkenness. McFarland, who was actually charged with disturbing the peace, appears in the August 12 police docket, along with J.M. Estes, the only person to be charged with drunkenness.[61] (A man named Ernest McIlwee—likely a misspelling of McElrath—was also arrested that morning.[62])

"Old Mike" was neither Arkansas's first nor only corpse to remain unburied for decades.[63] An earlier case involved "Tommy Moon," a man found dead in a railroad yard at Marianna (Lee Co.) in 1909, embalmed and kept in a local funeral home for fifty-three years. (It was widely but erroneously reported that he got his nickname from being found on a moonlit night by a man named Tommy.) He was believed to have died from malaria.[64]

Moon was still in residence at the Marianna funeral home in 1962 when the business was sold, and its new owner, wishing to be rid of the body, donated it to Little Rock's University of Arkansas Medical Center for research purposes, only to have it returned. The ensuing publicity caught the attention of Leona Berry Peck, who was four years old when her father, ill and seeking work, left home and was never heard from again. Peck's photos of her father provided a positive identification,[65] and the next month he was buried in Vanndale Cemetery (Cross Co.) with his true name and dates: Geo. C. Berry, 1876–1909.[66]

It can be difficult, today, to understand an earlier era's fascination with dead bodies. Both Old Mike and Charlie Moon might have ended up as sideshow attractions. Over the years, various carnivals, circuses, and museums attempted to buy their embalmed remains because the public would have paid to view them.[67] Equally strange is the tale of Peter Le Fevre's adopted niece who kept his bones—and, presumably, his skull with its oversized gold front teeth—in a drawer in her house after her uncle's unusually tall skeleton washed out of its grave long after his death in 1820.[68]

This desire to see and touch death could be related to Southern burial customs, done out of respect and to relieve the family, in which friends and neighbors washed and dressed the body, then sat up all night beside it.[69] Postmortem photography was common, as was the saving of personal mementos (such as locks of hair), while both funeral and graveside services gave mourners the chance to touch the body and to take a last, lingering look before burial.

TOMBSTONES OF AMPUTATED BODY PARTS

> If the union of heart and hand
> Death could untimely sever,
> When we meet in the angel land,
> We can love united forever.
>
> —JOHN A. COULTER, 1827–1857, CANE HILL CEMETERY (WASHINGTON CO.)

Judging from obituaries, life was once vastly more hazardous than it is today. In addition to deaths from infections and diseases that are now easily preventable, people faced dismemberment and death from such things as horse-drawn vehicles, farming machinery, hunting accidents, unregulated factory equipment, sawmill blades, and mining disasters. Job-related accidents were so common among railroad workers that supposedly in the late 1800s the Missouri, Kansas, and Texas freight depot, in Denison, Texas, had a graveyard reserved for the hands, fingers, and legs "mashed and mutilated by the cars" necessitating amputation.[70]

People lost appendages from a variety of accidents, not to mention complications from diabetes. Not all victims chose to have their amputated parts buried beneath tombstones, but at least a dozen such markers are found in Arkansas cemeteries. The inscriptions on these stones range from the vague, "Limb of I.C.E.," to the specific, "One hand of C.C. Humbard," illustrated with an outline of a left hand, representing the one Calvin Humbard had severed by a cotton baler (Carroll Co.).[71] Perhaps the most specific of all is the modern marker in Blackwell Cemetery (Van Buren Co.) that was placed there within the last few years: "Here lies the left foot of Grandpa J.J. Ward, it was removed around 1916 after an ax accident while chopping wood."

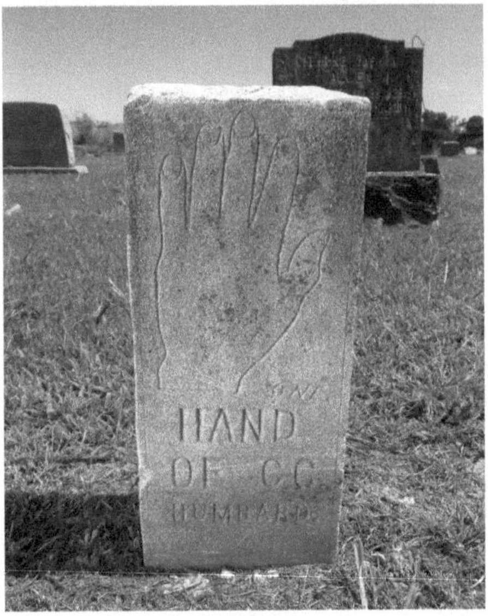

Fig 8.10. Calvin Humbard's amputated left hand has its own tombstone. Hale Cemetery (Carroll Co.).

Given the Christian belief that the physical body will rise at the time of the Resurrection, these stones might seem to be a way to enable amputees to eventually be buried beside their severed parts, and ultimately resurrected with them. However, this wasn't really necessary. New York City orator Rev. T. DeWitt Talmage, in a sermon published in Arkansas newspapers, offered a reassuring picture of what would happen during the Resurrection. "And now the air is darkened with the fragments of bodies that are coming together from opposite corners of the earth," he said in a lecture in 1891. "Lost limbs finding their mate—bone to bone, sinew to sinew—until every joint is reconstructed, and every arm finds its socket, and the amputated limb of the surgeon's table shall be set again at the point from which it was severed."[72]

Folklore, not religion, explains these small markers. "If you should have a part of the body amputated, be sure that it is straightened out and properly buried," wrote folklorist Otto Ernest Rayburn. "Carelessness may cause misery that medicine cannot reach."[73] Marking the burial of the hand, foot, arm, or leg made it easier to find when it became necessary to dig it up and reposition it in the grave to make it lie more comfortably. In an era before there were therapies to combat phantom limb pain (the sensation that the missing limb is contorting painfully, itching, burning, or being bitten by insects), this was the only known way to help a sufferer. Doing so gave the person actual physical relief, though usually only temporarily. This custom is known to have been practiced as late as the 1960s.[74]

The importance of proper burial is illustrated by the actions of Arthur Bone, whose leg was crushed by a tree during a big storm. Bone heeded the advice of a preacher relative who told him, "If you believe and you love God, you will walk on that leg," so Bone did as he was instructed. Unfortunately, this caused additional damage to the leg and it had to be amputated. Another family member gave him some practical advice, in that he would "feel everything that happened" to the leg if it wasn't buried properly. Bone had his leg embalmed, then stood it upright in a container and surrounded it with concrete. He buried the encased leg between his parents' headstones in Fredonia Cemetery (White Co.), where it could be easily found if needed.[75] The limb does not have a tombstone, and Bone is not buried in this cemetery.

Though phantom limb pain was real, and could be excruciating, the subject of digging up and repositioning arms and legs has its humorous side. Singer-songwriter and folklorist Jimmy Driftwood (born James Corbitt Morris, 1907–1998), who grew up in the Timbo community (Stone Co.), said, "I have actually known two old men who have experienced this, and we had to go out and dig their limbs up and straighten them out to stop the pain."[76]

Driftwood wrote and recorded a song on the subject, called "Straighten Out My Laig" (i.e., leg) about a man who broke his leg in two places after falling off a wagonload of moonshine. The amputated leg was buried in a crooked position, causing phantom pain in the victim's big toe. He pleads, in the song's chorus, for "Maude" to straighten out his leg in its grave. The final verse promises her,

> If you'll go down in the holler Maude, to straighten out my laig,
> I'll hold you tight and dance all night on my old wooden peg.
> We'll live a life of gladness, like we did in days of yore,
> 'Cause when you straighten out my laig it won't hurt any more.[77]

References to amputations turn up in unusual places, such as the nicknames "Peg Leg" and "Nub" found on headstones, or a photo-ceramic showing a person with an empty sleeve. The 1912 burial log kept by J.M. Moore, a Fayetteville (Washington Co.) gravedigger, shows that he charged fifty cents to bury Charles Hopkins's arm, amputated after Hopkins was shot, at a time when $8 was the fee to dig an adult's grave.[78] In 1891, James Dwyer was run over by a switch engine in Fort Smith (Sebastian Co.), which severed both of his legs and caused his death three days later. His wife paid $125 to have him washed, embalmed, dressed, casketed, and shipped to Fort Scott, Kansas, for burial. The undertaker's fee included a $10 charge for disinterring the legs and shipping them separately in a zinc box.[79]

The body parts mentioned in the stories above do not have grave markers, but others do. What follows are Arkansas limbs buried beneath their own tombstones:

> Limb of
> H. Earls
> 4–62

Henry Earls (1891–1969), New Hope Cemetery (Yell Co.), lost his leg below the knee from complications from diabetes.[80]

> Here lies the leg
> of Minnie Eoff

Found near the headstone shared by Minnie Eoff (1911–1969) and her husband in Liberty Cemetery (Newton Co.). Eoff lost a limb to diabetes in 1968.[81] The site was marked with a modern granite block some time between 2017 and 2020.

> Limb of I.C.E.

Found beside the grave of Iva C. Evans (1903–1914), Rambo Cemetery (Benton Co.).

Tony Finley
Left Arm
Juy [sic] 20 1960

Lewis Francis "Tony" Finley (1943–2019), Horatio Cemetery (Sevier Co.). Finley's arm was severed in an accident when he was sixteen years old.[82]

Alva's Arm
Amputated
Nov. 3, 1882

Alva Greer (1866–1893), Highland Cemetery, Ozark (Franklin Co.), is buried in the same plot, dying ten and a half years after he lost his arm in a sawmill accident. The stone is signed by M.L. Wright. Greer's family plot is filled with tombstones embellished with clasping hands and upwardly pointing ones. Greer's epitaph is oddly chosen, considering the loss of his appendage, as it begins, "Thy hands are clasped upon thy breast . . ."

One hand of C.C. Humbard

This small stone, showing an outline of a left hand, is found in Hale Cemetery (Carroll Co.). The letters BY-RD are below the inscription, possibly the signature of the carver. Calvin C. Humbard (1858–1938) and wife Martha are buried several rows distant from the hand.

LEG

Nothing is known about this, other than that it's among graves with the Miller surname, Shaver Campground Cemetery, Oxford (Izard Co.)

Arm of O.L. (Jufe) Nall

Mill Accident 1898

Oscar Lee "Jufe" Nall (1883–1946). The arm's grave is inside a woven wire fence in the Sheridan Cemetery (Grant Co.); Nall is buried elsewhere in the same cemetery.

Limbs of Dora Potter

This inscription is found on the marker Dora Gertrude Potter (1896–1972) shares with her husband in Mt. Zion Cemetery (Greene Co.).

A.B. Sosebee Leg

Arfastus Benivus Neab Sosebee (1872–1964) is buried in the same plot as his leg in Ozark's Highland Cemetery (Franklin Co.).

Sam's Leg

Sam Swindle (1910–1973), Scott-Wehunt Cemetery (Montgomery Co.). Swindle, suffering from osteomyelitis, was twelve when his leg was amputated on a kitchen table by a local doctor and a pharmacist. Swindle was buried next to his leg when he died sixty-one years later.[83]

Jesse Tabor's Foot

This is the first burial listed on signage at the entrance to Old Midway Cemetery (Marion Co.), but the grave is marked only with an uncarved fieldstone; Tabor's own burial site is unknown. Old Midway was created by combining three area cemeteries during the creation of Bull Shoals dam and lake, and Tabor's foot—actually, his entire leg, injured in a hunting accident—was removed from Yocham Bend cemetery between 1947 and 1951.[84] The Army Corps of Engineers originally marked these graves with wooden headboards, at which time the grave was identified as being that of Tabor's foot.[85]

"Here lies the left foot of Grandpa J.J. Ward, it was removed around 1916 after an ax accident while chopping wood."

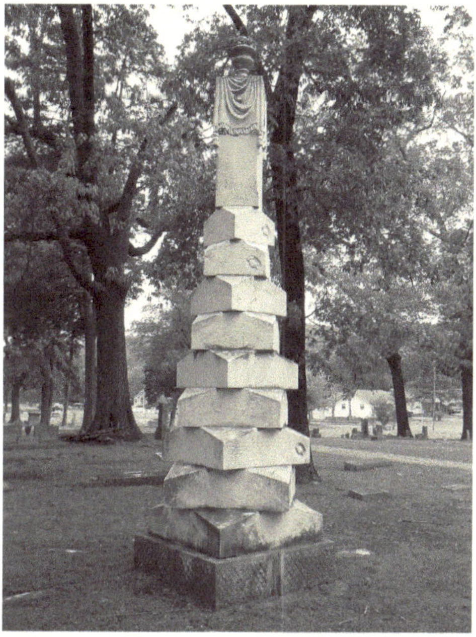

Fig 8.11. Members of the Smith and Ward families are buried radiating out from this central block pile. Greenwood Cemetery, Hot Springs (Garland Co.).

In the family plot of J.J. Ward (1874–1957), in Blackwell Cemetery, near Bee Branch (Van Buren Co.). The spot was marked with a cinderblock until about 2020. Oddly, the artwork on the stone shows the upturned sole of a right foot, not a left.

Lastly, there is something attached to a grave marker that, while not a body part, was once part of a man's body. Rising from the flat granite slab on Joseph Newman's grave in Fountain Lake's Rockdale Cemetery (2010, Garland Co.) is Newman's artificial hip, made of polished surgical steel.[86]

OTHER ARKANSAS ODDITIES

To thy dear memory, darling, and my own
I build in grief, this monumental stone.

All that it tells of life, in death, is thine,
All that it tells of death, in life, is mine.
For that which made thy pure spirit blest
In anguish deep has brought me great unrest.
You, dying, live to find a life divine
I, living, die till death shall make thee mine.

If the Smith and Ward families intended to commission a startlingly unusual marker for their shared plot in Hot Springs' Greenwood Cemetery (Garland Co.), they certainly succeeded. This Jenga-like pile of stacked marble blocks, over twelve feet high, is topped by a draped rectangular column that is in turn crowned with a three-dimensional urn full of marble flowers.

Some of the stacked blocks are embellished with carvings of little hands pointing to the six names (with death dates spanning 1870 to 1888, three of them in 1880) and the above epitaph, which, though unusual, is not original.[87] In-ground marble markers radiate out from the block pile like spokes on a wheel. It is a rare Arkansas example of a New England burial tradition known as a "pie."

A rough-hewn stone box crypt in Van Buren's Fairview Cemetery (Crawford Co.) is ordinary by Ozark burial standards, yet claims a whopper of an urban legend. According to a plaque attached to one end of the box, "Legend says this grave is one of DeSoto's men. Marks on headstone may be Masonic emblem," while a 1970 cemetery enumeration asserts, "It was here when the first white man came."[88] Online sources further burnish the myth by speculating that it could be a Viking grave, which would make that primitive emblem a rune, not a Masonic compass and square.

There is simply no basis for this far-fetched myth. Spanish explorer DeSoto and his soldiers came through Arkansas in 1541–1542. Roughly half of the six hundred soldiers who accompanied DeSoto died on this expedition, and the remainder had neither the energy nor the resources to carve stone crypts for their dead.[89] A more compelling argument is that Freemasonry was not known in Spain until the early 1700s. Immigrants to the Ozarks routinely created stone box crypts as well as necked discoid (head and shoulders) shapes, often in combination, as is found at one end of the box in Fairview Cemetery.

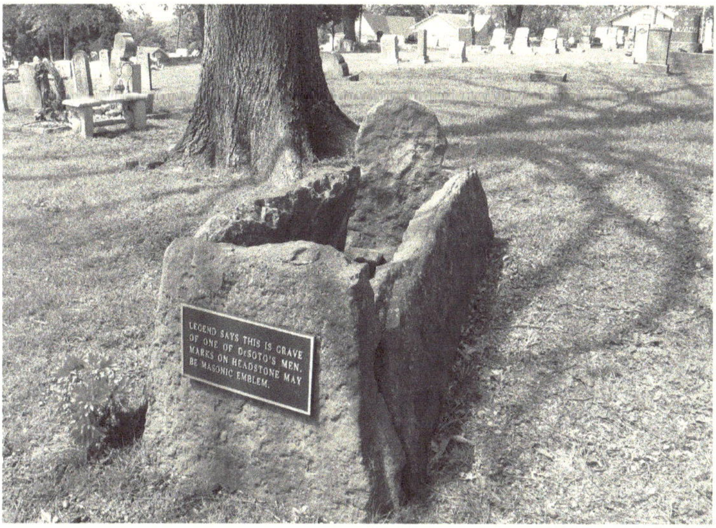

Fig 8.12. A box crypt mistakenly claimed to be the grave of one of DeSoto's explorers, in Fairview Cemetery, Van Buren (Crawford Co.).

Fairview's earliest recorded grave dates to 1816 and, according to cemetery history, "Community members dug the ['DeSoto'] grave up in the 1930s believing it was the site of buried treasure, as opposed to that of an actual burial site. The excavators discovered nothing more than 'bones and tacks' and presumably everything was reburied."[90]

> As I was walking across a field the other day I came to a field I thought was laying out, but I discovered it was a cotton patch. Down near the end I saw a grave and on the monument was a verse that read as follows: "Brother W.A. Barnard is dead; but not forgotten; if he had not died he would have hoed this cotton."
>
> —*FRANKLIN COUNTY NEWS*, JULY 7, 1916[91]

1. Oak Hill Cemetery, Booneville
(Logan)

2. Locksburg Cemetery **(Sevier)**

3. Harkey's Valley Cemetery
(Yell)

4. Walnut Lake Cemetery, Dumas
(Desha)

5. Whitley Cemetery, Cabot
(Lonoke)

6. Mount Holly Cemetery,
Little Rock
Oakland & Fraternal Cemetery,
Little Rock
(Pulaski)

7. Chickasawba, aka Founders Park,
Blytheville
(Mississippi)

8. Oaklawn Cemetery, Batesville
(Independence)

9. Oark Town Cemetery
(Johnson)

10. Arkansas River | **11.** Mississippi River

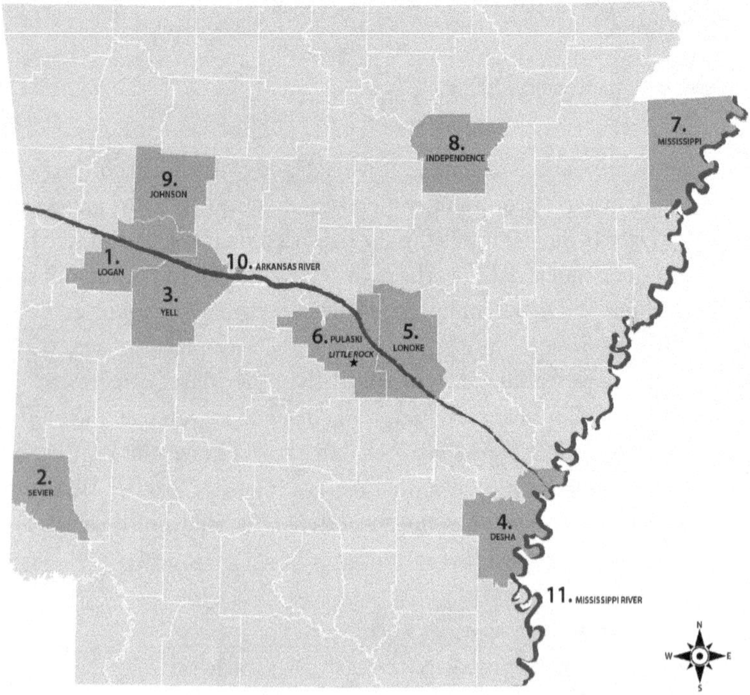

Major locations discussed in chapter 9.
Map by Red Rooster Design, Fayetteville, Arkansas.

Chapter 9

READING STONES, COLLECTING STORIES

On living tablets of the heart,
His virtues are engraved.
Then seek not in the works of art,
The record of his praise.

—ROBERT NICHOLS JEFFREYS, 1804–1850, TULIP CEMETERY (DALLAS CO.)

It would be a shame to miss what an older tombstone is telling us if we cannot fully make out an inscription, or if we misinterpret the symbolism found there. Still, there are ways of overcoming such problems. The first is by using noninvasive methods to either light up, or clean, a headstone to make it legible. The second is by using a guide to cemetery symbolism, rather than making assumptions. Such guesswork has caused family genealogists to surmise that Grandma served in the navy because there's an anchor on her headstone or, worse, that she was into Satanism after mistaking the Eastern Star emblem for a pentagram.

UNDERSTANDING GRAVE ORIENTATION

Why are Christians buried on an east-west axis, and why is this relevant when reading and photographing tombstones?

An east-west burial orientation is the norm in most parts of the country, and for most religious denominations. This comes from the Christian belief that the body will rise when Jesus returns—presumably from the east—at the Resurrection. (There are rare exceptions, such as burial on a north-south axis for someone who proudly refused to turn his back on the South, or the entirety of the oldest stone grave covers in Carroll County's Teeter cemetery,[1] whose north-south orientation has no explanation.) Bodies are positioned with their feet pointing toward the east so the supine body will rise facing that direction. Inscriptions, however, may be placed on either the east- *or* west-facing side of the marker, or sometimes both.

It helps to think of the grave as a bed, and the tombstone as its headboard. The writing on the oldest markers is usually placed on the west-facing, or reverse, side of the headboard or tombstone, the side that faces away from the bed or burial. Older markers are often covered in writing, including lengthy epitaphs in a very small typeface. Early visitors wanted to read these inscriptions without standing on the grave, which was both taboo and risky because, prior to the use of burial vaults, graves could collapse when their contents settled. Modern markers, however, place the inscriptions on the side directly above the bed, or burial, which is protected by a vault. As it is now the norm to use large typefaces and short inscriptions, visitors have no difficulty reading them from a distance.

Unfortunately, in recent times some cemetery groundskeepers have turned the older tablet-style markers around to face the opposite direction, making it impossible to know which side of the stone the burial is on. They have also removed footstones, which once gave a visual representation of the grave's length and, thus, the relative age of its occupant. Some modern cemeteries have begun to abandon the east-west grave orientation, perhaps to save space, and it is not a rule in Jewish and Catholic cemeteries.

Because the oldest markers generally have their inscriptions on the west-facing side of the stone, it pays to arrive in a graveyard around noon, or early afternoon, for the greatest legibility. Arrive too early and the sun, rising on the eastern side of the marker, will cause the inscription to be in shadow; arrive too late in the day and setting sun's afternoon light will bounce off the stone, overexposing the writing and making it difficult to read. It's also necessary to take daylight savings time into account when planning an arrival time. Winter visits are preferable for many reasons, including leafless trees casting fewer shadows on headstones, and less threat from ticks, chiggers, and snakes.

Even stones that are in shadow can be lit up on a sunny day by using a reflective surface, such as a large photo reflector, available where photographic equipment is sold, or with a full-length mirror. This is done by standing some distance from the stone and angling the reflective surface to direct a beam of light across the headstone, which can be difficult to do singlehandedly. Individual lines of writing can be illuminated by holding a bright flashlight perpendicular to the carving. Heavy encrustations of lichen can be lightly brushed away with a soft bristle brush before taking pictures, but first be sure that the marker is not loose in its base or socket, and do not scrub or put pressure on the stone.

No matter which side of the stone the writing is found on, be sure to check *both* sides. The backs of older tombstones sometimes hold additional artwork, the continuation of long epitaphs, the deceased's cause of death, a carver's signature, or the deceased's dying words. The backs of modern granite markers may contain lasered artwork, genealogy charts (including, in one instance, the deceased's twelve husbands and the dates she married them),[2] or poems written by grandchildren. There are even deliberate jokes, such as "Gone to Walmart," on the back of Cecil Rankin's marker (died 1996, Crawford Co.),[3] or Leo Ammons's marker (died 2006, Madison Co.).[4] The front of Ammons's marker notes that he "laughed often," while the reverse side offers proof: "I made a lot of deals in my lifetime . . . but I sure went in the hole on this one."

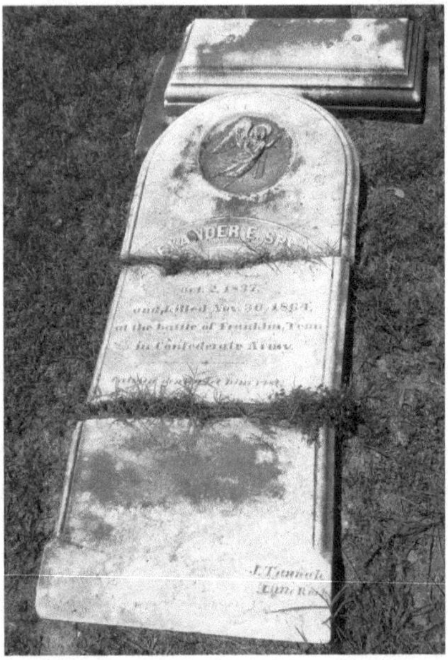

Fig 9.1. Alexander E. Spense's 1864 tombstone is signed, lower right corner, by Little Rock carver J. Tunnah, in Rose Hill Cemetery, Arkadelphia (Clark Co.).

CARVERS' SIGNATURES

Right up to the year 1900, it was common for tombstone carvers to sign their work. These signatures, also called makers' marks, are usually found near the front, bottom edge of a tablet-style stone. Unfortunately, this is exactly where breakage is most likely to occur, where stones that were reset in their bases have mortar obscuring this writing, or where writing may have sunk below ground level. On monument-style markers a signature might appear just about anywhere, though often located on the side of a stacked base.

Rosebrough Sons of St. Louis, the company that shipped more tombstones into Arkansas than any other, signed along the front lower left edge of their tablets. Both itinerant and established carvers tended to sign at the lower right edge but generally did not include a business location. Out-of-state monument companies sometimes did. F. Horn & Co. of St. Louis even included their street address on the first marker they sold in Jonesboro's city cemetery (Craighead Co.)[5] but not on subsequent ones as, presumably, customers now knew how to reach them.

With the exception of a few rural carvers, almost all signing stopped in the year 1900. This was a time when customers wanted granite, not locally quarried stone, something itinerant carvers could not supply. This led to the establishment, in larger towns and cities, of monument dealers who had granite markers shipped in from quarries as far away as Vermont and Georgia. Technology changed, too, from hand-carving with mallets and chisels to the use of sandblasters, pneumatic tools, and other industrial equipment.

SYMBOLISM

The difference between correctly interpreting the symbol on a headstone and completely misunderstanding it is, to steal and alter a quote by Mark Twain (who stole it from fellow humorist Josh Billings), the difference between lightning and lightning bug. Such misunderstandings can easily lead a genealogist astray, such as taking literally a carving of a Native American in a feathered headdress, which rather than being proof of Native American ancestry, means exactly the opposite. This emblem denotes membership in the Red Men fraternal lodge, which was "whites only" until 1974.

We owe it to our ancestors to correctly interpret their headstones just as, one day, we hope cemetery visitors will understand us through what we put on our markers. Numerous books have been written about cemetery symbolism, and there is no need to duplicate that information here. However, because certain symbols have caused confusion, the following is a guide to ones (all of which are found in Arkansas cemeteries) that are most commonly misunderstood.

Anchor: Unless "US Navy" or "United States Marines" is inscribed with it, the anchor represents hope: the hope of salvation, of the soul being safely in Heaven, of loved ones being reunited. Each of the three

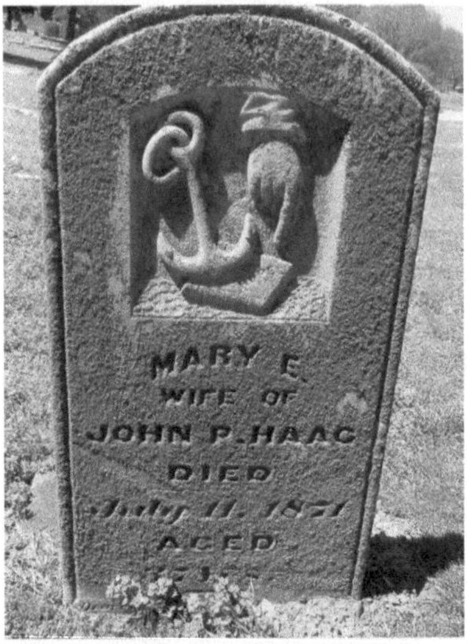

Fig 9.2. Symbols, used in combinations, can preach a sermon. Here God's hand points to an anchor (representing hope) resting on a Bible. Mary E. Haac (died 1871), Oak Cemetery, Fort Smith (Sebastian Co.).

theological virtues, Faith, Hope, and Charity, is portrayed holding a representative item, and Hope is always shown with an anchor. (Charity is rarely depicted, while statues of Faith show her with a Bible under one arm and her other hand pointing heavenward.) On tombstones, anchors are sometimes found in combination with doves, pointing fingers, and Bibles, and they also show up in epitaphs, such as the popular "Anchored safe where storms are o'er."

Broken columns and broken obelisks: Sometimes mistaken for vandalism, the snapped-off Corinthian column or Egyptian obelisk represents the life cut short by death. This is appropriate no matter how long the person's life was, and column height sometimes corresponds to the person's age. (A cluster of columns, of varying heights, may be used to denote the deaths of several children within one family.[6]) The column may be three-dimensional, its top portion missing or leaning against its base, or a bas-relief carving that, clearly, cannot be the work of vandals.

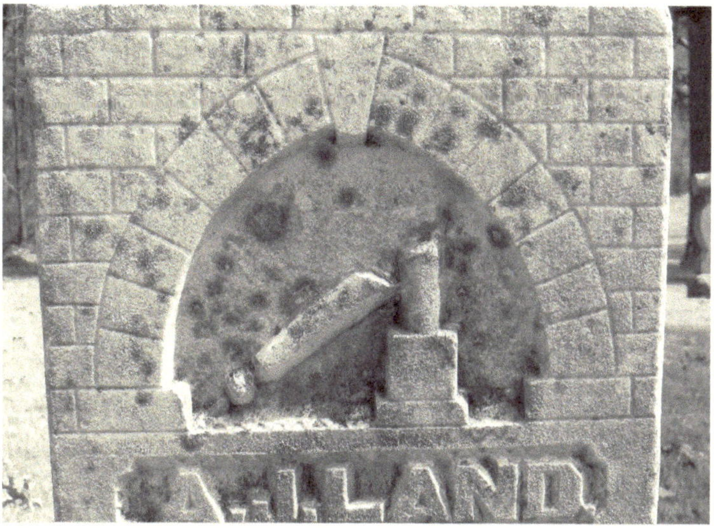

Fig 9.3. The broken obelisk represents the life cut short by death. A.L. Land (1843–1883) and son Edmund (1881–1882). IOOF Cemetery, now Eureka Springs Cemetery (Carroll Co.).

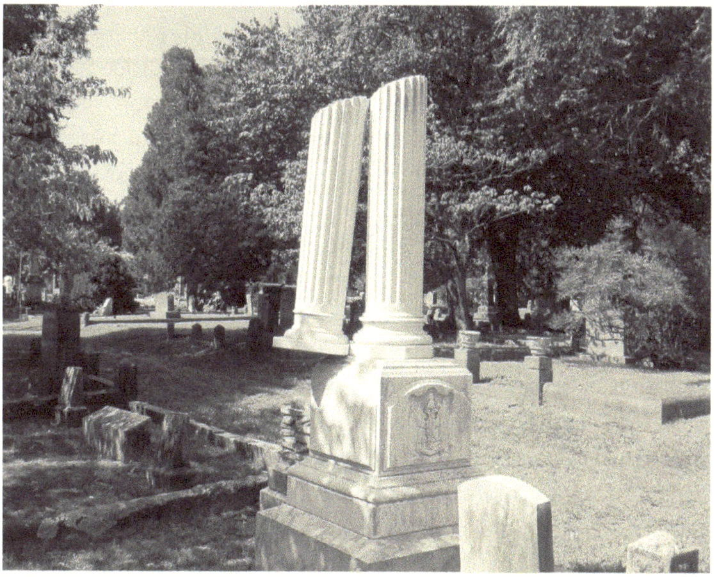

Fig 9.4. The broken column, like the obelisk, also represents the life cut short by death and is not the result of vandalism. R.S. Page (1855–1899). This is one of several three-dimensional, broken column markers in Mount Holly Cemetery, Little Rock (Pulaski Co.).

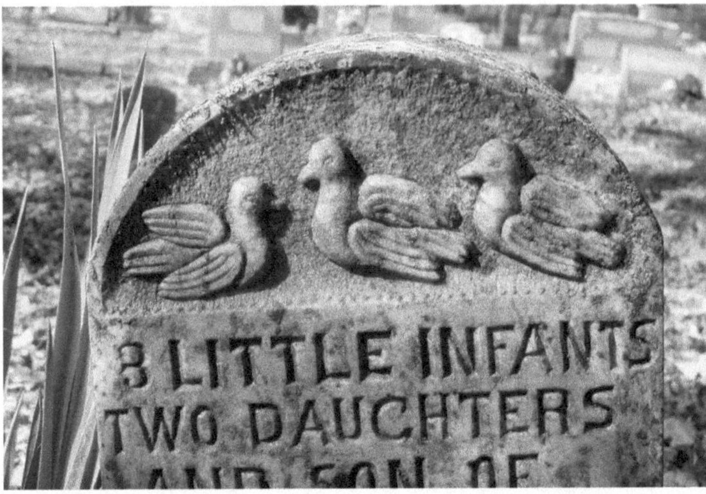

Fig 9.5. Doves represent the soul in flight, and multiple doves—or lambs or flowers—represent multiple deaths. The Howerton triplets (born and died 1899) are represented by three identical doves in Oark Cemetery (Johnson Co.).

Doubles and multiples: Deaths of a mother and child, usually in childbirth, are sometimes portrayed with paired emblems, such as a large and a small bird, two crowns, or a rose and a bud. Multiple emblems (cherubs, rosebuds, doves) are often used to represent the loss of multiple children. The headstone of thirteen-year-old Grant Earle McVey (died 1881, Carroll Co.), has a butterfly that has emerged from a chrysalis, as well as two tightly closed buds, tucked into one corner of the emblem. The buds represent Grant and his twenty-month-old brother, who died ten years earlier, and who does not have a tombstone.[7]

Doves: The dove conveys the soul to heaven or, when depicted with a bud, blossom, or leaf in its beak, represents the soul in flight. Children's burials sometimes show a three-dimensional dove with one broken wing, positioned at the base of a log or tree stump. While dimensional carvings of lambs portray them as living, and alert, the broken-winged doves are always dead.

Flowers: Though practically every type of flower can be found in funerary carvings, the most popular are lilies, representing death

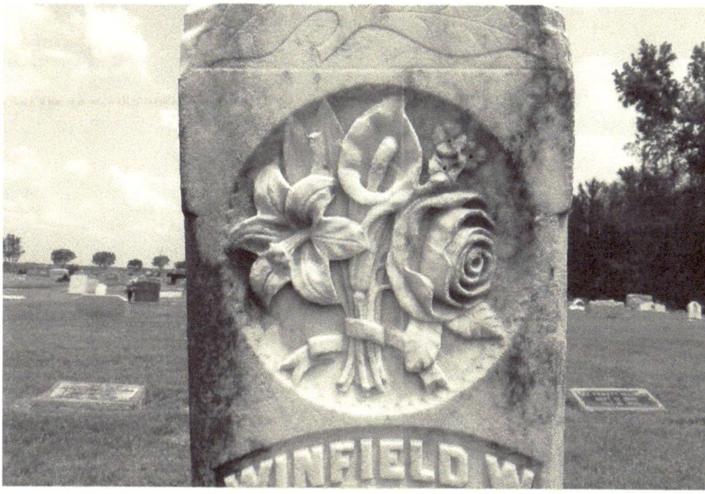

Fig 9.6. Flowers represent the beauty and brevity of life, with lilies, roses, and buds found most often, here combined with forget-me-nots. Winifield W. Holmes (1847–1897), Walnut Lake, Dumas (Desha Co.).

and resurrection; fully opened roses, representing adult lives; and buds for infants and children. Less common are lilies of the valley, forget-me-nots, and bleeding hearts, likely chosen for their names' significance, while poppies, used to make opium, are associated with sleep and death. Sunflowers are found in Catholic cemeteries and symbolize religious devotion because "the sun represents the divine light of God and the sunflower represents the devout striving toward God." Significantly, "when it matures, the flowers permanently face east" the same direction toward which most graves are oriented.[8] A few early Arkansas carvers re-created flowers they saw growing in nature, such as trillium, trout lilies, daffodils, dogwood, and primroses.

No matter what the flower, one depicted with a bent or snapped stem signifies the life cut short by death, blooming not in this world but in the next. Images of flowers separated from their stems go back, in this country, at least as far as the 1700s.

> I lay the Laurel wreath above
> The Cedar with its Sacred ties,

And place them with a husband's love
Where my lost "Lutie" lies.

Fresh Morning-glory buds I twine
With scarlet Woodbine laid beneath,
And mingled with them Eglantine
For my loved Lutie's Wreath.[9]

—LUCRETIA J. ("LUTIE") KEATTS, DIED SEPTEMBER 11, 1866, AGE FORTY-ONE, MOUNT HOLLY CEMETERY, LITTLE ROCK (PULASKI CO.)

Gates Ajar: Although its meaning may seem obvious—Heaven's gates opening to receive the incoming soul—this emblem is actually quite nuanced. It originated in a spiritualist novel by Elizabeth Stuart Phelps Ward, published after the Civil War, that gave comfort to the "helpless, outnumbering, unconsulted women" grieving their terrible losses in the war's aftermath.[10] A hugely popular best-seller, *The Gates Ajar* was eventually followed by two sequels, also having "gates" in their titles, which is significant because the books' healing message derives from the fact that God has not shut the gates "which bar heaven from our sight." This means that the deceased, in Heaven, can keep watch over the living and thus have not really left their loved ones behind.

Mail order companies such as Sears, Roebuck and Montgomery Ward sold grave markers with the gates ajar emblem. The symbol did not become popular on Arkansas tombstones until the 1900s and, in its earliest usage, was often combined with older iconography, which is why anchors, lambs, doves, roses, and clasping and pointing hands have all been depicted in the space above the gates, along with the emblems of just about every fraternal lodge. Though not common, crossed rifles denoting soldiers' deaths were also carved above the gates.

Hands: The Bible forbids making graven images, and perhaps for this reason God is not depicted on headstones. However, there is no prohibition against showing God's hand. This usually takes the form of a descending hand that grasps flowers or breaks a length of chain, slipping one link, representing the soul, onto a finger to convey to heaven.

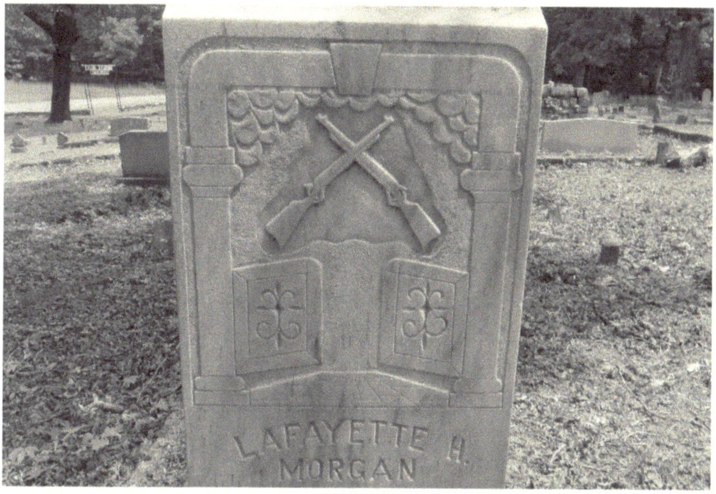

Fig 9.7. The gates ajar symbol, popularized after the Civil War, often includes older symbols (flowers, clasping hands, fraternal lodge emblems) positioned above the gates. Here, crossed rifles represent Lafayette H. Morgan (1890–1918), "Killed in Action," Harkey's Valley Cemetery (Yell Co.).

Upwardly pointing (human) fingers are a reminder of heaven, or call attention to such inscriptions as "We shall meet again" or "Gone Home." Clasping hands show the literal farewell between the living and the dead (a part of the funeral or burial service) because the hand that emerges from the left side of the emblem usually has straight, stiff fingers (the dead hand) with the opposite hand actively clasping it in farewell. Cuffs, though occasionally gender-specific, have no bearing on whether the deceased was male or female.

Fraternal organizations (discussed below) used identifying symbols or combinations of symbols. A number of these lodges included clasping hands in their emblems (or did in early versions, later simplified), including the Masons, Odd Fellows, United Mine Workers of America, the Western Catholic Union, the American Federation of Labor, and the Modern Brotherhood of America.

Occasionally one discovers an emblem not included in books on cemetery symbolism, and these are sometimes original depictions involving human hands. Examples include a hand grasping the handle of a walking stick (T.M. Baskin, 1807–1889, Harmony Cemetery, Johnson Co.), upraised hands in "peekaboo" position (Jonathan Cavaness,

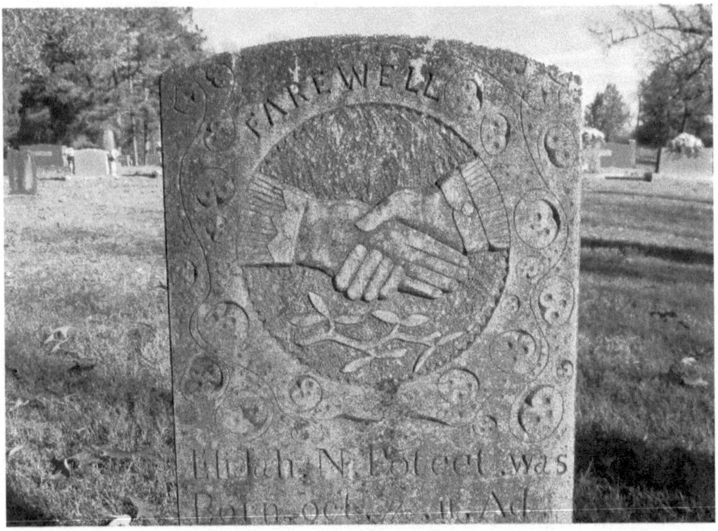

Fig 9.8. Clasping hands represent the farewell between the dead (with stiff fingers, on the left) and the living (actively clasping, on the right). Elijah N. Poteet (1812–1882), Harmony Cemetery (Johnson Co.).

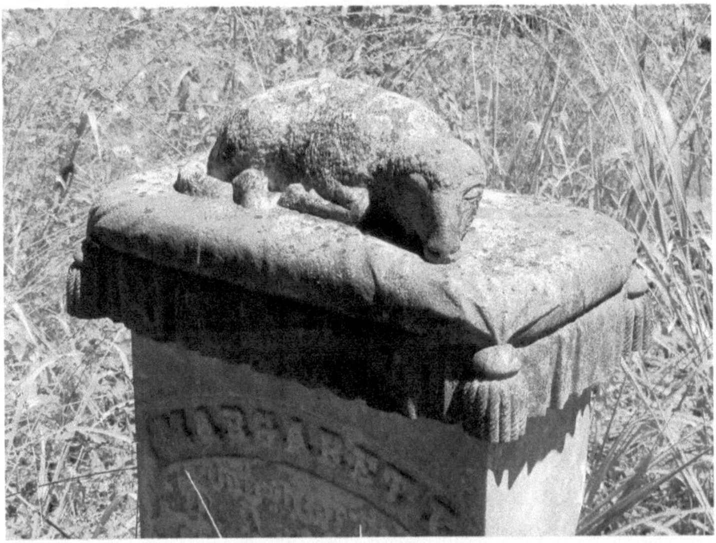

Fig 9.9. Lambs, said to represent innocence, are often found on children's gravestones but are a Christian symbol appropriate for all ages. Margaret Cherry (1858–1859), Whitley Cemetery, Cabot (Lonoke Co.).

1879–1880, Mount Pleasant Cemetery, Drew Co.), and a proffered handshake (James M. Hickman, 1823–1887, Eureka Springs' IOOF Cemetery, Carroll Co.). It's hard to know what was intended by the limp hand on the obelisk of William Gill (1861–1881) in Springdale's Bluff Cemetery (Washington Co.), a man crushed to death by a pile of lumber,[11] but Dr. John Hunt (1817–1894), buried in the same cemetery, leaves no doubt about the meaning of his emblem. A stylized hand points at the words, "Here is a hand for those in the dim future who aid in freeing the world from the slavery of priestcraft and superstition."

Lambs: Both three-dimensional and bas-relief carvings of lambs are commonly found on children's graves, said to represent innocence and purity, but the lamb is a Christian symbol (Jesus is the shepherd; his followers are his flock) and thus is appropriate for marking deaths at all ages. Some early carvers likely had never seen an actual lamb, and some lacked either the skill or the patterns needed to create realistic representations. As a result, some primitive carvings of lambs more closely resemble children's toys or hedgehogs, pigs, weasels, or floppy-eared bunnies; a few have understandably been mistaken for dogs.

Ropes: Symbolism guidebooks say that a rope represents eternity. Perhaps coincidentally, newspaper accounts of hangings would say that the condemned was "launched into eternity" at the end of the hangman's rope. In most cases, however, carvings of rope are merely decorative features that loop around an inscription panel or hang down the sides of a marker.

One possible exception is the three-dimensional carving of a thick twist of rope stretched across the top edge of Sam and Mose Vogel's shared monument in the Jewish section of Little Rock's Oakland and Fraternal Cemetery (both died 1901, Pulaski Co.). Just three months after father Mose's death, which necessitated son Sam going to work as an errand boy for a department store, Sam was killed on the job. Sam's epitaph compares his life to that of a bud just beginning to open and concludes:

> But just as it was opening,
> To the glory of the days

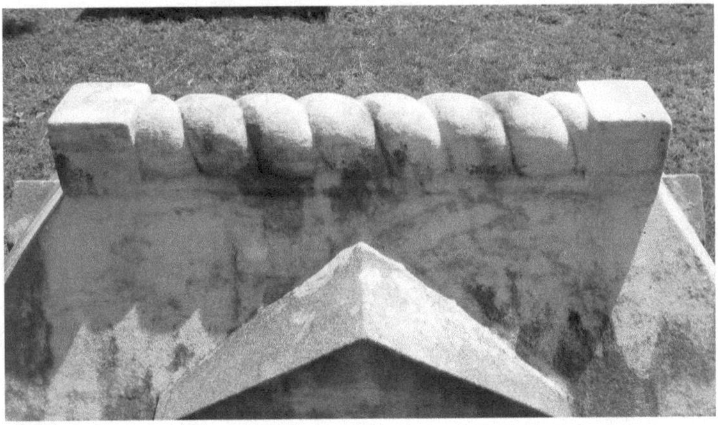

Fig 9.10. This cable-sized rope could symbolize the connection between father and son, or hint at how son Sam Vogel (1888–1901) died. Oakland and Fraternal Cemetery, Little Rock (Pulaski Co.).

Down came the heavenly angel
And took our bud away.

In reality, it was a freight elevator's three-quarter-ton counterweight that "came down" as the elevator's car rose in the shaft, a place Sam had been repeatedly warned to stay out of. But the sight was irresistible to the twelve-year-old, who hung over a railing in order to watch the car ascend, unaware of the descending counterweight, which struck him on the back of the head, killing him and pinning his body against the railing.[12] The rope carved on the Vogels' marker may represent the connection between father and son, joined together through eternity, but given how Sam died, it may literally represent the agent of his death.

Trees: The weeping willow, a popular funereal symbol in the 1800s, has a sorrowful name but also a backstory associating it with the Gospel of Jesus, "because the tree will flourish and remain whole no matter how many branches are cut off."[13] It presented problems for some early carvers who, once again, may never have seen a willow and who had difficulty carving the many long, delicate fronds that support the tree's deciduous leaves.

Although entire oak trees are not found in carvings, their leaves and acorns are. Sometimes only an acorn's empty cap is shown amid a cluster of oak leaves, suggesting that the acorn is now replanted and flourishing in Heaven. Even an illustrious life could be summed up by a single acorn, as in the case of Captain Andrew Randolph Porter's massive sandstone obelisk in Batesville's Oaklawn Cemetery (1847, Independence Co.). Porter was killed in the battle of Buena Vista, during the Mexican-American War, and his marker lengthily extols his intellect, virtues, and patriotism, which may explain why the acorn, perched at the top of his obelisk, is the size of a basketball.

Arkansas graveyards contain a few examples of the once-popular three-dimensional stone tree that has one or more dangling branches (representing death, sometimes of other family members). During the mid-1800s there was also a fad for "rustic" imagery such as stone tree limbs and twigs, carved to show intact bark, used on everything from plot curbing to benches and other stone furniture.[14] Small chairs—almost always rustic ones—represent the person no longer alive to sit there and are not intended for use by the living. All of these are separate from the often massive, limbless stone tree trunks placed on members' graves by popular insurance lodges, discussed below.

Fraternal lodges: Fraternalism flourished between the end of the Civil War and the Depression, a time when health and life insurance coverage was not readily available. The Odd Fellows' creed includes the injunction to bury the dead (which led to the establishment of cemeteries), while other fraternal lodges offered burial insurance to their members, end-of-life care, or burial space within a communal plot. People could join multiple lodges based on the benefits each one offered. (See chapter 2 for information on specific African American lodges.)

> The capstone is finished
> Our labour is o'er the sound
> Of the gavel shall hail us no more.
>
> —RICHARD DAVIS, 1823–1870, DAVIS CEMETERY, MT. JUDEA (NEWTON CO.)

The Free and Accepted Masons and the Independent Order of Odd Fellows (IOOF) are the best-known of the fraternal lodges, both having large memberships and both having survived the Depression. Neither one provided members with tombstones, but their emblems are found on grave markers everywhere: the compass and square on a Mason's marker, while the Eastern Star, the women's lodge, uses a five-pointed star. Odd Fellows use three links of chain and F-L-T (Friendship—Love—Truth) while their women's lodge, the Daughters of Rebekah, originally used a dove flying through a crescent moon surrounded by seven stars.

Though known as "secret" organizations, lodges' meeting times and locations were well publicized, and cities took pride in their numbers. A 1905 Little Rock directory listed the Masons and Scottish Rite Masons, Odd Fellows, Pythians (i.e., Knights of Pythias), Woodmen, Eagles, and Elks as all having lodge halls of their own, but numerous smaller lodges also used these halls for their meetings. The Order of Railway Conductors Hall allowed the Ancient Order of United Workmen (AOUW) and the Knights of Pythias chapters to meet there, along with various other railroad brotherhoods. These included the Brotherhoods of Locomotive Engineers, Firemen, and Trainmen, all three being separate lodges and just some of the railroad careers that had job-specific brotherhoods.[15]

Some lodges left a record of their existence on their members' tombstones in the form of symbols and enigmatic initials whose meanings were known only to initiates. Eastern Star markers sometimes include collections of letters arranged in circles: "F-A-T-A-L," which stands for "Fairest Among Thousands Altogether Lovely," A-M-R-Y, an anagram for "Mary" and FNDOZBTKC, which stands for "Fear not, daughter of Zion, Behold, the King cometh" (John 12:15). Masons who attain the rank of ancient grand master may put HTWSSTKS on their markers, which stands for "Hiram The Widow's Son Sent To King Solomon."

None of these lodge emblems attract attention quite like life-sized stone tree trunks and stacks of logs, sometimes depicted with axes, mauls, and splitting wedges carved on the emblem and, sometimes, also leaning against the trunks. These are the grave markers provided by the Modern Woodmen of America, the Woodmen of the

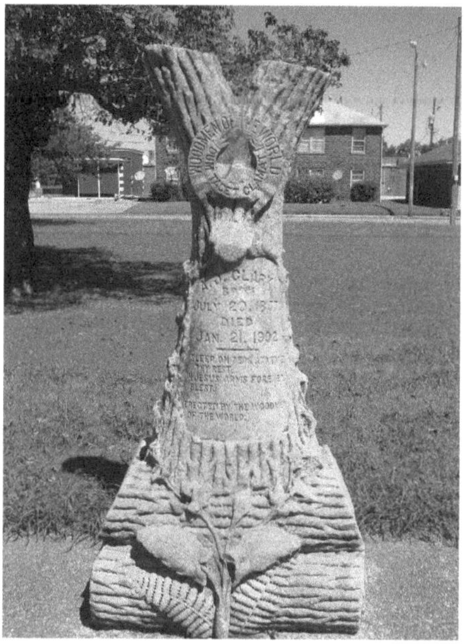

Fig 9.11. An example of one style of tombstone provided by the Woodmen of the World as a death benefit. A.J. Clark (1857–1902), Chickasawba, a.k.a. Founders Park Cemetery, Blytheville (Mississippi Co.).

World, and their adjacent women's fraternity, the Woodmen's Circle. To borrow the Woodmen of the World's motto, *Dum Tacet Clamet* ("Though silent, he speaks"), despite being literally silent, these headstones speak eloquently of the life that was cut down by death and, with their sheer presence in cemeteries across the country, of the popularity and importance of fraternalism.

These two organizations primarily sold life insurance. Initially the Woodmen of the World insured only white men in the prime of life, living in the healthiest states, and working the safest jobs.[16] They also offered the trappings of fraternalism, sponsoring brass bands, close order drill, oratorical contests, and special ceremonies when unveiling their members' tombstones. Though the tree trunk designs were originally supplied by the company, eventually local carvers began adding their own interpretations with additional symbolism. Arkansas's largest and strangest of these is the massive tree trunk, laid on

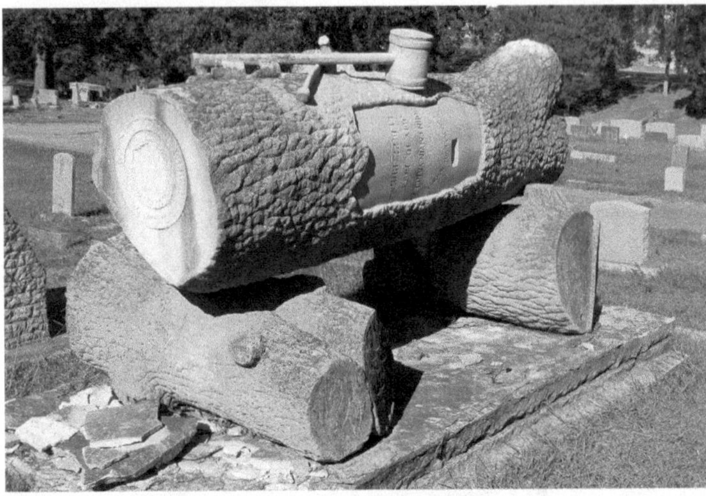

Fig 9.12. A massive, one-of-a-kind Woodmen of the World tree trunk marker on the grave of John Calvin Yancey (died 1907) in Oaklawn Cemetery, Batesville (Independence Co.).

its side atop two shorter stone logs, marking the grave of John Calvin Yancey in Batesville's Oaklawn cemetery (died 1907, Independence Co.). According to local legend this marker was carved at a nearby stone quarry and pulled to the cemetery by oxen.[17]

Families tended to insure only the husbands, whose loss would create the greatest hardship for dependents, but wives could also obtain insurance through their lodges. Children, having inexpensive burials and grave markers, did not require insurance, but there were a few rare exceptions. (As noted in chapter 2, the Black Supreme Royal Circle of Friends had a juvenile division that provided tombstones to children.) Huntsville's town cemetery contains a small, primitive tree trunk marker for one-year-old George W. Litterell (died 1884, Madison Co.) inscribed, "Infant of Woodcraft" while the Ashdown town cemetery has a marker for Emery Francis Thomas, aged three and a half (died 1909, Little River Co.). Thomas's stone has "Little Woodman" in raised letters across a small log, but neither example contains the emblem of any Woodmen lodges. Litterell's death came just one year after the Modern Woodmen of America was founded, and six years before the Woodmen of America was founded, so this inscription may be unrelated to either lodge.

The symbols used by fraternal lodges are complicated and can be confusing. For example, the Odd Fellows, the Knights of the Maccabees, and the Women's Beneficent Association all used emblems depicting shuttlecock-shaped tents, while the Odd Fellows occasionally used a hatchet emblem, easily mistaken for the Red Men (though the Red Men used a war bonneted Indian, and later an eagle and shield), while a drawn bow and arrow is the symbol of the Yeomen. Families sometimes created monograms of interlocking initials but so, too, did the Knights of Honor, who added the enigmatic OMA initials to their members' markers, either with or without their organization's full name.

No one outdid the Masons when it came to variety and complexity of symbols, such as Father Time counting the curls on the head of an unsuspecting virgin, or the inclusion of carved masonry tools like trowels and plumb bobs. The Masons' compass and square emblem was imitated by a number of other lodges, including the United Brotherhood of Carpenters and Joiners of America, the International Association of Machinists and Aerospace Workers (founded in 1888 and whites-only until 1950), and the Junior Order of United American Mechanics (JOUAM), the latter adding a tiny, flexed arm grasping a mallet to its otherwise identical copy of the Masonic emblem, for which it is often mistaken.

The JOUAM was one of several "nativist" lodges founded for the purpose of "keeping undesirable foreigners out of the country," including Catholics, Germans, and the Irish.[18] Both it and the Patriotic Order, Sons of America (another anti-immigrant lodge that also originated in Pennsylvania) had women's auxiliaries known as the Daughters of America. POS of A lodges are not known to have existed in Arkansas although their conferences were reported on in Arkansas newspapers, and an attempt was made to found a chapter in Little Rock.[19] The Red Men were another nativist lodge, later renamed the Improved Order of Red Men (IORM). Their members met in tribes, thus further confusing descendants finding "Kiowa tribe" on a great-grandfather's tombstone. The women's lodge was called the Degree of Pocahontas.

While these three lodges were also anti-Black, they are not the same as the Knights of the Ku Klux Klan, whose members, although

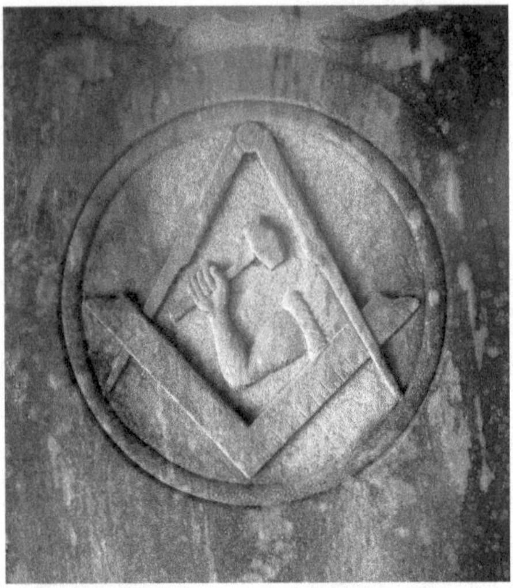

Fig 9.13. The Junior Order of United American Mechanics (JOUAM), founded, in part, to drive out foreigners, used an emblem mimicking the Masons' compass and square. W.W. Guinn (1881–1905), Oak Hill Cemetery, Booneville (Logan Co.).

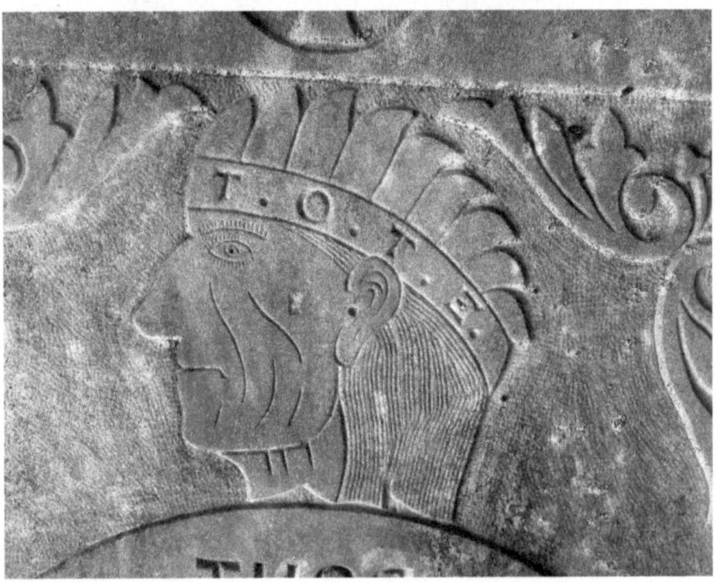

Fig 9.14. The Red Men fraternal lodge, though whites-only, used a Native American and, later, an eagle, as their emblem. Thomas Dillahunty (1859–1913), Lockesburg Cemetery (Sevier Co.).

secretive, publicly donned their robes and hoods to attend the funerals of fellow Klansmen. Their emblem, the blood-drop cross, has not been found on headstones in Arkansas, but the prominent initials "KKK" have been, on the grave of Joseph Brewster in Center Hill Cemetery, Paragould (died 1924, Greene Co.).

UNDERSTANDING ARCHAIC LANGUAGE

> Were the dead mindful of the devotion that the living pay them,
> We would bedew the graves of our sweet little babes with
> Our tears and disturb the repose of their ashes with our mighty orison.
>
> —ROBERT MOORE, 1869–1873, HIGHLAND CEMETERY, OZARK (FRANKLIN CO.)

"Consort" does not mean "concubine" and, despite what online dictionaries say, the non-reigning spouse of a monarch is not the only person entitled to be called a consort. When found on tombstones it merely means "spouse" and can rightly be used for either a woman or a man whose partner survives them. The term "relict" (literally, something that is left over) is found less often and means a widow or widower. "Nee" is French for "born" and is placed after a woman's married name, before giving her maiden one.

"Here rests the ashes of . . ." should never be taken literally. Cremation, while technically available from undertakers willing to transport bodies outside the state, was not available inside Arkansas until Denver Roller built the state's first facility at Conway in 1974. The word, however, is part of the language of the conventional graveside service ("ashes to ashes, dust to dust"), making it a poetic term for the earthly remains. Older columnar markers often have three-dimensional urns on top, but these, too, are symbolic and do not literally hold remains, cremated or otherwise.

It probably goes without saying, but our ancestors did not make jokes about death and dying. Still, because colloquial language changes over time, some older epitaphs are now unintentionally funny. "Gone to inhabit fairer climes, / Where streams of bliss fresh issue / From the throne" is one example;[20] so, too, is the verse about loved ones in Heaven, "Seated round the great white throne."[21] Some misspellings add humor: "Rest in pea's"[22] is this author's favorite, not to mention the frequent misspelling of "angel": "Gone to be an angle" and "We loved him yes we loved him / But the angles loved him more."

CLEANING STONES AND USING LIGHT

Although the Hippocratic oath does not include the injunction, "Do no harm" (Greek physician Hippocrates *did* write it, but in a text about epidemics), this should be the creed of anyone cleaning or repairing a tombstone, because it is so easy to do permanent damage. The question, "How do I clean a tombstone?" comes up repeatedly on Facebook's cemetery sites, where it is likely to set off a firestorm of arguments between conservationists urging the use of D/2—and nothing but D/2—and others endorsing harsh chemicals likely to cause injury to both the stone and the person cleaning it. The list of caustic products that people have touted is long and horrifying to anyone who has seen the damage caused by these substances or, just as distressingly, done by "professionals" using sandblasters and power washers. Such equipment, used on a high setting, can permanently wipe away inscriptions.

Tombstone cleaning is not without risks and should be undertaken only after getting permission (from family, a cemetery board, cemetery groundskeepers, or city government). Older monuments, ones made up of stacked stone bases, were usually assembled with mortar or lead strips between the bases and with interior metal pins connecting and securing the tiers. Over time, mortar degrades, lead strips fall out, and metal pins can become corroded, bent, or broken. If the monument is not level, as is caused by upheaval from tree roots, the result will be unsecured layers of stone that can topple. If this is suspected, move on and do not attempt to clean the marker.

If it is absolutely necessary to clean a tombstone, the only product endorsed by professional tombstone conservators is D/2 Biological

Solution, which works very slowly to kill plant growth.[23] The product, available online from stone conservation companies, works only when temperatures are above forty-five degrees. There are other products on the market that claim to clean tombstones but were not formulated for this job.

The following cleaning directions, using D/2, were written by Bob Young, whose Fayetteville, Arkansas, business, Gravestone Cleaning and Restoration, specializes in those services. While it is perfectly acceptable to simply spray a tombstone with D/2 without scrubbing, sometimes necessary when cleaning an unlevel marker, what follows is a more thorough method for getting results:

1. After making sure that the marker is stable, rinse it thoroughly with plain water and keep the stone wet throughout the cleaning process. Use a small plastic scraper (available in a hardware store's paint department) to remove encrustations of plant growth; use a bamboo skewer or soft toothbrush to clean out the lettering. Rinse again, from the top down.
2. Spray the stone with D/2 Biological Solution and let this stand for 10 to 15 minutes or more. (Try to spray downwind, so as not to inhale the mist.) Begin the cleaning process on other tombstones during this waiting period. Persons with sensitive skin should wear gloves, a face mask, or eye protection, as needed, but this is optional for most people using D/2.
3. Using a soft-bristle brush (preferably natural fibers or nylon, without colored bristles) scrub the stone, working from the bottom to the top. Be aware that the stone may change color—anything from mossy green to a bright orange or salmon pink—depending on the type and amount of biologicals growing on it. This color change is normal and may last a week or so before it disappears.
4. Rinse thoroughly with water from the top downward. Rescrub any areas that need special attention.
5. Spray the headstone completely with D/2 and you're finished! The D/2 will continue eliminating biologicals for weeks, being rinsed each time it rains. Expect to see improvement in several weeks' time.

A few final cautions: NEVER bring metal into contact with a tombstone—not scrapers, wire brushes, steel wool, or any other abrasive substances such as sandpaper. Black mold that has hardened on marble, resembling enamel paint, is difficult to remove and will require multiple applications of D/2 at intervals over a long period of time, although some remnant will always remain. When in doubt, contact a professional.

BASIC CEMETERY SAFETY

Exploring a cemetery comes down to some basic and probably obvious guidelines. Be mindful of safety, *especially* around the living. The dead are not likely to hurt you, though the uneven ground around their graves might. Carry a lot of drinking water and stay hydrated. Wear sunscreen and reapply it often or wear clothing that blocks sunlight, a wide-brimmed hat, and invest in a microfiber towel that, when wet, will keep your neck cool. Apply bug-repellant spray and be vigilant about removing ticks, which can carry a variety of illnesses, including Alpha-gal syndrome, which is on the rise. (Alpha-gal triggers an allergic reaction after eating beef, pork, and dairy products, with life-threatening consequences in some people.) Be sure to pack food, extra camera batteries, and basic gear: soft-bristled brushes, a photo reflector, a flashlight with a strong beam, a notebook and pen.

There are various apps that will help you find graveyards (including almost all of the ones mentioned in this book), such as Billiongraves and Find a Grave, but cell phones don't always get reception in isolated or mountainous areas. Download maps and directions in advance, carry a paper map of the state (available for free from visitor centers), and do not rely solely on cell phones for directions.

The Arkansas Historic Preservation Program has a free cemetery guide, titled "Grave Concerns: A Preservation Manual for Historic Cemeteries in Arkansas," which can be downloaded from their website: https://www.arkansasheritage.com/arkansas-historic-preservation-program. It is a hands-on guide to restoring a cemetery and includes the state cemetery laws and links to other resources.

Watch for snakes during warm weather, and be aware that wasp nests on tombstones can easily be mistaken for stone. Learn to identify, and avoid, ground hornets and fire ants. Wild animals, such as raccoons, are unlikely to be a threat, but a wild animal that is encountered in broad daylight and unafraid of humans could be rabid. If you have concerns about human dangers, carry pepper spray; wasp spray is also recommended because it shoots a long stream of chemicals. Last, but definitely not least, carry dog biscuits or pouches of wet dog food, in case you need to make friends with any stray dog that wants to keep you company in a graveyard. It never hurts to have biscuits handy with which to establish friendship.

A PARTING THOUGHT

Not everything that appears to be a tombstone is one. At the edge of a lawn fronting an abandoned building in Corning (Clay Co.) stands a tall stone marker with the words "Never can there be a substitute for a Monument" carved in Gothic lettering. Despite the fact that this stone incorporates such popular elements as tasseled drapery and a large stone book, it does not mark a grave but, instead, was created to display the skills of a now-vanished monument company. A lengthy inscription is carved on the front, written by three cemetery and monument associations.[24] It was good advertising in its day, and it also reflects the philosophy behind graveyard exploration: It is a constant source of inspiration.

–The Memorial Ideal–

A monument built of enduring granite or marble,
symbolic in design and reverent in purpose,
resting in surroundings of peace and beauty,
a tribute of respect and honor to the dead,
a constant source of inspiration to the living . . .

ARKANSAS CEMETERIES BY COUNTY

The following is a list, by county, of all the Arkansas cemeteries mentioned in this book, as well as several from outside the state.

ARKANSAS

Napoleon Island
"The old cemetery," at Arkansas Post [now gone]
Scull Cemetery, near Arkansas Post

ASHLEY

Flat Creek Cemetery
Hogue Cemetery

BAXTER

Big Flat Cemetery
Burnt Schoolhouse Cemetery
Fluty Cemetery
Galatia Cemetery
Mountain Home city cemetery

BENTON

Austin Cemetery, Best
Bozarth Cemetery
Dodson Cemetery, Bentonville
Georgia Cemetery

Ingram family graveyard, near Lowell
Oak Hill, Siloam Springs
Rambo Cemetery
Rest Haven Pet Cemetery, Bentonville
Rogers city cemetery
Silent Grove Cemetery

BOONE

Alpena town cemetery
Auman Cemetery
Bellefonte Cemetery
Capps Cemetery
Holmes Cemetery, Bellefonte
Rowland Family Cemetery, Valley Springs
Sexton Cemetery, a.k.a. Dark Hollow
Speer Cemetery
White Church Cemetery
White Oak Cemetery
Youngblood Cemetery

BRADLEY

McFarland Cemetery, at Banks
Palestine Cemetery

CALHOUN

Hampton town cemetery
New Hope Cemetery

CARROLL

Berryville city cemetery, formerly IOOF Cemetery
Carrollton Cemetery
Crescent Hotel, Eureka Springs
Denver town cemetery

Eureka Springs city cemetery, formerly IOOF Cemetery
Fair Grove, Green Forest
Great Passion Play, Eureka Springs
Hale Cemetery
Parker Cemetery, Green Forest
Rock Springs Cemetery
Teeter, a.k.a. Oak Hill Cemetery, near Green Forest

CHICOT

Hill Cemetery, Eudora
Hyner Cemetery, Sunnyside
Johnson family graveyard, Lakeport Plantation
Mount Caramel Cemetery
Old Lakeport Cemetery

CLARK

Golden Cemetery
Rose Hill Cemetery, Arkadelphia
Unity Cemetery, Arkadelphia

CLAY

Corning city cemetery
Richwoods Cemetery
Woodland Heights Cemetery, Rector

CLEBURNE

Aldridge Cemetery
Magness Cemetery

CLEVELAND

Humble Hope
New Cemetery, Rison

Rowell Cemetery
Smith-Morgan Cemetery, Kingsland
Union Cemetery, Rye

COLUMBIA

Harmony Cemetery, Rocky Mound

CONWAY

Bold Pilgrim Cemetery, Morrilton
Elmwood Cemetery, Morrilton
Petit Jean State Park

CRAIGHEAD

Jonesville Memorial Park Cemetery
Mount Sinai, Jonesboro
Oaklawn, Jonesboro
Temple Israel, Jonesboro
Thelma Holford Memorial Pet Cemetery, Jonesboro
Web mounds

CRAWFORD

Anton Peter Anderson Cemetery
Basham Memorial Cemetery, Mountainburg
Fairview Cemetery, Van Buren
Love Cemetery
Newberry Chapel Cemetery
Pevehouse Cemetery
Pope Cemetery

CRITTENDEN

Crittenden Memorial Park, Marion
George Berry Washington burial, Earle
Guerrant Cemetery

CROSS

Head and Shoulders Cemetery
Sawdust Hill community burial ground, in Parkin Archaeological State Park
Vanndale Cemetery

DALLAS

Bucksnort Cemetery
Delamar Cemetery
Hampton Springs
Oakland Memorial Cemetery, Fordyce
Tulip Cemetery

DESHA

Dumas Junior High School lawn, Dumas
Gill Gym, Dumas
McGehee town cemetery
Memorial Garden Cemetery [atop Native mound], inside Mound Cemetery
Mound Cemetery, a.k.a. Old Mound Cemetery, Arkansas City
Rohwer Relocation Camp Cemetery
Walnut Lake Cemetery, Dumas

DREW

Green Mount Cemetery, Coleman
Lacey Cemetery, Selma
Mount Pleasant A.M.E. Cemetery, a.k.a. Campground Cemetery
Mount Tabor Cemetery

FAULKNER

Cypress Valley Cemetery
Hendrix College, Conway

Martinville Cemetery
Oak Bowery Cemetery
Oak Grove, Conway
Red Hill Cemetery
Robinson Cemetery, Conway

FRANKLIN

Aetna Church Cemetery
Garden of Memories, Charleston
Garr Creek Cemetery
Highland Cemetery, Ozark
Hill family cemetery
Horner family cemetery
Nichols family cemetery, at rest stop beside I-40 westbound
Nixon Cemetery, Charleston
Kersey Cemetery
"Scab Graveyard"

FULTON

Agnos Cemetery
Elizabeth Cemetery
Flint Springs Cemetery
Grisso Cemetery
Union Cemetery

GARLAND

Beth Jacob Cemetery, Fountain Lake
Fourche Loupe Cemetery
Greenwood Cemetery, Hot Springs
Hollywood Cemetery, Hot Springs
Jewish Rest, Hot Springs
Memorial Gardens, Hot Springs
Pet Lawn, pet cemetery, inside Crestview Memorial Park, Hot Springs

Rockdale Cemetery, Fountain Lake
Showmen's Rest, Memorial Gardens, Hot Springs

GRANT

Ebenezer Cemetery, at Tull
Sheridan Cemetery

GREENE

Center Hill Cemetery, Paragould
Gainesville Cemetery
Linwood Cemetery, Paragould
Mount Zion Cemetery
Shiloh, a.k.a. Pioneer Cemetery, in Crowley's Ridge State Park
Sloan site, Native American

HEMPSTEAD

Huckabee Cemetery
Pioneer Cemetery, in Historic Washington State Park
Washington Presbyterian Cemetery, outside Historic Washington State Park

HOT SPRING

Oak Ridge Cemetery, Malvern
Strangers' Home Cemetery

HOWARD

Athens Cemetery, Newhope

INDEPENDENCE

Akron Cemetery
Convenience Cemetery

Oaklawn Cemetery, Batesville
Pine Grove Cemetery
Pioneer Cemetery, Batesville

IZARD

Shaver Campground Cemetery
No Bottom Cemetery

JACKSON

Eight Mile Cemetery
Gum Grove Cemetery, Newport
Nancy Redman burial, Jacksonport
Walnut Grove Cemetery, Newport

JEFFERSON

Bellwood Cemetery, Pine Bluff
Congregation Anshe Emeth Cemetery, in Bellwood
Old Town Cemetery, Pine Bluff
Oliver Cemetery, Pine Bluff
St. Joseph's Cemetery, Pine Bluff
Wright Cemetery, Pine Bluff

JOHNSON

Biggerstaff grave, Spadra
Brown Cemetery
Coal Hill Cemetery
Harmony Cemetery
Knoxville Bend Cemetery
Lone Pine Cemetery
Oakland Memorial Cemetery, Clarksville
Oark Cemetery
Ozone Cemetery
Pricetown Cemetery

Sacred Heart Cemetery, Clarksville
Sacred Heart Cemetery, Hartman
Yale Cemetery

LAFAYETTE

Boyds Hill/Union Hill/Galilee Cemetery
Conway Cemetery Historic State Park
Courthouse Cemetery, Lewisville
Old Town, a.k.a. Old Lewisville Cemetery
St. Mary's Cemetery, Bradley
Wilson Cemetery, at Lewisville

LAWRENCE

Cross Cemetery
Dry Creek Cemetery
John A. Rhea grave, Walnut Ridge
Shadowlawn Cemetery

LEE

Hawkins Chapel
John Patterson historical marker, east of Marianna
Morning Star Cemetery
Pilgrim Cemetery

LINCOLN

Lincoln Memorial Lawn Cemetery, Grady
Oak Grove, a.k.a. White Church Cemetery, Yorktown

LITTLE RIVER

Ashdown town cemetery
Campground Cemetery, Winthrop

LOGAN

Antioch Cemetery, Barber
Ellington Cemetery, Magazine
Graves Cemetery, Delaware
Hamby family cemetery, Booneville
Hopewell Cemetery, Carolan
Oak Hill Cemetery, Booneville
Paint Rock Cemetery

LONOKE

Butlarville Cemetery
Lonoke city cemetery
Plum Bayou Mounds
Sixteenth Section Cemetery
Sylvania Cemetery
Walters Chapel Cemetery, near Carlisle
Whitley Cemetery, Cabot

MADISON

Alabam Cemetery
Brashears Cemetery
Buckeye Cemetery
Farmer Cemetery, Hindsville
Huntsville town cemetery
Lower Wharton Creek Cemetery
Reeves Cemetery, Red Star
Walnut Grove Cemetery
Wesley town cemetery

MARION

Bruno Cemetery
Keesee Cemetery
Old Midway Cemetery
Yocham Bend, a.k.a. Yokum Bend Cemetery

MILLER

East Memorial Gardens, Texarkana
Mt. Sinai, inside Stateline Cemetery
Stateline Cemetery, Texarkana
Woodlawn Cemetery No. 2, in Stateline Cemetery

MISSISSIPPI

Blytheville Courthouse lawn war memorial
Chickasawba, a.k.a. Founders Park Cemetery, Blytheville
Ermen Cemetery, Osceola
Herman Davis State Park, Manila
Jackson mounds
McFadden Cemetery
Violet Cemetery, Osceola
Wilson, town center

MONROE

Ash Grove, a.k.a. Dark Corner
Shady Grove Cemetery, Clarendon

MONTGOMERY

Reed Cemetery
Scott-Wehunt Cemetery

NEVADA

Corinth Cemetery, Bodcaw
De Ann Cemetery, Prescott
Mount Moriah Cemetery
Mount Olive Cemetery
Mount Vernon Cemetery

NEWTON

Agee family cemetery, now called the Hasty town cemetery
Armstrong-Collins Cemetery
Buckhorn Cemetery
Buffalo Cemetery, outside Parthenon
Cowell Cemetery
Davis Cemetery, Mt. Judea
Liberty Cemetery
McFerrin Cemetery, near Compton
Moore Cemetery
Morris Cemetery
Mossville Cemetery
Plumlee Cemetery, Compton
Sand Hill Cemetery
Shaddox Cemetery
Smith Cemetery, Vendor

OUACHITA

Jewish Rest, Camden
Mount Willie, Camden
Oakland Cemetery, Camden

PERRY

McGhee Cemetery
St. Boniface church and cemetery, Bigelow

PHILLIPS

Magnolia Cemetery, Helena
Maple Hill Cemetery, Helena
Temple Beth El Cemetery, Helena

PIKE

Kirby Cemetery
Saline Cemetery

POINSETT

East family graveyard, Tyronza
Webber family cemetery, in Tyronza town cemetery

POLK

Cherry Hill Cemetery
Mount Calvary Cemetery, Mena

POPE

Atkins city cemetery
Brock Cemetery, Victor
God's Little Half-Acre
Lake Dardanelle State Park
Mount Zion Cemetery
Oakland Cemetery, Russellville

PRAIRIE

Czech National, south of Hazen
Hazen city cemetery
Russian Orthodox, Slovak
Slovak Catholic, a.k.a. Saints Cyril and Methodius Catholic cemetery, Slovak
White Church Cemetery, Des Arc
Zion Lutheran Cemetery, Ulm

PULASKI

Agudath Achim, in Oakland and Fraternal
B'nai Israel, in Oakland and Fraternal
Calvary Cemetery, Little Rock
Hebrew Burial Ground, Little Rock [now lost]
Mount Holly, Little Rock
Oakland and Fraternal, Little Rock
Pyeatte-Mason Cemetery, Maumelle

RANDOLPH

Duty Cemetery
Hite Cemetery
Masonic Cemetery, Pocahontas
Phillips-Reeves Cemetery, in Davidsonville Historic State Park
Scott Cemetery, in Davidsonville Historic State Park
Sharum Cemetery

SALINE

Fairplay Cemetery, Benton
Kentucky Cemetery
Stainer Cemetery

SCOTT

Chant Cemetery
Coop Prairie Cemetery
Duncan Cemetery, Waldron
Freedom Cemetery
Gipson Cemetery
Looper Cemetery
Pleasant Grove Cemetery

SEARCY

Campbell Cemetery
Canaan Cemetery
Hall Cemetery
Marshall city cemetery
Oak Grove Cemetery

SEBASTIAN

Cherokee African American Cemetery
Cross Cemetery, Greenland
Dayton Cemetery
Forest Park Cemetery, Fort Smith
Fort Smith Jewish Cemetery
Lone Star Cemetery, a.k.a. Eppler, in Fort Chaffee
Lovelace Cemetery, Witcherville
Lowrey-Rye Cemetery
Mountain View Cemetery, Hackett
National Cemetery, Fort Smith
Oak Cemetery, Fort Smith
Oak Valley Cemetery
Washington Cemetery, Fort Smith

SEVIER

Horatio town cemetery
Lockesburg Cemetery
Redmen Cemetery, De Queen

SHARP

Black Cemetery
Boles, a.k.a. Bowles Cemetery

ST. FRANCIS

Scott Bond Cemetery, a.k.a. Madison Cemetery, Forrest City
Forrest Park, Forrest City

STONE

Red Door Cemetery
Timbo Cemetery

UNION

Free Union Cemetery

VAN BUREN

Blackwell Cemetery, Bee Branch
Bradley Cemetery
Foster Cemetery, Scotland
Huie Cemetery
Hunter-Hill Cemetery
Pee Dee Cemetery

WASHINGTON

Bean Cemetery, Lincoln
Bluff Cemetery, Springdale
Brentwood Cemetery, Winslow
Cane Hill Cemetery
Evergreen Cemetery, Fayetteville
Friendship Cemetery, Springdale
Kidd family cemetery, Cane Hill
Lewis Cemetery
Mount Comfort, Fayetteville
Prairie Grove Cemetery
Reese Cemetery
Son's Chapel Cemetery, Fayetteville

Spring Creek Cemetery
St. Joseph's Cemetery, Tontitown
Strain Cemetery
Vineyard Cemetery, Evansville
White House Cemetery, Arnett
White Oak Cemetery
White Rock Cemetery, Dutch Mills
Wilson Cemetery, Springdale

WHITE

Beebe city cemetery
Crow Cemetery, Kensett
Fredonia Cemetery
Grissard Cemetery, El Paso
Gum Springs Cemetery
Oak Grove Cemetery, Searcy
Old Dogwood Cemetery
"Old Slave Cemetery"
US 67 N/167 near Judsonia

WOODRUFF

Augusta Memorial Park
Easton Cemetery, McCrory
Fakes Cemetery
Odd Fellows Cemetery, near McCrory
White Lake Cemetery

YELL

Harkey's Valley Cemetery
Harris Cemetery, Cotton Town
New Hope Cemetery
Oak Ridge, a.k.a. Nebo, Dardanelle
Sulphur Springs Cemetery

OUTSIDE ARKANSAS

COLORADO

Briggsdale Cemetery, Briggsdale (Weld Co.)

LOUISIANA

Goodrich's Landing (East Carroll Parish)
Lake Providence (East Carroll Parish)

INDIANA

Crown Hill, Indianapolis (Marion Co.)

MAINE

Hillside Cemetery, Yarmouth (Cumberland Co.)

MISSOURI

Calvary Cemetery, City of St. Louis
Jesse James farm burial, Kearney (Clay Co.)
Oak Lawn, West Plains (Howell Co.)
Rolla town cemetery (Phelps Co.)
Squibb Cemetery (Greene Co.)
Warsaw town cemetery (Benton Co.)
Weaver Cemetery, Ozark (Christian Co.)

NEW YORK

Albany Rural Cemetery (Albany Co.)

NORTH CAROLINA

Elmwood Cemetery, Charlotte (Mecklenburg Co.)

OHIO

Cedar Hill, Newark (Licking Co.)
Spring Grove, Cincinnati (Hamilton Co.)

OKLAHOMA

Showmen's Rest, Mt. Olivet Cemetery, Hugo (Choctaw Co.)

TENNESSEE

Elmwood Cemetery, Memphis (Shelby Co.)

TEXAS

Missouri, Kansas, and Texas railroad freight depot, Denison (Grayson Co.)
Rose Hill, Texarkana (Bowie County)

NOTES

INTRODUCTION

1. Dale Bumpers, *The Best Lawyer in a One-Lawyer Town: A Memoir* (New York: Random House, 2003), 177–78.

2. Accounts differ as to whether it was one or several tombstones.

3. Roy Reed, *Faubus: The Life and Times of an American Prodigal* (Fayetteville: University of Arkansas Press, 1997), 301–2.

4. Though buried in Pee Dee Cemetery (Van Buren Co.), thanks to genealogy websites, we know that her name was Mary Ann (Hargis) Humble Pistol[e] (1839–1929). Her husband Marion Pistole (1844–1896) is buried in Huie Cemetery (Van Buren Co.).

5. The grave of Virginia Clinton Kelley (1923–1994), mother of President Bill Clinton, could be added to this list due to the understated nature of her marker. However, signage throughout the cemetery points visitors to her grave in Hope's Rose Hill Cemetery (Hempstead Co.).

6. Four men are buried in their eponymous counties (Bradley, Cross, Logan, and Phillips), and all are in private or otherwise inaccessible graveyards.

7. The skeleton of Count Pulaski, who identified as male, has female characteristics; according to the BBC, testing confirmed an identical match between Pulaski's DNA and that of a female descendant. "Casimir Pulaski May Have Been Woman or Intersex, Study Says," BBC, April 6, 2019, https://www.bbc.com/news/world-us-canada-47842307.

8. *Weekly Arkansas Gazette* (Little Rock, AR), May 7, 1852, 1.

9. *Arkansas Democrat* (Little Rock, AR), December 31, 1919, 11.

10. Arkansas State Board of Health, Bureau of Vital Statistics, Registration District No. 538, Certificate of Death, # 1879; Wm. H. Waddle. "General disability" was listed as both his primary and secondary cause of death.

11. Abby Burnett and Vineta Wingate, "Samuel Doss' Death Halts 'The Giggling Granny,'" *Carroll County Historical Quarterly* 50, no. 1 (March 2005), 8–11.

12. This author has found cookie recipes in two Arkansas cemeteries: Neal marker, Garden of Memories Cemetery, Charleston (Franklin Co.) and on a bench in front of the Shearer marker, Magness Cemetery (Cleburne Co.).

13. Mrs. John B. Kittrell Sr., "The Spirit of the Gravestone," *Rivers and Roads and Points in Between* 1, no. 3 (1973), 33.

14. "Nathan Ellington, 1808–1890," *Wagon Wheels* 2, no. 1 (1982), 45–51.

15. Ellington Cemetery, Magazine (Logan Co.), family obelisk also contains the names of John Ellington (1766–1848) and John C. Ellington (1845–1862).

CHAPTER 1. AN OVERVIEW OF ARKANSAS CEMETERIES

1. Transcribed from a photo on Find a Grave; stone is in pieces and difficult to read in situ.

2. Juliet Morrow, "The Sloan Site," Arkansas Archaeological Survey, accessed January 18, 2023, https://archeology.uark.edu/who-we-are/50moments/sloansite/.

3. Jeannie M. Whayne, Thomas A. DeBlack, George Sabo III, and Morris S. Arnold, *Arkansas: A Narrative History* (Fayetteville: University of Arkansas Press, 2013), 67.

4. Dyan Bohnert, "Local Preservationists Restore Scull Cemetery," *Grand Prairie Historical Society Bulletin* 61, no. 2 (2018), 24–35; Bohnert acknowledges that Laclede could be buried either in Scull Cemetery or the Arkansas River bank, "probably the second place," but includes Laclede's modern tombstone in a cemetery enumeration titled "Known burials in Scull Cemetery."

5. Morris S. Arnold, interviewed by phone January 23, 2023, and January 3, 2024.

6. Morris S. Arnold, *Colonial Arkansas 1686–1804: A Social and Cultural History* (Fayetteville: University of Arkansas Press, 1991), 5.

7. Carl J. Ekberg and Sharon K. Person, *St. Louis Rising: The French Regime of Louis St. Ange de Bellerive* (Urbana: University of Illinois Press, 2015), 4, 58–63, 107–8, 225.

8. William E. Foley and C. David Rice. *The First Chouteaus: River Barons of Early St. Louis* (Urbana: University of Illinois Press, 1983), 23–24.

9. William E. Foley, "Laclede, Pierre De (1729–1778)," in *Dictionary of Missouri Biography*, ed. Lawrence O. Christensen, William E. Foley, Gary R. Kremer, and Kenneth H. Winn (Columbia: University of Missouri Press, 1999), 467–69.

10. Arnold, *Colonial Arkansas 1686–1804*, 169.

11. Morris S. Arnold, interviewed by phone January 23, 2023.

12. Both embalming and sealed metal coffins did not come into use until the mid-1800s and were unlikely to have been available to river travelers.

13. *Report of the Celebration of the Anniversary of the Founding of St. Louis, on the Fifteenth Day of February, A.D. 1847* (St. Louis, MO: Missouri Republican, printed by Chambers and Knapp, 1847), 13, contains an address by Wilson Primm stating that Chouteau saw the grave fifty years earlier, or 1797. J.F.D. [John F. Darby, identified from other sources], in "Territory and State; Col. Switzler's Address on the Early History of Missouri," *The Missouri Republican* (St. Louis, MO), March 11,

1872, 1, quotes Primm's address and the fifty-year time period; later in the article Darby says it was nine years later, which is likely a typo.

14. J.F.D., "Territory and State." *Missouri Republican*, 11 March, 1872, 1.

15. J.F.D., "Territory and State."

16. The 1820s or 1830s are the time periods most often estimated for the founding of Napoleon; naturalist Thomas Nuttall identified the location on a map he published in 1819, although he did not mention the presence of a town.

17. Richard G. Wood, "The Marine Hospital at Napoleon," *Arkansas Historical Quarterly* 14, no. 1 (1955), 42.

18. J.F.D., "Territory and State."

19. Seen as recently as 2022, according to Mark McElroy, interviewed by phone February 12, 2023.

20. A cemetery enumeration made in 1968 recorded the Smith marker and two others: A.D. Woodside, April 3, 1821–April 27, 1861, and J.J. Clark, born February 18, 1818, rest of stone missing. Typescript at the McGehee Branch Library Genealogy Room (Desha Co.), vertical file, "Cemetery" folder.

21. Dr. and Mrs. T.L. Hodges, "Possibilities for the Archaeologist and Historian in Eastern Arkansas," *Arkansas Historical Quarterly* 2, no. 2 (1943), 157–58.

22. J.F.D. "Territory and State."

23. Michael D. Hammond, "Arkansas Atlantis: The Lost Town of Napoleon," *Arkansas Historical Quarterly* 65, no. 3 (2006), 214–17.

24. The last person visited the few remaining houses in 1875.

25. J.F.D. "Territory and State"; "A Question of History," *Daily Arkansas Gazette* (Little Rock, AR), April 7, 1872, 2.

26. French Hill (James French Hill, US Representative), "Napoleon," essay delivered to the XV Club on January 10, 2002, unpaginated last page, shared by Morris S. Arnold.

27. Arnold, *Colonial Arkansas 1686–1804*, 17.

28. Morris S. Arnold, "Arkansas Post in 1832," *Grand Prairie Historical Society Bulletin* 61, no. 2 (2018), map drawn by Father Edward Saulnier in 1832, 5.

29. R.W. Dhonau, *A Collection of Early Arkansas Families, 1760–1820, On Family Charts* (Little Rock. AR: R.W. Dhonau, 1983), 224; map of the Post of Arkansas in 1820 was reconstructed from land records and is not original to 1820, nor does it show the current Scull Cemetery.

30. Boyd W. Johnson, ed., "A Visit to an Old Cemetery," *Grand Prairie Historical Society Bulletin* 6, no. 2 (1963), 23.

31. Clara Collins and Mrs. L. Oswald, enumerators, *Desha County, Arkansas Cemetery Records, Compiled in 1968 and 1969 by the Men and Women of Desha County* (McGehee, AR: M.M. Stroud, 1983), 113, 195; Napoleon Cemetery transcribed by Otis Howell; Facebook posts in 2023 claim to have seen at least one marble tablet at this site.

32. Ken Ziegenbein, blog post detailing visit made to Napoleon Island January 2009, accessed August 15, 2023, https://www.thundertrain.org/napoleon-012609-bb.html.

33. "Afloat in a Coffin," *Times Picayune* (New Orleans, LA), January 29, 1883, 1, reprinted from the *Vicksburg Herald* (Vicksburg, MS) January 27, 1883, 7.

34. "God's Acre. Something of the Little Graveyard Below Goodrich's Landing, La," *Times-Picayune* (New Orleans, LA), February 13, 1883, 9, reprinted from the *Vicksburg Herald* (Vicksburg, MS) February 10, 1883.

35. *Lonoke Democrat* (Lonoke, AR), February 23, 1882; *Arkansas Democrat* (Little Rock, AR), March 24, 1882, 4. This graveyard no longer exists, nor is its exact location known.

36. There are numerous accounts of bodies buried in wood yards; a good example: "A Deck Passenger's Death," *St. Louis Globe-Democrat* (St. Louis, MO) December 2, 1882, 12.

37. Duane Huddleston, "The Volant and Reindeer Early Arkansas Steamboats," *Pulaski County Historical Review* 24, no. 2 (1976), 32.

38. Hattie Ann Kelso, *Faulkner County, Arkansas Census of Cemeteries as of December 31, 1987* (Conway, AR: Faulkner County Historical Society, 1990), 544.

39. "White County's Top 25 Forgotten Cemeteries," *Historical Society News*, August 2002.

40. At least one of these cemeteries, Crow Cemetery at Kensett, has been restored since the article was written in 2002.

41. Sue Clark and Virginia McPhail, *Franklin County Cemeteries North of the Arkansas River* (N.p. 1995), 114; Scab Graveyard information provided by William Rupert Stephenson.

42. George Sabo III, *Ways of the Ancestors: Ancient Indians of Arkansas* (Fayetteville: Arkansas Archeological Survey, Popular Series No. 8, 2021), 9–10.

43. Morrow, "The Sloan Site."

44. Sabo, *Ways of the Ancestors*, 19.

45. Dan F. Morse, *Sloan: A Paleoindian Dalton Cemetery in Arkansas* (Fayetteville: University of Arkansas Press, 2018), 94.

46. Sabo, *Ways of the Ancestors*, 32.

47. Sabo, *Ways of the Ancestors*, 43.

48. Sabo, *Ways of the Ancestors*, 64–65.

49. Pierre-Francois-Xavier de Charlevoix, *Journal of a Voyage to North America Undertaken by Order of the French King*, Vol. 2 (London: R. and J. Dodsley, 1761), 247–48.

50. Marvin D. Jeter, ed., *Edward Palmer's Arkansaw [sic] Mounds* (Tuscaloosa: University of Alabama Press, 1990), 3.

51. Renamed in November 2022.

52. Martha Ann Rolingson, "Toltec Mounds Site," CALS Encyclopedia of Arkansas, accessed March 12, 2021, https://encyclopediaofarkansas.net/entries/toltec-mounds-site-413/.

53. National Register of Historic Places, Mound Cemetery, Arkansas City, Desha County, Arkansas, Site No. DE0002, Section 7, 1–3, accessed March 13, 2021, https://www.arkansasheritage.com/docs/default-source/national-registry/de0002-pdf.pdf?sfvrsn=e4a82928_0,.

54. National Register of Historic Places, Akron Cemetery, Newark vicinity, Independence County, Arkansas, [no Site No.], accessed August 14, 2023, Section 7, 1 https://www.arkansasheritage.com/docs/default-source/national-registry/in0619-pdf.pdf?sfvrsn=63ff2a9c_0.

55. Jeter, *Edward Palmer's Arkansaw Mounds*, 174.

56. Jeter, *Edward Palmer's Arkansaw Mounds*, 176.

57. "Arkansas Mounds with Historic Cemeteries on Them," compiled by Lela Donat, registrar of the Arkansas Archeological Survey, Fayetteville, Arkansas.

58. National Register of Historic Places, Augusta Memorial Park Historic Section, a.k.a. Crescent Hill Cemetery, Augusta, Woodruff County, Arkansas, Site No. WO0049, Section 7, 1, 3, accessed August 14, 2023 https://www.arkansasheritage.com/docs/default-source/national-registry/wo0049-pdf.pdf?sfvrsn=4ae3f0ce_0,.

59. Cindy Grisham, "Tyronza (Poinsett County)," CALS Encyclopedia of Arkansas, accessed July 5, 2021, https://encyclopediaofarkansas.net/entries/tyronza-poinsett-county-5561/. Palmer said there were once forty-two mounds; Grisham puts the number at forty-nine.

60. Jeter, *Edward Palmer's Arkansaw Mounds*, 346.

61. Cindy Grisham, *When Hope Grows Weary: Tyronza, Arkansas and Its Place in History* (Published by the author, 2013), 41–42, 153–54.

62. Information provided to the author by Grisham.

63. Jeter, *Edward Palmer's Arkansaw Mounds*, 238.

64. National Register of Historic Places, Mound Cemetery, Section 7, 1.

65. Jeter, *Edward Palmer's Arkansaw Mounds*, 239.

66. National Register of Historic Places, Mound Cemetery, Section 7, 2.

67. Ruth Polk Patterson, *The Seed of Sally Good'n: A Black Family of Arkansas, 1833–1953* (Lexington: University Press of Kentucky, 1985), 95.

68. Jeter, *Edward Palmer's Arkansaw Mounds*, 181.

69. F.M. McConnell, "White House Cemetery," *Flashback* 1, no. 3 (1951), 7.

70. Embarrassingly, I put this mistake into print without personally verifying the claim in my book *Gone to the Grave: Burial Customs of the Arkansas Ozarks, 1850–1950*.

71. Mrs. I.N. Barnett Sr., "Early Days of Batesville," *Arkansas Historical Quarterly* 11, no. 1 (1952), 15–16.

72. Lettering on the Marrs sisters' headstones in Prairie Grove (Washington Co.) has caused a similar misreading; both died in 1848 but were transcribed online as 1818.

73. "The History of Corning, AR: Corning Formerly Known as Hecht City Then Later as Carpenter's Station," no author, unpublished loose-leaf binder of town history found at the Piggott Public Library, quoting an 1892 edition of the local newspaper, 12.

74. National Register of Historic Places, Pyeatte-Mason Cemetery, Maumelle, Pulaski County, Arkansas, Site No. PU9990, accessed August 14, 2023, https://www.arkansasheritage.com/docs/default-source/national-registry/pu9990-pdf.pdf?sfvrsn=a83978ef_0 3–4.

75. National Register of Historic Places Fort Smith National Cemetery, Fort Smith, Sebastian County, Arkansas [no Site No. given], accessed August 14, 2023, https://www.arkansasheritage.com/docs/default-source/national-registry/sb0215-pdf.pdf?sfvrsn=7510a614_0.

76. W.J. Weaver, "Desecrated Grave Yards," in *Steep Hill and Jewish Cemeteries in Sebastian County, Arkansas with Some Abandoned Cemeteries* Sue Clark (N.p., n.d.), 1.

77. Thomas Nuttall, *A Journal of Travels into the Arkansa [sic] Territory* (Ann Arbor, MI: University Microfilms, 1966, originally published by Thos. M. Palmer, Printer, Philadelphia, PA, 1821), 141. Weaver (cited above) states that this early graveyard contained "two handsome marble slabs, one marking the grave of a young officer." Russell's present military marker could be a replacement.

78. Bill Black, Juliet Galonska, and Joe Crystal, preparers and consultants, *Cultural Landscape Report for Fort Smith National Historic Site* (Prepared by Fort Smith National Historic Site, Denver Service Center, National Park Service, US Department of the Interior, 1998), 6.

79. Sybil F. Crawford, "Mount Holly Cemetery," CALS Encyclopedia of Arkansas, accessed December 23, 2021, https://encyclopediaofarkansas.net/entries/mount-holly-cemetery-49/.

80. Rachel Silva, "Sandwiching in History: Oakland and Fraternal Cemetery," tour script, Arkansas Historic Preservation Program, 2010.

81. Lakresha Diaz, "Oakland-Fraternal Cemetery," CALS Encyclopedia of Arkansas, accessed June 10, 23, https://encyclopediaofarkansas.net/entries/oakland-fraternal-cemetery-7383/.

82. Felton D. Freeman, "Immigration to Arkansas," *Arkansas Historical Quarterly* 7, no. 3 (1948), 210–11.

83. Jaimie Metrailer, "Slovak (Prairie County)," CALS Encyclopedia of Arkansas, accessed August 14, 2023, https://encyclopediaofarkansas.net/entries/slovak-prairie-county-5362/.

84. Scott Van Laningham, ed., "St. Joseph's Cemetery at Tontitown," *Flashback* 51, no. 3 (2001), 9, reprinting an article from *Flashback* 15, no. 2.

85. Paul V. Canonici, *The Delta Italians: Their Pursuit of "The Better Life" and Their Struggle Against Mosquitoes, Floods, and Prejudice* (Published by the author, 2003), xiii.

86. Carolyn Gray LeMaster, *A Corner of the Tapestry: A History of the Jewish Experience in Arkansas, 1820s–1990s* (Fayetteville: University of Arkansas Press, 1994), footnote to chapter 1, 465.

87. Accounts differ about whether Fanny Block and the children arrived in 1826 or 1828.

88. LeMaster, *A Corner of the Tapestry*, 8–9.

89. LeMaster, *A Corner of the Tapestry*, 13. The date of the first burial in this cemetery is unknown.

90. National Register of Historic Places, Temple Beth El Cemetery, Helena, Phillips County, Arkansas, Site No. PO566, Sections 1–6, 4–6, accessed August 14, 2023, https://www.arkansasheritage.com/docs/default-source/national-registry/ph0566-pdf.pdf?sfvrsn=929609a9_0.

91. Diaz, "Oakland-Fraternal Cemetery."

92. It is hard to tell from this primitive carving whether the candelabra lacks candles or if they have burned down, leaving only short wicks.

93. Joshua L. Segal, *For an Eternal Memory: Ordinary and Unusual Jewish Cemetery Monuments and How to Create Them* (Nashua, NH: Jewish Cemetery Publishing, 2009), 65.

94. Joshua L. Segal, *A Field Guide to Visiting a Jewish Cemetery: A Spiritual Journey to the Past, Present and Future* (Nashua, NH: Jewish Cemetery Publishing, 2005), 51.

95. Segal, *A Field Guide to Visiting a Jewish Cemetery*, 51.

96. Joshua L. Segal, email to the author, March 16, 2023.

97. Menachem Benedek, 1890–1958, and Ruchel Benedek, 1889–1963 (first names are in Hebrew; translation and death dates provided by Find a Grave, although the transcriber, mistaking the symbolism of the menorah and pitcher, transposed the husband's and wife's dates), and Max Isken, 1882–1958, and Rose Isken, 1891–1983, Beth Jacob Cemetery at Fountain Lake (Garland Co.).

98. LeMaster, *A Corner of the Tapestry*, 53–54.

99. *Biographical and Historical Memoirs of Southern Arkansas* (Chicago: Goodspeed Publishing, 1890), a paragraph pertaining to the "secret orders" of Camden includes Elah Lodge No. 282, I.O.B.B., 648.

100. This monument contains the date October 20, 1945, found on what would have been the reverse side when viewed from the cemetery's original entrance.

101. National Register of Historic Places, Rohwer Relocation Center Site, Rohwer, Desha County, Arkansas [no Site No. given], accessed August 14, 2023, https://www.arkansasheritage.com/docs/default-source/national-registry/de0070-pdf.pdf?sfvrsn=ee5fe67f_0.

102. Raised letters on what would have been the back of the monument state that it is the work of camp "inhabitants" and dated October 1944.

103. "Wants U.S. to Take Over Cemetery," *Hope Star* (Hope, AR), October 16, 1961, 4.

104. Thelma Ellington Conner, "The Shadows of Rohwer," in *Inside View of Concentration Camps in Arkansas*, by Susan Gallion (Dumas Clarion, 2018), 68. This is an eighty-six-page large booklet sold at the McGehee museum.

105. "Wants U.S. to Take Over Cemetery," 24.

106. "News Briefs," *El Dorado Times* (El Dorado, AR), December 1, 1969, 7.

107. An inscription on the base of the largest modern granite memorial credits Sam Yutaka Yada (1905–1991) with working for "the national recognition and the preservation of this cemetery."

108. Russell E. Bearden, "Rohwer Relocation Center," CALS Encyclopedia of Arkansas, accessed May 1, 2023, https://encyclopediaofarkansas.net/entries/rohwer-relocation-center-369/.

109. Albert Marrin, *Uprooted: The Japanese American Experience During World War II* (New York: Borzoi/Alfred A. Knopf, 2016), 111, quoting an unnamed "inmate."

110. Russell E. Bearden, "Life Inside Arkansas's Japanese-American Relocation Centers," *Arkansas Historical Quarterly* 48, no. 2 (1989), 192.

111. Walter M. Imahara and David E. Meltzer, eds. *Jerome and Rohwer: Memories of Japanese American Internment in World War II Arkansas* (Fayetteville: University of Arkansas Press, 2022), quoting Kerry Yo Nakagawa, 96.

CHAPTER 2. AFRICAN AMERICAN GRAVEYARDS AND GRAVE MARKERS

1. P.P. (Philip Paul) Bliss, "Hallelujah 'Tis Done!," hymn written 1876.

2. On the mound is a stone tablet with "Father and Mother" in raised letters, evidence that Washington's first wife may also be buried there.

3. The photoceramic portrait was found by museum volunteer Thomas Machnitzki near the base of the statue and is now framed at the Crittenden County Museum at Earle.

4. National Register of Historic Places, George Berry Washington Memorial, Earle, Crittenden County, Arkansas, [no Site No.] 1994, accessed August 1, 2023, https://www.arkansasheritage.com/docs/default-source/national-registry/ct0098-pdf.pdf?sfvrsn=43106bb4_0 Section 7, 1–2.

5. Amount derived from online inflation calculators.

6. National Register of Historic Places, George Berry Washington Memorial, Section 8, 1–3.

7. There is a large angel statue on the grave of Daisy Marshall (1871–1910) near the entrance to Woodlawn Cemetery No. 2 in Texarkana (Miller Co.), a cemetery

sometimes mistakenly referred to as Black; however, the angel is on a white grave, and the two Black sections within Woodlawn are farther back from the entrance.

8. National Register of Historic Places, De Ann Cemetery Historic Section, Prescott, Nevada County, Arkansas, Site No. NE0076, Section 7, 1, 4, accessed August 16, 2023, https://www.arkansasheritage.com/docs/default-source/national-registry/ne0076-pdf.pdf?sfvrsn=5afd06ab_0.

9. Vennie Deas-Moore, "Treading on Sacred Grounds," in *Preservation of Historic Burial Grounds*, by Lynette Strangstad (Washington, DC: National Trust for Historic Preservation, 2003), 3.

10. "The DCC's Cemetery Project: 'Life Goes Goodbye,'" *Phillips County Historical Review* 37, nos. 1–2 (1999), 63–68 (an interview from the Delta Cultural Center's "The Cemetery Project: Oral Histories from the African American Community").

11. Carla Coleman, interviewed by phone, June 2020.

12. Oakland and Fraternal Historic Cemetery Park promotional brochure.

13. National Register of Historic Places, Oakland-Fraternal Cemetery, Little Rock, Pulaski County, AR, Site No. PU5892, Section 7, 5, accessed August 17, 2023, https://www.arkansasheritage.com/docs/default-source/national-registry/pu5892-pdf.pdf?sfvrsn=5aac62ef_0.

14. Joe Neal, "Fraternal Cemetery: Reflections on a Southern Negro Graveyard," *Pulaski County Historical Review* 25, no. 1 (1977), 4.

15. Neal, "Fraternal Cemetery," 1. The movie was *White Lightning*, released in 1973, starring Burt Reynolds.

16. Neal, "Fraternal Cemetery," 9–10.

17. Works Progress Administration, Historical Records Survey, Special Collections, University of Arkansas Libraries, Fayetteville; Early Settlers' Personal History Questionnaires: Malinda Sutton interview, born December 12, 1845 (Little River Co.), interviewed April 12, 1941.

18. George E. Lankford, ed., *Bearing Witness: Memories of Arkansas Slavery Narratives from the 1930s WPA Collections* (Fayetteville: University of Arkansas Press, 2003), Willis Winn, interviewed May 3, 1937, by Alex Hampton, 154.

19. Lankford, *Bearing Witness*, Louis Davis, undated interview by Mrs. Carrie Campbell, 433.

20. Lankford, *Bearing Witness*, John Bates, interviewed August 6, 1937, by William E. Smith, 317–18.

21. Grisso East Cemetery (Fulton Co.), Arkansas Gravestones, accessed August 15, 2023, https://arkansasgravestones.org/view.php?id=517578.

22. Extension Homemakers Council, *Cemeteries of Fulton County Arkansas* (N.p., 1999). Only enslaved person listed in the enumeration of Grisso (East), Map #25 is "Allie, slave of Martin Harber," although the book's index also lists "Slave of Jacob G." in this cemetery.

23. Jerry Harris Moore, interviewed by the author, October 2023.

24. Cherokee African American Cemetery, Find a Grave entry, accessed November 6, 2023, https://www.findagrave.com/cemetery/53426/cherokee-african-american-cemetery.

25. Alternate spellings are Wallage, Woolage, and Woodridge.

26. Governor Knauls, or Knowls (1905–1951), is buried in Washington Cemetery, Fort Smith (Sebastian Co.), but the author could not locate his headstone.

27. The exact date of this event is unclear, but Bond mentioned that his sons helped survey the land (two were in their twenties on the 1900 census). The whites-only Forrest Park Cemetery, at Forrest City, the county seat, was established in 1934, but contains headstones with death dates in the early 1900s.

28. Dan Rudd and Theo Bond, *From Slavery to Wealth: The Life of Scott Bond: The Rewards of Honesty, Industry, Economy and Perseverance*. Madison, AR: Journal Printing Company, 1917, 207–9.

29. Bond's death certificate states that he died in a Memphis hospital from internal injuries, sustained after being gored by a bull.

30. National Register of Historic Places, De Ann Cemetery Historic Section, Section 7, 2; Elizabeth Haltom, daughter of Prescott undertaker John D. Cornish, supplied the information about the ditch.

31. Mariah Fancher (March 10, 1841–August 19, 1901), Fancher-IOOF Cemetery, near Osage (Carroll Co.).

32. Fancher also has a footstone containing her initials, which led to a misconception that this was an infant's marker.

33. Another example is found in Lower Wharton Creek Cemetery (Madison Co.), a white cemetery that contains a number of Black burials, most of which have no inscribed markers, on the grave of Nelson York (1824–1917), whose marker has "(COLORED)" despite there being no other (white) Yorks with headstones in this cemetery.

34. Tom Clements (November 8, 1826–September 4, 1919), Mt. Zion Cemetery (Greene Co.); Find a Grave entry, accessed August 17, 2023, https://www.findagrave.com/memorial/39966864/tom-clements

35. Jenny Madden (1815–approx. 1903), Brown Cemetery (Johnson Co.).

36. "Former Slave Dies at Home on Rock Street," *Northwest Arkansas Times* (Fayetteville, AR), May 12, 1945, 4.

37. This is an error I regret having made in *Gone to the Grave* and have since corrected in the Encyclopedia of Arkansas entry on Evergreen Cemetery.

38. Bettina Lehovec, "The Slave Narrative Interviews of Miss Adeline Blakeley," *Flashback* 70, no. 2 (2020), 57; January 6, 2024, email from Ann (Wiggans) Sugg, whose mother oversaw Blakeley's burial.

39. "Funeral Service Held for Adeline Blakeley," *Northwest Arkansas Times* (Fayetteville, AR), May 15, 1945, 5.

40. Lehovec, "The Slave Narrative Interviews," 57.

41. Campbell Cemetery (Searcy Co.) marker is white marble not consistent with Civil War–era headstones, but not of recent vintage either.

42. Pevehouse, a.k.a. Peeveyhouse Cemetery.

43. Pope Cemetery (Crawford Co.).

44. Fairview Cemetery, Van Buren (Crawford Co.).

45. National Register of Historic Places, Fairview Cemetery, Van Buren, Crawford County, Arkansas, Site #CW0384, accessed November11, 2023, https://www.arkansasheritage.com/docs/default-source/national-registry/cw0384-pdf.pdf?sfvrsn=decf7b4_0.

46. Letty Horne (approx. 1792–1882), White Church Cemetery, Des Arc (Prairie Co.).

47. Susan Parks-Spencer, "Remembering the Lives of Robert Kidd and William Clingman Raper," *Flashback* 74, no. 1 (2024), 5.

48. Robert Kidd's original fieldstone marker in Bean Cemetery, Lincoln (Washington Co.), roughly inscribed "Bob K." is still on his grave. Two Little Rock newspapers published obituaries for Kidd, each putting his age at around a century.

49. Though no headstone has been located for him, Tandy Kidd is most likely buried in the Kidd graveyard near Cane Hill (Washington Co.) with other members of his family.

50. "Local Items," *Newark Journal* (Newark, AR), October 23, 1903, in *A History of Batesville and Independence County, Arkansas; Excerpts from Local and Regional Newspapers, Vol. 1, 1840–1907*, ed.Gary Perkey (Jonesboro, AR: Published by the author, 2012), 251. Note: no burial site has been found online for Evans.

51. Neal, "Fraternal Cemetery," 5.

52. "Mount Holly Cemetery," *Daily Arkansas Gazette* (Little Rock, AR), April 18, 1875, 4.

53. Mrs. John B. Kittrell Sr., "Misplaced Tombstones," *Rivers and Roads and Points in Between* 6, no. 2 (1978), 37.

54. Holly Almond, ed., *Brinkley Centennial Yearbook, 1872–1972* (Brinkley, AR: The Citizen).

55. Green Mount and Lacey Cemeteries (Drew Co.) have a large number of examples of Gumpert's work.

56. Holly Hope, "Historic Gravestone Iconography and Symbolism in Drew County," *Drew County Historical Journal* 32 (2017), 5–7. Some time after this was written, Gumpert (1909–1989) was identified by Marsha Winklepeck of Monticello (Drew Co.).

57. Theartis Early, interviewed by Evelyn Jackson Trammell, 2021. Early's father was the caretaker of St. Mary's Cemetery, Bradley. Bennie Ray Harris, grandson of a previous St. Mary's caretaker, interviewed by Evelyn Jackson Trammell, also verified McGuire's name.

58. In addition to the examples found in St. Mary's, there is one in Union Hill/Galilee/Boyds Hill Cemetery and two in Old Town (a.k.a. Old Lewisville) Cemetery (both Lafayette Co.).

59. This cemetery has no signage and goes by various names online: St. Mary's Cemetery, Bradley's town cemetery, or the African American section of the adjacent Walnut Hill Cemetery.

60. The club design, found the fewest times, may have been made with a small cake pan or Jell-O mold, as it does not show evidence of a strap handle. Online searches of vintage aluminum cookie cutters turned up an exact match for both the card suits and the star, a set made by Miro Aluminum Company. Ian W. Brown and students found examples of what appears to be the Miro Company's lion cookie cutter, used to embellish concrete markers in Tuscaloosa, Alabama, possibly an attempt to replicate the Supreme Royal Circle of Friends' emblem, which is a lion facing left.

61. McGuire's headstone reads: "Will J. McGuire, 7-4-1885—Passed after he was 90."

62. One tank has a concrete marker next to it for Dora Cozie (1870–1880).

63. *The History of Corning, AR; Corning, Formerly Known as Hecht City Then Later as Carpenter's Station*, unsigned, undated typescript donated to the Piggott Public Library by the Clay County Genealogical and Historical Society, 12.

64. Guy C. Vanderpool ed., *A Time to Every Purpose: The Photographs of Jesse L. Charlton, 1937–1954* (Texarkana, TX: Texarkana Museums System, 1999), unnumbered page, caption: "Glenwood Cemetery marker of Clemmie Farmer, with crockery and glass. Coastal Plain Land Tenure Study, 1954." The correct name of this cemetery is Mount Vernon, near Glenville (Nevada Co.).

65. National Register of Historic Places, Hampton Springs Cemetery (Black Section), Carthage, Dallas County, Arkansas, Site No. DA1, accessed August 16, 2023, https://www.arkansasheritage.com/docs/default-source/national-registry/da0004-pdf.pdf?sfvrsn=9a498fb9_0 1–2.

66. National Register of Historic Places, Hampton Springs Cemetery (Black Section), Carthage, Dallas County, Arkansas, Site No. DA1, 4.

67. There is no birth date on Taylor's marker.

68. John Michael Vlach, *The Afro-American Tradition in Decorative Arts* (Athens: University of Georgia Press, 1990), 139, 141.

69. Benford's birth year may be 1902; his death date is not legible.

70. Another example, though unrelated to these symbols, is found at Rohwer Relocation Center's cemetery on the side of the largest war memorial. The clock's hands appear to be set at ten minutes to five, but given the concrete's surface damage, could read twenty-five minutes past nine.

71. Forest Park Cemetery, Fort Smith (Sebastian Co.), has an uninscribed marker, possibly a footstone (name, dates unknown) containing the remnants of

a clock's internal gears; a similar example is embedded in the concrete marker of M.E. Andrews (1874–1938), Rowell Cemetery (Cleveland Co.).

72. David T. Beito, *From Mutual Aid to the Welfare State, Fraternal Societies and Social Services, 1890–1967* (Chapel Hill: University of North Carolina Press, 2000), 5–7.

73. Dick E. Browning, "Freemasons," CALS Encyclopedia of Arkansas, accessed August 1, 2023, https://encyclopediaofarkansas.net/entries/freemasons-4122/.

74. Laurel K. Gabel, "Ritual, Regalia and Remembrance: Fraternal Symbolism and Gravestones," *Markers* 11 (1994), 1.

75. Shumate is buried in Old Dogwood, a white cemetery, but this motto expresses the benefits conferred by all fraternal lodges.

76. "Form New Negro Insurance Firm," *Arkansas Democrat* (Little Rock, AR), June 20, 1919, 14; "Century Life Insurance Company Holds Annual Stockholders Meeting at Home Office," *The Black Dispatch* (Oklahoma City, OK), March 19, 1931, 2.

77. James Logan Morgan, ed., *Centennial History of Newport, Arkansas, 1875–1975* (Jackson County Historical Society, 1975), 49–53.

78. Beito, *From Mutual Aid to the Welfare State*, 223.

79. Clement Richardson, ed., "John Edward Bush," in *The National Cyclopedia of The Colored Race*, Vol. 1 (Montgomery, AL: National Publishing Co., 1919), 103.

80. Blake Wintory, *African American Fraternal Headstone Symbols in Arkansas: A Guide* (draft copy, June 6, 2018), 2, http://lakeport.astate.edu/wp-content/uploads/2018/06/Arkansas-Fraternal-Headstone-handout-June-2018.pdf.

81. Blake Wintory and Ashan R. Hampton, "Mosaic Templars of America," CALS Encyclopedia of Arkansas, accessed August 14, 2023, https://encyclopediaofarkansas.net/entries/mosaic-templars-of-america-1186/.

82. Carolyn Yancey Kent, "Supreme Royal Circle of Friends of the World," CALS Encyclopedia of Arkansas, accessed August 14, 2021, https://encyclopediaofarkansas.net/entries/supreme-royal-circle-of-friends-of-the-world-5861/.

83. Theda Skocpol and Jennifer Lynn Oser, "Organization Despite Adversity: The Origins and Development of African American Fraternal Associations," *Social Science History* 28, no. 3, (2004), 372.

84. Douglas Keister, August 4, 2020, Facebook post.

85. Beito, *From Mutual Aid to the Welfare State*, 11.

86. Angela Y. Walton-Raji, "American Woodmen—A Black Benevolent Society," *My Ancestor's Name* (blog), August 27, 2013, accessed August 16, 2023, http://myancestorsname.blogspot.com/2013/08/american-woodmen-black-benevolent.html.

87. A rare example of this organization's emblem is found on the grave of George Wilson (died 1931), Oak Cemetery, Fort Smith (Sebastian Co.).

88. "After Company Which Failed to Pay Claims," *Pine Bluff Daily Graphic* (Pine Bluff, AR), March 12, 1914, 5.

89. Benevolent and Protective Order of Elks, entry accessed November 16, 2023, https://en.wikipedia.org/wiki/Benevolent_and_Protective_Order_of_Elks.

90. "After Company Which Failed to Pay Claims," *Pine Bluff Daily Graphic* (Pine Bluff, AR), March 12, 12, 1914, 5, listing "some very high-sounding names among the fraternal orders" (presumably all African American).

91. Possibly a Black lodge that paralleled the Loyal Order of Ancient Shepherds (this emblem has not been found on Arkansas headstones).

92. Possibly a Black lodge that paralleled to the Ancient Order of Pyramids.

93. "After Company Which Failed to Pay Claims."

94. Wintory, *African American Fraternal Headstone Symbols*, 13, citing Bruce T. Bullion et al., *Condensed Report Fire, Life, Casualty and Fraternal 1923 Business, State of Arkansas Department of Insurance and Fire Preventions, 1923 Business* (Little Rock, AR, 1924), 53, http://lakeport.astate.edu/wp-content/uploads/2018/06/Arkansas-Fraternal-Headstone-handout-June-2018.pdf.

95. Marvin D. Jeter, ed., *Edward Palmer's Arkansaw [sic] Mounds* (Tuscaloosa: University of Alabama Press, 1990), 162.

CHAPTER 3. GRAVE MARKERS AND MORTUARY STRUCTURES

1. "Wife Kills Husband with Automobile Axle," hand-dated April 7, 1921, in *Yell County Historical and Genealogical Association Bulletin* 6, no. 2 (1981), 58.

2. Lola Person Cooper, comp., *Lest We Forget* (Typescript of Yell County history published by the author, 1972, reprinted 1979), 16.

3. *Cemeteries of Yell County, Arkansas*, Vol. 2 (Dardanelle, AR: Yell County Historical and Genealogical Society, 1994), 252; Burnett, Abby, "Murder Weapon Marks Grave," *AGS Quarterly* 43, no. 4 (Winter 2019)/44 no. 1 (Spring 2020), 13–15.

4. "Wife Kills Husband with Automobile Axle," 58.

5. Carrie Gardner (1892–1933) is buried in McGhee Cemetery (Perry Co.), not far from her sister Effie L. Conrade (1905–1974). Carrie's epitaph: "She was the sunshine of our home."

6. Photos of the existing piece of metal were shown to two mechanics who restore antique cars; both said the pipe was consistent with a Model T axle.

7. Robert Case Jr., interviewed by the author in Harris Cemetery, November 2022, and again by phone December 2022.

8. W.L. Lewsaw (1882–1909), Dry Creek Cemetery (Lawrence Co.).

9. Head and Shoulders Cemetery (Cross Co.) was named for the shape of these tablets, found there, though this cannot be verified as this cemetery is not identifiable using online sources.

10. Works Progress Administration, Historical Records Survey, Early Settlers' Personal History Questionnaire, Special Collections, University of Arkansas Libraries, Fayetteville; Question 46: "Tell of any early tombstone inscriptions."

11. Southwest Arkansas Regional Archives (SARA).

12. Southwest Arkansas Regional Archives, Historic Washington State Park; collection includes an undated headboard for P. Cox, and one for Z.A.S., presumably that of Zenobia Aurelia Sanders, dd. 1848.

13. Mary L. Kwas, *Thou Wert Dear to Us: A Record of Pioneer Cemetery, Washington, Arkansas* (Washington: Southwest Arkansas Regional Archives Foundation, 2011), 2.

14. "Mount Holly Cemetery," *Daily Arkansas Gazette* (Little Rock, AR) April 18, 1875, 3.

15. Sybil F. Crawford, *Jubilee: The First 150 Years of Mount Holly Cemetery, Little Rock, Arkansas* (Little Rock: Mount Holly Cemetery Association, 1993), 66–67.

16. Crawford, *Jubilee*, 1–2.

17. Huie and Hunter-Hill cemeteries (Van Buren Co.) have numerous examples of wooden markers, none with names or dates.

18. Abby Burnett, "Washington Monument Marble Quarry," CALS Encyclopedia of Arkansas, accessed August 20, 2023, https://encyclopediaofarkansas.net/entries/washington-monument-marble-quarry-14025/.

19. Vincent Anderson, "Lincoln's Memorial Stone from the Ozarks," November 14, 2018, accessed November 15, 2023, https://www.youtube.com/watch?v=URX-C6yTJmg&t=632s.

20. "Marble Cutting!," *Weekly Arkansas Gazette* (Little Rock, AR), November 1, 1850, 4.

21. "Honor to the Dead," *The Ouachita Herald* (Camden, AR), October 2, 1856, 3. Earliest advertisement found June 5, 1856, but earlier copies of the paper are missing.

22. "New Marble Yard," *Southern Shield* (Helena, AR), February 23, 1856, 1.

23. Brooks Blevins, *Hill Folks: A History of Arkansas Ozarkers and Their Image* (Chapel Hill: University of North Carolina Press, 2002), 18–19.

24. Holmes Cemetery, Bellefonte (Boone Co.); the carver spelled "far" as "for" on this marker and one for Weaver's daughter.

25. The largest and most diverse collections of combs are found in Holmes Cemetery at Bellefonte and Rowland Family Cemetery in Valley Springs (both Boone Co.), while Saline Cemetery (Pike Co.) contains a number of primitive examples.

26. Ric Finch, email to the author, May 14, 2020.

27. Shown to the author on condition that its location not be disclosed. The stone box is the length of an adult grave, so possibly the child's empty iron casket was found elsewhere and merely placed in the box crypt to dispose of it.

28. M. Ruth Little, *Sticks and Stones: Three Centuries of North Carolina Gravemarkers* (Chapel Hill: University of North Carolina Press, 1998), 242, 244.

29. "Last Chance to Get a Bargain in Tombstones," *Daily Arkansas Gazette* (Little Rock, AR), February 26, 1919, 8.

30. Joseph Hicks, "Concrete Folk Carved Gravestones of Eastern Tuscaloosa County, Alabama," in *A Survey of the Cemeteries of East Tuscaloosa County, Alabama*, ed. Ian W. Brown. Unpublished research conducted during the course "Marking Graves: Self and Society in Death," Blount Undergraduate Initiative 301 (Tuscaloosa: University of Alabama, Alabama Museum of Natural History, Gulf Coast Survey Archives, 2004), 8.

31. Ian W. Brown, email to the author, July 14, 2020.

32. C.U. M'Dowell, "Cheer Up! You've Better Outlook to Die Now as Tombstone Demand Booms," *The News Scimitar* (Memphis, TN), August 21, 1920, 1.

33. Barbara Rotundo, "Monumental Bronze," in *Cemeteries and Gravemarkers: Voices of American Culture*, ed. Richard E. Meyer (Ann Arbor: UMI Research Press, 1989), 263, 267.

34. *Catalogue of the Monumental Bronze Company* (Bridgeport, CT, October 1882), accessed August 20, 2023, https://archive.org/details/WhitebronzemonuooMonu/page/2/mode/2up.

35. Rotundo, "Monumental Bronze," 284.

36. Bill Plack and Ellis Michaels, "Known Tombstone Carvers of Pennsylvania," Pennsylvania USGenWeb Archives, Monumental Bronze Company, accessed August 20, 2023, http://www.usgwarchives.net/pa/1pa/tscarvers/monumental-bronze/monumental-bronze.htm.

37. Evergreen Cemetery, Fayetteville (Washington Co.).

38. Abby Burnett, "Evergreen Cemetery," CALS Encyclopedia of Arkansas, accessed August 20, 2023, https://encyclopediaofarkansas.net/entries/evergreen-cemetery-7426/

39. Gary Brown, interviewed by the author, August 2018. Brown, a former Clarendon undertaker, planned to restore the statue after recovering the detached hand but lost it in a house fire.

40. Annette Stott, *Pioneer Cemeteries: Sculpture Gardens of the Old West* (Lincoln: University of Nebraska Press, 2008), 229.

41. Mary Ollie Whitlow (1889–1900), Wesley town cemetery (Madison Co.).

42. J.K.P. Shelton's 1887 patent for a "monument or sign holder" is similar to the iron markers, but not an exact match.

43. Other examples are found in Flint Springs Cemetery and Union Cemetery (Fulton Co.), Moore Cemetery (Newton Co.), and Paint Rock Cemetery (Logan Co.).

44. Elizabeth Graham (1837–1928), Wilson Cemetery, Springdale (Washington Co.).

45. Ophelia Cleopatra Whitten Caldwell (1878–1899) and O.C. Caldwell, May 9–August 2, 1899, name and dates difficult to read but transcribed at Find a Grave, accessed August 20, 2023, https://www.findagrave.com/memorial/14057185/ophelia-cleopatra-caldwell.

46. Jeffrey A. Blakeley, "The Nineteenth Century Pottery Industry in Sebastian County, Arkansas," *Arkansas Historical Quarterly* 49, no. 1 (1990), 65–66.

47. Five generic box-style markers have been found in Coop Prairie, Looper, and Freedom Cemeteries (Scott Co.) and Lovelace Cemetery (Sebastian Co.). An unglazed ceramic box marker having a completely different profile is found in Nixon Cemetery (Franklin Co.) and may not be Caldwell's work.

48. Elsie Moran, October 26, 1916, Lovelace Cemetery, Witcherville, and Robert B. Wood, August 29–September 20, 1932, Dayton Cemetery (both Sebastian Co.).

49. Unsourced newspaper article dated March 31, 1935, on Find a Grave, accessed August 20, 2023, https://www.findagrave.com/memorial/52685436/john-harrison-caldwell.

50. Swannee Bennett and William B. Worthen, *Arkansas Made: A Survey of the Decorative, Mechanical, and Fine Arts Produced in Arkansas Through 1950* (Fayetteville: University of Arkansas Press, 2021), 148.

51. Sharum and Duty Cemeteries (Randolph Co.) and Fluty Cemetery (Baxter Co.).

52. Oak Valley Cemetery (Sebastian Co.).

53. Douglas Keister, *Stories in Stone: A Field Guide to Cemetery Symbolism and Iconography* (Salt Lake City, UT: Gibbs Smith, 2004), 87; Tammie Trippe-Dillon, *Grave Concerns: A Preservation for Historic Cemeteries in Arkansas* (Little Rock: Arkansas Historic Preservation Program, n.d.), 125, pdf accessed August 20, 2023.

54. Jessie Lie Farber, "Symbolism on Gravestones," Association for Gravestone Studies, accessed August 20, 2023, https://www.gravestonestudies.org/knowledge-center/symbolism#faqnoanchor.

55. "Mail," *White County Historical Society News*, February 2015, 9; Pine Grove Cemetery, near Floral (Independence Co.), photo submitted by a reader asking about the custom of using mussel shells to mark graves.

56. S.D. Dickinson, "Shells for the Dead," *The Old Time Chronicle, Folk History of Southwest Arkansas* 3, no. 11 (1990), 8–9.

57. In Mount Moriah Cemetery (Nevada Co.) spouses Jesse Hirst (1857–1923) and Susan Hirst (1868–1954) have individual shell covers; spouse Ausy Honea (1896–1937) has a shell cover, but wife Mary E. Honea (1891–1957) has a matching concrete mound with no shells.

58. Leonore Shoults, "Button Blank Industry," CALS Encyclopedia of Arkansas History and Culture, accessed August 20, 2023, https://encyclopediaofarkansas.net/entries/button-blank-industry-6577/.

59. Scott Akridge, email to the White County Historical Society and shared with the author, October 10, 2023. This author has found only one example, in Independence County, but has been told that punched shells have been seen in various cemeteries near both the White and Black Rivers.

60. Information provided by Carol Lawler, citing Find a Grave entry for Margaret Elizabeth Chunn, buried in Black Cemetery (Sharp Co.), accessed December 16/2023, https://www.findagrave.com/memorial/57138250/margaret-elizabeth-chunn.

61. Karla F.C. Holloway, *Passed On: African American Mourning Stories: A Memorial* (Durham, NC: Duke University Press, 2002), 210.

62. John Michael Vlach, *The Afro-American Tradition in Decorative Arts* (Athens: University of Georgia Press, 1990), 143.

63. "Children's Cemetery at Lakeport Plantation," November 7, 2018 blog post, Lakeport Plantation, https://lakeport.astate.edu/2018/11/.

64. Blake Wintory, *Images of America: Chicot County* (Charleston, SC: Arcadia Publishing, 2015), 19.

65. Juan Ignacio Blanco, Death Penalty USA; Executions 1607–1976, by state, accessed December 24/2024, https://deathpenaltyusa.org/usa1/state/arkansas.htm ?fbclid=IwY2xjawHH7zdleHRuA2FlbQIxMAABHeHsautMp-r9nVb -LFsos9URFOe-5W03uifW1QQIF8s80iwQVAKnCYVCNQ_aem _kOvTLbOpGrYg8qF1iRGuDg.

66. Parlee Taylor (1840–1877), buried in Stainer Cemetery (Saline Co.).

67. "The Murderous Poker, and How It Was Wielded by Tom Staner to Terminate the Existence of Two Women," *Daily Arkansas Gazette* (Little Rock, AR), May 22, 1877, 4; "Confession of a Murderer," *Saline County Digest* (Benton, AR), May 24, 1877, 1; "Tom Staner, the Saline County Murderer, Burns the Benton Jail and Makes a Bold Strike for Liberty—Is Severely Wounded and Recaptured," *Daily Arkansas Gazette* (Little Rock, AR), October 24, 1877, 4; "Satan's Recruit. Tom Staner, the Saline County Murderer, Dances the Aerial Quickstep," *Daily Arkansas Gazette* (Little Rock, AR) November 3, 1877, 4.

68. Adelia C. Kittrell and Curtis A. Houston, *Cemetery Records of Woodruff County: East of Cache River* (N.p., 1978), 72.

69. This author has also found grave houses just outside the Arkansas Ozarks in Craighead, Logan, White, and Yell Counties and, farther south, in Calhoun, Cleveland, Grant, Hot Spring, Lincoln, Nevada, Pike, Saline, Scott, and Union Counties; very likely others exist or have existed elsewhere across the state.

70. Cleveland Jacobs (1889–1890), Ebenezer Cemetery at Tull (Grant Co.).

71. Lula Lorraine Williams (died November 26, 1916), New Hope Cemetery (Calhoun Co.).

72. *Biographies of Van Buren County, Arkansas* (Clinton, AR: Van Buren County Historical Society, 1996), 181.

73. John Madison Graves, II (1930–1999) and Maggie Mae Faulkinbury Graves (1933–2020) are buried beneath a new, picket-sided house similar to an existing one in Graves Cemetery (Logan Co.), where two grave sheds, covering three burials, have since been removed.

74. Donald B. Ball, "A Reexamination of Gravehouse Origins in the Upland South: Misunderstood Examples of Folk Mortuary Hardware," paper presented to the Alabama Chapter of the Association for Gravestone Studies, spring meeting, April 27, 2013.

75. James K. Chrisman, *Death and Dying in Central Appalachia: Changing Attitudes and Practices* (Urbana: University of Illinois Press, 1994), 130–32.

76. William Maberry did not sign the headstones he carved, but a photo taken in his stone yard shows a headstone almost identical to Guffrey Agee's.

77. Abby Burnett, "Shelter for the Dead; Gravehouses Rare Find in Cemeteries," *The Morning News* (Springdale, AR), April 3, 2006, D Section. There is no explanation for why he did not create houses over the graves of two granddaughters buried in the Hasty (a.k.a. Agee) cemetery.

78. "Marvel Rhyne: Letters to Dear Joe," *The Journal* (Fort Smith Historical Society) 35, no. 1 (2011), 18.

79. Unsourced, undated typescript, courtesy of Teresa Harris and the Ouachita County Historical Society (Camden, Arkansas) that describes six "or more" caskets in disarray inside the vault.

80. Mrs. J.W. Meek, "A Plea for the Old Cemetery: Written for the Daughters of the Confederacy," believed to have been published in 1910, *The Sandyland Chronicle*, ed. Jerry McKelvy, 5, no. 2 (2005), 2, accessed August 20, 2023, https://sandyland.dreamhosters.com/2005-02.pdf.

81. *The History of Corning, AR: Corning Formerly Known as Hecht City Then Later as Carpenter's Station*, unsigned, undated typescript donated to the Piggott Public Library by the Clay County Genealogical and Historical Society, 13.

82. These once-popular statues, representing the infant Samuel at prayer, are in the form of a kneeling child. Other examples are found in Van Buren's Fairview Cemetery (Crawford Co.) and White Lake Cemetery (Woodruff Co.).

83. Ron. Romano, *Billboard Monuments of Maine: A Collection of Rare 1800s Gravestones* (Thomaston, Maine: Indie Author Books, 2020), 40–43, 48–50.

84. B. Craig Stinson, *A Brief History of Our Hill Family in America* (Blurb Creative Publishing Service, 2011), 111–12.

85. Kim Reynolds, "Frank 'Jelly' Nash (1887–1933)," CALS Encyclopedia of Arkansas, accessed August 20, 2023, https://encyclopediaofarkansas.net/entries/frank-jelly-nash-4067/.

86. National Register of Historic Places, Linwood Mausoleum, Paragould, Greene County, Arkansas, Site No. GE0270, Section 8, 3, 5–7, accessed August 20, 2023, https://www.arkansasheritage.com/docs/default-source/national-registry/ge0270-pdf.pdf?sfvrsn=71b8a5a_0.

CHAPTER 4. TOMBSTONE INSCRIPTIONS

1. Hite Cemetery, outside Pocahontas (Randolph Co.).

2. Eliza A. Smith (1850–1885), Richwoods Cemetery (Clay Co.). An identical, but unsigned, stone is in Oak Lawn Cemetery, West Plains, Missouri.

3. Ernest A. Nowell (1862–1877), Cypress Valley Cemetery (Faulkner Co.). An identical, but unsigned, version is found on the stone of James Thaddeus Reams (1870–1871), Rose Hill, Arkadelphia (Clark Co.).

4. Information from a public member tree for the Harry C. Hite on Ancestry, accessed August 20, 2023, https://www.ancestry.com/family-tree/person/tree/116716692/person/400156898497/facts. No tombstone has been found for this child.

5. If Harry Hite's child is the one referred to in Johnnie's epitaph, then Johnnie's stone wasn't purchased until at least fifteen years after he died.

6. Mary F. Johnson (1844–1859), Golden Cemetery (Clark Co.).

7. Rev. Stephen Carlile (1817–1860), Oak Grove Cemetery, Searcy (White Co.).

8. James Montgomery, "Servant of God, Well Done!," in *Greenland and Other Poems* (London: Printed by Strahan and Spottiswoode for Longman, Hurst, Rees, Orme and Brown, 1819).

9. Oak Grove Cemetery, Searcy (White Co.).

10. Below this one-liner are the initials F.M.S., name unknown, in Lewis Cemetery (Washington Co.).

11. Shaddox Cemetery, Pruitt (Newton Co.); stone signed by J.W. Robbins.

12. Malanthan Carver, son of Ben and B.E. Carver, February 2, 1873–October 27, 1888 [possibly 1883], Morris Cemetery (Newton Co.) near the Buffalo River; photo of headstone provided by Phillip Watkins, who was told by a Carver family member that Malanthan "was killed when a team of mules got away from him."

13. Extension Homemakers Council, *Cemeteries of Fulton County, Arkansas* (N.p., 1999). According to the preface, this stone is found among several unmarked graves atop a bluff in the southwest corner of Fulton County but does not give a cemetery name or directions for finding it.

14. Zebulon Jetton (1779–1865), Knoxville Bend Cemetery (Johnson Co.).

15. Jerry Lee Underwood (1952–1987), Gipson Cemetery (Scott Co.).

16. Moses Ford (died 1870), Love Cemetery (Crawford Co.). Stone is a replica of the original.

17. J.W. Meal (1822–1868), Spring Grove Cemetery, Cincinnati, Ohio.

18. Cowell Cemetery (Newton Co.).

19. Bellefonte Cemetery (Boone Co.).

20. Gum Springs Cemetery (White Co.).

21. Fair Grove Cemetery, Green Forest (Carroll Co.). Miller often included unusual information on the stones he carved.

22. Cooper's age is seventy on the 1870 census and seventy-three ten years later, in 1880; she died in 1892. Her stone was carved by Nick Miller, who seems to have encouraged clients to include unusual personal details on the stones he carved for them.

23. "Minié Ball," Wikipedia, accessed December 02/2023, https://en.wikipedia.org/wiki/Mini%C3%A9_ball.

24. Samuel E. Erwin (1843–1907), Find a Grave entry, accessed November 30, 2023, https://www.findagrave.com/memorial/86223716/samuel-erwin.

25. Allice L. Williams (October 22, 1870–October 15, 1882), White Rock Cemetery (Washington Co.)

26. The inscription actually reads, "A Survivor of the Mountain Meadow Masacree."

27. "A Peculiar Killing: An Old Texarkana Citizen Slain by a Bullet Fired at a Dog," *St. Louis Post-Dispatch* (St. Louis, MO), June 17, 1894, 1.

28. Found in Stone, Dallas, Independence, Lonoke, Jackson, and Baxter Counties, respectively.

29. Found in Cleveland, Conway, and Pope Counties, respectively.

30. Found in Boone, Monroe, Benton, Hot Spring, and Lawrence Counties, respectively.

31. Mourning family obelisk, Embry surname, Atkins city cemetery (Pope Co.).

32. Oak Grove Cemetery, Conway (Faulkner Co.).

33. Keesee Cemetery (Marion Co.).

34. Rolla, Missouri's town cemetery contains a zinc obelisk for Mary E. Godwin (1847–1849), who presumably died in childbirth. Cast inscription: "Jesus has named the little one. Rev. 2, C. 17. V". While no verse is given it is likely verse 17: ". . . I . . . will give him a white stone, and in the stone a new name written, which no man knoweth saving he that receiveth *it*."

35. US Bureau of the Census, *Thirteenth Census of the United States—1910*, Lafayette Township, Lonoke County, Arkansas, household of Infant Bea and his wife (African American, both born in South Carolina) and their two (named) teenaged children.

36. Brentwood Cemetery, Winslow (Washington Co.).

37. Mount Zion Cemetery (Pope Co.)

38. Reeves Cemetery, Red Star Road (Madison Co.).

39. Mountain View Cemetery, at Hackett (Sebastian Co.).

40. Linwood Cemetery, Paragould (Greene Co.).

41. Bold Pilgrim, near Morrilton (Conway Co.)

42. Martinsville Cemetery (Faulkner Co.)

43. Alpena Cemetery (Boone Co.).

44. Hite Cemetery, outside Pocahontas (Randolph Co.).

45. Glespy Sanders (1914–1956), Erple L. (Blair) Guffey (1918–1995), and Mamil Tyree (1918–1971), Elizabeth Cemetery (Fulton Co.).

46. Gladness Neal Breeding (1935–2008), Shady Grove Cemetery, Clarendon (Monroe Co.), and Mourning Womble Blasingame (1823–1893), Parker Cemetery (Carroll Co.).

47. Harmony Cemetery, Rocky Mound (Columbia Co.).

48. Chicot County (name and location withheld).

49. Paul W. Klipsch (1904–2002), Rose Hill Cemetery, Hope (Hempstead Co.). Klipsch was an engineer and inventor of high-fidelity speakers; "Bullshit"—his company's unofficial rallying cry—was printed on yellow buttons that Klipsch handed out at industry trade shows and that his employees (discreetly) wore to his funeral.

50. Douglas M. Byford (1942–2015), Chant Cemetery (Scott Co.).

51. Michael H. "Skymonkey" Reynolds (1953–no death date), Galatia (Baxter Co.).

52. Shawn Paul Lindsay (1974–2018), Alabam Cemetery (Madison County).

53. Edward Jason Allen, "E.J." (1977–2018), Alabam Cemetery (Madison Co.).

54. Butlerville Cemetery (Lonoke Co.).

55. "Destroyed," *Arkansas Democrat* (Little Rock, AR), April 28, 1880, 3.

56. "He Followed Them," *Arkansas Democrat* (Little Rock, AR), August 6, 1881, 4.

57. IOOF Cemetery, Berryville (Carroll Co.), modern marker placed on grave in the 1990s.

58. Abby Burnett, "Nick Miller, 1846?–1898," CALS Encyclopedia of Arkansas, accessed August 23, 2023, https://encyclopediaofarkansas.net/entries/nick-miller-5849/.

59. Edward Platt, died February 23, 1850, aged twenty-three, buried in Mount Holly Cemetery, Little Rock (Pulaski Co.).

60. Joseph H. Waite, died August 6, 1844, "Son of Col. Moses [&] Phebe Waite, of Hubbardston, Mass." buried in Sulphur Springs (Yell Co.); Ernestene [sic] Hudlow Gravelly, "Story of Sulphur Springs, Yell County, Arkansas," *Yell County Historical and Genealogical Association Bulletin* 7, no. 2 (1982), 112 (hand-numbered unpaginated issue).

61. Duane Huddleston, "The Volant and Reindeer Early Arkansas Steamboats," *Arkansas Historical Quarterly* 24, no. 2 (1976), 31.

62. "Obituary," *Arkansas Times and Advocate* (Little Rock, Arkansas Territory), July 24, 1833, 3, gives his cause of death as "congestive fever, which assumed a typhoid form" while the longer death notice, published in an unnamed Washington, Pennsylvania, newspaper, contains the quote given, in "Letters from a Steamboat Passenger," edited by Marion S. Craig, MD, and Dr. George E. Lankford, *Independence County Chronicle* 36, nos. 1 and 2, October 1994–January 1995, 17–18.

63. Craig and Lankford, "Letters from a Steamboat Passenger," 18, from an account written by another son, cited in the endnotes only as *History of the Acheson Family*, no name given.

64. Mary Acheson's implied criticism was not misplaced. Despite Drew's wealth (given to him by his father-in-law), he successfully kept the Acheson family from settling their son's estate and receiving his share of the business partnership(s).

65. Acheson is buried near the Bettis-Drew family plot of Governor Thomas S. Drew (1802–1879), who was originally buried in Texas but reinterred in Arkansas in 1923. Drew's obelisk mentions his own eventual impoverishment.

66. Though Hanks's little obelisk does not include birth or death dates, his death notice states that he died of pneumonia in February 1907; *Springdale News* (Springdale, AR), February 15, 1907, reprinting an undated item from the *Prairie Grove Herald* (Prairie Grove, AR).

67. Smith Cemetery, Vendor (Newton Co.).

68. Oakland Memorial Cemetery, Clarksville (Johnson Co.).

69. A variation on this verse ("She tasted of life's bitter cup / Refused to drink the portion up . . .") is found in Massachusetts, on the grave of four-year-old Caroline Newcomb, died 1812.

70. This consolation is occasionally found on adults' markers, such as Mary Fannie Curry (1853–1907), Union Cemetery (Cleveland Co.), who has this epitaph: "Under a deep turf of daisies, / Our dearest has folded her arms on her breast, / They wanted new angels to praise him in heaven, / And mama dear mama was called with the rest."

71. Jahve Sooter (February 3, 1887–August 26, 1888), Marshall town cemetery (Searcy Co.).

72. Lola (October–November 1888) and Leroy (September–October 1892) Baggett, Spring Creek (Washington Co.).

73. Mansel H. Bryant (August 20, 1913–June 28, 1914), Capps Cemetery (Boone Co.).

74. Infant son of B.E. Patton, died August 6, 1911, White Oak Cemetery (Boone Co.).

75. Stone broken, no legible name or dates, Highland Cemetery, Ozark (Franklin Co.).

76. Hopewell Cemetery, Carolan (Logan Co.).

77. Nixon Cemetery (Franklin Co.); inscription also found in Nixon Cemetery for Demps Williams (1893–1894)

78. J.H. Williams (February 2, 1891–March 18, 1899), Aetna Church Cemetery (Franklin Co.).

79. White Rock Cemetery, Dutch Mills (Washington Co.).

80. William R. Grace (1829–1910 or 1918; stone is broken across last number), Atkins City Cemetery (Pope Co.).

81. J.P. Penn (1833–1894), Augusta Memorial Park (Woodruff Co.).

82. Buffalo Cemetery (Newton Co.).

83. Nancy Redman grave near Jacksonport (Jackson Co.); listed on Find a Grave as Jacksonport Cemetery.

84. Though broken, this appears to be Jesse Brazil's original concrete marker (1829–1870), now piled behind his military headstone, Campground Cemetery, Winthrop (Little River Co.).

85. Sarah Carlton (1862–1885), Buffalo Cemetery, Parthenon (Newton Co.).

86. Nin A. Gray (1853–1879) and son Ernest (Jan. 6–18, 1879), Evergreen Cemetery, Fayetteville (Washington Co.).

87. Sarah P. Gibson (1870–1900), Antioch Cemetery, Barber (Logan Co.)

88. Hassie Morrison (1893–1919), New Hope Cemetery (Calhoun Co.).

89. Rush R. Batterton (1902–1920), Fourche Loupe Cemetery (Garland Co.)

90. Antinette N. Blackwell (1851–1881), Unity Cemetery, Arkadelphia (Clark Co.). The verse is obscured after the word "calmly." Bryant likely wrote "Consumption" between the 1820s and 1850s; he is better known for "Thanatopsis," another poem about death.

91. Meredith Wilkerson (January 20, 1839–January 16, 1954), Augusta Memorial Park (Woodruff Co.).

92. Auman Cemetery, near Alpena (Boone Co.). Despite this name, Pearl was a boy.

93. Wm. Lang (1864–1914), Kersey Cemetery (Franklin Co.).

94. Charles Russo (1887–1919), St. Joseph's Cemetery, Pine Bluff (Jefferson Co.).

95. Oaklawn Cemetery, Jonesboro (Craighead Co.).

96. Jefferson Pierce (1888–1900), Smith Cemetery, Vendor (Newton Co.).

97. Lilly V. Howerton (1881–1885), Rock Springs Cemetery (Carroll Co.).

98. Demoss Dillahunty (1884–1888), Violet Cemetery at Osceola (Mississippi Co.).

99. Wanda Carson McGehee, *Ancestors Inside the Gates, Fort Chaffee, Sebastian County, Arkansas*, catalogued by Sue Clark McGehee (N.p., 1992), 30. Note: Lone Star, a.k.a. Eppler Cemetery is on government property and not accessible to the public.

100. "A Shocking Accident," *The Pulaski Citizen* (Pulaski, TN), April 3, 1884, 3.

101. Coal Hill Cemetery (Johnson Co.).

102. McFerrin Cemetery, near Compton (Newton Co.).

103. *Fayetteville Daily* (Fayetteville, AR), June 26, 1905, 2. (Note: Article has no headline.)

104. "Gave Her Life for Little One" and "Negro Girl Saved Baby's Life, but Lost Her Own Under Car," *Arkansas Democrat* (Little Rock, AR), May 23, 1905, 1, 4.

105. "Monument to Heroic Act," *Daily Arkansas Gazette* (Little Rock, AR), May 25, 1905, 7.

106. "Why Not a Carnegie Medal in Catherine Lawson's Case?," *Daily Arkansas Gazette* (Little Rock, AR), May 31, 1905, 4.

107. "Gave Her Life for Little One"; "Suits Are Settled," *Daily Arkansas Gazette* (Little Rock, AR), November 2, 1905, 3.

108. *Clay County Courier* (Corning, AR), March 2, 1906, 2. Age determined from Trager's headstone in Elmlawn Cemetery, Little Rock (Pulaski Co.).

109. Sacred Heart Cemetery, Clarksville (Johnson).

110. "Fast Train Strikes Girls: Frances Spanke Killed and Mary [sic] Oberle Injured at Iron Bridge: An Act of Heroism," *Clarksville Democrat* (Clarksville, AR), May 14, 1914, reprinted in *Johnson County Historical Society Journal* 30, no. 2 (2004), 16–17 ["Article submitted by Lance Spanke"].

111. "Carnegie Hero Fund Commission Case Minute[s], Class—Train, #1387," *Johnson County Historical Society Journal* 30, no. 2 (2004), 17–21.

112. The application for the Carnegie medal says Francis's original name was Frances Beiner, but she appears on the 1910 census as "Francis Bayor, granddaughter."

113. The name is spelled Zeblon Jetton on the tombstone and Zebulon in online documentation (1779–1865), Knoxville Bend Cemetery (Johnson Co.).

114. Walters Chapel Cemetery, Carlisle (Lonoke Co.).

115. Local lore has it that someone scratched a sentence on Bogard's stone, condemning him for spitting in a man's face but, if true, this graffiti is not visible today.

116. The stone is signed, "Lilly, Fort Smith," and is the work of Isom Daniel, who, with his family, lived near Charleston (Franklin Co.) in the early 1870s but moved to Fort Smith by 1880, where he produced work for the Lilly company.

117. Wes Goodner, "Waldron War," CALS Encyclopedia of Arkansas, accessed September 8, 2023, https://encyclopediaofarkansas.net/entries/waldron-war-2819/.

118. Doris Dewberry, "Oark and Some of It's [sic] Pioneers," *Johnson County Historical Society Journal* 25, no. 1 (1999), 4–5; Arkansas Archaeological Survey, Site Survey Form for State Site No. 3J0376, Site Documentation for Ozark National Forest, Horner Cemetery.

119. Basham Memorial Cemetery, Mountainburg (Crawford Co.).

120. Jesse Woodson James (1847–1882), buried on the Jesse James farm, Kearney (Clay Co.) Missouri.

121. "Another Tragedy: Shawnee Again the Scene of a Horrible Affair," *The Shawnee Herald* (Shawnee, OK), January 3, 1902, 5.

122. Anton Peter Anderson Cemetery (Crawford Co.).

123. "Serious Trouble at a Dance," *The Southern Standard* (Arkadelphia, AR), February 3, 1899, 1.

124. "The Ashley Township Tragedy: Further Particulars—The Deliberate Murder of a Constable's Posse," *Daily Arkansas Gazette* (Little Rock, AR), November 8, 1873, 4.

125. "The Ashley Township Tragedy: Arrest of Eight of the Ringleaders—They Are Lodged in Jail," *Daily Arkansas Gazette* (Little Rock, AR), November 9, 1873, 4.

126. "The Ashley Township Tragedy," 4.

127. *Eagles on the Prairie: A Historic View of Lonoke and Lonoke County Through One Man, James P. Eagle Jr. and His Family* (Lonoke, AR: Lonoke County Museum, n.d.), 44–53.

128. Nancy Snell Griffith, "Eagle Murders of 1873," CALS Encyclopedia of Arkansas, accessed August 23, 2020, https://encyclopediaofarkansas.net/entries/eagle-murders-of-1873-15623/.

129. "$400 Reward!" *Daily Arkansas Gazette* (Little Rock, AR), February 9, 1871, 4.

130. Farmer Cemetery, near Hindsville (Madison Co.), yet another example of unusual information found on tombstones carved by Nick Miller.

131. Sylvanus Hinds (1843–1863), Farmer Cemetery, Hindsville (Madison Co.).

132. Susan Ferrandiz, letter to the author, September 28, 2020, regarding her husband's family, stating that the Hinds family is found on the 1870 and 1880 censuses in Missouri.

133. Information provided by Youngblood family researchers Vineta Wingate and Dorothy Quaife.

134. Mountain Home cemetery (Baxter Co.).

135. "Marion County Man Killed by Officer in Café Shooting," *Baxter Bulletin* (Mountain Home, AR), April 11, 1947, 1; "Young Man Killed Here Last Week Resisting Arrest" and "Circuit Court Had Unusually Heavy Docket," *The Mountaineer Echo* (Yellville, AR), April 10, 1947, August 1 and 14, 1947, 1; Kennedy's brothers were found guilty of assault on an officer (receiving two-year prison sentences, suspended for good behavior) and resisting arrest, a fifty-dollar fine.

136. "More About the Henry Conway Grave," reprinting an undated, unsourced newspaper clipping found at Arkansas Post (likely published August 1935), *Grand Prairie Historical Society Bulletin* 6, no. 3 (1963), 53–54.

137. Though easily found in the Richard Hill Cemetery, the marker is not necessarily on Deny's grave: A landowner removed the headstones, brush-hogged the land, and put the stones back, but there is no guarantee that they were returned to their original locations.

138. "A Tale of Horror," *Ft. Smith Weekly New Era* (Fort Smith, AR), December 1, 1871, taken from the *Tri-Weekly*, November 20, 1871, 2; "Horrid Crime in Franklin County—Speedy Justice Administered to the Murderer," *Van Buren Press* (Van Buren, AR), November 28, 1871, 2.

139. "Capt. Whisler, Funston Fiend, Dies by Own Hand: Latest Chapter in Bloody Story of Looting of Army Bank," *Leavenworth Weekly Times* (Leavenworth, KS), January 17, 1918, 3.

140. "Influenza Epidemic Took Toll," in *Insight 2000: A Millennium Project of the Southwest Times Record*, ed. Nancy Steel (Southwest Times Record, 2000), 88.

141. Alabam Cemetery (Madison Co.).

142. Both inscriptions, as well as a stone with "asshole" below a man's name, are all found on markers with birth, but not death, dates and are presumed to have been chosen by the person, who is still living. Wayne Everett Strickland chose "I am a busy man I don't have time for this" for his marker in Prairie Grove's cemetery (Washington Co.) long before he died in 2005.

143. *Richland Beacon* (Rayville, LA), December 23, 1876, 2.

144. "A Deadly Resolution: Suicide of a Son of Senator W. Jasper Blackburn: Love and Whisky the Compound Which Produced His Distemper," *The Times-Picayune* (New Orleans, LA), December 18, 1876, 1; "A Sunday Evening Suicide: A Sad Social History," *The Ouachita Telegraph* (Monroe, LA), December 22, 1876, 2.

145. The Hambys are buried in their family graveyard just off Highway 23, south of Booneville (Logan Co.).

146. Matthew 5:10 and 11.

147. Newspapers refer to Jetton and Fuller as friends of the Hambys, but there were other connections. Micajah Hamby, the boys' father, sold land to the Hopewell church to create a cemetery; Fuller's father was one of the church's trustees, and a Hamby child was one of the earliest burials there.

148. Walter H. Watts, "The Plot That Backfired," *Booneville Democrat* (Booneville, AR), May 11, 1978. This article, while containing errors, states that the Logans were warned, and the Hambys purposely hoped to view the bodies.

149. Justitia, "The Sequel; The Logan County Assassins Murder Their Friends by Mistake," *Arkansas Democrat* (Little Rock, AR), September 16, 1881, 1.

150. "Personal and General," *Batesville Guard* (Batesville, AR), September 21, 1881, 1.

151. "Paris, Ark," *Daily Arkansas Gazette* (Little Rock, AR), May 5, 1886, 6.

152. The State of Arkansas vs. Bun Fuller, June 6, 1886, Vol. E, 56, Paris Courthouse (Logan Co.).

153. Watts, "The Plot that Backfired."

154. Walter H. Watts, "The Hambys Answer 'The Plot that Backfired,'" *Booneville Democrat* (Booneville, AR), May 25, 1978.

155. IOOF Cemetery, Eureka Springs; the verses are from Psalms 147:3 and John 15:13, respectively.

156. Jerry Akins, *Hangin' Times in Fort Smith: A History of Executions in Judge Parker's Court* (Little Rock, AR: Butler Center Books, 2012), 214–17. Note: his name is given here as John Pointer (except when using the alias George L. Longley), but he has John Coleman Poynter on his headstone.

157. June Westphal, "Wayward John Poynter: Part I," *Carroll County Historical Quarterly* 52 (2008), 15–17. Article does not cite sources.

158. "John Poynter Executed," *Kansas City Times* (Kansas City, MO), September 21, 1894, 5.

159. The epitaph, on a broken tombstone, contains five additional verses, some of which repeat the dying words as a refrain.

160. "Homicide on the River," *The Daily Picayune* (a.k.a. *Times-Picayune*, New Orleans, LA), November 12, 1870, 2. News story calls victim Thomas Moore, but a related item on the same page calls him Edward.

161. Oakland Cemetery, Camden (Ouachita Co.).

162. Mary Anne Cruse, *Bessie Melville or Prayer Book Instructions Carried Out Into Life: A Sequel to "the Little Episcopalian,"* 1858 [publication date corrected by Google books], headnote to chapter 1.

163. Oak Grove Cemetery, Searcy (White Co.).

164. Buckeye Cemetery (Madison Co.).

165. Carrollton Cemetery (Carroll Co.).

166. Mattie Collier (1867–1946), who shares her husband's stone, has these dying words: "I'm going to a better Home."

167. Reese Cemetery (Washington Co.).

168. "Reese Cemetery," *Flashback* 5, no. 4, (1955), 891, unpaginated issue with page numbers written in by hand. Since this publication, Dickerson's marker has broken off just below the line, "Mother have I sined [sic] today?" which, according to this article, originally concluded, "She sweetly said, then passed away."

169. Speer Cemetery (Boone Co.).

170. Uriah Rackley (1831–1906), Redmen Cemetery, De Queen (Sevier).

171. Agnos Cemetery (Fulton Co.).

172. Polly Helen Evans (1878–1897), Agnos Cem. (Fulton Co.).

173. Austin Cemetery, at Best (Benton Co.).

174. Mrs. J.A. [Jeannetta Ann] Reed (1842–1912), Reed Cemetery (Montgomery Co.).

175. "Billy Rice Laid to Rest," *Daily Arkansas Gazette* (Little Rock, AR), March 12, 1902, 2: "Burial Scene at Funeral of Minstrel Billy Rice," *St. Louis Daily Republic* (St. Louis, MO), March 15, 1902, Part II, 1. Photo taken at the event shows four women, all wearing large hats, among the otherwise all-male gathering.

176. Abby Burnett, "'Well Boys, I've Told My Last Joke': The Life and Career of Minstrel Billy Rice, 1844(?)–1902," *The Record*. (Journal of the Garland County Historical Society) 59 (2018), 3.1–3.12.

CHAPTER 5. PORTRAITS AND PERSONALITIES

1. Albert Pike, "Every Year," in *Hymns to the Gods, and Other Poems* (Little Rock, AR: F.W. Allsopp, 1916 [originally published 1881]).

2. Frank Tillar (1861–1911), Oakland and Fraternal (Pulaski Co.).

3. Herman Billingslea, age seventeen [no dates given], Augusta Memorial Park (Woodruff Co.).

4. "A Magnificent Monument: The Tribute to be Placed Over the Grave of Angelo Marre," *Arkansas Democrat* (Little Rock, AR), September 19, 1889, 4.

5. Douglas Keister, *Stories in Stone: A Field Guide to Cemetery Symbolism and Iconography* (Layton, UT: Gibbs Smith, 2004), 48, 62.

6. "Angelo Marre," *Daily Arkansas Gazette* (Little Rock, AR) citing the *Memphis Avalanche*, February 20, 1889, 2.

7. *The Osceola Times* (Osceola, AR) citing the *Vidette* (Augusta, AR), March 2, 1889, 1.

8. "Angelo Marre Dead, the Fatal Result of a Singular Case of Blood Poisoning," *Daily Arkansas Gazette* (Little Rock, AR), February 19, 1889, 4.

9. Xera, "Angelo Marre, 'Requiescat in Pace,'" *Arkansas Democrat* (Little Rock, AR), February 21, 1889, 4.

10. "Angelo Marre Dead," 4.

11. Found across Arkansas, including Elva Shoup (1854–1892), Augusta Memorial Park (Woodruff Co.), Harriet Fowlkes (1897–1925), Greenwood Cemetery (Garland Co.), and Beaulah Barker (1870–1898), Hawkins Chapel (Lee Co.); to be fair, it has been found on the grave of Thomas A. Thorn (1846–1885), Gainesville (Greene Co.), modified to read, "think what a husband and father should be. . . ."

12. One variation, found in Squibb Cemetery, Greene County, Missouri, adds the line, "Lou's obedience, Margaret's open heart" before the last line.

13. This signature has been found on only one stone, whose typography and symbolism match other markers found throughout Scott County.

14. Information about Willis Ambrose Keithley carving daughter Victory (listed on the 1870 census as Victoria) Keithley's tombstone comes from Maudie Standridge Boyd, Find a Grave entry, accessed May 22, 2024, https://www.findagrave.com/memorial/7359855/victory-b-keithley.

15. James Blachowicz, lecture given at the Association for Gravestone Studies' annual conference, Granville, Ohio, 2010.

16. "Some Women Marble Cutters," *The Monumental News, an Illustrated Monthly Monumental Art Journal* 51, no. 12 (1939), 120, reprinting the article from an earlier, undated issue believed to be 1901, accessed September 6, 2023, https://quarriesandbeyond.org/article_list_2.html.

17. US Bureau of the Census, *Tenth Census of the United States—1880*. Washington, DC: United States Census Office, Jackson County, Arkansas.

18. "Miss Lucy J. Daniel," *The Monumental News, an Illustrated Monthly Monumental Art Journal* 7, no. 1 (1895), 92.

19. Plumlee signed a single marker, which makes it possible to identify his work based on his distinctive lettering style.

20. Shared with the author by descendants.

21. William Plumlee photo, in the collection of the Boone County Heritage Museum, Harrison, Arkansas.

22. Lakresha Diaz, "Oakland-Fraternal Cemetery," CALS Encyclopedia of Arkansas, accessed September 5, 2023, https://encyclopediaofarkansas.net/entries/oakland-fraternal-cemetery-7383/.

23. National Register of Historic Places, Oakland-Fraternal Cemetery, Little Rock, Pulaski County, Arkansas, Site # PU5892, Section 7, 17, accessed September 6, 2023, https://www.arkansasheritage.com/docs/default-source/national-registry/pu5892-pdf.pdf?sfvrsn=5aac62ef_0.

24. Frank Key, *The First 30 Years: A History of Lewisville, Arkansas from 1883–1913* (Washington, AR: Etter Printing Co., 1996), 16.

25. US Bureau of the Census, *Ninth Census of the United States—1870*. Washington, DC: United States Census Office, Lafayette County, Arkansas.

26. Wilda Knight, ed., *Lafayette County, Arkansas: Pieces of Its Past and Its People* (Lafayette County Historical Society, 2002), 20, 34–35.

27. "Condensed Telegrams," *Daily Arkansas Gazette* (Little Rock, AR), September 8, 1893, 6, announcing the death of Judge Cassius Leigh, "the oldest and wealthiest lawyer in Lafayette County."

28. Arkansas Reports: Cases Determined in the Supreme Court of Arkansas, Vol. 64, Leigh v. Evans, opinion delivered April 17, 1897, and denied a rehearing.

29. Arkansas State Board of Health, Bureau of Vital Statistics, Registration District No. 137, State File No. 11294, William Graham Hayes, Morrilton (Conway Co.), October 17, 1952.

30. Jerry McKelvy, ed., "The Doctor, the Disobedient Daughter, and the Preacher's Son: The Rest of the Story About William Graham Hayes and Libbie Lucille Brownlee Hayes," *The Sandyland Chronicle* 8, no. 10 (2008), 1–3, accessed September 6, 2023, https://sandyland.dreamhosters.com/2008-10.pdf.

31. *Helena Weekly Clarion* (Helena, AR), April 14, 1869, 3, advertisement for Mayo and Newman, undertakers.

32. *Biographical and Historical Memoirs of Eastern Arkansas* (Chicago: Goodspeed Publishing, 1890), 766, biography of H.P. Coolidge (deceased).

33. 1870 Census, Phillips Co., St. Francis township

34. *The Courier-Journal* (Louisville, KY), January 1, 1891, 30, and February 14, 1939, 6, reporting both 1854 and 1855 as the starting date of the company.

35. Sybil F. Crawford, *Jubilee: The First 150 Years of Mount Holly Cemetery, Little Rock, Arkansas* (Little Rock, AR: Mount Holly Cemetery Association, 1993), 71.

36. *The Semi-Weekly Clarion* (Jackson, MS), August 22, 1871, 1.

37. Kimberly McCollum and Willy Bearden, *Images of America: Elmwood Cemetery* (Charleston, SC: Arcadia Publishing, 2016), 67.

38. Crawford, *Jubilee*, 71, states that it's not known if Anderson, Venn did the actual carving of these markers, but Peyton's marker is signed, and their placement in the cemetery was overseen by a representative of the company. Mary's marker was made two years after her death, suggesting that it was likely carved in Italy.

39. These include two versions in Albany Rural Cemetery, Albany, New York, and ones in Crown Hill Cemetery, Indianapolis, Indiana, Cedar Hill, Newark, Ohio, Calvary Cemetery in St. Louis, Missouri, and Abney Park Cemetery, London, England.

40. "Art," *Arkansas Democrat* (Little Rock, AR), November 8, 1878, 1.

41. "Miss Mary C. Watkins," *Daily Arkansas Gazette* (Little Rock, AR), October 4, 1878, 4.

42. Douglas Keister, *Forever Dixie: A Field Guide to Southern Cemeteries and Their Residents* (Salt Lake City, UT: Gibbs Smith, 2008), 74.

43. Carol A. Grissom, *Zinc Sculpture in America, 1850–1950* (Newark: University of Delaware Press, 2009), 555–62, referencing Brookin statue, 562.

44. "Dr. Kilgore Crash Victim," *El Dorado Times* (El Dorado, AR), April 7, 1964, 15.

45. *Lonoke Democrat* (Lonoke, AR), July 9, 1925.

46. "Death of Mrs. Duffie," *Arkansas Democrat* (Little Rock, AR), October 9, 1904, 1. A small marker next to the statue has Duffie's name, "and infant."

47. John Deering, "George Edward Fisher (1923–2003)," CALS Encyclopedia of Arkansas, accessed December 6, 2020, https://encyclopediaofarkansas.net/entries/george-edward-fisher-2502/.

48. Jennifer Atkins Gordeeva, "Rosemary Beryl Snook 'Snooky' Fisher (1927–1983)," CALS Encyclopedia of Arkansas, accessed August 27, 2023, https://encyclopediaofarkansas.net/entries/rosemary-beryl-snook-snooky-fisher-457/.

49. *Monuments[,] Tombstones and Markers* (Montgomery Ward and Co., 1929), unpaginated last page (28), accessed August 6, 2023, https://quarriesandbeyond.org/articles_and_books/pdf/montgomery_ward_monument_catalog_1929.pdf.

CHAPTER 6. PRIVATE GRAVES IN PUBLIC PLACES

1. Oliver and Wright cemeteries are located at the perimeter of the University of Arkansas at Pine Bluff's Simmons Bank Field, a sixteen-thousand-seat stadium.

2. The four members of the Steel a.k.a. Steele family have death dates spanning 1860–1875.

3. William B. Dumas (1841–1892) and son Arthur P. Dumas (dates unknown), Dumas Junior High School, 315 South College Street, Dumas (Desha Co.), graves commemorated by the town with a small marble plaque in 1930, and with modern granite markers and a flagpole in 2002.

4. Andrew Marvell (1621–1678), "To His Coy Mistress," written mid-1600s, published posthumously in 1681.

5. Mike Polston, "Davidsonville (Randolph County)," CALS Encyclopedia of Arkansas, accessed May 26, 2025, https://encyclopediaofarkansas.net/entries/davidsonville-randolph-county-6069/.

6. John Hudson Tiner, "Bad Days Near Black Rock: The Disappearance of Davidsonville," *The Ozarks Mountaineer* 19, no. 10 (1971), 20–21.

7. "Parkin Archaeological State Park," brochure, Arkansas State Parks, 2014.

8. "Adrienne Dumont (1700–1800)" Find a Grave memorial states that "her grave is actually on Stout's Point," accessed September 9, 2023, https://www.findagrave.com/memorial/46948208/adrienne-dumont.

9. Fred W. Allsopp, *Folklore of Romantic Arkansas*, Vol. 1 (New York: The Grolier Society, 1931), 193.

10. Allsopp, *Folklore of Romantic Arkansas*, 193, endnote citing "Thwaites" as the source for the counter story.

11. Morris S. Arnold, *Colonial Arkansas 1686–1804: A Social and Cultural History* (Fayetteville: University of Arkansas Press, 1991), 18, 113 and footnote, 185–86, putting Petit Jean's death in 1732.

12. Courtney Moore Clements, "Legend of Petit Jean," CALS Encyclopedia of Arkansas, accessed September 9, 2023, https://encyclopediaofarkansas.net/entries/petit-jean-legend-3474/.

13. Ruby Erwin Livingston, "Traces of Early Explorers," *Arkansas Democrat* (Little Rock, AR), November 27, 1921, 6, claiming that the Petit Jean story "was brought up from Louisiana by slaves long ago."

14. Mary L. Kwas, *Thou Wert Dear to Us: A Record of Pioneer Cemetery, Washington, Arkansas* (Washington: Southwest Arkansas Regional Archives Foundation, 2001), 1.

15. Mary L. Kwas, research associate, Arkansas Archeological Survey, email to the author, December 13, 2011.

16. Kwas, *Thou Wert Dear to Us*, 49.

17. Kwas, *Thou Wert Dear to Us*, 2–3.

18. Ricky Vermillion, "The Story of Herman Davis," *Craighead County Historical Quarterly* 7, no. 4 (1969), 15.

19. Tennessee State Board of Health, Bureau of Vital Statistics, Registration District No. 28005 [US Veterans' Hospital No. 88], Registration No.32, Herman Davis.

20. Margaret Smith Ross, "Herman Davis: Forgotten Hero," *Arkansas Historical Quarterly* 14, no. 1 (1995), 51–61.

21. "Davis Fund Nears $1,000," *The Courier News* (Blytheville, AR), August 11, 1967, 1.

22. Information on Visquesney, and the Otis Henry statue, accessed September 9, 2023, https://doughboysearcher.weebly.com/texarkana-texas.html.

23. Otis Henry was born June 22, 1843, in Denison, Texas.

24. Both the 1900 and 1910 censuses show that Susan Wilder gave birth five times, with only one child surviving.

25. Robert W. Meriwether, "Hendrix College," in *Faulkner County: Its Land and People*, ed. Doris B. Dolan, Hattie Ann Kelso, and Corinne H. Robinson (Faulkner County Historical Society, 1986), 257–58; Bill Lynch, "Captain William W. Martin," *Arkansas Historical Quarterly* 11, no. 1 (1952), 228.

26. Lynch, "Captain William W. Martin," 53–54.

27. "Martinville," in *Faulkner County: Its Land and People*, ed. Doris B. Dolan, Hattie Ann Kelso, and Corinne H. Robinson (Faulkner County Historical Society, 1986), 306–7.

28. Martinville Cemetery, twenty-one miles north of Conway, is all that now remains of the town. Martin's tombstone was placed on the grave a year after his

death, according to "Martinville," *Log Cabin Democrat* (Conway, Faulkner Co.), November 9, 1912, 2.

29. "Martin Dormitory at Hendrix Is Dedicated: Tribute Is Paid Memory [sic] of Philanthropist and College Benefactor," *Arkansas Democrat* (Little Rock, AR), October 27, 1919, 8; "Martin Hall Dedicated; And Body of Captain Martin Laid to Rest on Hendrix College Campus," *Arkansas Daily Gazette* (Little Rock, AR), October 28, 1919, 2.

30. "Hendrix Campus," *Faulkner County, Arkansas Census of Cemeteries as of December 31, 1987*, Faulkner County Historical Society (Conway, Arkansas), 1990, 686.

31. "Children's Cemetery at Lakeport Plantation," Lakeport Plantation, November 7, 2018, https://lakeport.astate.edu/2018/11/.

32. Blake Wintory, *Images of America: Chicot County* (Charleston, SC: Arcadia Publishing, 2015), 19.

33. Edgar Harold Lloyd memorial, Find a Grave, accessed September 9, 2023, https://www.findagrave.com/memorial/7179237/edgar-harold-lloyd.

34. "Here and There in Arkansas," *Hope Star* (Hope, AR), December 31, 1948, 4.

35. Edward L. Underwood and Karen J. Underwood, *Forgotten Tales of Arkansas* (Charleston, SC: History Press, 2012), 101–109.

36. Cindy Grisham, "Wilson (Mississippi County)," CALS Encyclopedia of Arkansas, accessed September 9, 2023, https://encyclopediaofarkansas.net/entries/wilson-mississippi-county-4294/.

37. "Little Cemetery at Bassett Will Receive His Body," *The Courier News* (Blytheville, AR), September 29, 1933, 1.

38. "Resting Place of Founder and Wife," photo caption, *The Courier News* (Blytheville, AR), October 10, 1950, Section C, 15. Perhaps R.E.L. Wilson's body was moved to the town square when wife Elizabeth Beall Wilson died in 1943.

39. "John Patterson," *Phillips County Historical Quarterly* 1, no. 1 (1962), 1–6.

40. W.E. Orr, "Judsonia's Unknown Child's Grave," *White County Heritage* 24, 1986, 76–78.

41. Jeanni Brosius, "Legends Abound Over Girl's Grave," *Arkansas Democrat Gazette* (Little Rock, AR), June 19, 2011, https://www.arkansasonline.com/news/2011/jun/19/legends-abound-over-girls-grave-20110619/.

42. David E. Harkins, *Haunted Graveyards of the Ozarks* (Charleston, SC: History Press, 2013), 108–11; Orr, "Judsonia's Unknown Child's Grave," 77–78.

43. The plaque for the unmarked Ingram graves is at the intersection of Phillips and Primrose Roads, southeast of Lowell but technically in the unincorporated Accident community.

44. Abby Burnett, "Moses Tran Clegg (1876–1919)," CALS Encyclopedia of Arkansas, accessed September 9, 2023, https://encyclopediaofarkansas.net/entries/moses-tran-clegg-8854/.

CHAPTER 7. ANIMALS—ON AND IN GRAVES

1. National Register of Historic Places, Maple Hill Cemetery, Phillips County, Arkansas, Site #PHO290, 6–7, accessed September 9, 2023, https://www.arkansasheritage.com/docs/default-source/national-registry/pho290-pdf.pdf?sfvrsn=cb1bd150_0.

2. "Through the Exchanges," *Daily Arkansas Gazette* (Little Rock, AR), February 25, 1893, 4.

3. *Pine Bluff Weekly Press Eagle* (Pine Bluff, AR), February 21, 1893, 2.

4. "An Insurance Suit," *Daily Arkansas Gazette* (Little Rock, AR), January 10, 1894, 2.

5. "A Fatal Quarrel," *Daily Arkansas Gazette* (Little Rock, AR), August 7, 1884, 1, concerning Moore's shooting of Warren J. Smiser; "Our Specials" *Daily Arkansas Gazette* (Little Rock, AR), October 15, 1887, 1, reported Moore's acquittal.

6. "Warren Smizer Dies from His Wounds—Political Points," *Daily Memphis Avalanche* (Memphis, TN), August 7, 1884, 1.

7. "When Doctors Disagree," *St. Louis Post Dispatch* (St. Louis, MO), February 19, 1893, 22.

8. "Examination Postponed," *Daily Arkansas Gazette* (Little Rock, AR), February 18, 1893, 3.

9. Children's ages determined from the 1900 Census, Nashville, Tennessee, giving John's birth date as November 1881 and Catherine's as September 1888.

10. "An Insurance Suit," 2.

11. "The True Wife Ignored," *St. Louis Post-Dispatch* (St. Louis, MO), April 29, 1895, 7; Robertson is called Robinson in the St. Louis newspapers.

12. "Won by the Insurance Company," *The Southern Standard* (Arkadelphia, AR), January 19, 1894, 1.

13. "Won by a Woman: Jury in Federal Court Gives Minnie Robinson a Verdict for $5,902.13," *Daily Arkansas Gazette* (Little Rock, AR), May 3, 1896, 2.

14. One account of Moore's death includes Pedro being present at Moore's sparsely attended funeral and, later, discovered dead from grief atop Moore's grave, https://mydeltaworld.com/2019/08/20/pedro-is-waiting/.

15. "A Prophetic Dream," *Daily Arkansas Gazette* (Little Rock, AR), February 25, 1893, 4.

16. Douglas Keister, *Stories in Stone: A Field Guide to Cemetery Symbolism and Iconography* (Salt Lake City, UT: Gibbs, Smith, 2004), 72.

17. *Arkansas Daily Gazette* (Little Rock, AR), March 30, 1882, 4.

18. "Eagles Acquitted," *Arkansas Democrat* (Little Rock, AR), August 27, 1898, 1.

19. The three names are C.E. Booe (December 6, 1863–April 25, 1898), W.H. Booe (February 12, 1862), and W.K. Booe (April 28, 1836).

20. Sara Eagle Briggs, an Eagle descendant, says the two families share more than burial proximity: "They had shops or offices in the same building, too" from a Facebook gravestone site discussing the (different) Eagle murders of 1873.

21. "Killed in Bed," *The Memphis Appeal-Avalanche* (Memphis, TN), March 30, 1891, 1. Accounts differ as to whether "Miss Eagle" was Charlie's sister, half sister, or stepsister.

22. "Coroner and Magistrate Decide That Killing Was Justifiable," *Arkansas Democrat* (Little Rock, AR), January 22, 1903, 6.

23. *Clay County Courier* (Corning, AR), December 11, 1903, 3.

24. Martin Van Buren ("Mart") Vowell memorial on Find a Grave, accessed September 9, 2023, https://www.findagrave.com/memorial/8910151/martin-vanburen-vowell.

25. "Death Penalty for Mart Vowell," *Newport Daily Independent* (Newport, AR), September 11, 1903, 1.

26. Tina Easley, "Hanging Day 1904," accessed September 9, 2023, http://www.usgennet.org/usa/ar/county/greene/hanging.htm.

27. "The Mart Vowell Case," *Arkansas Democrat* (Little Rock, AR), June 10, 1904, 4.

28. "Speech Delivered by Gov. Davis at Hardy." *Daily Arkansas Gazette* (Little Rock, AR), August 7, 1904, 12.

29. "Grave of a Man and his Horse Killed by a Train: Walnut Ridge, Arkansas," Atlas Obscura, accessed September 9, 2023, https://www.atlasobscura.com/places/grave-of-a-man-and-his-horse-killed-by-a-train.

30. Probate documents of John A. Rhea, Walnut Ridge courthouse (Lawrence Co.).

31. "Death of J.A. Rhea, Walnut Ridge," *Daily Arkansas Gazette* (Little Rock, AR), February 16, 1893, 2.

32. "Miscellaneous Items," *Batesville Guard* (Batesville, AR), March 5, 1884, 4.

33. W.G.H., "Sent Up for Fifteen Years: Other Crimes and Criminals," *Daily Arkansas Gazette* (Little Rock, AR), May 10, 1884, 4.

34. "Mrs. Elizabeth Burel Lawrence Count's Foremost Woman," *The Blade* (Walnut Ridge, AR), March 22, 1912

35. "They Lost All," *Daily Arkansas Gazette* (Little Rock, AR), April 4, 1893, 4.

36. "Blood Feud at Walnut Ridge," *Lawrence County Historical Journal* 17, no. 1 (2013), 7–29.

37. "Salesman Killed in a Folding Bed," *Daily Arkansas Gazette* (Little Rock, AR), March 12, 1910, 1.

38. Information attributed to Nancy Feroe, Find A Grave memorial, accessed September 9, 2023, https://www.findagrave.com/memorial/133312371/mitchell-vernon-herzberger.

39. More is learned about the dog than the daughter from their matching headstones: "Infant dau. of W.Y. and N.C. Lane, Aug. 14, 1904" and "Our dog Trip, Born in Georgia, Died Aug. 29, 1904."

40. "Sheba Greeter Dog," Arkansas Gravestones, accessed September 9, 2023, https://arkansasgravestones.org/view.php?id=733144.

41. Angela Swanlund, "Ronald Gene Simmons," CALS Encyclopedia of Arkansas, accessed December 4, 2024, https://encyclopediaofarkansas.net/entries/ronald-gene-simmons-3731/.

42. Joyce Zeller, *Hidden History of Eureka Springs* (Charleston, SC: History Press, 2011), 50–51.

43. Abby Burnett, "Eureka Springs, Arkansas: A Town with Purrfect Workers," *The Ozarks Mountaineer* 45, no. 5 (1997), 39–41.

44. Heather Zbinden, programs and website coordinator, Central Arkansas Library System (CALS), Little Rock, email to the author, March 2023, and email from Mark Christ, head of adult programing, CALS, March 2023, both of whom have researched the Rohwer Relocation Center.

45. Clara Collins and Mrs. L. Oswald, enumerators, *Desha County, Arkansas Cemetery Records, Compiled in 1968 and 1969 by the Men and Women of Desha County* (McGehee, AR: Marion McKinney Stroud, 1983), 28, 195.

46. Bob Keen, "Gypsy Tragedy On Evansville Creek," *Flashback* 47, no. 1 (1997), 31–34.

CHAPTER 8. SEERS, CIRCUS FOLK, ECCENTRICS, AND GRAVEYARD ODDITIES

1. Dehorn's grave marker gives his birth date as May 11, 1872, and his age as seventy-two; his death certificate gives his birth date as October 10, 1863, and his age as seventy-one, corrected to read eighty-one.

2. J.E. Browning, "William M. DeHorn: A Most Remarkable Man," *Rivers and Roads and Points in Between* (28 (2001/2002), 11–12.

3. US Bureau of the Census, *Fifteenth Census of the United States—1930*. Washington, DC: United States Census Office, Woodruff Co., De View Township, District 0013; US Bureau of the Census, *Sixteenth Census of the United States—1940*. Woodruff Co., Patterson Township, Enumeration District 74–14, sheet 4-A.

4. Arkansas State Board of Health, Bureau of Vital Statistics, Registration District No. 666, State File No. 108, William Dehorne, Patterson (Woodruff), November 11, 1944.

5. "Inventory," Caroline Dye probate records, Jackson County Courthouse, Jackson County Probate Court, filed December 30, 1918, Box 159.

6. "Caroline Dye Passes Away," *Newport Daily Independent* (Newport, AR), September 27, 1918, 2.

7. US Bureau of the Census, *Tenth Census of the United States—1880*. Washington, DC: United States Census Office, Jackson County, Bird Township, Mart Dye household.

8. "Old Negro Seer Had Much Money on Premises," *Arkansas Democrat* (Little Rock, AR), October 2, 1918, 4.

9. Caroline Dye probate records, Jackson County Courthouse, Jackson County Probate Court, filed November 22, 1918, box 159, unnumbered bill from W.S. Hubble, undertaker and embalmer, dated November 12, 1918.

10. John Quincy Wolf, "Aunt Caroline Dye: The Gypsy in 'The St. Louis Blues,'" *Southern Folklore Quarterly* 33, no. 4 (1969), 339–40.

11. Wolf, "Aunt Caroline Dye," 341.

12. "Caroline Dye Passes Away."

13. John Quincy Wolf, cited above, claimed that her headstone was inscribed, "The Sunbeam of the World" and that it gave her age as 108.

14. Mayes's cause of death was told to the author by a descendant; his is not the only epitaph to mention hearing a voice say, "weep not."

15. Bill, Simmons, "Thousands Line Up to See 'Sign from God' in Window," *Baxter Bulletin* (Mountain Home, AR), October 28, 1987, 10 A.

16. Robert Anderson, "Weird Tales: Tragedy Is Crossed by Miracle," *Arizona Daily Star* (Tucson, AZ), December 26, 1987, 70. This is similar to an event in Akron, Ohio, in 1926, after a young man was killed and a star-like light was seen in his family's home, attracting hundreds of visitors. Two weeks later the victim's father took out a newspaper announcement stating that his house was not haunted, did not have ghosts, and, though the light still shone, was now closed to the public. *Akron Beacon Journal* (Akron, OH), January 19, 1926, 28.

17. Michael Kammen, *Digging Up the Dead: A History of Notable American Reburials* (Chicago: University of Chicago Press, 2010), 22–23.

18. Burney McClurkan, "The Saracen Window," *Jefferson County Historical Quarterly* 2, no. 4 (1970), 3.

19. Morris S. Arnold, *The Rumble of a Distant Drum: The Quapaws and Old World Newcomers, 1673–1804* (Fayetteville: University of Arkansas Press, 2000), 147–48, citing Protestant missionary Timothy Flint, who published his account in 1826.

20. Joseph Patrick Key, "Sarasin (?–1832?)," CALS Encyclopedia of Arkansas, accessed December 14, 2023, https://encyclopediaofarkansas.net/entries/sarasin-1756/.

21. Bob Lancaster, *The Jungles of Arkansas: A Personal History of the Wonder State* (Fayetteville: University of Arkansas Press, 1989), 32, footnote 2 cites George Gray to the secretary of war, *Territorial Papers of the United States*, Vol. 20, 476, quoted material from Clarence Edwin Carter, editor.

22. James W. Leslie, *Saracen's Country: Some Southeast Arkansas History: Based on Articles for the Pine Bluff Commercial* (Little Rock, AR: Rose Publishing Co., 1974), 126–28.

23. McClurkan, "The Saracen Window," 4.

24. Ronald Fuller, interviewed by phone, May 23, 2024.

25. Andy Gotlieb, "Brooksville Family's Life a 3 Ring Circus," *Tampa Tribune* (Tampa, FL), January 18, 1994, 82.

26. "Mrs. Forrestina Campbell," *The Madison County Record* (Huntsville, AR), August 23, 1973, 8.

27. Jim Tackett, Fayetteville, Facebook post and Facebook message to author, December 2020.

28. Phillip Steele, *White River Red: A Legend in Her Own Time*, typography and design by Jan Cooper [booklet] (Fayetteville, AR, 1995), 6.

29. Marge Lyon (a.k.a. "Marge of Sunrise Mountain Farm"), "White River Red Is Tiny but Quite a Gal, Marge Finds," *Chicago Tribune* (Chicago, IL), March 19, 1950, part 7, 4.

30. Forrestina Bradley Campbell memorial, Find a Grave, accessed September 17, 2023, https://www.findagrave.com/memorial/39475902/forrestina-campbell.

31. Steele, *White River Red*, 10–11; Denele Campbell, "The 'Otherness' of Forrestina Bradley Campbell aka White River Red," *Flashback* 73, no. 1 (2023), 2–21.

32. Both terms used in Palace Museum advertisement, *Star Tribune* (Minneapolis, MN), October 17, 1897, 7.

33. "Biggest Man in World Dead," *Daily Arkansas Gazette* (Little Rock, AR), November 13, 1903, 1.

34. "Biggest Man in World Dead."

35. "At the Palace Museum," *Star Tribune* (Minneapolis, MN), October 17, 1897, 24.

36. "Glenwood's Fat Man, Charged with Non-Support," *Neenah Daily Times* (Neenah and Menasha, WI), September 29, 1903, 1.

37. "Heavy Man Dead," *Topeka Daily Herald* (Topeka, KS), November 18, 1903, 2; correct embalming fluid determined by Brashears Funeral Home, Huntsville, AR.

38. "Father Refused to Bury Son," *Daily Arkansas Gazette* (Little Rock, AR), November 15, 1903, 3; Trickey's father died in 1872, and his mother—who had remarried—in 1884.

39. "Big Man Buried," *Newport Weekly Independent* (Newport, AR), November 20, 1903, 1.

40. The first recorded burial in the Walnut Grove Annex (a.k.a. the potters' field) is 1905, so perhaps it had not been established at the time of Trickey's death.

41. Jerry McKelvey, "DeAnn Cemetery in Prescott," *The Sandyland Chronicle* 7, no. 1 (2007), 2–3, accessed September 18, 2023, https://sandyland.dreamhosters.com/2007-01.pdf

42. "Dixie Is Dead," *Nashville News* (Nashville, AR), December 24, 1910, 1.

43. "Enraged Lion Claws Small Girl to Death," *The Courier News* (Blytheville, AR), October 31, 1951, 6.

44. Arkansas State Board of Health, Bureau of Vital Statistics, Registration District No. 501, State File No. 13136, Maria de la Luez Campa, Mena (Polk), December 4, 1951.

45. "Several Ferocious Beasts at Large in Arkansas," *Spokane Chronicle* (Spokane, WA), October 31, 1951, 49.

46. Newspaper accounts called this the Melville-Reise Shows. Elmwood Cemetery also contains a marker for John King, a member of the John Robinson Circus, "Killed at Charlotte N.C. Sept. 27, 1880 by the elephant Chief."

47. Sue Shell Chrisco, "Izard County Cemetery Preservation Association," *Izard County Historian* 41, no. 4 (2016), 2–3.

48. Susan S. "Susie" Harvell, 1853–pre-1900, No Bottom Cemetery (Izard Co.).

49. No dates given for these deaths; buried in Boles a.k.a. Bowles Cemetery (Sharp Co.).

50. Roger Larry Mawson, Cross Cemetery, Greenland (Sebastian Co.); Mawson is buried next to his parents, Saysell and Pebble Mawson.

51. "Some People Who Survive," *Houston Post* (Houston, TX), September 13, 1900, 4.

52. "Lone Star Lines," *Shiner Gazette* (Shiner, TX), October 17, 1900, 2.

53. Embalming became an accepted practice following the Civil War, but doctors had begun experimenting with the process prior to that; the first US patent for an embalming process (using injected arsenic and alcohol) was in 1856. See Robert W. Habenstein and William M. Lamers, *The History of American Funeral Directing* (Milwaukee, WI: Bulfin Printers, 1955), 327.

54. "Board Bill Causes a Double Tragedy," *Daily Arkansas Gazette* (Little Rock, AR), May 23, 1913, 1. Surname is spelled Stevens in this account.

55. Both plates spell White's nickname as "Whitty" and E.V.'s surname as "Stevans." Posts on Facebook's Arkansas Tombstones page, in 2024, add that these graves were a town legend, and that the descendant who marked them had a 1913 letter stating that a relative, headed to Banks in search of work, was believed to have been killed in a gunfight.

56. "Unknown Man Buried at De Ann Cemetery," *The Nevada News* (Prescott, AR), March 23, 1911, reprinted in *The Sandyland Chronicle* 3, no. 11 (2003), 3, accessed September 18, 2023, https://sandyland.dreamhosters.com/2003–11.pdf.

57. Jerry McKelvey, "Old Mike Put to Rest after 64 Years," *The Sandyland Chronicle* 3, no. 3 (2003), 1–2, reprinting (untitled, unsourced) original newspaper story dated August 21, 1911, https://sandyland.dreamhosters.com/2003-03.pdf.

58. Billy Burton, "Prescott's Old Mike Finally Buried . . . Interred Monday After 64 Years," *Hope Star* (Hope, AR), May 16, 1975, 1.

59. Comments left by visitors on the Old Mike page, Nevada County Depot and Museum website, accessed September 18, 2023, http://depotmuseum.org/search.php?keyword1=Old+Mike&andor2=AND&keyword2=&andor3=AND&

keyword3=&andor4=AND&keyword4=&andor5=AND&keyword5=&Search=Begin+Search.

60. John Teeter, "Old Mike," fact sheet at the Depot Museum, Prescott, dated April/May 2001, 39, original source unknown.

61. Mike Nichols, "The Mystery of Prescott's Ol' Mike," *The Old Time Chronicle* [unnumbered Vol. 9], 10–12, 42, citing the *(Daily) Arkansas Gazette* (Little Rock, AR), August 12, 1911, 7.

62. "City News," *Daily Arkansas Gazette* (Little Rock, AR), August 12, 1911, 7. McIlwee was charged with petty larceny.

63. The body of an indigent woman was used to demonstrate embalming techniques in Searcy (White Co.) in 1891, then displayed in the windows of mercantile stores, for a month, by local undertaker John Neal, who eventually buried her at his own expense. Abby Burnett, *Gone to the Grave: Burial Customs of the Arkansas Ozarks, 1850–1950* (Jackson: University Press of Mississippi, 2014), 236–37.

64. "53-Year-Old Body Again Identified," *Hope Star* (Hope, AR), September 4, 1962, 3.

65. "Woman Has Claimed Body at Marianna," *Hope Star* (Hope, AR), September 26, 1962, 1.

66. Berry's full name is George Clark Berry. Geo. C. Berry memorial, Find a Grave, accessed December 31, 2023, https://www.findagrave.com/memorial/8620300/george-clark-berry.

67. "53-Year-Old Body Again Identified"; Burton, "Prescott's Old Mike Finally Buried"; McKelvy, "'Old Mike' Put to Rest," 2.

68. Mary P. Fletcher, "A Sketch of Peter Le Fevre," *Arkansas Historical Quarterly* 13, no. 1 (1954), 87–89.

69. Abby Burnett, "Funeral Customs, Traditional (Ozark Mountains)," CALS Encyclopedia of Arkansas, accessed September 18, 2023, https://encyclopediaofarkansas.net/entries/funeral-customs-traditional-7338/.

70. "A Curious Graveyard, in Which Is Buried Only the Amputated Legs and Fingers of Railroad Men," *Dallas Morning News* (Dallas, TX), May 3, 1891, 10.

71. "Humbard," *History and Families of Carroll County, Arkansas*, Carroll County Historical and Genealogical Society (Paducah, KY: Turner Publishing, 2003), 102.

72. T. DeWitt Talmage, "Talmage's Sermon: The Burial and the Resurrection of Jesus, the Christ," in *The Southern Standard* (Arkadelphia, AR), April 3, 1891, 1 and the *Fayetteville Weekly Democrat* (Fayetteville, AR), April 10, 1891, 4.

73. Otto Ernest Rayburn, *Ozark Country* (Fayetteville: University of Arkansas Press, 2021, reprint of 1941 edition), 196.

74. Joy Russell, "Ribbon Ridge Graves," *Madison County Musings* 19, no. 1 (2000), 44.

75. Unnamed speaker in "Our Lost Pioneers," DVD produced in White County (presumably by the White County Historical Society).

76. One of these was likely Silas Bennett Lawrence (1855–1945), wounded in a shootout in 1898, his arm buried in the Timbo Cemetery while he is buried in Oklahoma. Driftwood's quote taken from his introduction to "Straighten Out My Laig," on "Voice of the People" [Monument record label, 1963] YouTube, accessed September 18, 2023, https://www.youtube.com/watch?v=vbo-vSxHOCo.

77. Jimmy Driftwood, "Straighten Out My Laig," recorded on "Voice of the People," Monument record label, 1963.

78. Burial log of J.F. Moore, Evergreen Cemetery, Fayetteville (Washington Co.), found in the Evergreen papers, University of Arkansas, Special Collections.

79. Birnie Brothers funeral home records, Fort Smith public library, genealogy room, record dated February 1, 1891. Dwyer's legs were severed on Friday, January 30; he died on Sunday, February 1, so presumably the legs were buried in Fort Smith and had to be exhumed when the body was shipped to Kansas the following Tuesday, February 3.

80. Jeff Koone, Facebook contact with the author, giving information on Earls.

81. Information provided by Anice Bunch in phone call with the author, February 2017, at which time the burial was not marked.

82. "Lewis Francis 'Tony' Finley" memorial, Find a Grave, accessed September 18, 2023, https://www.findagrave.com/memorial/29691478/lewis-francis-finley.

83. Sam Swindle (1910–1973) memorial, Find a Grave, accessed September 18, 2023, https://www.findagrave.com/memorial/25294438/sam-swindle.

84. Cemetery is spelled "Yokum Bend" in the Army Corps of Engineers paperwork.

85. Vicki A. Roberts, *Marion County Cemeteries* (Yellville, AR, 2008), 120–121; George Smith, "A Cemetery Is Dying" and "Old Midway Cemetery," photo essay, *Baxter Bulletin* (Mountain Home, AR), September 9, 1971, 1 and Section C, 1.

86. Rockdale Cemetery is inaccessible and Newman's steel hip has not been verified by this author; information from Find a Grave, accessed October 22, 2023, https://www.findagrave.com/memorial/47258148/joseph-harvey-newman.

87. Henry Howe, *Historical Collections of Ohio, in Three Volumes: An Encyclopedia of the State*, Vol. 11 (Columbus, OH: Henry Howe and Son, 1891), 368; verse written by Col. Donn Piatt for his wife, Louise Kirby Piatt, died 1864 (Logan Co., Ohio).

88. Susan Stevenson Swinburn and Doris Stevenson West, comps., *History in Headstones: A Complete Listing of All Marked Graves in Known Cemeteries of Crawford County, Arkansas* (Van Buren, AR: Press-Argus, 1970), 119.

89. Jeffrey M. Mitchem, "Hernando de Soto (1500?–1542)," CALS Encyclopedia of Arkansas, accessed November11, 2023, https://encyclopediaofarkansas.net/entries/hernando-de-soto-1770/.

90. National Register of Historic Places, Fairview Cemetery, Van Buren, Crawford County, Arkansas, Site #CW0384, accessed November 11, 2023, https://

www.arkansasheritage.com/docs/default-source/national-registry/cw0384-pdf .pdf?sfvrsn=decf7b4_0. Information provided by Willie Shaw.

91. Cathy Barnes, comp., *The Grim Reaper's Footsteps Across the Nation as Mentioned in the Clay County (AR) Courier Newspaper 1893–1925* (Conway, AR: Arkansas Research, 2002), 21. Presumably apocryphal as no W.A. Barnard has been found online.

CHAPTER 9. READING STONES, COLLECTING STORIES

1. Teeter Cemetery, a.k.a. Oak Hill, contains over a dozen stacked-stone cairn grave covers, many of them over seven feet in length, all oriented north-south.

2. Melba Agnes Burks (1943–2011), Fairplay Cemetery at Benton (Saline Co.), had thirteen marriages over the course of her sixty-eight years, including one man whom she married twice.

3. Cecil I. Rankin (1919–1996), Newberry Chapel Cemetery (Crawford Co.).

4. Leo Ammons (1914–2006), Walnut Grove Cemetery (Madison Co.).

5. Sarah E. Culberhouse (1833–1881) and Thomas Culberhouse (1836–1895), Jonesboro City Cemetery (Craighead Co.). Typeface is different on Thomas's side of the marker and was likely inscribed much later by a different carver.

6. Three Rector children (aged two days, two months, and three years, respectively) in Hollywood Cemetery, Hot Springs (Garland Co.), and four Pike children (aged two days, five months, under one year, and one and a half years old, respectively) in Mount Holly Cemetery, Little Rock (Pulaski Co.) have graves marked with a cluster of columns, each representing a child.

7. Grant Earle McVey (1867–1881), Eureka Springs IOOF Cemetery; brother Shirley died in Missouri at a time when the family faced financial and medical difficulties, and no tombstone has been found, online, for him.

8. Douglas Keister, *Stories in Stone: A Field Guide to Cemetery Symbolism and Iconography* (Salt Lake City, UT: Gibbs Smith, 2004), 54–55.

9. Morning glory blossoms open and close in a day, and represent life's brevity. Woodbine is associated with honeysuckle; Eglantine is the common name for sweet briar rose; both are very fragrant.

10. Elizabeth Stuart Phelps [Ward], *Chapters from a Life* (Boston, MA: Houghton, Mifflin, 1896), 97.

11. *Fayetteville Weekly Democrat* (Fayetteville, AR), August 11, 1881, 3.

12. "Sammie Vogel: Accidentally Killed by a Freight Elevator This Morning," *The Arkansas Democrat* (Little Rock, AR), July 22, 1901, 1.

13. Keister, *Stories in Stone*, 67.

14. "The Rustic Movement and the Tree Stump Gravestone," *Gravely Speaking* (blog), accessed December 14, 2023, https://gravelyspeaking.com/2020/04/22/the-rustic-movement-and-the-tree-stump-gravestone/.

15. "The 1905 'New Handy Map of Little Rock,'" *Pulaski County Historical Review* 34, no. 4 (1986), 92.

16. Keister, *Stories in Stone*, 188–89.

17. This marker includes two massive stone tools carved across its upper surface, a crossed maul and ax, both many times larger than actual tools.

18. Joyce M. Tice, "Junior Order of United American Mechanics," Tri-Counties Genealogy and History: A Pictorial Catalog of Commemorative Flagholders and Plaques of Organizations and Military, accessed September 21, 2023, https://www.joycetice.com/flaghold/flag040.htm.

19. "Be a Recruiting Officer for the Patriotic Order United Sons of America," *Arkansas Democrat* (Little Rock, AR), March 24, 1917, 10 (classified ad).

20. Tommie M. Turner and infant (died 1906), Lone Pine Cemetery (Johnson Co.).

21. Samuel McCampbell (1832–1892), Son's Chapel Cemetery, Fayetteville (Washington Co.).

22. Sarah Patterson, died 1890, Buckhorn Cemetery (Newton Co.); inscription reads: "Ma She Rest In pea's. Amen."

23. The US Department of Veterans Affairs (VA) oversees the National Cemeteries and, while they do not endorse specific products, D/2 is named on their "Cleaning Government-Furnished Headstones and Markers" site, accessed January 6, 2024, https://www.cem.va.gov/hmm/cleaning.asp.

24. "A Joint Declaration of Principles and Objectives by the American Cemetery Association, Inc., American Monument Association, Inc., Monument Builders of America, Inc., with Recommended Specifications for Memorial Work," n.p., n.d., in the author's collection.

BIBLIOGRAPHY

[N.p. = no publisher; n.d. = no date]

Akins, Jerry. *Hangin' Times in Fort Smith: A History of Executions in Judge Parker's Court*. Little Rock, AR: Butler Center Books, 2012.

Allsopp, Fred. W. *Folklore of Romantic Arkansas*. Vol. 1. New York: The Grolier Society, 1931.

Almond, Holly, ed. *Brinkley Centennial Yearbook, 1872–1972*. Brinkley, AR: The Citizen, 1972.

Anderson, Vincent. "Lincoln's Memorial Stone from the Ozarks in Baxter County, Arkansas." Ozarks' History. YouTube, accessed November 15, 2023. https://www.youtube.com/watch?v=URX-C6yTJmg&t=632s.

Arkansas Archaeological Survey, Site Survey Form for State Site No. 3J0376, Site Documentation for Ozark National Forest, Horner Cemetery.

Arkansas Reports: Cases Determined in the Supreme Court of Arkansas, Vol. 64, Leigh v. Evans, opinion delivered April 17, 1897.

Arkansas State Board of Health, Bureau of Vital Statistics, Registration District No. 137, State File No. 11294, William Graham Hayes, Morrilton (Conway Co.), October 17, 1952.

Arkansas State Board of Health, Bureau of Vital Statistics, Registration District No. 501, State File No. 13136, Maria de la Luez Campa, Mena (Polk), December 4, 1951.

Arkansas State Board of Health, Bureau of Vital Statistics, Registration District No. 538, Certificate of Death, # 1879; Wm. H. Waddle, Pocahontas (Randolph Co.), December 29, 1919.

Arkansas State Board of Health, Bureau of Vital Statistics, Registration District No. 666, State File No. 108, William Dehorne, Patterson (Woodruff), November 11, 1944.

Arnold, Morris S. "Arkansas Post in 1832." *Grand Prairie Historical Society Bulletin* (Arkansas County) 61, no. 2 (2018).

Arnold, Morris S. *Colonial Arkansas, 1686–1804: A Social and Cultural History*. Fayetteville: University of Arkansas Press, 1991.

Arnold, Morris S. *The Rumble of a Distant Drum: The Quapaws and Old World Newcomers, 1673–1804*. Fayetteville: University of Arkansas Press, 2000.

Barnes, Cathy, comp. *The Grim Reaper's Footsteps Across the Nation as Mentioned in the Clay County (Arkansas) Courier Newspaper 1893–1925*. Conway: Arkansas Research, 2002.

Barnett, Mrs. I.N., Sr. "Early Days of Batesville." *Arkansas Historical Quarterly* 11, no. 1 (1952).

Bearden, Russell E. "Life Inside Arkansas's Japanese-American Relocation Centers." *Arkansas Historical Quarterly* 48, no. 2 (1989).

Beito, David T. *From Mutual Aid to the Welfare State, Fraternal Societies and Social Services, 1890–1967*. Chapel Hill: University of North Carolina Press, 2000.

"Benevolent and Protective Order of Elks." Wikipedia. Accessed November 16, 2023. https://en.wikipedia.org/wiki/Benevolent_and_Protective_Order_of_Elks.

Bennett, Swannee, and William B. Worthen. *Arkansas Made: A Survey of the Decorative, Mechanical, and Fine Arts Produced in Arkansas Through 1950*. 2nd edition, Vol. 1. Fayetteville: University of Arkansas Press, 2021.

Biographical and Historical Memoirs of Eastern Arkansas. Chicago: Goodspeed Publishing Company, 1890.

Biographies of Van Buren County, Arkansas. Clinton, AR: Van Buren County Historical Society, unnumbered Vol. I, 1996.

Birnie [Brothers] Funeral Home Records, Fort Smith (Sebastian County), Special Collections, Fort Smith Public Library.

Black, Bill, Juliet Galonska, and Joe Crystal, preparers and consultants. *Cultural Landscape Report for Fort Smith National Historic Site*. Prepared by Fort Smith National Historic Site, Denver Service Center (National Park Service, US Department of the Interior); 1998.

Blakeley, Jeffrey A. "The Nineteenth Century Pottery Industry in Sebastian County, Arkansas." *Arkansas Historical Quarterly* 49, no. 1 (1990).

Blevins, Brooks. *Hill Folks: A History of Arkansas Ozarkers and Their Image*. Chapel Hill: University of North Carolina Press, 2002.

"Blood Feud at Walnut Ridge." *Lawrence County Historical Journal* 17, no. 1 (2013).

Bohnert, Dyan. "Local Preservationists Restore Scull Cemetery." *Grand Prairie Historical Society Bulletin* (Arkansas County) 61, no. 2 (2018).

Browning, J.E. "William M. DeHorn: A Most Remarkable Man." *Rivers and Roads and Points in Between* (Woodruff County Historical Society), 28 (2001/2002).

Bumpers, Dale. *The Best Lawyer in a One-Lawyer Town: A Memoir*. New York: Random House, 2003.

Burnett, Abby. "Eureka Springs, Arkansas: A Town with Purrfect Workers." *The Ozarks Mountaineer* 45, no. 5 (1997).

Burnett, Abby. *Gone to the Grave: Burial Customs of the Arkansas Ozarks, 1850–1950*. Jackson: University Press of Mississippi, 2014.

Burnett, Abby. "Murder Weapon Marks Grave." *AGS Quarterly* 43, no. 4 (Winter 2019)/44, no. 1 (Spring 2020).

Burnett, Abby. "'Well Boys, I've Told My Last Joke': The Life and Career of Minstrel Billy Rice, 1844(?)–1902." *The Record* (Journal of the Garland County Historical Society), 59 (2018).

Burnett, Abby, and Vineta Wingate. "Samuel Doss' Death Halts 'The Giggling Granny.'" *Carroll County Historical* 50, no. 1 (March 2005).

Campbell, Denele. "The 'Otherness' of Forrestina Bradley Campbell aka White River Red." *Flashback* 73, no. 1 (2023).

Canonici, Paul V. *The Delta Italians: Their Pursuit of "The Better Life" and Their Struggle Against Mosquitoes, Floods, and Prejudice.* Published by the author, 2003.

"Carnegie Hero Fund Commission Case Minute[s], Class—Train, #1387." *Johnson County Historical Society Journal* 30, no. 2 (2004).

Catalogue of the Monumental Bronze Company. Bridgeport, CT, October 1882. Internet Archive. Accessed August 20, 2023. https://archive.org/details/Whitebronzemonu00Monu/page/2/mode/2up.

Cemeteries of Yell County, Arkansas. Vol. 2. Dardanelle, AR: Yell County Historical and Genealogical Society, 1994.

Central Arkansas Library System (CALS). Charlevoix, Pierre-Francois-Xavier de. *Journal of a Voyage to North America Undertaken by Order of the French King.* Vol. 2. London: R. and J. Dodsley, 1761.

"Children's Cemetery at Lakeport Plantation." Lakeport Plantation. November 7, 2018. https://lakeport.astate.edu/2018/11/.

Chrisco, Sue Shell. "Izard County Cemetery Preservation Association." *Izard County Historian* 41, no. 4 (2016).

Chrisman, James K. *Death and Dying in Central Appalachia: Changing Attitudes and Practices.* Urbana: University of Illinois Press, 1994.

Clark, Sue, and Virginia McPhail. *Franklin County Cemeteries North of the Arkansas River.* N.p., 1995.

Collins, Clara, and Mrs. L. Oswald, enumerators. *Desha County, Arkansas Cemetery Records, Compiled in 1968 and 1969 by the Men and Women of Desha County.* McGehee, AR: Marion McKinney Stroud, 1983.

Conner, Thelma Ellington. "The Shadows of Rohwer." In *Inside View of Concentration Camps in Arkansas*, by Susan Gallion. Dumas Clarion, 2018.

Cooper, Lola Person, comp. *Lest We Forget.* Typescript of Yell County History published by the author, 1972, reprinted 1979.

Coste, Wilhelmine. "Facing Death; Photoceramic Gravestone Portraits and Immigrant Religious Identity, 1880–1960. *Markers* 40 (2025).

Crawford, Sybil F. *Jubilee: The First 150 Years of Mount Holly Cemetery, Little Rock, Arkansas.* Little Rock, AR: Mount Holly Cemetery Association, 1993.

Cruse, Mary Anne. *Bessie Melville or Prayer Book Instructions Carried Out Into Life: A Sequel to "The Little Episcopalian."* New York: E.P. Dutton, 1893 [original copyright 1853].

"The DCC's Cemetery Project: 'Life Goes Goodbye.'" *Phillips County Historical Review* 37, nos. 1–2 (1999).

Deas-Moore, Vennie. "Treading on Sacred Grounds." In *Preservation of Historic Burial Grounds*, by Lynette Strangstad. Washington, DC: National Trust for Historic Preservation, 2003.

Dewberry, Doris. "Oark and Some of It's [sic] Pioneers." *Johnson County Historical Society Journal* 25, no. 1 (1999).

Dhonau, R.W. *A Collection of Early Arkansas Families, 1760–1820, On Family Charts*. Little Rock, AR: R.W. Dhonau, 1983.

Dickinson, S.D. "Shells for the Dead." *The Old Time Chronicle, Folk History of Southwest Arkansas* 3, no. 11 (1990).

Dye, Caroline. Probate records, Jackson County Courthouse, Jackson County Probate Court, Box 159, bill filed November 22, 1918; "Inventory" filed December 30, 1918.

Eagles on the Prairie: A Historic View of Lonoke and Lonoke County Through One Man, James P. Eagle Jr. and His Family. Lonoke, AR: Lonoke County Museum, n.d.

Ekberg, Carl J., and Sharon K. Person. *St. Louis Rising: The French Regime of Louis St. Ange de Bellerive*. Urbana: University of Illinois Press, 2015.

Extension Homemakers Council. *Cemeteries of Fulton County Arkansas*. N.p., 1999.

Farber, Jessie Lie. "Symbolism on Gravestones." Association for Gravestone Studies. Accessed August 20, 2023. https://www.gravestonestudies.org/knowledge-center/symbolism#faqnoanchor.

Fletcher, Mary P. "A Sketch of Peter Le Fevre." *Arkansas Historical Quarterly* 13, no. 1 (1954).

Foley, William E. "Laclede, Pierre De (1729–1778)." In *Dictionary of Missouri Biography*. Edited by Lawrence O. Christensen, William E. Foley, Gary R. Kremer, and Kenneth H. Winn. Columbia: University of Missouri Press, 1999.

Foley, William E., and C. David Rice. *The First Chouteaus: River Barons of Early St. Louis*. Urbana: University of Illinois Press, 1983.

Freeman, Felton D. "Immigration to Arkansas." *Arkansas Historical Quarterly* 7, no. 3 (1948).

Gabel, Laurel K. "Ritual, Regalia and Remembrance: Fraternal Symbolism and Gravestones." *Markers* 11 (1994).

"Grave of a Man and his Horse Killed by a Train: Walnut Ridge, Arkansas." Atlas Obscura. Accessed January 22, 2024. https://www.atlasobscura.com/places/grave-of-a-man-and-his-horse-killed-by-a-train.

Gravelly, Ernestene Hudlow. "Story of Sulphur Springs, Yell County, Arkansas." *Yell County Historical and Genealogical Association Bulletin* 7, no. 2 (1982).

Grisham, Cindy. *When Hope Grows Weary: Tyronza, Arkansas and Its Place in History*. Published by the author, 2013.

Grissom, Carol A. *Zinc Sculpture in America, 1850–1950*. Newark: University of Delaware Press, 2009.

Habenstein, Robert W., and William M. Lamers. *The History of American Funeral Directing*. Milwaukee, WI: Bulfin Printers, 1955.

Hall, Donald B. "A Reexamination of Gravehouse Origins in the Upland South: Misunderstood Examples of Folk Mortuary Hardware." Paper presented to the Alabama Chapter of the Association for Gravestone Studies, April 27, 2013.

Hammond, Michael D. "Arkansas Atlantis: The Lost Town of Napoleon." *Arkansas Historical Quarterly* 65, no. 3 (2006).

Harkins, David E. *Haunted Graveyards of the Ozarks*. Charleston, SC: History Press, 2013.

Hicks, Joseph. "Concrete Folk Carved Gravestones of Eastern Tuscaloosa County, Alabama." In *A Survey of the Cemeteries of East Tuscaloosa County, Alabama*. Edited by Ian W. Brown. Unpublished research conducted during the course "Marking Graves: Self and Society in Death," Blount Undergraduate Initiative 301 (Tuscaloosa: University of Alabama, Alabama Museum of Natural History, Gulf Coast Survey Archives, 2004).

"The History of Corning, AR: Corning, Formerly Known as Hecht City Then Later as Carpenter's Station." Unsigned, undated typescript donated to the Piggott Public Library by the Clay County Genealogical and Historical Society.

Hodges, Dr., and Mrs. T.L. "Possibilities for the Archaeologist and Historian in Eastern Arkansas." *Arkansas Historical Quarterly* 2, no. 2 (1943).

Holloway, Karla F.C. *Passed On: African American Mourning Stories: A Memorial*. Durham, NC: Duke University Press, 2002.

Hope, Holly. "Historic Gravestone Iconography and Symbolism in Drew County." *Drew County Historical Journal* 32 (2017).

Howe, Henry. *Historical Collections of Ohio, in Three Volumes: An Encyclopedia of the State*. Vol. 11. Columbus, OH: Henry Howe and Son, 1891.

Huddleston, Duane. "The Volant and Reindeer Early Arkansas Steamboats." *Arkansas Historical Quarterly* 24, no. 2 (1976).

"Humbard." *History and Families of Carroll County, Arkansas*. Carroll County Historical and Genealogical Society. Paducah, KY: Turner Publishing, 2003.

Imahara, Walter M., and David E. Meltzer, eds. *Jerome and Rohwer: Memories of Japanese American Internment in World War II Arkansas*. Fayetteville: University of Arkansas Press, 2022.

"Influenza Epidemic Took Toll." In *Insight 2000: A Millennium Project of the Southwest Times Record*, edited by Nancy Steel. Southwest Times Record, 2000.

Jeter, Marvin D., ed. *Edward Palmer's Arkansaw [sic] Mounds*. Tuscaloosa: University of Alabama Press, 1990.

JimmyDriftwoodfan. "Jimmy Driftwood—Voice of the People 09 Straighten Out My Laig." [Monument record label, 1963] YouTube. Accessed September 18, 2023. https://www.youtube.com/watch?v=vbo-vSxHOCo.

"John Patterson." *Phillips County Historical Quarterly* 1, no. 1 (1962).

Johnson, Boyd W., ed. "A Visit to an Old Cemetery." *Grand Prairie Historical Society Bulletin* 6, no. 2 (1963).

"A Joint Declaration of Principles and Objectives by the American Cemetery Association, Inc., American Monument Association, Inc., Monument Builders of America, Inc., with Recommended Specifications for Memorial Work." Pamphlet, no publication information.

Kammen, Michael. *Digging Up the Dead: A History of Notable American Reburials.* Chicago: University of Chicago Press, 2010.

Keen, Bob. "Gypsy Tragedy on Evansville Creek." *Flashback* 47, no. 1 (1997).

Keister, Douglas. *Forever Dixie: A Field Guide to Southern Cemeteries and Their Residents.* Salt Lake City, UT: Gibbs Smith, 2008.

Keister, Douglas. *Stories in Stone: A Field Guide to Cemetery Symbolism and Iconography.* Salt Lake City, UT: Gibbs Smith, 2004.

Kelso, Hattie Ann. *Faulkner County, Arkansas Census of Cemeteries as of December 31, 1987.* Conway, AR: Faulkner County Historical Society, 1990.

Key, Frank. *The First 30 Years: A History of Lewisville, Arkansas from 1883–1913.* Washington, AR: Etter Printing, 1996.

"Kings's Prairie View, Reese, Mt. Olive, White House, Low Gap cemeteries." *Flashback* 5, no. 4 (1955).

Kittrell, Adelia C., and Curtis A. Houston. *Cemetery Records of Woodruff County: East of Cache River.* N.p., 1978.

Kittrell, Mrs. John B., Sr. "Misplaced Tombstones." *Rivers and Roads and Points in Between* 6, no. 2 (1978).

Kittrell, Mrs. John B., Sr., "The Spirit of the Gravestone." *Rivers and Roads and Points In Between* 1, no. 3 (1973).

Knight, Wilda, ed. *Lafayette County, Arkansas: Pieces of Its Past and Its People.* Lafayette County Historical Society, 2002.

Kwas, Mary L. *Thou Wert Dear to Us: A Record of Pioneer Cemetery, Washington, Arkansas.* Washington: Southwest Arkansas Regional Archives Foundation, 2011.

Lancaster, Bob. *The Jungles of Arkansas: A Personal History of the Wonder State.* Fayetteville: University of Arkansas Press, 1989.

Lankford, George E., ed. *Bearing Witness: Memories of Arkansas Slavery Narratives from the 1930s WPA Collections.* Fayetteville: University of Arkansas Press, 2003.

Lehovec, Bettina. "The Slave Narrative Interviews of Miss Adeline Blakeley." *Flashback* 70, no. 2 (2020).

LeMaster, Carolyn Gray. *A Corner of the Tapestry: A History of the Jewish Experience in Arkansas, 1820s–1990s.* Fayetteville: University of Arkansas Press, 1994.

Leslie, James W. *Saracen's Country: Some Southeast Arkansas History: Based on Articles for the Pine Bluff Commercial.* Little Rock, AR: Rose Publishing, 1974.

Little, M. Ruth. *Sticks and Stones: Three Centuries of North Carolina Gravemarkers.* Chapel Hill: University of North Carolina Press, 1998.

Lynch, Bill. "Captain William W. Martin." *Arkansas Historical Quarterly* 11, no. 1 (1952).

"Mail." *White County Historical Society News*, February 2015.

Marrin, Albert. *Uprooted: The Japanese American Experience During World War II*. New York: Borzoi/Alfred A. Knopf, 2016.

"Marvel Rhyne: Letters to Dear Joe." *The Journal* (Fort Smith Historical Society), 35, no. 1 (2011).

McClurkan, Burney. "The Saracen Window." *Jefferson County Historical Quarterly* 2, no. 4 (1970).

McCollum, Kimberly, and Willy Bearden. *Images of America: Elmwood Cemetery*. Charleston, SC: Arcadia Publishing, 2016.

McConnell, F.M. "White House Cemetery." *Flashback* 1, no. 3 (1951).

McGehee, Wanda Carson. *Ancestors Inside the Gates, Fort Chaffee, Sebastian County, Arkansas*. Catalogued by Sue Clark McGehee. N.p., 1992

McKelvey, Jerry. "DeAnn Cemetery in Prescott." *The Sandyland Chronicle* 7, no. 1 (2007). Accessed September 18, 2023. https://sandyland.dreamhosters.com/2007-01.pdf.

McKelvy, Jerry. "The Doctor, the Disobedient Daughter, and the Preacher's Son: The Rest of the Story About William Graham Hayes and Libbie Lucille Brownlee Hayes." *The Sandyland Chronicle* 8, no. 10 (2008). https://sandyland.dreamhosters.com/2008-10.pdf.

McKelvey, Jerry. "Old Mike Put to Rest after 64 Years." *The Sandyland Chronicle* 3, no. 3 (2003). https://sandyland.dreamhosters.com/2003-03.pdf.

McNerney, Michael J. *A Shape in Time and Space: The Migration of the Necked Discoid Gravemarker—The Illinois Sample*. Tuscaloosa, AL: Borgo Publishing, 2017.

Meek, Mrs. J.W. "A Plea for the Old Cemetery: Written for the Daughters of the Confederacy." *The Sandyland Chronicle* 5, no. 2 (2005). https://sandyland.dreamhosters.com/2005-02.pdf.

Meriwether, Robert W. "Hendrix College." In *Faulkner County: Its Land and People*, edited by Doris B. Dolan, Hattie Ann Kelso, and Corinne H. Robinson. Faulkner County Historical Society, 1986.

"Minié Ball." Wikipedia. Accessed January 22, 2024. https://en.wikipedia.org/wiki/Mini%C3%A9_ball.

"Miss Lucy J. Daniel." *The Monumental News, an Illustrated Monthly Monumental Art Journal* 7, no. 1 (1895).

Montgomery, James. "Servant of God, Well Done!" In *Greenland and Other Poems*. London: Printed by Strahan and Spottiswoode for Longman, Hurst, Rees, Orme and Brown, 1819.

Monuments[,] Tombstones and Markers. Montgomery Ward and Co., 1929. Quarries and Beyond. Accessed August 6, 2023. https://quarriesandbeyond.org/articles_and_books/pdf/montgomery_ward_monument_catalog_1929.pdf.

Moore, J.F. Burial log. Fayetteville Evergreen Cemetery Association Records: Odd Fellows and Masons Cemetery Book, Vol. 1. University of Arkansas library, Special Collections.

"More About the Henry Conway Grave." *Grand Prairie Historical Society Bulletin* 6, no. 3 (1963).

Morgan, James Logan, ed. *Centennial History of Newport, Arkansas, 1875–1975*. Jackson County Historical Society, 1975.

Morse, Dan F. *Sloan: A Paleoindian Dalton Cemetery in Arkansas*. Fayetteville: University of Arkansas Press, 2018.

"Nathan Ellington, 1808–1890." *Wagon Wheels* 2, no. 1 (1982).

Neal, Joe. "Fraternal Cemetery: Reflections on a Southern Negro Graveyard." *Pulaski County Historical Review* 25, no. 1 (1977).

Nichols, Mike. "The Mystery of Prescott's Ol' Mike." *The Old Time Chronicle, Folk History of Southwest Arkansas* (1996).

"The 1905 'New Handy Map of Little Rock.'" *Pulaski County Historical Review* 34, no. 4 (1986).

Nuttall, Thomas. *A Journal of Travels into the Arkansa [sic] Territory*. Ann Arbor, MI: University Microfilms, 1966, originally published by Thos. M. Palmer, Printer, Philadelphia, PA, 1821.

Orr, W.E. "Judsonia's Unknown Child's Grave." *White County Heritage* 24 (1986).

"The Otis Henry Memorial." E.M. Visquesney Doughboy Database. Accessed January 22, 2024. https://doughboysearcher.weebly.com/texarkana-texas.html.

Parks-Spencer, Susan. "Remembering the Lives of Robert Kidd and William Clingman Raper." *Flashback* 74, no. 1 (2024).

Patterson, Ruth Polk. *The Seed of Sally Good'n: A Black Family of Arkansas, 1833–1953*. Lexington: University Press of Kentucky, 1985.

Perkey, Gary, ed. *A History of Batesville and Independence County, Arkansas: Excerpts from Local and Regional Newspapers, Vol. 1, 1840–1907*. Jonesboro, AR: Published by the author, 2012.

Phelps [Ward], Elizabeth Stuart. *Chapters from a Life*. Boston, MA: Houghton, Mifflin, 1896.

Pike, Albert. "Every Year." In *Hymns to the Gods, and Other Poems*. Little Rock, AR: F.W. Allsopp, 1916 (originally published 1881).

Plack, Bill, and Ellis Michaels. "Known Tombstone Carvers of Pennsylvania." Pennsylvania USGenWeb Archives. Accessed January 27, 2024. http://www.usgwarchives.net/pa/1pa/tscarvers/monumental-bronze/monumental-bronze.htm.

Rayburn, Otto Ernest. *Ozark Country*. Fayetteville: University of Arkansas Press, 2021, reprint of 1941 edition (New York: Duell, Sloan and Pearce).

Reed, Roy. *Faubus: The Life and Times of an American Prodigal*. Fayetteville: University of Arkansas Press, 1997.

Report of the Celebration of the Anniversary of the Founding of St. Louis, on the Fifteenth Day of February, A.D. 1847. St. Louis: Missouri Republican, printed by Chambers and Knapp, 1847.

Richardson, Clement, ed. "John Edward Bush." In *The National Cyclopedia of the Colored Race*. Vol. 1. Montgomery, AL: National Publishing Co., 1919.

Roberts, Vicki A. *Marion County Cemeteries*. Yellville, AR, 2008.

Romano, Ron. *Billboard Monuments of Maine: A Collection of Rare 1800s Gravestones*. Thomaston, ME: Indie Author Books, 2020.

Ross, Margaret Smith. "Herman Davis: Forgotten Hero." *Arkansas Historical Quarterly* 14, no. 1 (1995).

Rotundo, Barbara. "Monumental Bronze." In *Cemeteries and Gravemarkers: Voices of American Culture*, edited by Richard E. Meyer. Ann Arbor: UMI Research Press, 1989.

Rudd, Dan, and Theo Bond. *From Slavery to Wealth: The Life of Scott Bond: The Rewards of Honesty, Industry, Economy and Perseverance*. Madison, AR: Journal Printing Company, 1917.

Russell, Joy. "Ribbon Ridge Graves." *Madison County Musings* 19, no. 1 (2000).

"The Rustic Movement and the Tree Stump Gravestone." Gravely Speaking. Accessed January 22, 2024. https://gravelyspeaking.com/2020/04/22/the-rustic-movement-and-the-tree-stump-gravestone/.

Sabo, George, III. *Ways of the Ancestors: Ancient Indians of Arkansas*. Fayetteville: Arkansas Archeological Survey, Popular Series No. 8, 2021.

Segal, Joshua L. *A Field Guide to Visiting a Jewish Cemetery: A Spiritual Journey to the Past, Present and Future*. Nashua, NH: Jewish Cemetery Publishing, 2005.

Segal, Joshua L. *For an Eternal Memory: Ordinary and Unusual Jewish Cemetery Monuments and How to Create Them*. Nashua, NH: Jewish Cemetery Publishing, 2009.

Silva, Rachel. "Sandwiching in History: Oakland and Fraternal Cemetery." Tour script, Arkansas Historic Preservation Program, 2010.

Skocpol, Theda, and Jennifer Lynn Oser. "Organization Despite Adversity: The Origins and Development of African American Fraternal Associations." *Social Science History* 28, no. 3, 2004.

"Some Women Marble Cutters." *The Monumental News, an Illustrated Monthly Monumental Art Journal* 51, no. 12 (1939). Accessed September 6, 2023. https://quarriesandbeyond.org/article_list_2.html.

Spanke, Lance. "Fast Train Strikes Girls: Frances Spanke Killed and Mary [sic] Oberle Injured at Iron Bridge: An Act of Heroism." *Johnson County Historical Society Journal* 30, no. 2 (2004).

Steele, Phillip. *White River Red: A Legend in Her Own Time*. Typography and design by Jan Cooper [booklet]. Fayetteville, AR, 1995.

Stinson, B. Craig. *A Brief History of Our Hill Family in America*. Blurb Creative Publishing Service, 2011.

Stott, Annette. *Pioneer Cemeteries: Sculpture Gardens of the Old West.* Lincoln: University of Nebraska Press, 2008.

Swinburn, Susan Stevenson, and Doris Stevenson West, comps. *History in Headstones: A Complete Listing of All Marked Graves in Known Cemeteries of Crawford County, Arkansas.* Van Buren, AR: Press-Argus, 1970.

Talmage, T. DeWitt. "Talmage's Sermon: The Burial and the Resurrection of Jesus, the Christ." *The Southern Standard* (Arkadelphia, AR), April 3, 1891.

Teeter, John. "Old Mike." Fact sheet at the Depot Museum, Prescott, dated April/May 2001, original source unknown.

Tennessee State Board of Health, Bureau of Vital Statistics, Registration District No. 28005 [US Veterans' Hospital No. 88, Memphis, TN], Registration No. 32, Herman Davis, Shelby County, TN, January 5, 1923.

Tice, Joyce M. "Junior Order of United American Mechanics." Tri-Counties Genealogy and History: A Pictorial Catalog of Commemorative Flagholders and Plaques of Organizations and Military. Accessed September 21, 2023. https://www.joycetice.com/flaghold/flag040.htm.

Trippe-Dillon, Tammie, *Grave Concerns: A Preservation for Historic Cemeteries in Arkansas.* Accessed August 20, 2023. Little Rock: Arkansas Historic Preservation Program, n.d., 125. .pdf.

Underwood, Edward L., and Karen J. Underwood. *Forgotten Tales of Arkansas.* Charleston, SC: History Press, 2012.

Unger, Robert. *The Union Station Massacre: The Original Sin of J. Edgar Hoover's F.B.I.* Kansas City, MO: Andrews McMeel Publishing.

"Unknown Man Buried at De Ann Cemetery." *The Sandyland Chronicle* 3, no. 11 (2003). https://sandyland.dreamhosters.com/2003-11.pdf.

US Bureau of the Census. *Ninth Census of the United States—1870.* Lafayette County, Arkansas. Washington, DC: United States Census Office.

US Bureau of the Census. *Tenth Census of the United States—1880.* Washington, DC: United States Census Office, Jackson County, Arkansas.

US Bureau of the Census. *Thirteenth Census of the United States—1910.* Lafayette Township, Lonoke County, Arkansas.

US Bureau of the Census. *Fifteenth Census of the United States—1930.* Woodruff County, Arkansas. Washington, DC: United States Census Office.

US Bureau of the Census. *Sixteenth Census of the United States—1940.* Woodruff County, Arkansas.

Vanderpool, Guy C., ed. *A Time to Every Purpose: The Photographs of Jesse L. Charlton, 1937–1954.* Texarkana, TX: Texarkana Museums System, 1999.

Van Laningham, Scott, ed. "St. Joseph's Cemetery at Tontitown." *Flashback* 51, no. 3 (2001).

Vermillion, Ricky. "The Story of Herman Davis." *Craighead County Historical Quarterly* 7, no. 4 (1969).

Vlach, John Michael. *The Afro-American Tradition in Decorative Arts*. Athens: University of Georgia Press, 1990.

Walton-Raji, Angela Y. "American Woodmen—A Black Benevolent Society." *My Ancestor's Name* (blog), August 27, 2013. http://myancestorsname.blogspot.com/2013/08/american-woodmen-black-benevolent.html.

Weaver, W.J. "Desecrated Grave Yards." In *Steep Hill and Jewish Cemeteries in Sebastian County, Arkansas with Some Abandoned Cemeteries*. Sue Clark, n.d., 1.

Westphal, June. "Wayward John Poynter: Part I." *Carroll County Historical Quarterly* 52, no. 3 (2008).

Whayne, Jeannie M., Thomas A. DeBlack, George Sabo III, and Morris S. Arnold. *Arkansas: A Narrative History*. Fayetteville: University of Arkansas Press, 2013.

"White County's Top 25 Forgotten Cemeteries." *Historical Society News*, August 2002.

"Wife Kills Husband with Automobile Axle." Newspaper clipping, hand-dated April 7, 1921. *Yell County Historical and Genealogical Association Bulletin* 6, no. 2 (1981).

Wintory, Blake. *African American Fraternal Headstone Symbols in Arkansas: A Guide*. Draft copy, June 6, 2018. http://lakeport.astate.edu/wp-content/uploads/2018/06/Arkansas-Fraternal-Headstone-handout-June-2018.pdf.

Wintory, Blake. *Images of America: Chicot County*. Charleston, SC: Arcadia Publishing, 2015.

Wolf, John Quincy. "Aunt Caroline Dye: The Gypsy in 'The St. Louis Blues.'" *Southern Folklore Quarterly* 33, no. 4 (1969).

Wood, Richard G. "The Marine Hospital at Napoleon." *Arkansas Historical Quarterly* 14, no. 1 (1955).

Works Progress Administration. Historical Records Survey, Special Collections, University of Arkansas Libraries, Fayetteville; Early Settlers' Personal History Questionnaires: Malinda Sutton interview, born December 12, 1845 (Little River Co.), interviewed April 12, 1941.

Zeller, Joyce. *Hidden History of Eureka Springs*. Charleston, SC: History Press, 2011.

ADDITIONAL ONLINE SOURCES

Central Arkansas Library System (CALS). Encyclopedia of Arkansas. Edited by Guy Lancaster. www.encyclopediaofarkansas.net

Bearden, Russell E. "Rohwer Relocation Center." CALS Encyclopedia of Arkansas. Accessed May 1, 2023. https://encyclopediaofarkansas.net/entries/rohwer-relocation-center-369/.

Browning, Dick E. "Freemasons." CALS Encyclopedia of Arkansas. Accessed August 1, 2023. https://encyclopediaofarkansas.net/entries/freemasons-4122/.

Burnett, Abby. "Evergreen Cemetery." CALS Encyclopedia of Arkansas. Accessed August 20, 2023. https://encyclopediaofarkansas.net/entries/evergreen-cemetery-7426/.

Burnett, Abby. "Funeral Customs, Traditional (Ozark Mountains)." CALS Encyclopedia of Arkansas. Accessed September 18, 2023. https://encyclopediaofarkansas.net/entries/funeral-customs-traditional-7338/.

Burnett, Abby. "Moses Tran Clegg (1876–1919)." CALS Encyclopedia of Arkansas. Accessed September 9, 2023. https://encyclopediaofarkansas.net/entries/moses-tran-clegg-8854/.

Burnett, Abby. "Nick Miller, 1846?–1898." CALS Encyclopedia of Arkansas. Accessed August 23, 2023. https://encyclopediaofarkansas.net/entries/nick-miller-5849/.

Burnett, Abby. "Washington Monument Marble Quarry." CALS Encyclopedia of Arkansas. Accessed August 20, 2023. https://encyclopediaofarkansas.net/entries/washington-monument-marble-quarry-14025/.

Clements, Courtney Moore. "Legend of Petit Jean." CALS Encyclopedia of Arkansas. Accessed September 9, 2023. https://encyclopediaofarkansas.net/entries/petit-jean-legend-3474/.

Crawford, Sybil F. "Mount Holly Cemetery." CALS Encyclopedia of Arkansas. Accessed December 23, 2021. https://encyclopediaofarkansas.net/entries/mount-holly-cemetery-49/.

Deering, John. "George Edward Fisher (1923–2003)." CALS Encyclopedia of Arkansas. Accessed December 6, 2020. https://encyclopediaofarkansas.net/entries/george-edward-fisher-2502/.

Diaz, Lakresha. "Oakland-Fraternal Cemetery." CALS Encyclopedia of Arkansas. Accessed August 14, 2023. https://encyclopediaofarkansas.net/entries/oakland-fraternal-cemetery-7383/.

Goodner, Wes. "Waldron War." CALS Encyclopedia of Arkansas. Accessed September 8, 2023. https://encyclopediaofarkansas.net/entries/waldron-war-2819/.

Gordeeva, Jennifer Atkins. "Rosemary Beryl Snook 'Snooky' Fisher (1927–1983)." CALS Encyclopedia of Arkansas. Accessed August 27, 2023. https://encyclopediaofarkansas.net/entries/rosemary-beryl-snook-snooky-fisher-457/.

Griffith, Nancy Snell. "Eagle Murders of 1873." CALS Encyclopedia of Arkansas. Accessed August 23, 2020. https://encyclopediaofarkansas.net/entries/eagle-murders-of-1873–15623/.

Grisham, Cindy. "Tyronza (Poinsett County)." CALS Encyclopedia of Arkansas. Accessed July 5, 2021. https://encyclopediaofarkansas.net/entries/tyronza-poinsett-county-5561/.

Grisham, Cindy. "Wilson (Mississippi County)." CALS Encyclopedia of Arkansas. Accessed September 9, 2021. https://encyclopediaofarkansas.net/entries/wilson-mississippi-county-4294/.

Kent, Carolyn Yancey. "Supreme Royal Circle of Friends of the World." CALS Encyclopedia of Arkansas. Accessed August 14, 2021. https://encyclopediaofarkansas.net/entries/supreme-royal-circle-of-friends-of-the-world-5861/.

Key, Joseph Patrick. "Sarasin (?–1832?)." CALS Encyclopedia of Arkansas. Accessed February 14, 2023. https://encyclopediaofarkansas.net/entries/sarasin-1756/1.

Metrailer, Jaimie. "Slovak (Prairie County)." CALS Encyclopedia of Arkansas. Accessed August 14, 2023. https://encyclopediaofarkansas.net/entries/slovak-prairie-county-5362/.

Mitchem, Jeffrey M. "Hernando de Soto (1500?–1542)." CALS Encyclopedia of Arkansas. Accessed November 11, 2023. https://encyclopediaofarkansas.net/entries/hernando-de-soto-1770/.

Polston, Mike. "Davidsonville (Randolph County)." CALS Encyclopedia of Arkansas. Accessed June 2, 2025. https://encyclopediaofarkansas.net/entries/davidsonville-randolph-county-6090/.

Reynolds, Kim. "Frank 'Jelly' Nash (1887–1933)." CALS Encyclopedia of Arkansas. Accessed August 20, 2023. https://encyclopediaofarkansas.net/entries/frank-jelly-nash-4067/.

Rolingson, Martha Ann. "Toltec Mounds Site." CALS Encyclopedia of Arkansas. Accessed March 12, 2021. https://encyclopediaofarkansas.net/entries/toltec-mounds-site-413/.

Shoults, Leonore. "Button Blank Industry." CALS Encyclopedia of Arkansas. Accessed August 20, 2023. https://encyclopediaofarkansas.net/entries/button-blank-industry-6577/.

Swanlund, Angela. "Ronald Gene Simmons." CALS Encyclopedia of Arkansas. Accessed December 4, 2024. https://encyclopediaofarkansas.net/entries/ronald-gene-simmons-3731/.

Wintory, Blake, and Ashan R. Hampton. "Mosaic Templars of America." CALS Encyclopedia of Arkansas. Accessed August 14, 2023. https://encyclopediaofarkansas.net/entries/mosaic-templars-of-america-1186/.

National Register of Historic Places Nominating Forms

Akron Cemetery, Newark vicinity, Independence County, Arkansas, [no Site No.]. Accessed August 14, 2023. https://www.arkansasheritage.com/docs/default-source/national-registry/in0619-pdf.pdf?sfvrsn=63ff2a9c_0.

Augusta Memorial Park Historic Section, a.k.a. Crescent Hill Cemetery, Augusta, Woodruff County, Arkansas, Site No. WO0049. Accessed August 14, 2023. https://www.arkansasheritage.com/docs/default-source/national-registry/wo0049-pdf.pdf?sfvrsn=4ae3f0ce_0,.

De Ann Cemetery Historic Section, Prescott, Nevada County, Arkansas, Site No. NE0076. Accessed August 16, 2023. https://www.arkansasheritage.com/docs/default-source/national-registry/ne0076-pdf.pdf?sfvrsn=5afd06ab_0.

Fairview Cemetery, Van Buren, Crawford County, Arkansas, Site No. CW0384. Accessed November 11, 2023. https://www.arkansasheritage.com/docs/default-source/national-registry/cw0384-pdf.pdf?sfvrsn=decf7b4_0.

Fort Smith National Cemetery, Fort Smith, Sebastian County, Arkansas [no Site No.]. Accessed August 14, 2023. https://www.arkansasheritage.com/docs/default-source/national-registry/sb0215-pdf.pdf?sfvrsn=7510a614_0.

George Berry Washington Memorial, Earle, Crittenden County, Arkansas, [no Site No.]. Accessed August 1, 2023. https://www.arkansasheritage.com/docs/default-source/national-registry/ct0098-pdf.pdf?sfvrsn=43106bb4_0.

Hampton Springs Cemetery (Black Section), Carthage, Dallas County, Arkansas, Site No. DA1. Accessed August 16, 2023. https://www.arkansasheritage.com/docs/default-source/national-registry/da0004-pdf.pdf?sfvrsn=9a498fb9_0.

Linwood Mausoleum, Paragould, Greene County, Arkansas, Site No. GE0270. Accessed August 20, 2023. https://www.arkansasheritage.com/docs/default-source/national-registry/ge0270-pdf.pdf?sfvrsn=71b8a5a_0.

Maple Hill Cemetery, Phillips County, Arkansas, Site No. PHO290. Accessed September 9, 2023. https://www.arkansasheritage.com/docs/default-source/national-registry/ph0290-pdf.pdf?sfvrsn=cb1bd150_0.

Mound Cemetery, Arkansas City, Desha County, Arkansas, Site No. DE0002. Accessed March 13, 2021. https://www.arkansasheritage.com/docs/default-source/national-registry/de0002-pdf.pdf?sfvrsn=e4a82928_0,.

Oakland-Fraternal Cemetery, Little Rock, Pulaski County, Arkansas, Site No. PU5892. Accessed September 6, 2023. https://www.arkansasheritage.com/docs/default-source/national-registry/pu5892-pdf.pdf?sfvrsn=5aac62ef_0.

Pyeatte-Mason Cemetery, Maumelle, Pulaski County, Arkansas, Site No. PU9990. Accessed August 14, 2023. https://www.arkansasheritage.com/docs/default-source/national-registry/pu9990-pdf.pdf?sfvrsn=a83978ef_0.

Rohwer Relocation Center Site, Rohwer, Desha County, Arkansas [no Site No.]. Accessed August 14, 2023. https://www.arkansasheritage.com/docs/default-source/national-registry/de0070-pdf.pdf?sfvrsn=ee5fe67f_0.

Temple Beth El Cemetery, Helena, Phillips County, Arkansas, Site No. PO566. Accessed August 14, 2023. https://www.arkansasheritage.com/docs/default-source/national-registry/ph0566-pdf.pdf?sfvrsn=929609a9_0.

INDEX

Note: Enslaved Black people, known only by their first names, have been indexed together under "enslaved individuals" as well as separately, using surnames of their enslavers.

ABOUT THE AUTHOR

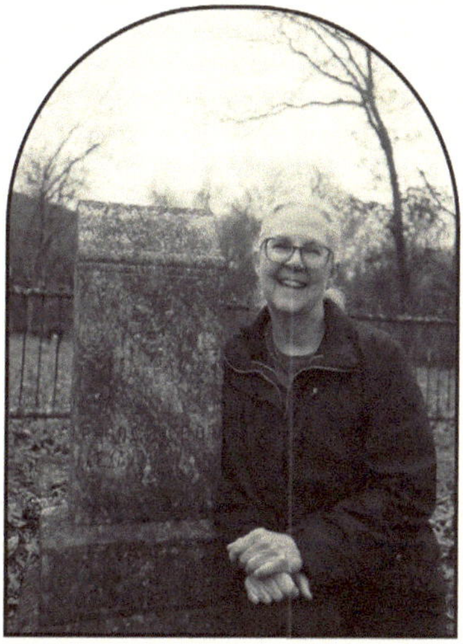

Photo by Don House

Abby Burnett is an independent researcher who, as seen in the Arkansas Educational Television Network's 2010 documentary *Silent Storytellers*, studies such things as long-lost burial customs, tombstone symbolism, epitaphs, and the work of early stone carvers. Her book *Gone to the Grave: Burial Customs of the Arkansas Ozarks, 1850–1950* was published in paperback in 2015 by the University Press of Mississippi. She has written entries on graveyards, stone carvers, and early medicine for the online CALS Encyclopedia of Arkansas, in addition to doing public speaking on all aspects of burial in Arkansas, her adopted state for the past forty years.